Social Research Methodology and Publishing Results:

A Guide to Non-Native English Speakers

Candauda Arachchige Saliya
Sri Lanka Institute of Information Technology, Sri Lanka

A volume in the Advances in
Knowledge Acquisition, Transfer,
and Management (AKATM) Book
Series

Published in the United States of America by
IGI Global
Information Science Reference (an imprint of IGI Global)
701 E. Chocolate Avenue
Hershey PA, USA 17033
Tel: 717-533-8845
Fax: 717-533-8661
E-mail: cust@igi-global.com
Web site: http://www.igi-global.com

Library of Congress Cataloging-in-Publication Data

Names: Saliya, Candauda Arachchige, 1962- editor.
Title: Social research methodology and publishing results : a guide to
  non-native English speakers / edited by Candauda Arachchige Saliya.
Description: Hershey, PA : Information Science Reference, [2023] | Includes
  bibliographical references and index. | Summary: "The focus of this book
  is not only on doing research as course work, but also to organise and
  conduct the whole research process with a view to publishing important
  results. The editor's own 7Ps model (Saliya, 2021), will be improved by
  adding three more essential elements to match the purpose of this book
  to include activities such as Planning (research design), Programming
  (time frames, co-ordinating and budgeting) and Publishing. The 10
  elements are identified as; 1. Paradigm; Positivism, Interpretivism,
  Constructivism and Critical thought etc. 2. Perspective; Marxism,
  Power-knowledge, Feminism, Structuralism, Bourdieu's theory etc. 3.
  Purpose; Articulating research problem, constructing hypothesis etc. 4.
  Previous knowledge; literature review, Knowledge gap and significance
  etc. 5. Planning: Research resign 6. Programming; Ethical issues, timing
  and budgeting etc. 7. Plot (strategies); Quantitative methods,
  Introducing commonly used software and their strengths and weaknesses,
  Qualitative methods, Mixed methods and Quantitative Vs Qualitative
  debate etc etc. 8. Procedures (methods); Gathering/collecting, recording
  and storing data/evidence via surveys, interviews, observations and
  exploring insights etc. 9. Persuasion (drawing conclusions); Developing
  cogent arguments, methods of reasoning such as deduction, induction and
  abduction etc. 10. Publishing; Selecting journals, writing abstracts,
  addressing issues raised by reviewers. This exercise is not a smooth
  process that moves from one stage to another, or a sequential process
  like peeling an onion, layer by layer; nor is it a process that starts
  from roots of ontology and epistemology and spreads like a tree growing
  upwards for methodology, it is not a straitjacket where the researcher
  is confined to a particular box"-- Provided by publisher.
Identifiers: LCCN 2022043758 (print) | LCCN 2022043759 (ebook) | ISBN
  9781668468593 (hardcover) | ISBN 9781668468630 (paperback) | ISBN
  9781668468609 (ebook)
Subjects: LCSH: Social sciences--Research--Methodology. |
  Research--Methodology.
Classification: LCC H62 .S67374 2023 (print) | LCC H62 (ebook) | DDC
  300.72--dc23/eng/20221103
LC record available at https://lccn.loc.gov/2022043758
LC ebook record available at https://lccn.loc.gov/2022043759

This book is published in the IGI Global book series Advances in Knowledge Acquisition, Transfer, and Management (AKATM) (ISSN: 2326-7607; eISSN: 2326-7615)

British Cataloguing in Publication Data
A Cataloguing in Publication record for this book is available from the British Library.

All work contributed to this book is new, previously-unpublished material.
The views expressed in this book are those of the authors, but not necessarily of the publisher.

For electronic access to this publication, please contact: eresources@igi-global.com.

Advances in Knowledge Acquisition, Transfer, and Management (AKATM) Book Series

ISSN:2326-7607
EISSN:2326-7615

Editor-in-Chief: Murray E. Jennex, San Diego State University, USA

MISSION

Organizations and businesses continue to utilize knowledge management practices in order to streamline processes and procedures. The emergence of web technologies has provided new methods of information usage and knowledge sharing.

The **Advances in Knowledge Acquisition, Transfer, and Management (AKATM) Book Series** brings together research on emerging technologies and their effect on information systems as well as the knowledge society. **AKATM** will provide researchers, students, practitioners, and industry leaders with research highlights surrounding the knowledge management discipline, including technology support issues and knowledge representation.

COVERAGE

- Cognitive Theories
- Cultural Impacts
- Information and Communication Systems
- Knowledge Acquisition and Transfer Processes
- Knowledge Management Strategy
- Knowledge Sharing
- Organizational Learning
- Organizational Memory
- Small and Medium Enterprises
- Virtual Communities

IGI Global is currently accepting manuscripts for publication within this series. To submit a proposal for a volume in this series, please contact our Acquisition Editors at Acquisitions@igi-global.com or visit: http://www.igi-global.com/publish/.

The Advances in Knowledge Acquisition, Transfer, and Management (AKATM) Book Series (ISSN 2326-7607) is published by IGI Global, 701 E. Chocolate Avenue, Hershey, PA 17033-1240, USA, www.igi-global.com. This series is composed of titles available for purchase individually; each title is edited to be contextually exclusive from any other title within the series. For pricing and ordering information please visit http://www.igi-global.com/book-series/advances-knowledge-acquisition-transfer-management/37159. Postmaster: Send all address changes to above address. Copyright © 2023 IGI Global. All rights, including translation in other languages reserved by the publisher. No part of this series may be reproduced or used in any form or by any means – graphics, electronic, or mechanical, including photocopying, recording, taping, or information and retrieval systems – without written permission from the publisher, except for non commercial, educational use, including classroom teaching purposes. The views expressed in this series are those of the authors, but not necessarily of IGI Global.

Titles in this Series

For a list of additional titles in this series, please visit:
http://www.igi-global.com/book-series/advances-knowledge-acquisition-transfer-management/37159

Phenomenology Research Design for Novice Researchers
Barbara Ann Turner (Walden University, USA)
Information Science Reference • ©2023 • 300pp • H/C (ISBN: 9781799895701) • US $215.00

Knowledge Management and Research Innovation in Global Higher Education Institutions
Lawrence J. Jones-Esan (York St. John University, UK) Vipin Nadda (University of Sunderland, UK) and Kendra S. Albright (Kent State University, USA)
Information Science Reference • ©2023 • 249pp • H/C (ISBN: 9781668436523) • US $210.00

Innovative Technologies for Enhancing Knowledge Access in Academic Libraries
Tlou Maggie Masenya (Durban University of Technology, South Africa)
Information Science Reference • ©2022 • 317pp • H/C (ISBN: 9781668433645) • US $215.00

Understanding, Implementing, and Evaluating Knowledge Management in Business Settings
Tereza Raquel Merlo (University of North Texas, USA)
Business Science Reference • ©2022 • 307pp • H/C (ISBN: 9781668444313) • US $215.00

Cases on Developing Effective Research Plans for Communications and Information Science
María-Victoria Carrillo-Durán (University of Extremadura, Spain) and Margarita Pérez Pulido (University of Extremadura, Spain)
Information Science Reference • ©2022 • 466pp • H/C (ISBN: 9781668445235) • US $215.00

Handbook of Research on the Global View of Open Access and Scholarly Communications
Daniel Gelaw Alemneh (University of North Texas, USA)
Information Science Reference • ©2022 • 435pp • H/C (ISBN: 9781799898054) • US $165.00

For an entire list of titles in this series, please visit:
http://www.igi-global.com/book-series/advances-knowledge-acquisition-transfer-management/37159

701 East Chocolate Avenue, Hershey, PA 17033, USA
Tel: 717-533-8845 x100 • Fax: 717-533-8661
E-Mail: cust@igi-global.com • www.igi-global.com

Table of Contents

Detailed Table of Contents

Section 1
Research Process and Philosophy

Chapter 1

The research process is not a smooth process that moves from one stage to another, or a sequential process growing from the roots of ontology and epistemology towards the data collection and analytical techniques and interpretations. The existentialist position of the interpretive/reformist paradigm is that reality is subjective and multiple, that it does not exist independently in the human mind. Their epistemological stance is that the available knowledge depends on the researcher's thoughts and desires. That is, "knowledge" is created by the seeker and deploying a specific methodology which is not necessarily a sequential set of "stages", a "step-by-step" course or a "layer-by-layer" peeling activity like peeling-off an onion.

Chapter 2

This chapter aims to provide a simple but a complete idea about the difficult concepts in the research field. Research paradigm is a concept which is difficult for new researchers to understand and memorize. This chapter covers the key concepts in the research paradigm: ontology, epistemology, and methodology. Researchers can understand these concept and decide the best paradigm to investigate different phenomena. To make these difficult concepts simple, this chapter has been organized with brief explanations and graphs.

    *Nagalingam Nagendrakumar, Sri Lanka Institute of Information
       Technology, Sri Lanka
    Naduni Madhavika, Sri Lanka Institute of Information Technology, Sri
       Lanka*

The debate of application of research philosophy in social science research is trending. One side takes the positivism while another side depends on interpretivism, some other believes critical realism and the rest stand with pragmatism. Yet, the understanding on and interpretation of ontological argument and epistemological positioning of the pragmatism is criticized. Accordingly, the authors are motivated to critically argue that gap with empirical research evidence from management disciplines in Sri Lanka. The pragmatism followers contend that all beliefs, knowledge, and scientific concepts are provisional and defined by their practical application in ongoing experience, not by their correspondence with antecedent truth or reality (Carlsen and Mantere, 2007). Hence, recent social sciences studies are rooted in pragmatic ideas, practice-based approaches thereby harvesting the intersubjective knowledge. Thus, this chapter acknowledges the paradox of whether the definition of pragmatism could be universal or differs contextually research scholars.

    *Candauda Arachchige Saliya, Sri Lanka Institute of Information
       Technology, Sri Lanka*

The purpose of this chapter is to summarize the philosophical developments in the academic research field and provide a framework for non-native English-speaking budding researchers. Revealing the philosophical stance of the authors of a research paper is crucial in understanding their arguments. Therefore, an understanding of this historical evolution is useful in justifying authors' choices and presenting them clearly in the research report. Authors' perceptions of different theories, perspectives, and worldviews influence and affect many aspects of research, and it is important to mention personal stances on them in the research report at the very beginning. The choice of underpinning philosophy is significantly influenced by the author's psychosocial, economic, and cultural backgrounds. Multivism is a dynamic position of a researcher who is not confined to the bipolar-disordered extremism of objectivism and subjectivism of ontology, epistemology, methodology, and methods.

Chapter 5
*Kenneth Peprah, University of Business and Integrated Development
Studies, Ghana*

Philosophy is a science of knowledge, and it concentrates on epistemology, ontology, axiology, and methodology. However, researchers have understated the role of philosophy, even though it is very interwoven with research. This chapter is to position data analysis in philosophy and show its epistemological and ontological underpinnings using the philosophy of perception. The methods are a desk study, literature reviews, and lecture notes. Traditionally, the definition of knowledge is 'justified true belief' (JTB). The JTB is placed in the context of empiricism, rationalism, and/or dualism. These are further linked to ontological materialism, idealism, and dualism. The chapter has tried to draw a relationship with perception's direct realism, indirect realism, and dualism respectively. In conclusion, knowledge is justified by good evidence (empiricism) and reason (rationalism). The chapter recommends researchers utilise the philosophy of the sciences in order to improve on their research.

Section 2
Research Methods and Literature Review

Chapter 6
*Krishantha Wisenthige, Sri Lanka Institute of Information Technology,
Sri Lanka*

The framework of methods and techniques that the researcher has chosen to conduct the research is described as research design. In social science research, it is required to collect evidence relevant to the research problem, especially evidence required to evaluate a problem, to test the theory, or to describe a phenomenon. Successful research designs should be able to provide research insights that are accurate and unbiased. This chapter covers the type of research designs, and names key characteristics of a good research design; neutrality, reliability, validity, and ability for generalization as well as qualitative, quantitative, mix method research, and fix and flexible research designs.

Chapter 7
Kavita Gupta, The Maharaja Sayajirao University of Baroda, India

A research design is a deliberate, well-organized technique that a researcher follows when conducting a scientific study. It is the coexistence of previously identified elements with any additional knowledge or data that leads to a reasonable end result. In simpler terms, research design is a glue that keeps the research endeavor together. The present chapter focuses on quantitative research design, qualitative research design and mixed method design. This chapter will help the budding researcher to have a deeper understanding of research designs therein enabling the researcher to utilize them for their purpose of research.

Chapter 8

Thulitha Wickrama, University of Nebraska, Lincoln, USA
Michael J. Merten, University of Nebraska, Lincoln, USA
Nuwanthi Tharaka Perera, Girne American University, Cyprus

A literature review is a summary of existing literature on topics of interest to the study. It provides proof of a gap in the literature that must be filled by the current study. Having a thorough literature review is the first step in planning a new research project. There are several critical reasons for writing a literature review. First, it is to identify the practical problem. Second, it is to identify the theoretical problem. The researcher should examine the literature about the problem area; both the theoretical literature and research literature. This helps to identify specific research purposes, questions, or testable hypotheses. Published research often makes specific suggestions for future research in the last section of their articles. This chapter on the literature review will provide a step-by-step method to write an effective literature review.

Chapter 9

Peterson K. Ozili, Central Bank of Nigeria, Nigeria

This chapter examines the acceptable R-square in social science empirical modelling with particular focus on why a low R-square model is acceptable in empirical social science research. The paper shows that a low R-square model is not necessarily bad. This is because the goal of most social science research modelling is not to predict human behaviour. Rather, the goal is often to assess whether specific predictors or explanatory variables have a significant effect on the dependent variable. Therefore, a low R-square of at least 0.1 (or 10 percent) is acceptable on the condition that some or most of the predictors or explanatory variables are statistically significant. If this condition is not met, the low R-square model cannot be accepted. A high R-square model is also acceptable provided that there is no spurious causation in the model and there is no multi-collinearity among the explanatory variables.

Section 3
Quantitative Research Strategies

Chapter 10

*Sai Priyanka Pagadala, Indian Agricultural Research Institute, New
Delhi, India*
Sangeetha V., Indian Agricultural Research Institute, New Delhi, India
Venkatesh P., Indian Agricultural Research Institute, New Delhi, India
*Girish Kumar Jha, Indian Agricultural Research Institute, New Delhi,
India*

Social science research deals with the highly complex phenomenon guided by
various latent and interrelated constructs. As these constructs are invisible and
not directly measurable, social scientists employ highly sophisticated multivariate
analytical techniques that can simplify a complex data pattern to derive meaningful
conclusions. Structural equation modeling (SEM) is a methodology used to represent,
estimate, and test a network of relationships among variables. It is an integrated
model for hypothesis testing and constructs' validity. This chapter deals with the
various aspects of the SEM methodology, starting from describing the statistical
algorithms used, the role of theory, measurement and structural model, stages in
testing model validity, etc., meticulously explained in simple terms to provide with
a basic understanding of this intricate technique.

Chapter 11

*Sanath Jayawardena, Sri Lanka Institute of Information Technology, Sri
Lanka*
*R. A. R. C. Gopura, Department of Mechanical Engineering, University
of Moratuwa, Sri Lanka*

In the introduction, what decision making is and the significance of the decision
making was introduced. Few popular decision-making techniques were listed out
and three rational techniques were discussed in a nutshell. Then Professor Saaty's
seminal work, Analytical Hierarchical Process (AHP) was described, starting with
the evolution of AHP and moving towards its practice through a four-step process.
The AHP generates weights on a relative ratio scale with an input of measurements
on a standard scale and due to the normalization process linearity of the results
was destroyed. Finally, the four-step analytical hierarchical process was illustrated
through an example of the selection of a job. During the progression, outcomes of
the key theoretical aspects have been touched on without providing proof.

Analytic Network Process (ANP) is a generalized form of the Analytical Hierarchical Process (AHP). AHP is an objective theory of deriving the decision makings on absolute scale values starting from subjective relative measurements perhaps on tangible or intangible or a mix of both rated by the experts. A consistency measure of the relative ratings is verified with a consistency ratio to assure the ratings of the experts are consistent. The clustering of criteria/sub-criteria with inner and outer dependencies as well as feedback is taken into account in ANP. In ANP rather than a hierarchical process, a network structure is assumed and all nodes in the network are treated equally with interaction between nodes and grouping into clusters. A super-matrix is constructed, then normalized it to get weighted super matrix and raised it to a sufficient power to converge this into a unique eigen vector representing the final weights in limit super-matrix. Step by step iterations of ANP was demonstrated with a selection of car example.

Chapter 13

Although LGC modeling is gaining popularity in some disciplines, it has not been widely employed in social-epidemiological studies. This paper presents an introduction to the latent growth curve (LGC) technique within a structural equation modelling (SEM) framework as a powerful tool to analyze change in individual attributes over time (e.g., behaviors, attitudes, beliefs, and health) and potential correlates of such changes. The rationale for LGC analysis and subsequent elaboration of this statistical approach are discussed. For illustrations, Mplus (version 8, Muthén & Muthén, 2012) software and depressive symptoms as the individual outcomes attribute are used. The limitations of traditional analytical methods are also addressed. Particularly, the chapter considers socio-contextual factors as correlates of change in the outcomes variable, and examines the dynamic systematic relationship with the socioeconomic factors (however, these correlates can also be factors other than social-context).

Conducting qualitative research is an art. A skilled artist produces a high-quality piece of artwork using experience, tools, and intrinsic attributes developed over the years. In the same manner, a qualitative researcher produces a high-quality piece of research. Novice researchers need to gradually develop understanding and practice the fundamentals of qualitative research. In this context, the current chapter provides guided practical sessions, and research problems for experimentation and to improve their research capabilities. Conceptual sessions address interview technologies, recording tools, transcribing standards, coding, memoing, categorizing, and development of themes, which are the fundamentals in the grounded theory approach. The guided practical sessions that are selected carefully to make the targeted research group more comfortable and familiar with the coding process focus on the application of grounded theory approach for researchers to get a better understanding of concepts while clearing potential doubts in applications.

This chapter is an attempt to provide a basic understanding to law researchers of doctrinal legal research. The chapter is drafted in such a manner that it will give a systematic approach to acquainted with the doctrinal legal research. It includes the brief historical background, purpose, and steps to conduct doctrinal legal research, tools that are used, advantages and limitations, and summing up with a conclusion. The author has tried his best effort to give all the relevant tools, however, there were limitations due to the huge expansion of information and technology, e.g. social media. These limitations restrain the author to stick to more traditional tools of research.

Section 4
Research Results

This chapter is written with behavioural science students and emerging scholars in mind. Behavioural science in this context includes but is not limited to management sciences, social sciences, psychology, education, and any discipline that deals with human actions. The chapter is written to sharpen the knowledge and skills of students in these areas in writing a good quality research report (at advanced undergraduate level), thesis, or dissertation (at postgraduate level). The chapter has valuable hints that will guide behavioural science students and emerging scholars in writing good quality research reports, theses, or dissertations. The hints will also be helpful for supervisors and mentors in guiding and assessing their student's work. A research project, thesis, or dissertation is essential for graduation from tertiary institutions. The need, therefore, to write good quality research reports requires that students possess the necessary knowledge and skills in writing.

Chapter 17

Ltifi Moez, College of Science and Humanities, Shaqra University, Saudi Arabia & Higher Business School, Sfax University, Tunisia

Scientific publication is an essential aspect of technical, medical, social, economic, and other progress. New advances in human knowledge in any field are communicated to the rest of the world through publications. Scientific research is universal, so it is essential that this communicated knowledge is accurate, valid, reproducible, and practically useful. Researchers and scientists dream of publishing their work in high impact journals. To make these dreams come true, it is essential to learn, follow, and know the basic principles of research methodology and scientific publication. In this chapter book on the basis of the author's experiences and knowledge, the author presents a personal opinion on how to publish a chapter book in a high impact journal. The author talks about how to carry out good research, the design of the manuscript preparation, the respect of the editorial policy of the journal, the likely results, and the reasons for failure or success. The author provides the competitive weapons of publication in the form of advice, recommendations, and explanations, in order to achieve scientific success.

Chapter 18

Michael J. Merten, University of Nebraska, Lincoln, USA
Amanda Terrell, University of Arkansas, Fayetteville, USA

This chapter will provide valuable information to readers about several important issues in the publishing process. This chapter will concentrate on issues specific to: (1) selecting the appropriate journal for a manuscript; (2) writing effective abstracts that convey the main points of a manuscript; and (3) effectively addressing issues and comments raised during the peer review process. This chapter will discuss the importance of identifying a potential journal early in the writing process and reassessing goodness of fit once the manuscript is complete. Additionally, this chapter suggests ways to construct effective abstracts that provide an accurate picture of what the paper is about, which allows readers to determine whether or not they are interested in reading the article further. Lastly, this chapter will provide step-by-step instruction for researchers to effectively address comments that journal reviewers have provided, including the importance of addressing all comments thoroughly and the organization and presentation of the authors' comments in response to the reviewers.

Preface

We designed this book to help budding researchers speaking other languages. The experience that authors have gathered over years of work in research including teaching, guiding, and supervising the research work of graduate/postgraduate/doctoral students in the fields of management, business, and education have repeatedly showed some common qualities as successful researchers such as;

- sharp in thinking to identify researchable problems and study frameworks
- integrative in designing to relate problems to previous studies/knowledge
- pragmatic in approach to apply realistic research strategies/traditions
- skillful in technologies to apply appropriate methods
- professional in character to adhere international standards and ethical guidelines and
- proficiency in presenting research findings through publishable materials

The chapter contributors to this edited book have gained these proficiencies, qualities and skills through extensive experiences in teaching, doing rigorous research and publishing quality articles. As the title of this book suggests, with the target audience in mind, the authors exemplify the above characteristics by using more illustrations and simple language, hence this book enables the beginner to become Master of Research, especially to non-native English-speaking academics.

This book consists of 18 chapters are distributed as follows;

Section 1: Research Process and Philosophy: Chapters 1, 2, 3, 4 and 5
Section 2: Research Methods and Literature Review: Chapters 6, 7, 8 and 9
Section 3: Research Strategies/Traditions: Chapters 10, 11, 12, 13, 14 and 15
Section 4: Research results: Chapters 16, 17 and 18

It is our expectation that non-native English-speaking budding academics will enjoy research and gain an adequate understanding of the research methodology and methods from this book and apply them in a productive manner in both your work and everyday life. I take this opportunity to thank all the contributors and reviewers and, extent my greatest gratitude to IGI Global publishers for making this task a success.

CHAPTER DESCRIPTIONS

Section 1: Research Process and Philosophy

"Choosing a paradigm is important because it allows you to start forming research questions (RQs). This is useful, even if your questions start off vague" (Gournelos, Hammonds and Wilson, 2019, p. 8).

Describing the researchers' stances/positions on his/her worldviews at the outset of a research report is important and helpful to understand the interpretations/discussions of the research findings and evaluate conclusions drawn from research. The choice of underpinning philosophy is significantly influenced by the author's psychosocial, economic and cultural backgrounds. The Chapters in this section would be helpful to critically analyze the salient features and developing cogent arguments from researchers' personal perspectives and worldviews.

Multivism of ontology, epistemology, methodology and methods (Chapter 4) and *Cross-functional* process of conducting research (Chapter 1) are two terms introduced in this section.

Chapter 1: Integrated-Flexible Research Methodology: An Alternative Approach

Candauda Arachchige Saliya, *Sri Lanka Institute of Information Technology, Sri Lanka*

This chapter discusses the practical research process followed by many social researchers. In this chapter, the research elements/activities/process are presented in a form of Ven diagram illustrating the *Integrated-flexible* manner of conducting the research process in practice. It is not really a novel methodology, but an alternative presentation of the manner research is conducted by many researchers. This chapter also attempts to connect post-positivist ideologies with quantum physics.

The author attempts to justify this approach in association with theories such as quantum mechanics, social constructivism, critical thought, pseudoscience and pragmatism etc., hence making his argument very cogent and plausible.

Chapter 2: Paradigm; Positivism, Interpretivism, Pragmatists and Critical Thought

Nisha Jayasuriya, *Sri Lanka Institute of Information Technology, Sri Lanka*

This chapter aims to provide a simple but complete idea about the complex philosophical concepts in the social research field. It covers the key concepts in the research paradigm: ontology, epistemology, and methodology. Researchers can understand these concepts and decide the best approach to investigate different phenomena. To make these difficult concepts simple, this chapter has been organized with simple explanations, graphs and video links.

Chapter 3: Pragmatism Paradigm for Social Science Research

Nagalingam Nagendrakumar, *Sri Lanka Institute of Information Technology, Sri Lanka*
    Naduni Madhavika, *Sri Lanka Institute of Information Technology, Sri Lanka*

This chapter helps budding researchers to understand a paradigm called *pragmatism*. The chapter could be read quite easily, even if one has only a minimal background on the topic of combining qualitative and quantitative methods. To provide a basic understanding to the 'pragmatism paradigm', the chapter is concisely summarized.

Chapter 4: Research Philosophy: World-views, Perspectives and Theories

Candauda A Saliya, *Sri Lanka Institute of Information Technology, Sri Lanka*

This chapter summarizes the historical developments of research philosophy in the academic field and provide a simple framework for non-native English-speaking budding researchers. Understanding of this historical evolution is useful in justifying authors' choices and presenting them clearly in the research report. It is important to mention your stances on them in the research report at the very beginning. This chapter coins the term *Multivism* which is about dynamic positions of a researcher in contrasts to the bipolar-disordered extremism of objectivism and subjectivism of ontology, epistemology, methodology and methods.

Chapter 5: Social Science Philosophy Behind Data Analysis With Special Reference to Philosophical Perception

Kenneth Peprah, *SDD-UBIDS, Ghana*

This chapter discusses about the nature of the social sciences, human beings, their occupied environments, and, activities which are the targets of any study.

Hence, when it comes to the application of scientific methods in the sciences, there are divided opinions in the social sciences. One school of thought believes that the social sciences should use the same scientific methods and quantification just as the natural sciences; and, the other school of thought disagrees and advocates the use of qualitative/language methods. This chapter provides further grounds to the concept of *Multivism*.

Section 2: Research Methods and Literature Review

Different academic scholars have identified different research designs. These designs are basically grouped into two categories for research purposes, namely basic or fundamental design designs and applied research designs. It may be necessary to redesign the research problem (the first step 'decided' earlier) after reviewing the literature which is traditionally considered to be the second step in this process. Similarly, other steps are also supposed to be revisited back and forth as the research proceed.

The researcher does not have to be confined to a rigid framework that specifies a specific starting point where academic research should begin. This does not mean that you have to complete one task at a time and do the other. For example, literature review may be followed by reconsideration of the research problem or vice versa. These tasks should be repeated to select the optimal method.

Designs can be broadly classified into three types: Quantitative, Qualitative and Mixed method.

Chapter 6: Research Design

Krishantha Wisenthige, *Sri Lanka Institute of Information Technology, Sri Lanka*

The research design refers to the way that you choose to integrate the different components of the study in a coherent and logical way, thereby, ensuring you will effectively address the research problem; it constitutes the blueprint for the collection, measurement, and analysis of data. This chapter outlines different approaches for designing research.

Chapter 7: Research Design and Methods in Social Sciences Research

Kavita Gupta, *The Maharaja Sayajirao University of Baroda, India*

Research Design is a set of decisions about what, where, when, how much, and how to conduct an inquiry or research project. In this chapter, the three types of research designs, that is, Quantitative, Qualitative and Mixed method with respect to menstrual health are being discussed in detail. In order to achieve Sustainable development goals, maintenance of menstrual health is essential. Research in this area is very important in understanding menstrual experiences, and their intersections with physical, mental, and social health.

Chapter 8: Writing a Literature Review

Thulitha Wickrama, *University of Nebraska, Lincoln, USA*
    Michael J Merten, *University of Nebraska, Lincoln, USA*
    Nuwanthi Tharaka Perera, *Girne American University, Turkey/Cyprus*
    A literature review is a summary of the existing knowledge in the field regarding the topic. A literature review helps to identify the practical problem as well as the theoretical problem, and then to identify specific research purposes, questions, or testable hypotheses. Having a thorough literature review is the first step in planning a new research project. This chapter provides a comprehensive knowledge about what is a literature review, why we need a literature review, important facts to consider when writing a literature review and steps of writing a literature review.

Chapter 9: The Acceptable R-square in Empirical Modelling for Social Science Research

Peterson K Ozili, *Central Bank of Nigeria, Nigeria*
    This paper examines the acceptable R-square in empirical social science research. It focuses on why a low R-square model is acceptable in empirical social science research. As a general principle, an econometric model is considered to have a high predictive power if the model has a high R-square.
    Many social scientists get worried when their models report a very low R-square, below 0.6 (or 60 percent when expressed in percentage), and their worry is further amplified when they learn that statisticians and scientists in the pure sciences will dismiss a model as "weak", "unreliable" and "lacking a predictive power". In this paper, this issue is addressed and shows that empirical modelling in social science has a different purpose compared to empirical modelling in the pure science.

Section 3: Research Strategies: Quantitative and Qualitative

Acceptance of research results, regardless of the strategy used, is based on the validity/consistency/confirmability and reliability/credibility of the research data and methods used. Validity and reliability are the concepts of the quantitative tradition, and accordingly the qualitative concepts are confirmability and credibility. The detailed study of these concepts should be done in accordance with the chosen research method, using specific sources. The chapters 10, 11, 12 and 13 provides very advanced application of quantitative strategy. Chapter 14 is on Grounded Theory which is considered as 'rigorous' application of qualitative approach while chapter 15 is a kind of qualitative desk-research: A library-based Doctrinal legal research.

Chapter 10: An Overview of Structural Equation Modeling and Its Application in Social Sciences Research

Sai Priyanka, *Pagadala Indian Agricultural Research Institute, India*
   Sangeetha V, *Pagadala Indian Agricultural Research Institute, India*
   Venkatesh P, *Pagadala Indian Agricultural Research Institute, India*
   Girish Kumar, *Pagadala Indian Agricultural Research Institute, India*
   The advantage of Structural Equation Modeling (SEM) is its ability to incorporate both quantitative and qualitative data (in coded form) for analysis. This framework is an integration that combines Measurement Theory from Psychology, Factor analysis from Psychology and statistics, Path analysis from biology (epidemiology), Regression modeling from statistics and Simultaneous equations from Econometrics. Therefore, in existing literature SEMs are also known as Covariance structure analysis, Analysis of Moment Structures (AMOS), Analysis of Linear Structural Relationships (LISREL), and Causal modelling. This chapter provides an overview of this advanced quantitative technique.

Chapter 11: Analytical Hierarchical Process in Decision Making: AHP

T S S Jayawardena, *University of Moratuwa, Sri Lanka*
   RARC Gopura, *University of Moratuwa, Sri Lanka*
   The analytical hierarchical process (AHP) is widely used in cost-benefit analysis, strategic planning, research and development priority setting and selection, technology choice, investment priority, priority for development criteria, evaluation of telecommunication service, and other evaluation of alternatives.

   The AHP was first coined by Thomas L. Saaty, as "A scaling method for priorities in hierarchical structures" in 1977. Subsequently, a large number of papers were published explaining and illustrating the analytic hierarchical process. Then the AHP concept was so appealing to many types of research, that researchers started to use it intensively in their research. Professor Saaty's seminal scholarly publication in 1988 has been rewarded with more than 84,400 citations.

Chapter 12: Analytical Network Process in Decision Making

T S S Jayawardena, *University of Moratuwa, Sri Lanka*
  C S Jayawardena, *University of Moratuwa, Sri Lanka*

The author of the previous chapter (Chapter 11) confesses that the analytical hierarchical process (AHP) suffers from a serious limitation in assuming independence among the decision-making criteria as well as the absence of feedback between layers. In real-world decision-making problems especially in complex decisions, cross-dependency among criteria and alternatives as well as feedback is inevitable. This circumstance paved the way for the development of a much more generic framework by the same originator, Prof. Saaty, in 1996 and it is called Analytical Network Process (ANP). In ANP, the multilayered structure can view much as a network structure rather than a hierarchy when modeling due to interdependencies of higher-level elements from lower-level elements, and also of the elements within the same level. Hence the name was derived as Analytical Network Process. ANP also allows the inclusion of all the relevant criteria (tangible or intangible, objective or subjective, etc.) including clustered sub-criteria that can help in arriving at an optimal decision.

Chapter 13: Estimating Latent Growth Curve Models (LGCM): An Introduction

KAS Wickrama, *University of Georgia, USA*

This chapter provides an overview of latent growth curve modeling (LGCM), and demonstrates the strengths of this approach via a practical illustration with Mplus software. A LGCM estimation can be considered as two different processes capturing intra- and inter- change; a latent initial level and a latent slope, then growth factors estimate the average trajectory and variation across individuals' trajectories. Therefore, a LGM allows researchers to examine individual trajectories over time and their inter-individual variations simultaneously and to investigate how these trajectories are associated with predictors and distal outcomes.

Chapter 14: Simple Guide to Conduct Qualitative Research Using Grounded Theory Method

A Ranasinghe MW Amaradasa, *The University of Fiji, Fiji*

Conventional research is conducted to describe research problems with the help of existing theoretical framework. The "Grounded Theory" approach minimizes advocates the use of any theoretical framework other than methods followed in the process of building a new concept. The concept is established using original data gathered from original primary sources.

The foundation for using the grounded theory approach is data gathered from surveys and interviews which should be designed very carefully to capture the original data while maintaining neutrality to avoid any bias. The author does not intend to describe survey design and interview design in this chapter, but it is important to note the criticality of their designs to conduct quality qualitative research.

Chapter 15: Doctrinal Legal Research: A Library-based Research

Gaurav Shukla, *The University of the South Pacific, Fiji*

In this research methodology one doesn't have to work or collect data from the field rather the researcher composes a descriptive and detailed analysis of legal rules and regulations, case laws, juristic writings, etc from primary and secondary sources. The doctrinal legal method revolves around gathering information, organizing them, and describing the law.

This chapter provides the readers with the tools that are traditional as well as contemporary for conducting doctrinal legal research. Its purpose and steps to conduct are elaborated in the later part of the chapter followed by the advantages and limitations of doctrinal legal research. This chapter will help the law researcher to explore the doctrinal legal research method which has been useful for attorneys, judges, etc, this method helps to examine legal theories and doctrines and provide the solution to legal problems with lesser time.

Section 4: Research Results

It is a known fact that publishing a paper in a journal is harder than gaining a PhD. The main reason for this difficulty is the time it takes for peer review and the inability to submit a manuscript to several journals simultaneously. Almost all scholarly journals have a peer-review process, a quality control mechanism in which one to four scholars who are faculty experts in the author's field evaluate each article. These peer reviewers identify inadequacies, misinterpretations, and errors; provide recommendations to the author for improvement; and aid the editor in making a decision about the value of the work.

Chapter 16: Basics of Research Report Writing for Behavioural Science Students and Emerging Scholars

Bassey Asuquo Bassey, *University of Calabar, Calabar, Nigeria*
Valentine Joseph Owan, *University of Calabar, Calabar, Nigeria*

This chapter was written primarily to guide emerging scholars, students and early career researchers on the basic constituents of a research report for a thesis, projects, dissertation and other related documents. The theme of this chapter is twofold; for students writing research projects, theses and dissertations and for supervisors and mentors in guiding and assessing their students' work. The need to adopt best practices in research reports and supervise students' theses motivated the authors to write this chapter.

Chapter 17: Scientific Publication Guide for Non-native English-speaking Researchers

Ltifi Moez, *Shaqra University & Sfax University, Tunisia*

The objective of this chapter is to help researchers produce a manuscript of high scientific quality in order to meet the requirements of the impacted journals and succeed in their publications. The scientific quality, experience, writing capacity ... vary from one researcher to another. Even the most experienced scientists sometimes forget the requirements of scientific research as well as the requirements of the journals, which generally results in a lower level of their productions. In this chapter, the author presents the essential requirements and how to manage researchers' knowledge in order to achieve a solid publication with high impact.

Chapter 18: Publishing; Selecting Journals, Writing Abstracts, and Addressing Issues Raised by Reviewers

Michael J Merten, *University of Nebraska, Lincoln, USA*
    Amanda Terrell, *University of Arkansas-Fayetteville, USA*

The process of selecting a journal to review and publish your manuscript involves a series of considerations and decisions. The primary concern is whether a journal's subject area encompasses a potential publication's topic and scientific approach. This is not always readily apparent and may require a decision-making process. This chapter provides good insight on how to organise a journal submission by selecting right journals, writing correct Abstracts, and addressing issues raised by reviewers.

Candauda A. Saliya
Sri Lanka Institute of Information Technology, Sri Lanka
1 February 2023

Section 1
Research Process and Philosophy

Chapter 1
Integrated–Flexible Research Methodology:
An Alternative Approach

Candauda Arachchige Saliya
https://orcid.org/0000-0002-9239-1648
Sri Lanka Institute of Information Technology, Sri Lanka

ABSTRACT

The research process is not a smooth process that moves from one stage to another, or a sequential process growing from the roots of ontology and epistemology towards the data collection and analytical techniques and interpretations. The existentialist position of the interpretive/reformist paradigm is that reality is subjective and multiple, that it does not exist independently in the human mind. Their epistemological stance is that the available knowledge depends on the researcher's thoughts and desires. That is, "knowledge" is created by the seeker and deploying a specific methodology which is not necessarily a sequential set of "stages", a "step-by-step" course or a "layer-by-layer" peeling activity like peeling-off an onion.

It is more practical to follow a continuous interaction progression by reconsidering, revising, and revisiting activities to achieve more presentable cogent arguments. Therefore, a dynamic research process is presented as a integrated-flexible vigorous set of activities as a Ven diagram by adding the activity of publishing as a critical element of the research process.

DOI: 10.4018/978-1-6684-6859-3.ch001

INTRODUCTION

Social Research is defined as a systematic in-depth study about social issues and the way we understand the world. It is, in fact,

"...a never-ending journey of discovery, because the 'knowledge' that is presented today as 'new' can be nullified by another 'new' discovery tomorrow. Such negatives occur frequently and inevitably, reminding us of the impermanent nature of the world" (Saliya, 2022, p. 7).

Common knowledge is generated from critical discourses among scholars holding different world views. However, the *falsification principle* proposed by Karl Popper (1959 in McLeod, 2020) argues that the possibility of falsifying a scientific theory is an essential feature for knowledge to be scientific. Meanwhile, more modern scholars such as Mano Sinham (2020) reject this falsification requirement as a myth and suggest abandoning it.

Every type of research, either of natural sciences (biology, chemistry, mathematics, etc.) or social sciences (economics, political science, accounting, history, and aesthetics etc.), it is scientific because they follow a systematic process; methodological.

Academic research is basically of two types; quantitative and qualitative and, recently a third type (mixed method) came by combining these two to add more rigor. Traditionally, only quantitative research using numbers were considered as scientific but today qualitative inquiry, which goes beyond dealing with numbers, too is also considered as valid, dependable, credible, and therefore scientific. The 'knowledge' discovered through academic research should be published in indexed journals/conferences or as book chapters in edited books published by reputed publishers. Otherwise, such discoveries would be wasted; "publish or perish", they say.

SOCIAL RESEARCH AND QUANTUM MECHANICS

Contradicting positivist scientism, the analogy between evolution and quantum mechanics and sociology has demonstrated that quantum mechanics has an individual and a social consciousness for material objects (Nakmanson, 2003). Positivism, which is based on empiricism is challenged by post-positivist paradigms such as interpretivism, constructivism, pragmatism and critical thought. Empiricism is based on sensory experiences, through five senses, but certain things such as gravitation or any other attraction, which is felt towards the earth, cannot be smelled, tasted, touched, heard or seen with our five sensatory organs. There are certain things that cannot be cognized or apprehended through five senses. Therefore, the positivist-objectivist concept about *single* "truth" and *existence* of "reality" independent of the observer is convincingly disputed by post-positivists based on a subjectivist nature of *multiple* "truths" and *relative* "realities" and, sometimes even reject their existence.

This perspective coincides well with Einstein's theory of relativity and quantum mechanics which argue that certain observations are mental constructs and could vary when they are observed (see double slit experiment; Nakmanson, 2003). They argue that observations can control the behavior of material objects and, acknowledged that space and time are inextricably connected and, also reject the existence of gravity, hence reality too.

It is surprising to watch the wave–particle duality of light and the way observations can control the behavior of material objects, see the you tube video in Box 1.

Box 1.

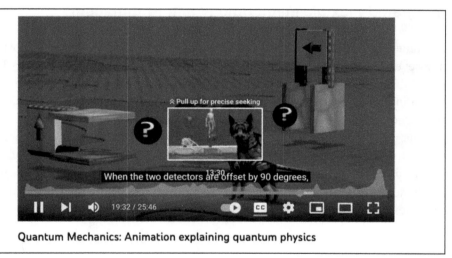

Quantum Mechanics: Animation explaining quantum physics

https://www.youtube.com/watch?v=iVpXrbZ4bnU

Many researchers in social science (for example; Denzin and Lincoln, 2005; Saunders et al, 2019; Guba, 2018) suggest that the research process is a sequential, step by step or a straight line series of activities comprised with stages. This approach is rigid and grounded on a single truth (positivist) and, even contradictory to their post-positivist ideology. Therefore, this chapter proposes a dynamic approach to follow the different activities/functions of conducting social research; integrated-flexible methodology which would be in line with post-positivist subjectivist ideology.

Integrated-Flexible Approach and Theories of Reasoning

In social research, three methods have been used to reach conclusions: induction, deduction and abduction. Deduction is a derivation, about proving something while induction attempts to generalize observations based on empirical evidence. However, abduction, by contrast, merely supposes that something might be the case in order to introduce a new idea or to understand a new phenomenon (Bude, 2004). The existing research methodologies are about following a strict adherence to principles, a step-by-step process, to arrive at an assured derivation or testing a theory or generalization of observations. It is time to abandon this straight jacket type positivist approaches. Researchers should be able to and capable of starting research from any 'stage' or 'step' of research activities without following a sequential or peeling of layers like an onion, to break free from the narrow frames imposed by traditional logic.

Integrated-Flexible Methodology and Pragmatism

Prominent sociologists such as Max Weber and George Simmel rejected positivism and several forms of empirical and rational thought while Charles Sanders Peirce, father of pragmatism, introduced the concept of abduction inferencing (abduction reasoning) as an alternative to David Hume but complementary to (in parallel with) the induction and deduction logics.

The positivism lies on one corner, interpretivism lies on another corner while the realism and pragmatism shares both features and critical paradigm stands in the middle providing critical insight towards emancipation and equality. The direction of single headed arrows indicates evolutionary progression and double headed arrows indicates a critical approach towards all three paradigms (Figure 1).

Figure 1. Interrelationship of paradigms

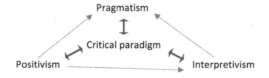

The pragmatism may lie anywhere on the continuum, but it will take different shapes based on the research type. If it is exactly in-between the two extremes, it becomes a balanced pragmatism, if it lies towards the left side the pragmatism effort is highly exposed to positivism and if it is vice versa the pragmatism effort is highly exposed to interpretivism. The critical paradigm lies in the middle providing critical insight towards all three paradigms and can belong to any paradigm according to the circumstances but towards human emancipation and equal rights. It is not realistic to decide the paradigm to which the researcher belongs at the beginning of the research as the *onion* suggests. The researcher should be free to decide the paradigm at a later stage to interpret the research results and construct cogent arguments more plausibly, convincingly and produce 'publishable' conclusions. Hence the integrated-flexible research approach is more practical.

Integrated-Flexible Approach and Human Dynamism

Wilhelm Dilthey (1725) argued that scientific explanations did not reach the inner nature of phenomena endorsing of G. B. Vico's argument (1725) that life should also be taught to defend themselves on many sides of the controversy. Because man has a free and brilliant style of expression, they are able to build arguments that are more logical and of the most optimal accuracy. These ideologies also provide plausible grounds that single rigid set of principles are not very helpful for social researchers to conduct their research. They are, as free and brilliant human beings, capable of deploying the research process to suit the circumstances and, cross through the various "stages" or "steps" or "layers" of the research process freely towards presenting cogent arguments/conclusions.

Integrated-Flexible Methodology and Pseudoscience

Pseudoscience consists of statements, beliefs, or practices that claim to be both scientific and factual but are incompatible with the scientific method. The errors of human reasoning can be subject to pseudoscience and irrationality. Pseudoscience is described as an 'imitation of real science'. As social constructivism insists that the knowledge is socially situated and built by interacting with others, so do the research process. The activities; stages, steps and layers of a research process could interact with each other to construct knowledge in the constructivism paradigm. Social constructism focuses on the objects created through the social interaction of a group, while the worldview of social reformism focuses on the learning of an individual as a result of his or her interactions within a group. Strong social reformism as a philosophical approach suggests that the natural world has little or no role in the construction of scientific knowledge.

Many researchers insist that research methods and knowledge are co-evolving (Varga, 2018).

The Integrated-flexible vigorous research methodology model facilitates this co-evolving cointegrated function between research methods, practices and knowledge.

Alternative Approach

The website shown in Box 2 provides a useful insight on such a research methodology. This chapter promotes alternative approaches for doing research to such traditional sequential-linear approaches such as the research onion and research tree.

The integrated-flexible research methodology is more appropriate to a wider range of research types. Table 1 shows this diversity.

Box 2.

Source: https://www.scribbr.com/dissertation/methodology/

Table 1. Diversity of academic research types

Aspect	FIELD	LAB/CLOSED STUDIES	ENVIRONMENT BASED	SOCIAL STRUCTURE	HUMAN STUDIES	PRODUCTS & PROCESSES
Purpose	Discovery	Double slit experiment	Flora & fauna species	Cause & effect relationships		The wheel
	Developments	Quantum physics	Artificial rain	Policy formulations	Coronary-artery stents	Information technology
	Explanations			Social injustice	Biographies	Cancerous effects
	Predictions	Comets & Asteroids	Climate change	Millennium goals		Hazards
Approach	Observations		Direct Observations	Ethnography	Surveys/Interviews	Market surveys
	Experiments	Robotics	Satellites		Thought experiments	Electronics and mechanicals
	Implementations	Green houses		Action research		
	Historical	Confirming	Excavations, Longitudinal studies and Generalising etc.			Effects of chemicals
Strategy	Statistical analyses	Descriptive analysis		Regression analysis	Multivariate analysis	Significance Tests
	Logical arguments	Proving or falsifying		Grand & Conspiracy theories		Complement & Substitute goods
	IT based	Software developments, simulations and algorithm etc.				

Source: Saliya, 2022

In this light, Saliya (2022) suggests that a researcher does not have to be confined to a rigid framework that specifies a specific starting point and stage by stage sequential approach because the depth and complexity of research plans can vary significantly.

Many models are discussed so far such as *onions (Saunders et al., 2019)*, *Trees* and *7Ps* (Saliya, 2021) and *10Ps* (Saliya, 2022). The 10Ps model encompasses elements such as **P**aradigm, **P**erspective, **P**urpose, **P**revious knowledge (literature review), **P**lanning and **P**rogramming, **P**lot (strategies), **P**rocedures (methods), **P**ersuasion (drawing conclusions) and finally **P**ublishing. This model has been reproduced as Integrated-flexible methodology using a Ven diagram.

Integrated-flexible Model of Research Process

Traditionally, academic research follows the following activities;

1. Identifying a research problem
2. Reviewing literature
3. Selecting methods for data management and analyses
4. Organizing results with discussions and finally,
5. Drawing conclusions

When novice researchers do real research, it seems not practical to implement this process in such a linear-sequential manner;

"...it may be necessary to redesign the research problem (the first step 'decided' earlier) after reviewing the literature which is traditionally considered to be the second step in this process. Similarly, other steps are also supposed to be revisited back and forth as the research proceed." (Saliya, 2022, p. 47).

As pointed out before with the support of numerous literature, the positivist approach for research is not a smooth process that moves from one stage to another, or a sequential process like peeling-off an onion, layer by layer, or like a tree growing from the roots of ontology and epistemology. Therefore, a dynamic research process is presented as a integrated-flexible vigorous set of activities as shown in Figure 2.

Also, it is practical to follow a continuous interaction by reconsidering, revising, and revisiting activities to achieve more presentable cogent arguments. On the other hand, as Saliya suggests, in post positivist paradigms,

"...it is of great value to select and justify the methodology of a research report in a practical as well as philosophical way, because the paradigm to which the researcher belongs may influence and obscure the observations and conclusions. It is important

to understand that these element lenses are not an unalterable alignment, but a flexible program that should change the order from time to time and lead to more successful results." (2022, p. 47).

Figure 2. The Integrated-flexible total process of doing research and publishing results
Source: Saliya (2022)

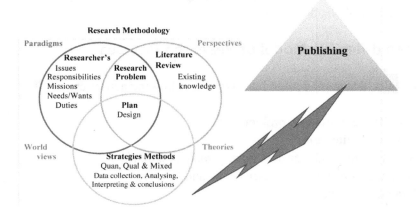

REFERENCES

Alvesson, M. & Sköldberg, K. (2009). Reflexive Methodology: New Vistas for Qualitative Research. London. Sage

Bude, H. (2004). The art of interpretation. In U. Flick, E. von Kardorff, & I. Steinke (Eds.), *A companion to qualitative research.* Sage.

Creswell, J. W. (2007). *Qualitative Inquiry and Research Design; Choosing among five traditions.* Sage.

Denzin, N. K., & Lincoln, Y. S. (2005). *The landscape of qualitative Research: theories and issues.* Sage.

Gournelos, T., Hammonds, J. R., & Wilson, M. A. (2019). *Doing Academic Research: A Practical Guide to Research Methods and Analysis.* Sage.

Gournelos, T., Hammonds, J. R., & Wilson, M. A. (2019). *Doing Academic Research: A Practical Guide to Research Methods and Analysis., Taylor & Francis Group.* Routledge.

Gray, E. D. (2018). Doing Research in the Real World (4t ed.). London, Sage.

Guba, E. (1990). *The Paradigm Dialog.* Sage.

Guba, E. G., & Lincoln, Y. S. (1988). Do inquiry paradigms imply inquiry methodologies? In D. M. Fetterman (Ed.), *Qualitative approaches to evaluation in education: Thesilent scientific revolution* (pp. 89–115). Praeger.

Guba, E. G., & Lincoln, Y. S. (1989). What is This Constructivist Paradigm Anyway? In *Fourth Generation Evaluation.* Sage.

Guba, E. G., & Lincoln, Y. S. (1994). Competing paradigms in qualitative research. In N. K. Denzin & Y. S. Lincoln (Eds.), *The Handbook of Qualitative Research* (3rd ed., pp. 105–117). Sage.

Guba, E. G., & Lincoln, Y. S. (2005). *Paradigmatic controversies, contradictions, and emerging confluences. The SAGE handbook of qualitative research. N. K. Denzin and Y. S. Lincoln.* Sage.

Gummesson, E. (2003). All research is interpretive! *Journal of Business and Industrial Marketing, 18*(6/7), 482–492. https://doi.org/10.1108/08858620310492365

Helen, E. L. (1990). *Science as Social Knowledge: Values and Objectivity in Scientific Inquiry.* Princeton University Press.

Mario, L. (2013). *Brilliant Blunders: From Darwin to Einstein - Colossal Mistakes by Great Scientists That Changed Our Understanding of Life and the Universe.* Simon & Schuster.

Maxwell, J. A. (2013). *Qualitative research design: An interactive approach.* SAGE.

Maykut, P. S. (1994). *Beginning Qualitative Research: A Philosophic and Practical Guide.* Falmer Press.

McLeod, S. A. (2020), May 01). Karl popper - theory of falsification. *Simply Psychology.* https://www.simplypsychology.org/Karl-Popper.html

Nakhmanson, R. (2003). Quantum mechanics as a sociology of matter *Quantum Physics.* https://doi.org/ doi:10.48550/arXiv.quant-ph/0303162

O'Leary, Z. (2005). *Researching real-world problems.* Sage.

O'Leary, Z. (20014). *The essential guide to doing research.* London: Sage.

Popper, K. (1959). The Logic of Scientific Discovery (2002 pbk; 2005 ebook ed.). Routledge.

Saliya, C. A. (2017), Doing Qualitative Case Study Research in Business Management, International Journal of Case Studies Journal ISSN (2305-509X), 6 (12), pp. 96 – 111.

Saliya, C. A. (2021). Conducting Case Study Research: A Concise Practical Guidance for Management Students. *International Journal of KIU*, *2*(1), 1–13. https://doi.org/10.37966/ijkiu20210127

Saliya, C. A. (2022). Doing Social Research and Publishing Results. Springer. https://link.springer.com/book/10.1007/978-981-19-3780-4

Saunders, M., Lewis, P., Thornhill, A., & Bristow, A. (2019). Research Methods for Business Students Chapter 4: Understanding research philosophy and approaches to theory development. Harlow, United Kingdom. Pearson.

Varga, L. (2018). Mixed methods research: A method for complex systems. In E. Mitleton-Kelly, A. Paraskevas, & C. Day (Eds.), *Edward Elgar handbook of research methods in complexity science* (pp. 34–39). Edward Elgar Publishing.

Chapter 2
Paradigm:
Positivism, Interpretivism, Pragmatists, and Critical Thought

Nisha Jayasuriya
Sri Lanka Institute of Information Technology, Sri Lanka

ABSTRACT

This chapter aims to provide a simple but a complete idea about the difficult concepts in the research field. Research paradigm is a concept which is difficult for new researchers to understand and memorize. This chapter covers the key concepts in the research paradigm: ontology, epistemology, and methodology. Researchers can understand these concept and decide the best paradigm to investigate different phenomena. To make these difficult concepts simple, this chapter has been organized with brief explanations and graphs.

INTRODUCTION

Research philosophy and methodology are some critical aspects that make research sound and successful. A researcher who conducts the study without a proper understanding of these concepts may end up doing an incomplete study. Hence, the simple approach used in this chapter will be useful for novel researchers to make sure that they are following the correct systematic approach in conducting this study. Following the correct approach will essentially be helpful for the researchers in publishing their articles in reputed journals and conferences.

DOI: 10.4018/978-1-6684-6859-3.ch002

This chapter aims to provide a simple but complete idea about the difficult concepts in the research field. It covers the key concepts in the research paradigm: ontology, epistemology, and methodology. Researchers can understand these concepts and decide the best approach to investigate different phenomena. To make these difficult concepts simple, this chapter has been organized with simple explanations, graphs and video links.

RESEARCH PARADIGM

A new researcher who is curious about social problems thinks about giving solutions through conducting research. There is a novel and fresh idea like a seed to grow. This curious researcher, like a planter, needs to find appropriate soil and fertilizer to grow this seed and this process is like selecting a research paradigm for the study.

There is no one method to plant your seeds, but there are several methods. Like that, a researcher can see the problem from different angles. These different viewpoints we can see as research paradigms. So, once you have a research idea, you should think what the best way to grow the idea and get a solution for the research question. It is like finding a proper ground to plant your seeds. If you select the wrong place, you will not get the expected crop. Same as a plant if you do not select the correct respondents your findings may not be valuable.

In the field of research, the research paradigm is called the way you understand the reality of the world. A paradigm is based on assumptions about 1) ontology, 2) epistemology, 3) and methods (Figure 1). These elements can be identified as the foundation of research and it is very important to have a clear understanding to make a systematic study successful. Paradigm contains important assumptions about the way the researcher sees the world. The research approach, strategy, and methodology are part of this assumption and are based on the selection of the researcher (Saunders, et al., 2012). Therefore, this chapter focuses on discussing this belief system in detail.

Ontology

Everyone wears their glasses when they see the world. People make different assumptions about reality based on their experiences and assumptions. Same as that, ontology can be identified as the nature of our belief about reality (Saunders, et al., 2012). Before starting the study researchers have some assumptions about reality and how it exists. E.g., Is everything and everyone temporary? So, the answer is yes, everything temporary, or no, they are not. Whatever your answer, it is based on your experiences and assumptions. It explains the way you see the world.

Figure 1. Research Paradigm (Video Link for research paradigm: https://www. youtube.com/watch?v=8xvpxBVCo0c&t=137s)
(Image source: Royal Queen Seeds, 2023)

Accordingly, the researcher also has some assumptions about a different phenomena such as world hunger, poverty, gender issues, company performances etc. Accordingly ontology concern the nature of social realities (Bryman & Bell, 2011). While some researchers believe there should be only one reality which can be generalized to everyone (a single verified reality), other researchers may believe in the existence of multiple realities (socially constructed multiple realities). According to these assumptions, ontology can be identified in two streams objectivism and subjectivism (Figure 2).

Figure 2. Ontology

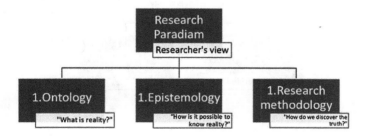

Epistemology

Epistemology is the concept of knowledge and supports to decision of how and from where to gather knowledge. As the researcher's sight of the world and knowledge affect his or her data interpretation, it is necessary to have a clear philosophical standpoint from the beginning of the research. For example, is the world consisting of only things which feel to our five senses or is there a different world out there which we have not even noticed? Someone may be curious about knowing the truth about the world reality. However, sometimes things we feel in our five senses are misleading. For example, a straight stick submerged in water looks bent. If someone thinks it is bent, then they mistake about how the world is.

According to Buddhism none of our senses is guaranteed to present what the world is. One may identify something in a square shape and filled with paper as a book based on their previous experience. A newborn baby who has no experience does not realize it as a book. However, when that baby gets old, he will get to know from others that thing is a book and start to believe them. Hence, knowledge can be identified as a combination of reality and belief. However, there is a reality out there which cannot feel by the five senses and is difficult to understand.

In the field of research, epistemology focuses on how knowledge is gathered from which sources. Researchers are highly confident about their view of the world and their knowledge strongly influenced the interpretation of data. Based on these knowledge differences there are several research philosophies emerged in the world. Positivism and interpretivism can be considered as initial approaches and considering some drawbacks of these basic methods, some contemporary philosophies also enter into the field (Figure 3).

Figure 3. Basic research philosophies

Positivism

In the positivist philosophy, the researcher believes that research needs to be independent of the researcher. Researchers observed the phenomenon that exists independently and does not participate or disturb what is happening (Saunders, et al., 2012). Most scientific or quantitative studies use positivism as a philosophy.

Positivist methodology relies heavily on experimentation. As a results sometime positivism mistakenly considered as a synonymous with science and the scientific (Bryman & Bell, 2011). Positivists try to identify cause and effect relationship between phenomena. Positivism entail both a deductive approach (2) and an inductive strategy (Bryman & Bell, 2011). First, the researcher may identify independent and dependent variables based on theories or past studies. Then hypotheses are proposed. Then the collected data is analyzed using the statistical method and the proposed hypothesis is confirmed or rejected depending on these results. The epistemological position of positivism is that of objectivism. Researchers observe the objectives to study phenomena that happened independently without interfering with them. Due to reality being expected to be context-free, the positivist expects different researchers who work in different times and places should convey the same conclusion about phenomena. Accordingly, the positivism philosophy expects once a relationship is established using a statical method it should be able to generalize to another study. That means if the same systematic approach is followed in a different context the results of that study should be the same as the previous study. For example, if it could identify A caused B, then a theory will be formulated for wider applicability. To generalize the results, the researcher should follow a systematic process strictly. In this process, research needs to be independent of the researcher and the sample should be probabilistic.

Positivistic research is quantitative. Here, the researcher believes that any human behaviour can be studied and predicted quantitatively. While using the positivist philosophy the researchers control all the other factors that can ruin the research by their impact. However, to have a controlled environment the researchers must conduct the study in a laboratory environment like scientific experiments. However, human behaviour is difficult to study in controlled environments. This makes it difficult for social scientists to use positivism in the study.

A similar viewpoint to positivism was carried out by Karl Marx in his communism concept. Accordingly, everyone in the world should be treated equally without considering the different capabilities and motivations of people. On one hand, this concept would benefit society by reducing the income disparity among people. However, on the other hand, it mistreats the people who are dedicated and motivated toward personal and economic development by treating the same as others who are not that dedicated.

The criticism of positivism caused the emergence of post-positivism philosophy. This can be identified as an attempt to overcome the weaknesses in positivism. This position can be identified as critical realism. It assumes reality exists independently. However, due to the complexity of social phenomena; using only one method cannot be captured perfectly. Therefore, it recognizes the possibility of including the researcher's own beliefs and values in what they observed.

Box 1.

As example, Tom wants to know what factors effect on customer satisfaction in the hotel they operate. To understand what factors behind customer satisfaction, he has studied the a past study conducted in this field and found that service quality, cleanliness, food quality and location attractiveness work as the factors behind it. This study followed positivism philosophy and quantitative approach. Data has been collected from a representative sample. Due to the generalizable nature of this research, Tom can expect the same outcome even he has conducted similar study in his hotel.

Video Link: https://www.youtube.com/watch?v=zUh5mAekUfA

Interpretivism

Interpretivism argues against the existence of universally identical truth. Human behaviours have been shaped by culture, history, situation factors and lived experiences. Therefore, the possibility of expecting the same results in all the phenomena without considering the above factors cannot be considered a valid approach. Further, in the interpretation of the data collected, the researcher works subjectively by adding their values and beliefs (Saunders, et al., 2012). The conclusions are mainly based on the interpretation of the researcher. In this approach, the social realities can be approached from different angles by different people. Taking interpretivism stance mean the researcher will come up with a surprising finding or at least finding that appear surprising (Bryman & Bell, 2011).

This view can be justified by taking the application of communism as an example. The idea related to communism is presented by Karl Marx considering his viewpoints and predictions to the world. Capitalism was criticized and focus was given to providing more freedom to the labour force through communism. Even though the idea is so noble, the communist approach was not generated equally results throughout the world. Even though capitalism was criticized some countries developed under capitalism and made sure that everyone had good living standards. On the other hand, there were some countries following the concepts of communism, but people had to do so many sacrifices. Further, countries which were developed under strict rules later tend to get more freedom and are open to competition and private ownership. Treating everyone seems to go against the nature of human beings who always have eager for development. This can be considered a good example to accept the differences and different capabilities of human beings which cannot fix into a single frame. In the field of research as well, this concept applies. The results applied to one region may not as it is generalized to the entire world.

This concept can be further explained through Buddhism as well. Accordingly, what people feel is subjective to the previous experience you had. When you see a bar of chocolate in a shop you might want to buy it. However, if you do not know the taste of chocolate before, even though you saw it, it will not create liking in your mind. People in different countries identified different tastes as their favourites and they have different parameters for beauty as well. All these depend on the experience and teaching they received and generated in their mind.

Interpretivism research is more toward qualitative researchers. In these studies data was collected through open-ended interviews, observations, field notes, personal notes, documents, etc. In the data collection and interpretation, the researchers expected to see the phenomenon as the participants rather than researchers. The approaches to analysing data are inductive. In this approach, researchers try to discover the patterns in the data by collapsing them into themes and developing theories. This is opposite to the deductive approach.

The criticism of interpretivism is caused by its soft nature. The use of a limited sample which does not represent the entire population and lack of objectivity makes this method weak in the field of research. However, researchers in this field disagree with the "soft" claim about this method highlighting this method demands a systematic, rigorous and attention in details approach. Further, while positivism has some advantages some phenomena are best described through an interpretive paradigm.

Box 2.

A researcher would like to study about the agricultural waste in developing countries. Due to inadequate studies in this field, it is very difficult to identify what are the elements impact on increase the waste. Further, the researcher has doubt that the context studies in developed countries are not applicable to the developing countries beyond the climate differences. Hence the researcher employed interpretivism concept and used semi-structured interviews to collect data. Based on the data collected from farmers in the country, the researcher has identified what factors behind the agricultural waste and developed a conceptual framework.

Video Link: https://www.youtube.com/watch?v=FybkUMplAlI

Pragmatism

Though there are basic two paradigms there are several other paradigms that emerged from these two. One of such paradigms that emerged in the social science research field is pragmatism, which is the mixed method of research. Pragmatism do not take a certain position to judge what makes a research is good (Sekaran & Bougie, 2016). This blended approach can be considered a consequence of the debate in the field about the best method for conducting research (Saunders, et al., 2012). Researchers could overcome the drawbacks of each method by using both methods for the study. Further, pragmatism can identify as an answer to the debate in selecting between positivism or interpretivism philosophy. Choosing between one position and the other is somewhat unrealistic in practice.

Pragmatism focuses more on practical aspects of reality rather than theories. Thus, the selection of epistemology and ontology should be based on the research question that needs to be answered. This concept avoids the researchers engaging in pointless debate about the best philosophy. Accordingly, researchers can select the appropriate way to do research based on their interests and the different practices will give a different meanings.

Box 3.

A researcher has identified the digital usage of women entrepreneurs as an understudied area. Due to unavailability of past literature, he thought of conducting in-depth interviews with the entrepreneurs and discuss what kind of tactics they have applied to make their business success. Then, using those findings he developed a conceptual framework and tested it covering a representative sample of women entrepreneurs in the entire country.

Video Link: https://www.youtube.com/watch?v=W_SDL07BmVo

Critical Theory

This philosophy believes that no object can be researched without being affected by the researcher. This concept goes against the belief that positivism bears related to the objectivity of the findings. Further, the generalizing concept in positivism is also criticized in this method. This philosophy is assumed that reality exists, however it has been shaped by different social factors like culture, religion, gender, ethics, and political environment. Hence, it is not possible to find a universal truth related to a social phenomenon. Another speciality of this philosophy is this study not to merely explain or understand society but to change it. In that sense, this philosophy is different to both positivism and interpretivism philosophies. Mainly the critical theory focuses on lighting up the beliefs and actions that limit human freedom.

In critical theory, most qualitative data is gathered even quantitative data also be used. Methodologies employed in critical theory are critical ethnography, critical discourse analysis, action research, ideology critique, etc.

Video Link - https://www.youtube.com/watch?v=WHJ_3uesiDQ

Research Methods

In the previous section, we discussed research methodology which consists of theoretical and philosophical assumptions about research. In this section, we will discuss the research methods which consist of practical steps necessary for the data collection and interpretation of data. Practising the 'correct' method is important for the validation of the research. When presenting research before a scholarly audience or publishing in an indexed journal, the correct method/approach followed for the research is very much important. Therefore, the researcher needs to understand the methods include two stages, the stage of data collection and the stage of data interpretation. (Figure 4)

Figure 4. Research Methodology

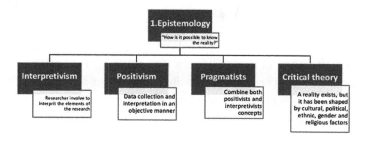

Data Collection Methods

In the field of research, the researchers can consider about two types of data. They are primary data and secondary data.

Primary data refers to the information and evidence gathered by the researcher for the current research purpose. These data have not been collected and stored before the research for another purpose. The researcher originally collected these data for his/her study. The main source of primary data in field research is surveys, interviews, discussions, and observations.

Secondary data refers to the data already collected and stored for another purpose. Researchers use data stored in the central bank, world bank or other reliable sources and analyzed them to find hidden links in these data sets. In addition to them, the researchers used past research, newspapers, reports and books as secondary data sources.

Any research needs a combination of these data to conduct the study. However, researchers should be able to identify the main types of data that they are required to collect. The decision about the type of data can be taken after considering the research problem and objectives. For example, if researchers focused on analyzing the perfume advertisements published in newspapers within a 10-year time duration, the research mainly depends on the secondary data. On the other hand, if the researcher wishes to study the reasons behind agricultural waste from farmers' perspectives, then the primary data should be collected from the farmers through interviews or survey methods.

Method of Interpretation

The collection of data is the important first step of the research. The next stage entails the challenges of what to do with the body of data, and data collected. Sometimes researchers develop a hypothesis and test them. However, by testing the hypothesis the purpose of social science research is fulfilled. The reason is data by itself does not tell anything. Therefore, even in a quantitative or qualitative study, researchers should interpret the findings. What the data tell us is what we interpret them to tell us. However, these interpretations need to be meaningful. Arbitrary interpretation will not add value to the study. Thus, social science researchers could get the support of theories to make sense of data, evidence and patterns. The researcher would get more acceptance for interpreting their findings beyond the statistical interpretations and linking to the relevant theoretical framework and practical context. There is no unified approach to interpreting data. However, researchers should be able to tell the reader the many stories told by the data. Further, he/she should be able to add credibility to the interpretation to make their claims sensible to the reader.

Video Link - https://www.youtube.com/watch?v=rWGyTOR0KVQ

CONCLUSION

Most of the researchers get confused in the selection of appropriate research methodology. This book chapter provides a simple guide to them in identifying the ideal method for their study. Further, researcher should identify that there is more than one approach in doing research. These different approaches support researchers to conduct diverse studies which match with their different viewpoints. These methodologies are not stagnant and growing gradually and new approaches come to the field of study. It is valuable for researcher to know different approaches and philosophies which will shape up the researches into ideal form.

SUMMARY

- The research paradigm consists of ontology, epistemology and research methodology.
- The selection of each method will be based on the viewpoint of the researcher and the nature of the study.
- Most quantitative studies go in line with the positivism concept while qualitative studies go with interpretivism.

REFERENCES

Bryman, A., & Bell, E. (2011) Business Research Methods. Oxford University Press.

Royal Queen Seeds (2023) *Get 1 Free Cannabis Seed With Your Order - Royal Queen Seeds.* Retrieved: https://www.royalqueenseeds.dk/free-seeds/201-1-free-cannabis-seed.html

Saunders, M., Lewis, P., & Thornhill, A. (2012) *Research methods for business students, International Journal of the History of Sport.* Pearson Education Limited.

Sekaran, U., & Bougie, R. (2016). *Research Methods for Business.* Wiley & Sons Ltd., doi:10.1007/978-94-007-0753-5_102084

Chapter 3
Pragmatism and Non-Native English Speakers:
Pragmatism Paradigm for Social Science Research

Nagalingam Nagendrakumar

(iD) https://orcid.org/0000-0002-3396-7854

Sri Lanka Institute of Information Technology, Sri Lanka

Naduni Madhavika

(iD) https://orcid.org/0000-0002-7613-1512

Sri Lanka Institute of Information Technology, Sri Lanka

ABSTRACT

The debate of application of research philosophy in social science research is trending. One side takes the positivism while another side depends on interpretivism, some other believes critical realism and the rest stand with pragmatism. Yet, the understanding on and interpretation of ontological argument and epistemological positioning of the pragmatism is criticized. Accordingly, the authors are motivated to critically argue that gap with empirical research evidence from management disciplines in Sri Lanka. The pragmatism followers contend that all beliefs, knowledge, and scientific concepts are provisional and defined by their practical application in ongoing experience, not by their correspondence with antecedent truth or reality (Carlsen and Mantere, 2007). Hence, recent social sciences studies are rooted in pragmatic ideas, practice-based approaches thereby harvesting the intersubjective knowledge. Thus, this chapter acknowledges the paradox of whether the definition of pragmatism could be universal or differs contextually research scholars.

DOI: 10.4018/978-1-6684-6859-3.ch003

INTRODUCTION

This chapter helps a budding researcher in understanding the "pragmatism paradigm". The chapter could be read quite easily, even if one has only a minimal background on the topic of combining qualitative and quantitative methods. To provide a basic understanding to the 'pragmatism paradigm', the chapter is concisely summarized, which serves as an introductory chapter.

Figure 1. Continuum Visualization of Pragmatism

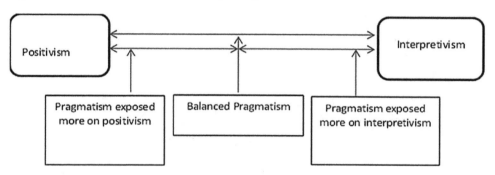

"Pragmatism" Overview

The ontological, epistemological, and axiological stances derive and direct the research philosophies. All research philosophies are "ism" driven (positivism, interpretivism, realism, pragmatism and many more). When we take as a continuum the positivism lies on the one extreme and interpretivism lies on the other extreme while the realism and pragmatism hang in-between the two. However, it must be noted that the "ism" travels throughout the continuum (figure 1). Here our job is to investigate only one "ism" *i.e.,* pragmatism. The pragmatism may lie anywhere on the continuum, but it will take different shapes based on the point on which you hang your research. If you hang it exactly in-between the two extremes, it becomes balanced pragmatism, if you lie towards the left-hand side your pragmatism effort is highly exposed to positivism and if it is vise-versa your pragmatism effort is highly exposed to interpretivism. Moving on the continuum and taking a decision on the point of pragmatism is totally depends on your experience.

The experience directs your point on the line based on the philosophical underpinnings *i.e.,* your ontology, epistemology, and axiology. The two extremes go with their own set of assumptions, but pragmatism does not stick to any of them individually but argues all are connected to a situation. Accordingly, it could take any form on the line. Figure 2 illustrates the significance of ontological, epistemological, and axiological stance of the pragmatist. You can see the area is not equally divided among the three since all can play different role in different magnitude in different situations in pragmatism. That is how, it is argued that pragmatist is free to travel either direction on the continuum.

Figure 2. Philosophical Underpinnings of Pragmatism

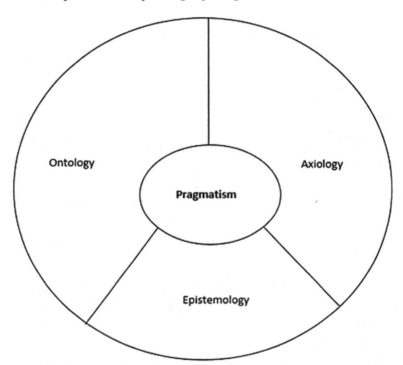

According to the pragmatism philosophy, all beliefs, knowledge, and scientific concepts are provisional and defined according to their usage in ongoing experience, not in accordance with antecedent truths or reality. Many contemporary frontiers of organization studies are rooted in pragmatics. Rational cognition and rational purpose cannot be separated according to pragmatism as a theory of truth. It is impossible to separate people's beliefs and knowledge from their contexts of use and actions. As far as recent reforms of New Public Sector Financial Reporting System (NPSFRS) by Sri Lanka incorporating the International Public Sector Accounting Standards (IPSAS) are concerned, Nagendrakumar (2017) argues that reform must be looked at pragmatist point of view. Many attempts of NPSFRS reforms in the world failed since it was approached based on truth and reality that exist in the private sector. That is accrual accounting practices have well established in the private sector. New public financial management tries to incorporate the private sector accrual accounting practices to the public sector. Once the private sector practices are taken into the public sector the reforms fail since the real practice goes away from the truth and reality but engaged with the ongoing practices and experience of the public sector.

Further, Madhavika et al (2022), conducted a study with the aim of operationalizing resilience through collaboration having considered a case of Sri Lankan tea supply chains during Covid 19. The study adopted pragmatism viewpoint where they had gathered data using self-administered questionnaires and structured interviews which enabled the authors in digging deep into the research problem and better understanding the roots of the research problem. This study findings suggested that all the subcomponents of collaboration positively impacted on tea supply chain resilience during the Covid-19 while the sub-components connectivity and coordination have the highest positive impact on tea supply chain resilience while the other three sub-components: information sharing, integration and visibility have significant but relatively less positive impact on supply chain resilience.

Having said that it is important to posit the way a pragmatist maps his/her project (Figure 3). The Figure 3, depicts a mind map for a budding researcher who tries to understand the paradigm of "Pragmatism". Accordingly, the paradigm of "Pragmatism", has the ontological stance of believing that there is no single "real world" and all individuals are allowed in having their own unique interpretation of the respective world. The epistemological stance believe that one cannot argue of having a best way of knowing how the reality exists and that reality could both be known subjectively and objectively. The aim of pragmatism paradigm is to answer the varied research questions being raised while addressing a research problem in both in depth and in breadth. Thus, the pragmatism paradigm employs mixed method approach, which enables the researcher in adopting both a subjective and objective stance depending on the research questions that are complex and requires in depth exploration, along with quantification to fully address the problem.

In spite of the fact that the world exists independently of mind or not independently of mind, the knowledge people have of it is always interpretive and is based on teleological weapons of the mind, which are tools to cope with the worlds where they live (William James, 1910). Therefore, 'knowledge' cannot be described in privileged terms that hold forever, but only in conjectures based on previous experiences, which are tested in future encounters. So, knowledge becomes a part of continuous refinement and reflection of ongoing experience of the world. In the absence of further inquiry, truth is always provisional and fallible. As with everything else in life, people are entitled to believe in provisional truths, regardless of whether they are scientific or not. As a result, it is argued that pragmatism concentrates on practicality of the phenomenon not whether it is an eternal truth or not.

Figure 3. Mind Map for Pragmatism

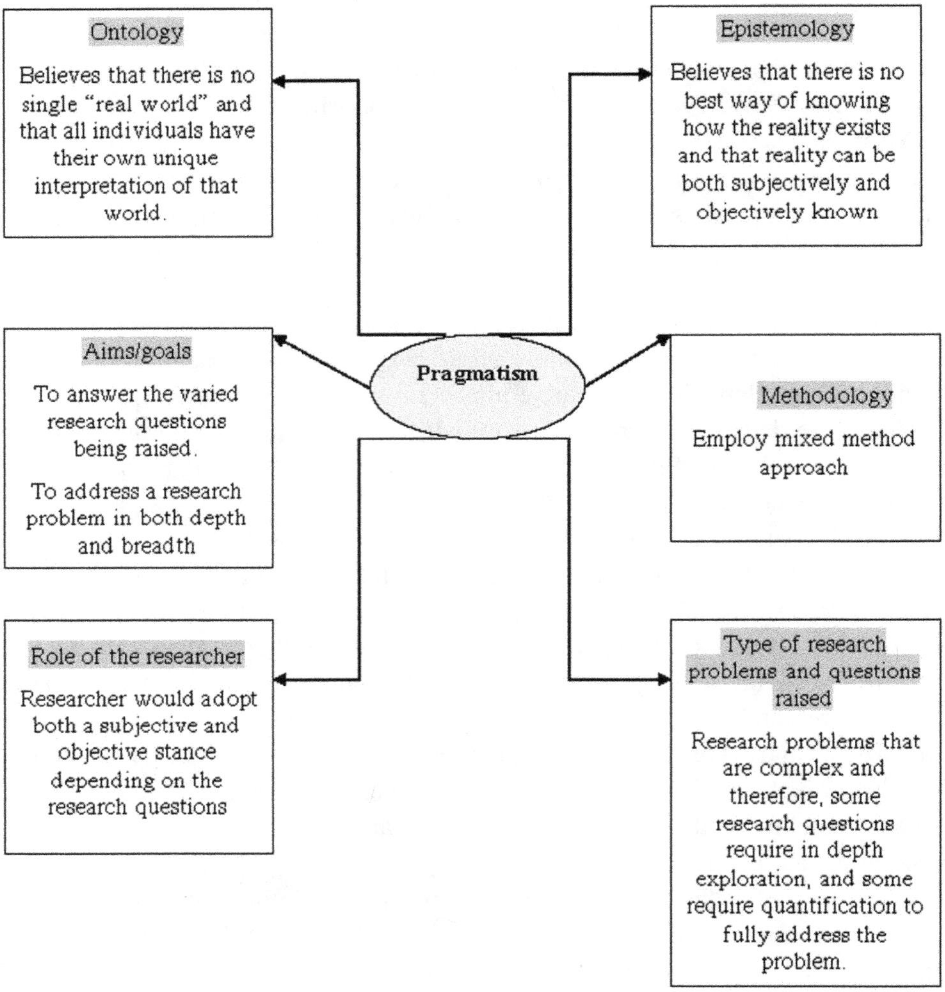

Ontology
Believes that there is no single "real world" and that all individuals have their own unique interpretation of that world.

Epistemology
Believes that there is no best way of knowing how the reality exists and that reality can be both subjectively and objectively known

Pragmatism

Aims/goals
To answer the varied research questions being raised.
To address a research problem in both depth and breadth

Methodology
Employ mixed method approach

Role of the researcher
Researcher would adopt both a subjective and objective stance depending on the research questions

Type of research problems and questions raised
Research problems that are complex and therefore, some research questions require in depth exploration, and some require quantification to fully address the problem.

HISTORICAL OVERVIEW OF PRAGMATISM PHILOSOPHY

Pansiri (2005) explains that pragmatism originates from the Greek word "pragma," which means action. Philosophers of pragmatism maintain that human actions cannot be separated from the experiences of the past and the beliefs derived from them. There is therefore an intrinsic link between human thoughts and human actions. The results of past actions help people predict the consequences of future similar actions. People determine what actions to take based on the potential consequences of those actions in the pragmatic philosophy, we can never experience the same situation twice, so we have provisional beliefs about the possible outcome of a given situation, which means that the way we act in a particular situation is inherently provisional as well (Morgan, 2014).

Pragmatism is a philosophy movement, which is originally stem from in the US in the late 19th century. An early 1870s discussion group in Cambridge, Massachusetts brought together the founders of pragmatism, including the philosopher Charles Sanders Peirce, the psychologist William James, Chauncey Wright, the jurist Oliver Wendell Holmes Jr., and the philosopher and lawyer Nicholas St. Johns Green, to form this distinctly American philosophical doctrine. As philosophers, educators, and social reformers, John Dewey, George Herbert Mead, Arthur F. Bentley, philosopher, sociologist, and psychologist contributed to the development of the doctrine over the last century. The doctrine has been further developed by academics and non-academics alike (Maxcy 2003; Morgan 2014; Pansiri 2005; Ormerod 2006). In rejecting traditional assumptions about reality, knowledge, and inquiry, these scholars started the pragmatism movement. A single scientific method is not sufficient for accessing reality in social science inquiry, as the pragmatist colleagues reject this idea (Maxcy, 2003). Saliya's (2021; 2022) flexible models of research methodology too would belong to pragmatism paradigm.

PRAGMATISM PARADIGM

Pragmatists claim that the process of knowledge acquisition is a continuum compared to that of positivism and constructivism where they believe in the extremes of objectivity and subjectivity. Positivistic researchers are camouflaged with natural scientist's stance and who claim that objective knowledge could be gathered through empirical evidence and testing hypotheses. Subjectivist are camouflaged with social scientist's stance who claims that the knowledge is relative and reality is complicated. When one is clear with the positivist and subjectivist stances and basics of pragmatism it enables the pragmatist to select the research design and the respective methodology depending on its suitability and practicality in addressing the selected research question. Thus, abductive reasoning which dwells between both deduction and induction is associated with pragmatism. This enables the pragmatistic research to get active engagement in data creation along with theoretical developments which would have the practical consequences (Goldkuhl 2012; Morgan 2007).

Dewey's idea of social inquiry has also been examined in light of pragmatism's methodological frameworks (Dillon et al. 2000). According to Dewey, a pragmatist would see actual issues that arise in social contexts, define them properly, and then launch an investigation to find solutions. Nagendrakumar et. al (2022) came out with a myth where they argued that the Sri Lankan government and the political actors believed that the economic crisis and the resultant bankruptcy status was due to Easter Sunday attack and the COVID 19. Researchers wanted further to dig into and see the practical side of it by selecting one sector of the economy (hotel industry). This study concentrated on corporate social responsibility (CSR) which is the subjective part of the study and the next the financial performance (FP) which is the objective part of the study. The qualitative part of the CSR words which were found in the annual reports were converted to objective form using Nila units. Then the CSR in objective form was analyzed with FP which is already been an objective form. The hypothesis was then tested. Finally, they concluded that the bankruptcy was prevalent even before the Easter Sunday attack and COVID 19. The practical consequence of this study is that it first eliminates the myth and directs the economic role players to go even before the Easter Sunday attack in searching and recommending solutions to the crisis. Accordingly, as per Dewey, a research problem is only viable for investigation if it is socially placed. He also maintains that investigations should be spontaneous, contextual, and based on difficulties. According to Dewey's philosophy, enquiries are evaluative as well as interrogations of theory and practice. Dewey's work has been utilized to point out the flaw in most investigations, which is choosing the approach without having a firm grasp of the issue. Dewey suggests that the researcher should study the topic from numerous viewpoints based on the goal or objective of the inquiry once the problem has been discovered and its dimensions have been clearly defined (Dillon et al. 2000).

It is argued by followers of the metaphysical paradigm that realism and constructivism are inherently incompatible (Kuhn, 1977). Pragmatism, on the other hand, takes a middle road through these assumptions. The first argument pragmatists make regarding reality is that there is a reality that exists apart from human experience. It can be said that all knowledge of the world is socially constructed, but that some versions are more likely to be correct based on individual experiences. As a result, you are free to believe whatever you want, but there are some beliefs that are more likely to meet the needs and goals of your life. Alternatively, the world has an obstinate quality (Blumer, 1969), in which some lines of action are continued, and others are obstructed.

In terms of epistemology, pragmatism contends that all knowledge of the world is based on experience. Philosophies of knowledge emphasize truth, which contrasts sharply with this approach. Pragmatists also believe that all knowledge is social knowledge, along with the belief that the world is both real and socially constructed. The world that we live in today is shaped and shaped by generations of previous generations. Any knowledge you gain is inescapably shaped by the social experiences you have had since infancy. Since individual experience creates individual knowledge, pragmatics confirm that knowledge is unique, but they also note that much of it comes from social experiences, so much knowledge is socially shared.

The philosophical assumptions related to methodology are devoted more to explaining why one would prefer one approach over another, as well as producing one form of knowledge over another, than to defining research methods. A realism and constructivist approach to qualitative methods, for example, does not directly relate to the question of how to combine qualitative and quantitative methods (Lincoln & Guba, 1985; Smith & Heshusius, 1986). Therefore, if you conduct surveys or observe participants, you do not need to believe in an external reality or deny the existence of truth. A qualitative researcher is more likely to use constructivist assumptions than a quantitative researcher. A pragmatist believes humanism, subordination to action, values emerge, experiment in real life experiences, high faith in democratic and social values, researcher is the manipulator, flexible instrumentations, reality lies in its utility, and great power of man. Madhavika et al (2021), conducted a study in testing the misleading fallacy of, higher the chemical fertilizer higher the yield therefore, better the income be. The authors had used the pragmatism viewpoint in understanding the research problem where the data were collected in a data triangulation, where a controlled experiment, two series of interviews and two sets of questioners were utilized. Controlled experiment included getting yield and soil samples tested for the controlled experiment plots while interviews were analyzed using thematic analysis and data collected through the survey was analyzed using descriptive and correlation. The approach had allowed the authors in digging deep into the research problem by having done real life experiment.

FIVE-STEP MODEL FOR UNDERSTANDING PROBLEM SOLVING (PRESENTED BY DEWEY (1933) AND REVISED BY MORGAN (2014))

Dewey's five step model of inquiry explains that before you act on a problem, you need to have developed novel belief that these action steps would enable in addressing the problem. However, the nature of the said belief would change based on the experiences of true outcomes encountered by the researcher. The concept of warranted beliefs was introduced by Dewey (1986) and referred to beliefs that result from the consequences of actions. By separating these beliefs from speculative beliefs about how certain actions might affect the outcome, they are differentiated from purely speculative beliefs.

Figure 4. Five-step Model for Understanding Problem Solving

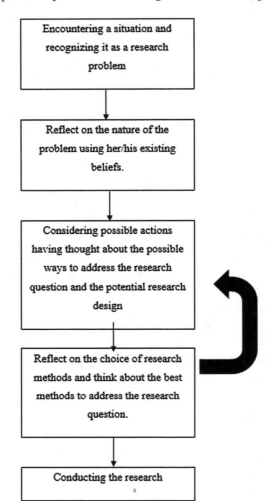

To begin applying this model (figure 4), you must first encounter a situation and recognize it as a research problem. It would, however, be outside the researcher's current expertise. Due to this, there will be no way for the researcher to address the research problem. After reflecting on the nature of the problem, the researcher would formulate a hypothesis. In some cases, reflecting on a problem may lead to redefining the research question in a new way and developing a new version of the problem. Next, consider possible actions, i.e., how the research question could be addressed and potential research design considerations. After the researcher has chosen the method and decided on the best means of addressing the research question, he or she would reflect on the choice of research methods. By working through this process, a researcher may be forced to rethink the choice of methodology, which might force them to revise the choice of research design, which might then force them to reconsider the research question. Research may proceed through several stages before the researcher begins conducting the research, including designing the research, selecting the methods, reflecting on the decisions, and reconsidering the research question. This process is referred to as "abduction" in pragmatism, and it is based on an if-then relationship, according to Morgan (2014), in which researchers reflect on the nature of the problem and conclude, based on their reflections, that if you act a certain way, you are likely to produce a certain outcome. In his work on the logic of science, Charles Sanders Peirce coined the term "abduction.". To differentiate it from the well-known inductive type of inference, Peirce introduced the term (Peirce, 1878). Peirce's writings on abduction are commonly criticized for failing to provide a coherent picture. The main difference between his conception of abduction and the modern one is that, according to the latter, abduction belongs to the "context of justification"—the stage of scientific inquiry in which we evaluate theories. In Peirce's view, abduction was appropriate to be considered in the context of discovery, the stage of inquiry which enables us to develop theories that can then be evaluated later. "Abduction involves forming hypotheses to explain the world," he writes (Peirce, 1934). The essence of abduction is to develop an if-then formula, in which you determine that by acting in one way, you will likely result in another. For example, one can decide to buy a used car if a guarantee is received on covering the necessary repairs.

CONCLUSION

"Any problem of scientific inquiry that does not grow out of actual (or 'practical') social conditions is factitious; it is arbitrarily set by the inquirer" (Dewey 1938, p. 499). The purpose of this chapter is to emphasize the value of pragmatism as a research paradigm in social science. To achieve fruitful outcomes from their studies, budding researchers can adopt this paradigm. As a result of bringing together a variety of perspectives, we argue in favor of pragmatism as a tool for engaging marginalized and oppressed communities and fostering macro and micro discourse.

REFERENCES

Blumer, H. (1969). *Symbolic interactionism: Perspective and method*. Prentice-Hall.

Carlsen, A., & Mantere, S. (2007). Pragmatism. In *International Encyclopedia of Organization Studies*. Sage publications.

Dewey, J. (1938). *Logic: The Theory of Inquiry*. Henry Holt.

Dewey, J. (1986). How we think: A restatement of the relation of reflective thinking to the educative process. In *John Dewey: The Later Works, 1925–1953* (Rev. ed., Vol. 8). Southern Illinois University Press.

Dillon, D. R., O'Brien, D. G., & Heilman, E. E. (2000). Literacy research in the next millennium: From paradigms to pragmatism and practicality. *Reading Research Quarterly, 35*(1), 10–26. doi:10.1598/RRQ.35.1.2

Goldkuhl, G. (2012). Pragmatism vs interpretivism in qualitative information systems research. *European Journal of Information Systems, 21*(2), 135–146. doi:10.1057/ejis.2011.54

Guba, E. G., & Lincoln, Y. S. (2005). Paradigmatic controversies, contradictions, and emerging confluences. In N. K. Denzin & Y. S. Lincoln (Eds.), *The SAGE handbook of qualitative research* (3rd ed., pp. 191–215). Sage.

James, W. (2000). What pragmatism means. In J. J. Stuhr (Ed.), *Pragmatism and the Classical American Philosophy: Essential Readings and Interpretive Essay* (2nd ed., pp. 193–202). Oxford University Press.

Kuhn, T. S. (1977). The essential tension: Tradition and innovation in scientific research. In *The essential tension: Selected studies in scientific tradition and change* (pp. 225–239). University of Chicago Press. doi:10.7208/chicago/9780226217239.001.0001

Lincoln, Y. S., & Guba, E. G. (1985). *Naturalistic inquiry*. Sage. doi:10.1016/0147-1767(85)90062-8

Madhavika, N., Jayasinghe, N., Ehalapitiya, S., Wickramage, T., Fernando, D., & Jayasinghe, V. (2022). Operationalizing resilience through collaboration: The case of Sri Lankan tea supply chain during Covid-19. *Quality & Quantity*. doi:10.100711135-022-01493-8 PMID:35971419

Madhavika, W.D.N., Nagendrakumar, N., Colombathanthri, P.S.H., Rathnayake, R.M.T., Jayaweera, J.H.M.P.S.B., & Buddhika M.S. (2021). "Resource Optimization in Paddy Cultivation, for Developing Countries; A Sector Synergetic Approach " *Alinteri Journal of Agricultural Science,* vol.36, Issue 2, 2021, pp.122 131, EBSCO, 22/09/2021, doi:10.47059/alinteri/V36I2/AJAS21124

Maxcy, S. J. (2003). Pragmatic threads in mixed methods research in the social sciences: The search for multiple modes of inquiry and the end of the philosophy of formalism. In A. Tashakkori & C. Teddlie (Eds.), *Handbook of Mixed Methods in Social and Behavioral Research* (pp. 51–89). Sage.

Morgan, D. L. (2007). Paradigms lost and pragmatism regained: Methodological implications of combining qualitative and quantitative methods. *Journal of Mixed Methods Research*, *1*(1), 48–76. doi:10.1177/2345678906292462

Morgan, D. L. (2014). *Integrating Qualitative and Quantitative Methods: A Pragmatic Approach*. Sage. doi:10.4135/9781544304533

Nagendrakumar, N. (2017). Public Sector Accounting and Financial Reporting Reforms: Public Entities Perspectives, Sri Lanka. *International Journal on Governmental Financial Management*, *17*(1), 17–34.

Nagendrakumar, N., De Silva, L. M. H., Weerasinghe, R. M., Pathirana, T. D., Rajapaksha, C. M., Perera, K. R., & Kaneshwaren, S. (2022). Corporate social responsibility and financial performance: A study of the tourism industry in Sri Lanka. *Corporate Ownership & Control, 19*(4), 103–110 (B rank). doi:10.22495/cocv19i4art9

Ormerod, R. J. (2006). The history and ideas of pragmatism. *The Journal of the Operational Research Society*, *57*(8), 892–909. doi:10.1057/palgrave.jors.2602065

Pansiri, J. (2005). Pragmatism: A methodological approach to researching strategic alliances in tourism. *Tourism and Hospitality Planning and Development*, *2*(3), 191–206. doi:10.1080/14790530500399333

Peirce, C. S. (1878). Illustrations of the Logic of Science. *Popular Science Monthly*, *13*, 470–482.

Peirce, C. S. (1934). Pragmatism and Abduction. In C. Hartshorne & P. Weiss. Cambridge, (eds). The Collected Papers of Charles Sanders Peirce, Vol. 5, Pragmatism and Pragmaticism [sic],180-212. Harvard University Press.

Saliya, C. A. (2021). Conducting Case Study Research: A Concise Practical Guidance for Management Students. *International Journal of KIU*, *2*(1), 1–13. doi:10.37966/ijkiu20210127

Saliya, C. A. (2022). *Doing Social Research: A Guide to Non-native English Speakers*. Springer., https://link.springer.com/book/10.1007/978-981-19-3780-4

Smith, J. K., & Heshusius, L. (1986). Closing down the conversation: The end of the quantitativequalitative debate among educational inquirers. *Educational Leadership, 15*(1), 4–12. doi:10.3102/0013189X015001004

Thompson, A. (1997). Political pragmatism and educational inquiry. In F. Margonis (ed.) Philosophy of Education, pp. 425–34. Urbana: Philosophy of Education Society.

Chapter 4
Research Philosophy:
Paradigms, World Views, Perspectives, and Theories

Candauda Arachchige Saliya
iD https://orcid.org/0000-0002-9239-1648
Sri Lanka Institute of Information Technology, Sri Lanka

ABSTRACT

The purpose of this chapter is to summarize the philosophical developments in the academic research field and provide a framework for non-native English-speaking budding researchers. Revealing the philosophical stance of the authors of a research paper is crucial in understanding their arguments. Therefore, an understanding of this historical evolution is useful in justifying authors' choices and presenting them clearly in the research report. Authors' perceptions of different theories, perspectives, and worldviews influence and affect many aspects of research, and it is important to mention personal stances on them in the research report at the very beginning. The choice of underpinning philosophy is significantly influenced by the author's psychosocial, economic, and cultural backgrounds. Multivism is a dynamic position of a researcher who is not confined to the bipolar-disordered extremism of objectivism and subjectivism of ontology, epistemology, methodology, and methods.

HISTORICAL DEVELOPMENT

The origins of Western philosophy go back to the ancient Greek philosophers such as Plato (424-348 BC) and Aristotle (384-322 BC). Research and knowledge were highly valued by these philosophers; Socrates (470-399 BC) has said that 'there is

DOI: 10.4018/978-1-6684-6859-3.ch004

only one good; knowledge, and one evil; ignorance and Aristotle has mentioned that 'the educated differ from the uneducated, as the living from the dead'. In fact, this seems to be in line with the teachings in the Eastern philosophers such as of Gautama Buddha (563-483 BC) who called this evil of ignorance as 'avijja' about 100 years before Aristotle (Saliya, 2010).

Awareness of the authors'/researchers' philosophical stance is crucial in understanding their arguments. Therefore, an understanding of this historical evolution is useful in justifying your choices and presenting them clearly in the research report. Awareness and understanding of the different theories, perspectives and worldviews influence and affect many aspects of research, and it is important to mention your stances on them in the research report at the very beginning. The choice of underpinning philosophy is significantly influenced by the author's socio-economic and cultural background.

PARADIGMS AND WORLDVIEWS

"Choosing a paradigm is important because it allows you to start forming research questions (RQs). This is useful, even if your questions start off vague" (Gournelos et al., 2019, p. 8)

Paradigm is the entire sets of beliefs, values, techniques that are shared by members of a community (Kuhn, 2012). Guba and Lincoln (1994) who are leaders in the field define a paradigm as a basic set of beliefs or worldview that guides research action or an investigation. Paradigms are thus important because they provide beliefs and dictates, which, for scholars in a particular discipline, influence what should be studied, how it should be studied, and how the results of the study should be interpreted. The paradigm defines a researcher's philosophical orientation and, as we shall see in the conclusion to this paper, this has significant implications for every decision made in the research process, including choice of methodology and methods. And so a paradigm tells us how meaning will be constructed from the data we shall gather, based on our individual experiences, (i.e. where we are coming from). It is therefore very important, that when you write your research proposal, you clearly state the paradigm in which you are locating your research.

Scholars have identified three main paradigms: positivism, interpretivism / constructivism and critical thinking. Pragmatism is also cited by some scholars as the latest paradigm shift. Positivists aim to explore, explain, evaluate, predict, or test theories. The goal of interpretivists as well as constructivists is to understand human behavior. Critical theorists aim to critique social reality, liberate, empower people, and propose solutions to social problems. The pragmatic paradigm refers to a worldview that focuses on 'what works' rather than what might be considered absolutely and objectively 'true' or 'real.' Early pragmatists rejected the idea that social inquiry using a single scientific method could access truths regarding the real world.

Critical realism is a branch of philosophy that distinguishes between the 'real' world and the 'observable' world. The basis of this theory is that 'reality' cannot exist or be excluded from human cognitions, theories and creations. By interpreting the world scientifically through cause-and-effect mechanisms, it contradicts / alternates the methods of empiricism and fundamentalism.

Pseudoscience and Social Constructivism

Born in 1984 and still in his early career, Maarten Boudry is best known for his skepticism and critical attitude towards pseudoscience. He studies the errors of human reasoning, which can be subject to pseudoscience and irrationality. Pseudoscience is described as an 'imitation of real science'. Social constructivism is a sociological theory of knowledge in which human development is socially situated and knowledge is built by interacting with others. Like constructism, social constructivism states that people work together to create something.

Social constructism focuses on the objects created through the social interaction of a group, while the worldview of social reformism focuses on the learning of an individual as a result of his or her interactions within a group. Strong social reformism as a philosophical approach suggests that the natural world has little or no role in the construction of scientific knowledge.

PERSPECTIVES AND THEORIES

A theory is a reasonable or scientifically acceptable general principle or a set of principles that explain a particular phenomenon. Perspective is basically the way we look at things or our point of view. Both theories and perspectives are highly subjective; depends on the observer. For example, some might see university as a place to have fun, whereas some may see it as an academic ground with too many ethical restrictions. Furthermore, it is also important to note that these terms have different meanings in different contexts. In philosophy, it refers to a point of view, opinions or beliefs while in visual arts in it refers to different angles.

The figure 1 illustrates a comparative integration of paradigm, worldview, perspective and theory.

Figure 1. Comparative Integration of Paradigm, Worldview, Perspective and Theory

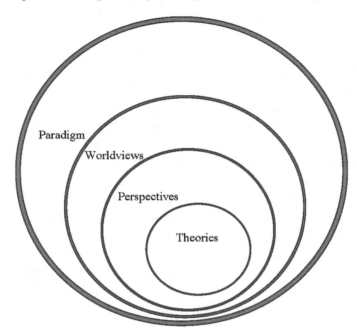

Paradigm Comparison

Objectivity, reliability, validity and generalizability are the keywords used by positivists in their vocabulary whereas non-positivists, often guide qualitative research, may employ terms such as 'credibility', 'transferability', 'dependability' and 'conformability' (Guba and Lincoln, 2005).

Positivism, Post-Positivism and Interpretivism

The basis of the positivist paradigm is positivism. Positivism was a social research philosophy introduced in 1848 by Auguste Comte. According to this view, the researcher begins the process of discovery with theory and tests hypotheses using deductive reasoning using statistical techniques. Their ontological belief is that an objective reality exists and can be known through research in contrast to post-positivists who concede that reality can never be known but some accumulated efforts in discovering what is real (Bailey 2007).

Interpreters and reformers in the post-positivist paradigm argue that 'truth' is 'creation' and that it is created in the minds of individuals and among people in a culture. The interpretivist/constructivist paradigm assumes that there are multiple realities; subjective understandings), and a naturalistic set of methodological procedures (Denzin and Lincoln, 2005). The epistemological stance of positivists is that the five senses must be based on unbiased sensible observations and experience should not be influenced the researcher's feelings or values.

Positivism is a belief that knowledge is exclusively derived from sensory experiences, verified data ("facts") collected using *five senses* are known as empirical evidence; thus positivism is based on empiricism. Does this mean that the senses do not play any role in the creation of knowledge beyond the empirical evidence built on the five senses? In fact, it is important to examine in depth whether observation or experience can be obtained only by the five senses without the sense of mind.

The existentialist position of the interpretive / reformist paradigm is the belief in the existence of the world, that reality is relative / subjective, that it does not exist independently, but that it exists as multiple collectively created realities in the human mind. Their epistemological stance is that the available knowledge depends on the researcher's thoughts and desires. That is, 'knowledge' is created by the seeker and what is sought by a specific methodology.

Pragmatism

At the beginning of the twentieth century, the German sociologists Max Weber and George Simmel rejected positivism and several forms of empirical and rational thought emerged. Charles Sanders Peirce: father of pragmatism, introduced the concept of abduction inferencing (abduction reasoning) as an alternative to David Hume but complement to (parallel to) the induction and deduction logics.

Critical Theory

The epistemological position in critical reality is that the researcher is not independent of what he is researching and discusses the findings of the research through his or her values. Bailey (2007) argues that one of the most important values often included in such critical research is the desire to eliminate social injustice. In that sense, fundamentalists and interpretation / reformists are mere observers and judges while the critical researchers are aiming at *just society*. The prevailing general understanding is that researchers in the critical paradigm often want to describe, educate, understand, and change how powerful groups oppress the weak, the poor, the discriminated. They seem to hold opportunistic interpretations of reality, the existence of 'truth', the fact that truth is absolute and relative, that there is only one truth or that there are multiple truths, and that 'truth' can be found or not.

Differences in these assumptions cannot be ruled out as mere philosophical differences. The philosophical positions of these researchers are critical to the practical investigation of research-problems as well as the interpretation of findings and policy choices. The table 1 presents a comparative evolution of paradigms and theories.

Table 1. Comparative evolution of philosophies and theories.

Paradigm	Positivist/Post-positivist	Interpretivist/Social Constructivist	Critical
Theories/ Perspectives and Contributors	Empiricism, Scientific method: Francis Bacon (1561-1626), Rationalism: Rene Descartes (1596-1650) Liberalism: John Locke (1632-1704), Positivism: Auguste Comte (1798-1857) Post-positivism; Max Weber (1864–1920) and George Simmel (1858–1918).	Naturalism: David Home (1711-1776) Idealism: Johann Fichte (1762-1814) Protestantism: Max Webber (1864-1920) Pragmatism: Charles Sanders Peirce (1839-1940), William James (1842 –1910) Symbolic interactionism: G. H. Mead (1863-1931), Herbert Blumer (1900-1987)	Materialism: Georg Hegel (1770-1831) Marxism: Karl Marx (1818-1883) Friedrich Nietzsche (1844-1900), Power-knowledge: Michael Foucault (1926-84) Cultural capital: Pierre Bourdieu (1930-2002) Deconstructivism: Jacques Derrida (1930-2004
	Liberal Naturalism: Emmanuel Kant (1724-1804), Middle-range thinking: Robert Merton (1910-2003), Falsificationism: Karl Popper (1902-1994)		

Sources: Updated on Laughlin, 1995; Saliya, 2017; Saliya, 2022

In the early 20th century, several forms of practical philosophy emerged, combining the basic understanding of empirical (experience-based induction) and rationalist (concept-based deduction) thought. Charles Pierce's (1839–1914) major contributions were the addition of the concept of abduction to the logic of deduction and induction. These three forms of reasoning serve as the basic conceptual basis for empirically based scientific methodology.

LIBERALISM AND NATURALISM/REALISM

Liberalism is a political and moral philosophy based on liberty, consent of the governed and equality before the law. These ideas were first drawn together and systematized as a distinct ideology by the English philosopher John Locke, generally regarded as the father of modern liberalism. Locke's fame is attributed to the suggestion that human knowledge is the experience of a person's life experiences accumulated on a *blank sheet of paper*. This implies that liberalism and realism are based on empiricist principles. Beginning with 'A Treatise of Human Nature', David Hume (1711-1776) attempted to create a naturalistic science of man that examined the psychological basis of human nature. Hume argued against *innatism* which is a philosophical and epistemological doctrine that the mind is born with ideas, knowledge, and beliefs. Therefore, Hume is aligned with empiricism and liberalism against rationalism and of innatism. Hume argued that inductive reasoning and belief in *causality* cannot be justified rationally but resulted from customs and mental habits. No one can be certain that one event causes another but only experience the "constant conjunction" of events.

Wilhelm Dilthey (1833-1911), a hermeneutic philosopher, argued that scientific explanations does not reach the inner nature of phenomena and, that the most plausible way of understanding thoughts, feelings, and desires was humanist knowledge. This view confirms G. B. Vico's argument (1725) that man has a free and brilliant style of expression, they are able to build more logical and convincing arguments to defend of both sides in the controversy which are actually bogus and rhetoric.

NEWTONIAN AND QUANTUM MECHANICS

Newton's theory of gravitation and Einstein's theory of relativity are not sensitive to the five senses. Although gravity or any other attraction is felt towards the earth, we do not feel the smell, taste, touch, to see with our eyes or to hear. According to Raoul Nakhmanson (2003), the wave function is purely a mental construct. Einstein called these so-called non-material 'matter waves', 'Gespenster Felders' (demon fields). However, they control the behavior of material objects. They argue that there is no sensory evidence of gravity or any other attraction toward the earth. It may not be a pull in the center of the earth, but, as Einstein put it, and acknowledged by modern physicists; special relativity argued that space and time are inextricably connected, and they do not acknowledge the existence of gravity.

The wave-particle duality is a mind-body one. In the real 3D-space there exists only the particle, the wave exists in its consciousness. If there are many particles, their distribution in accordance with the wave function represents a real wave in real space. Many worlds, Schrödinger cat, Great Smoky Dragon, etc. exist only as virtual mental constructions (Nakhmanson, 2003).

Thomas Young's (1773-1829) 'Double-slit experiment' (1801) shows that 'light' can display characteristics of both waves and particles. In 1927, Davisson and Germer demonstrated that electrons show the same behavior and further development of this experiment surprised people by demonstrating that this duality depends on 'observation'; when observed, electrons behave as particles and when not under observation the same electrons behave as waives (https://youtu.be/Jqm4f55soJQ). There are several Youtube videos available in internet for example;

You can get a clear idea of this by watching the amazing videos such as (figures 2a & 2b);

Figure 2a. Double Slit Experiment
https://www.youtube.com/watch?v=A9tKncAdlHQ

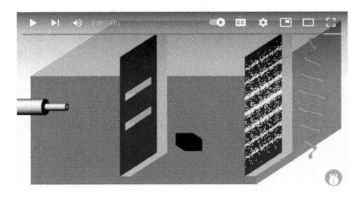

Figure 2b. Double Slit Experiment
https://www.youtube.com/watch?v=0ui9ovrQuKE

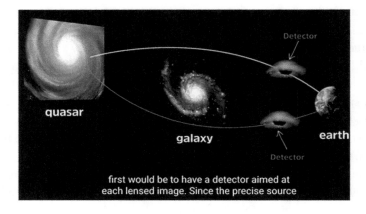

Evolution and Quantum Mechanics

Raoul Nakhmanson (2003) argues that the analogy between evolution and quantum mechanics and sociology gives rise to the idea that quantum mechanics has an individual and a social consciousness for material objects. Like biological objects they are able to receive, to work on, and to spread semantic information. In general-meaning we can name it 'consciousness'. The important ability of consciousness is ability to predict future. He goes on to say that the wave-particle duality (figure 3b) is the same as the mind-body duality. Only the particle exists in real three-dimensional space. The wave exists in consciousness (figure 3a). If there are many particles, their distribution represents a real wave in real space according to the wave function.

Figure 3a. Consciousness
https://www.youtube.com/watch?v=uva6gBEpfDY

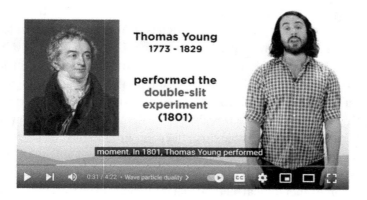

Figure 3b. Consciousness
https://www.youtube.com/watch?v=O6g-7rUgrdg

DEDUCTION, INDUCTION AND ABDUCTION

Classical era of research methodology has been fairly documented from the time of Francis Bacon (1561-1626) who led the advancement of both natural philosophy and the "scientific" method. Bacon has been called the father of *empiricism* that is the possibility of scientific knowledge based only upon *inductive reasoning* and *observations*. 'Skepticism' (a doubt towards knowledge claims that are seen as mere belief or dogma) nature of this original Baconian method motivated him to formulate the modern *scientific method* presented in his book Novum Organum (1620) or 'New Method' which led for *deductive derivation*.

In contrast to these developments (i.e. scientific deduction and empirical induction), in 1870s the term '*abduction*' was coined by Charles Sanders Peirce. However, today 'abduction' means a logical reasoning or 'context of justification' but for Peirce's 'abduction' was the process of forming explanatory hypotheses and that encompasses all the operations of integrating theories and conceptions. However, Gerhard Schurz defends abduction in the Peircean spirit that abduction leads to make most promising explanatory conjecture which is then subject to further test (Schurz 2008). Therefore, it is more cogent to assert that deduction tests the hypotheses explained by abductive conjectures, and induction finally draws conclusions on the tested and verified hypotheses. Therefore, Deduction proves that, for logical reasons, something must be the case; induction demonstrates that there is empirical evidence that something is truly so; abduction, by contrast, merely supposes that something might be the case. It therefore abandons the solid ground of prediction and testing in order to introduce a new idea or to understand a new phenomenon (Bude, 2004).

In other words, Charles Sanders Peace emphasizes that deduction is a mathematical derivation or some other logical method that is intended to prove certain conclusions. Also, using the security of generalization (as an alternative to the certainty of deduction) from the induction process, one seeks to present empirical evidence to prove something truly so. In contrast, the abduction method introduces a discovery by conjecture, which goes beyond these derivations and inferences, such as looking at right and wrong in theories and/or creating or predicting theories. What is happening in this conjecture is simply arguing that something might (might be). Therefore, in order to introduce a new idea or to understand a new phenomenon, abductive conjecture rejects the theory of rigid stubborn positivist deductive certainty and the flexible humanistic interpretive judgments of induction methods.

Grounded theory is a qualitative research approach which uses all these three reasoning methods as illustrated in the Figure 3 chapter 14.

PERSPECTIVES AND THEORIES

Marx 's critical theories of society, economics, and politics, collectively understood as Marxism (Karl Marx 1818-1883), suggest that human societies develop through class conflict. In the capitalist mode of production, this shows the conflict between the ruling classes (known as the bourgeoisie) who control the means of production and the working class (known as the proletariat) who activate these means by selling their labor power for wages. Using a critical approach known as historical materialism,

Marx predicted that capitalism, like previous socio-economic systems, would cause internal tensions and cause these systems to self-destruct and be replaced by a new system known as the socialist mode of production.

Perspectives are a set of rules or theories that apply to the interpretation of a phenomenon, a framework of its own. For example, in a car accident, the driver of one car may have one view, another driver or passenger may have another view, and each observer may have slightly different perspectives on their location and distance. Holding a single strict worldview may enable an American to disregard other perspectives, and may be unnecessarily confusing, confusing, and perhaps adaptable by worldviews.

Snyder (2015) asserts that low wage labour or sweatshops is often described as self-evidently exploitative and immoral. But for defenders of sweatshops might describe it as the first rung on a ladder toward greater economic development. On the other hand, in another perspective, it can be described as enhancing productivity or wealth maximisation and such excessive explanations would lead to too much noise.

Critical Education

It should be noted that the notion that today, any theory not based on the senses or experience is not currently rejected as non-scientific or not scientifically convincing. Anthony Giddens (1938-), who is known for his theory of structuration and his holistic view of modern societies, argues that because mankind is constantly using science to discover and research new things, mankind will not move beyond the second metaphysical phase.

Paulo Reglus Neves Frier (1921-1997) was a Brazilian educator and philosopher who was a leading consultant in critical education. He is best known for his book, 'Pedagogy of the Oppressed', which is considered as one of the books on which his critical educational movement is based. 'Critical teaching' is a philosophy of education and the social movement. It developed concepts from critical theory and related traditions and applied to the field of education and the study of culture.

Quantitative or Qualitative Boxes

O'Leary (2004; 2005) explains that the purpose of the knowledge varies from just 'building understanding' to 'action change within a system' to 'emancipate through action' or further to 'expose the systems. Therefore, the research methodologies could vary from 'basic' to 'applied/evaluative' to 'participatory' or further to 'critical/ radical ethnography' accordingly.

Therefore, it is not so enlightening or logical for academic researchers to be trapped in quantitative or qualitative boxes. Therefore, the mixed methods school emerged combining the different elements of these two traditions in different ways facilitating many different strategies for exploring the vast world around us.

CLASSIFICATION OF WORLDVIEWS

Emerging worldviews from the 18th century onwards can be divided into four basic categories according to their basic positions and/or periods of introduction:

1. Classic worldviews (18th century)
2. Modern worldviews (1800–1950)
3. Post-modern worldviews (1900–1990)
4. Dynamic worldviews (since 1980)

Classical worldviews consist of research approaches based on extremely abstract theoretical creations, such as idealism, materialism, rationalism, and positivism. Modern classical worldviews consist of research approaches based on theories such as Marxism, naturalism/realism, and symbolic interactionism. Postmodern worldviews, identified as theories that evolved in the post-industrialization period, consist of major research strategies such as phenomenology, critical sociology, ethnography, and neo-pragmatism. Among these worldviews, dynamic worldviews have their place because they are separated from dual or bipolar interpretations such as idealism and materialism, quantitative and qualitative research, and free market economic policies and centrally planned economic policies. Theories related to paradigms such as critical thinking and pragmatism belong to this set of dynamic worldviews (Saliya, 2010, 2017).

Dynamic Perspectives

Dynamic perspectives could be attributed to the theories introduced in the late 20thcentury, such as middle-range thinking (Laughlin, 1995) from the interpretive paradigm, anti-realism (Dummett, 1978) (position involving either the denial of the objective reality or the insistence that we should be agnostic about their real existence) from the positivistic end and mixed method research (Johnson & Onwuegbuzie, 2004) and emergent methods (Hesse-Biber & Leavy, 2011) from interpretive and critical paradigms respectively. These theories could be identified as further developments of modern and post-modern schools of thought rather than from classical grand theories. Researchers in these schools seem more dynamic and enjoying the liberty of interchanging their positions between different beliefs according to the situation. Therefore, these theories are categorized under the name of dynamic perspective in this thesis. Justification of emergence of middle class within Marxian analysis (Gray et. Al., 1996) also falls into this category and named as 'Marxism after USSR'.

Emergent methods, according to Hesse-Biber and Leavy, are the logical conclusion to paradigm shifts, major evolutions in theory and new conceptions of knowledge and the knowledge-building process, and they see that emergent method as hybrid that "they often borrow and adopt methods from their own disciplines or can cross disciplinary boundaries to create new tools and concepts...in order to answer complex and often novel questions" (p. xii). Scholars from mixed methods school of thought position mixed methods research "as the natural complement to traditional qualitative and quantitative research, to pragmatism" (Johnson & Onwuegbuzie, 2004, p. 14).

Modernism, Postmodernism and Surrealism

The main difference between modernism and postmodernism is that modernism is characterized by the radical break from the traditional forms of prose and verse whereas postmodernism is characterized by the self-conscious use of earlier styles and conventions.

D.H. Lawrence, Virginia Wolf, James Joyce, W.B Yeast, Sylvia Plath, F. Scott Fitzgerald, William Faulkner, and Ernest Hemingway are some notable modernist authors. James Joyce's Ulysses, Faulkner's As I Lay Dying and Virginia Woolf's Mrs. Dalloway, T. S. Eliot's The Waste Land are some notable literary works that epitomize modernism.

Some notable writers in postmodernism include Vladimir Nabokov, Umberto Eco, John Hawkes, Richard Kalich, Giannina Braschi, Kurt Vonnegut, William Gaddis, John Barth, Jean Rhys, Donald Barthelme, E.L. Doctorow, Don DeLillo, Ana Lydia Vega, Jachym Topol and Paul Auster.

The Surrealists sought to give form to the irrational side of the human nature, to express the contents of the unconscious mind as described by Sigmund Freud. They employed dreamlike imagery full of strange juxtapositions. Surrealism is a very eccentric and thought-provoking movement of art and literature that has manifested into all aspects of thought and views today. Interestingly enough it seems to be closely related to the philosophical stance that postmodernism claims as well. Surrealism is evident in everyday life and the original art movement has stakes in pop culture today as we can see with many celebrities and famous artist in the mainstream. In today's world there is a large need for expression of the individual and surrealism helps provoke this need of the individual to stand out and to create their own self-identity.

ONTOLOGY AND EPISTEMOLOGY: OBJECTIVIST, SUBJECTIVIST AND DYNAMIC STANCES OF REALITY

Ontology relates to a central question of whether social entities need to be perceived as objective or subjective. Ontology and epistemology are two different ways of viewing the research philosophy. Ontology in business research can be defined as 'the science or study of being' and it deals with the nature of reality. Ontology is a system of belief that reflects an interpretation of an individual about what constitutes a fact. In simple terms, ontology is associated with what we consider as reality. Recent increasing popularity of mixed method methodology has paved a way to detach researchers from the bipolar-disordered extremist assumptions of basic philosophical stances on ontology, epistemology, methodology and methods and I call that position '*multivist*'. The Table 2 summarizes these differences.

Table 2. Types of Philosophical Stances

	Philosophical Stance		
	Objectivist	**Subjectivist**	**Multivist**
Ontology	Single truth	Multiple truth	Single or Multiple truth
Epistemology	Independent of the researcher	Biased towards researcher's values	Depends on the type of research
Methodology	Mainly quantitative	Mainly qualitative	No preference
Analysis	Primarily statistical	Mainly Thematic	No preference
Reasoning	Primarily deductive	Primarily inductive	Deductive/inductive and abductive

Objectivism (or positivism) and subjectivism can be specified as two important aspects of ontology. Objectivism assumes that social entities exist in reality external to social actors and social phenomena and their meanings have an existence that is independent of social actors.

Contrarily, subjectivism (also known as constructionism or interpretivism) perceives that social phenomena are created from perceptions and consequent actions of those social actors.

Multivist

Multivist position moves alone this bipolar continuum of assumptions according to the research type and researcher's psychosocial and cultural backgrounds.

Multivist researchers follow most liberal approaches towards human behavior and, political, social, sexual and economic issues. They are critical thinkers and working towards social justice and emancipation of all suppressions. They reject all kinds of discriminations and extremisms and, appreciate cultural diversity and equality in gender, race, color, religion and income/wealth etc., in the society.

Multivists value rational compromised consensus over democratic popular harmony. Democratic choices have not only been proven correct always in the past but sometimes had caused disasters and massacres. They value humanism over nationalism or patriotism.

REFERENCES

Bailey, C. A. (2007). *A Guide to qualitative field research*. Sage. doi:10.4135/9781412983204

Bude, H. (2004). The art of Interpretation. In U. Flick, E. von Kardorff, & I. Steinke (Eds.), *A companion to qualitative research*. SAGE.

Denzin, N. K., & Lincoln, Y. S. (2005). *The landscape of qualitative Research: theories and issues*. Sage.

Dummett, M. (1978). *Truth and Other Enigmas*. Harvard University Press.

Gournelos, T., Hammonds, J.R., & Wilson, M.A. (2019). Doing Academic Research: Perlego.

Gray, R., Owen, D., & Adams, C. (Eds.). (1996). Accounting and Accountability Changes and Challenges in Corporate Social and Environmental Reporting. Prentice Hall. ISBN 9780131758605

Guba, E. G., & Lincoln, Y. S. (1994). Competing paradigms in qualitative research. In N. K. Denzin & Y. S. Lincoln (Eds.), *The Handbook of Qualitative Research* (3rd ed., pp. 105–117). Sage.

Guba, E. G., & Lincoln, Y. S. (2005). *Paradigmatic controversies, contradictions, and emerging confluences. The SAGE handbook of qualitative research. N. K. Denzin and Y. S. Lincoln*. Sage.

Hesse-Biber., S. (2011). *The practice of Qualitative Research*. Sage.

Johnson, R. B., & Onwuegbuzie, A. J. (2004). Mixed Methods Research A Research Paradigm Whose Time Has Come. *Educational Researcher, 33*(7), 14–26. doi:10.3102/0013189X033007014

Kuhn, T. S. (2012). *The Structure of Scientific Revolutions*. University of Chicago Press. doi:10.7208/chicago/9780226458144.001.0001

Laughlin, R. C. (1995). *Middle Range Thinking*. Accounting, Auditing and Accountability.

Nakhmanson, R. (2003). Quantum mechanics as a sociology of matter. eprint arXiv:quant-ph/0303162. https://ui.adsabs.harvard.edu/abs/2003quant.ph.3162N/abstract

O'Leary, Z. (2004). *The essential guide to doing research*. Sage.

O'Leary, Z. (2005). *Researching real-world problems*. Sage.

Peirce, C.S. (1878). How to Make Our Ideas Clear. *Popular Science Monthly, 12*, 286–302.

Saliya, C. A. (2010). *The Role of bank lending in sustaining income/wealth inequality in Sri Lanka*. [PhD Thesis, Auckland University of Technology, New Zealand.] https://openrepository.aut.ac.nz/handle/10292/824

Saliya, C. A. (2012). The oldest profession. *Accounting, Auditing & Accountability Journal, 25*(6), 1072–1072. doi:10.1108/09513571211250279

Saliya, C. A. (2017). Doing Qualitative Case Study Research in Business Management. *International Journal of Case studies, 6* (12), pp. 96 – 111. http://www.casestudiesjournal.com/Volume%206%20Issue%2012%20Paper%2010.pdf

Saliya, C. A. (2022). Doing social research and publishing results. Springer. https://link.springer.com/book/10.1007/978-981-19-3780-4

Saliya, C. A., & Wickrama, K. A. S. (2021). Determinants of Financial Risk Preparedness. *Advances in Climate Change Research*. Advance online publication. doi:10.1016/j.accre.2021.03.012

Schurz, G. (2008). Patterns of abduction. *Synthese, 164*(2), 201–234. doi:10.100711229-007-9223-4

Snyder, J. (2015). Exploitation and Sweatshop Labour: Perspectives and Issues. *Society for Business Ethics*. 20(2), 187– 213. . doi:10.5840/beq201020215

ADDITIONAL READING

Creswell, J. W. (2007). *Qualitative Inquiry and Research Design; Choosing among five traditions*. Sage.

Czarniawska, B. (2004). *Narratives in finance science research: Introducing qualitative methods*. Sage., doi:10.4135/9781849209502

Czarniawska-Joerges, B. (1992). *Exploring Complex Organizations*. Sage.

Gummesson, E. (2003). All research is interpretive! *Journal of Business and Industrial Marketing, 18*(6/7), 482–492. doi:10.1108/08858620310492365

Mario, L. (2013). Brilliant Blunders: From Darwin to Einstein - Colossal Mistakes by Great Ontology Vs Epistemology: https://study.com/academy/lesson/ontology-vs-epistemology-differences-examples.html

NormanP. (2020). *Positivism*. Youtube. https://www.youtube.com/watch?v=8QkVqT3EPyk

Norman, P. (2020). *Constructivism* - Research Paradigm. Youtube. https://www.youtube.com/watch?v=EDEXXvpbOIM

Norman, P. (2020). *Critical paradigm*. Youtube. https://www.youtube.com/watch?v=Xx9JM1gcc3E

Norman, P. (2020). *Interpretivism*. Youtube. https://www.youtube.com/watch?v=FybkUMplAlI

Norman, P. (2020). *Paradigms*. Youtube. https://www.youtube.com/watch?v=URWcOJWfSnI

Norman, P. (2020). *What is Interpretivism*. Youtube. https://www.youtube.com/watch?v=FybkUMplAlI

Norman, P. (2021). Ontology, epistemology, and axiology (2021). Youtube. https://www.youtube.com/watch?v=AhdZOsBps5o

Practical Guide to Research Methods and Analysis (1st ed.). Routledge. doi:10.4324/9780429263552

Scientists That Changed Our Understanding of Life and the Universe. London.

Singham, M. (2020). *The Idea That a Scientific Theory Can Be 'Falsified' Is a Myth. It's time we abandoned the notion*. Policy & Ethics.

Chapter 5

Social Science Philosophy Behind Data Analysis With Special Reference to Philosophical Perception

Kenneth Peprah

https://orcid.org/0000-0002-2074-8054

University of Business and Integrated Development Studies, Ghana

ABSTRACT

Philosophy is a science of knowledge, and it concentrates on epistemology, ontology, axiology, and methodology. However, researchers have understated the role of philosophy, even though it is very interwoven with research. This chapter is to position data analysis in philosophy and show its epistemological and ontological underpinnings using the philosophy of perception. The methods are a desk study, literature reviews, and lecture notes. Traditionally, the definition of knowledge is 'justified true belief' (JTB). The JTB is placed in the context of empiricism, rationalism, and/or dualism. These are further linked to ontological materialism, idealism, and dualism. The chapter has tried to draw a relationship with perception's direct realism, indirect realism, and dualism respectively. In conclusion, knowledge is justified by good evidence (empiricism) and reason (rationalism). The chapter recommends researchers utilise the philosophy of the sciences in order to improve on their research.

DOI: 10.4018/978-1-6684-6859-3.ch005

1. INTRODUCTION

In practice, on the one hand, the social sciences carry out their duty simply as science. The duty includes the use of ontology, epistemology, axiology, and, methodology. On the other hand, by the nature of the social sciences, human beings, their occupied environments, and, activities are the targets of study. Hence, when it comes to the application of scientific methods in the sciences, there are divided opinions in the social sciences. One school of thought believes that the social sciences should use the same scientific methods and quantification just as the natural sciences; and, the other school of thought disagrees and advocates the use of qualitative/language methods (Gerring, 2001). Yet, there is a recent movement in the social sciences that uses mixed methods (combined quantitative and qualitative scientific methods) (Gerring, 2001; Giddings, 2006; Pelto, 2015).

The complexities and diversities within the social sciences are many and deep (Gerring, 2001). A further division is the one between the materialists (physical data) and idealists (mental data) (Rose & Brown, 2015). This particular dichotomy is more often than not a major challenge to students of post-graduate research. For instance, the written and submitted post-graduate theses contain pieces of evidence of the confusion of students. Moreover, during the oral defence of the post-graduate thesis (viva voce), the presentations and responses to questions show the frustrations of students. During such difficulties, students find refuge in the term "it is perception studies".

Therefore, this paper is an attempt to contribute to the solution to this problem. This paper argues that perception is first about perceived reality. Going forward, it is the nature of this reality, that is contentious. The argument, according to Rose and Brown (2015), is as to whether we perceive material reality (materialism) or mental/immaterial reality (idealism). Secondly, there is the standpoint of pragmatic realism, which is the usefulness or necessity in a situation and not necessarily a hybrid (Putman, 2020).

2. EPISTEMOLOGY OF DATA ANALYSIS
- WHAT IS KNOWLEDGE?

An epistemology is a scientific study of knowledge; the study of the theory of knowledge; or the science of knowledge. It deals with the main issue of mind possession of knowledge. The root words of epistemology are in Greek "episteme" meaning knowledge, and "logia [logos]" referring to science, study, doctrine, or giving an account (Steup & Neta, 2020; Kivunja & Kuyini, 2017). Epistemology tries to answer the most critical question in philosophy, that is, how do we know what we know (L'Amour, n.d.). This implies that under epistemology, the concept "knowledge" is contested in terms of what it means to be knowledge, accounts for knowledge, or what can be known (Pojman, 2001). By doing so, epistemology shows the linkages between the knower (researcher) and the known (research object). There is a separation between the epistemic subject (knower) and the epistemic object (known); that is, a distinction between the knower and the known (Fenstermacher, 1994). For knowledge to occur and the mind to possess it, earlier philosophers set three conditions: justification, truth, and belief. These conditions form the traditional theory of knowledge, or tripartite theory of knowledge (Jenkins & Steup, 2017). Figure 1 shows the traditional definition of knowledge in an answer to the question: what is knowledge? Hence, knowledge is justified by true belief [JTB]. That is, the belief has to be justified and it has to be true.

Figure 1. Diagrammatic representation of the tripartite theory of knowledge

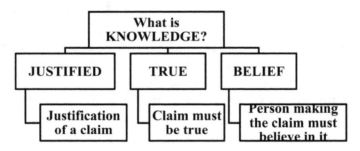

Generally, epistemology deals with propositional knowledge (Truncellito, n.d.). Hence, the philosophy of science does not consider technical knowledge (knowledge of know-how) or knowledge by familiarity. The basis of propositional knowledge is belief, truth, and justification.

2.1. Belief as an Aspect of Knowledge

A belief is a human concept and is considered to be a propositional attitude of truth, an epistemic object, the object of knowledge, shared knowledge, or, a claim known to be a fact (Rigo-Lemini & Martinez-Navarro, 2017; Truncellito, n. d.; Mastin, 2009; Jenkins & Steup 2017). In Figure 2, human beings are capable of possessing a belief and expressing it in a way to qualify as a propositional attitude. Therefore, a belief is an object of epistemology as well as knowledge; and it is a shared domain, or simply a fact.

Figure 2. Diagrammatic representation of belief

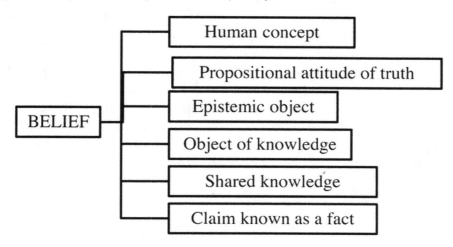

2.2. Truth as an Aspect of Knowledge

The second condition of knowledge in the traditional sense is truth. So what is truth? Answers to this simple question are varied. The literature discusses three types of truth: the correspondence theory of truth; the coherence theory of truth; and the pragmatic theory of truth (Pojman, 2001; Rutten, n. d.). Figure 3 displays the second condition of knowledge as truth, which requires that a belief must be true to constitute the basis for knowledge. This implies that false beliefs cannot be the basis of knowledge.

Figure 3. Diagrammatic representation of truth as a condition of knowledge

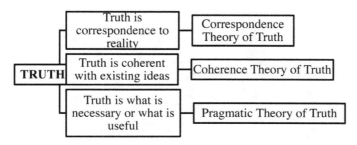

For example, the claim that the Earth is flat. For this to form the basis of knowledge, it must either correspond to reality, cohere with existing notions, or be a very useful claim for human progress. It turns out that this claim does not match up with reality, adheres to existing notions about the shape of the Earth, or is useful for any purpose. However, it shows that a belief can be false irrespective of how long it has existed and has been used and misused. Another belief, which later turned out to be false, is that the Earth is at the centre of the universe and the Sun revolves around it. It took a lot of time and human progress in technology to make this claim false. The essence of true belief is the fact that falsehood cannot be a basis for knowledge (JTB) (Mclaughlin, n. d.; Baima, 2015; Barnett, n. d.). A belief is true unless there is a prima facie fact that makes a belief untrue (Snare, 1974). Further and better facts in the future can indeed make an existing true belief false. Hence, a revelation of those further and better facts shall falsify the existing true belief. Until then, it is a true belief, on prima facie. In Greek, the term prima facie means "on/at first viewing" (Herlitz, 1994, p. 391).

2.3 Justification as an Aspect of Knowledge

The third and final condition of knowledge is justification. In addition, it has epistemic justification. It answers the question, "Is the person making the claim justified in believing the truth of the claim?". This question takes the discussion to the next and final level of knowledge where a true belief has to be justified. Therefore, research analyses use collected data to justify a true belief. From Figure 4, justification offers support for a true belief. It implies that the foundation of a true belief is the justification it has as knowledge. Justification is, therefore, the pillar on which a true belief stands. The two processes of justification of true belief are the use of good evidence and reason. Hence, in the data analysis, either good quality evidence, reasonable evidence, or both justify a true belief. In terms of epistemology, empiricism uses pieces of good evidence, and rationalism employs reason to justify a true belief.

Figure 4. Diagrammatic representation of justification as a condition of knowledge

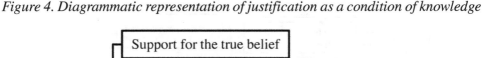
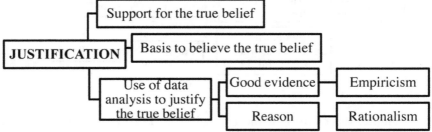

2.4 Means or Methods of Knowledge Acquisition

Knowledge as defined as [JTB] comes in two broad categories under epistemology: empiricism and rationalism. On the one hand, empiricism postulates that knowledge is acquired using the five senses from the external world around the researcher (Markie, 2004). Thus, sensory experience is the only or main source of knowledge. The sensory experience is a perceptual experience [an elaboration later]. In addition, experience and observation happen within the external world as material or physical things [a clarification later]. From Figure 5, empiricism is also a posteriori [after experience], synthetic [data analysis], and requires the use of induction in order to respond to epistemological questions or problems. Hence, in an empirical study of perception, a researcher operates under "direct realism". In addition, the perception problem of "illusion" affects this form of knowledge production in research. This implies that a researcher is not capable of knowing the research object in its entirety (illusion). The problem of illusion is a sceptical attack on the possibility of knowledge. In the same vein, the sceptical argument of such knowledge being affected by illusion should also come out equally strong. On the other hand, rationalism declares that reason is the only or main source of knowledge acquisition (Markie, 2004).

Figure 5. Diagrammatic representation of epistemology branches

EPISTEMOLOGY	
Empiricism	**Rationalism**
PERCEPTUAL EXPERIENCE	*REASONING*
Sensory experience	Mind
A Posteriori	Deduction, analytic
Induction, synthetic	A priori
Based on our senses	Innate Ideas
Direct	Indirect
PERCEPTION	
Illusion	Hallucination

Knowledge comes out as a product of the application of the human mind. Knowledge is accumulative and builds on innate ideas already existing in the human mind. Therefore, it is a priori and deductive reasoning, or application of the mind. Hence, it is analytic [known by the application of the mind based on innate concepts already existing in the mind] (Markie, 2004). Therefore, in research using rationalism, a researcher works with the notion of indirect realism. In addition, a skeptical attack on rationalism-indirect realism is the perception problem of hallucination. The attack is that researchers perceive research objects, which do not exist.

3. PHILOSOPHICAL ONTOLOGY OF DATA ANALYSIS: WHAT EXISTS?

Philosophical ontology is the scientific study of reality, existence, or, being in the world (Moon & Blackman, 2014; Uddin & Hamiduzzaman, 2009). Hence, it relates to the fundamental nature of reality, existence, being, or becoming (Kivunja & Kuyini, 2017). It is usually a shared domain of conceptualization [in information studies], and it answers the question: what is real, or, what exists? (Guarino, Oberle, & Staab, 2009; Neuhaus, 2017). Ontology comes from two Greek words: "onto" meaning existence, or, being real, and, "logia" [logos], which is study, or, science. Therefore, from the root words, ontology refers to a study of existence or science of reality. With reference to knowledge [JTB], ontology deals with the nature of belief, the existence of belief, or the reality of belief (Dudovskiy, n.d.). In addition, ontology refers to the taxonomy of reality, that is, the organisation of reality, and in this context, the organisation or taxonomy of belief in JTB. Ontology describes the essence of belief in terms of the existence or reality of such a belief (Peperzak, 2007). In addition, it denotes the general characteristics of belief, or, the features of reality constituting belief; and, the linkages between the parts forming the belief. In this context, ontology goes beyond belief and the languages used in describing belief. It is a fundamental nature of belief and the features that come together to form the belief, as well as the relationships between the various features (Schalley, 2019). Therefore, ontology deals with stuff, that constitutes the existence, or, the reality of belief; and, whether this stuff is material, or, immaterial stuff, or, even both.

3.1 Various Forms of Existence or Being

Figure 6 shows the three main branches of ontology: materialism, idealism, and dualism. The linkages thereof with philosophical perception are indicated in Figure 6. Materialism as an ontology depends on external metaphysics just as idealism rests on internal metaphysics.

3.2 Material or Physical Existence

On the one hand, materialism carries the notion that reality, existence, or being is physical stuff, which has its own being irrespective of the knowledge of a researcher [knower] of it. The material world is external to the consciousness of a researcher [knower]. This means a separation between a knower and a known or two distinct beings in the material world. Hence, what is real is material or physical [materialism].

3.3 Mental Existence or Being

On the other hand, idealism presupposes that no physical world [reality, being] exists; rather, reality or existence is made up of immaterial stuff, often referred to as sense-datum [data]. In other words, the human mind exists or is real and not any physical stuff. In terms of philosophical perception, direct realism matches up with the material world, and indirect realism corresponds to ontological idealism.

Figure 6. Diagrammatic representation of the linkage between philosophical ontology and perception.

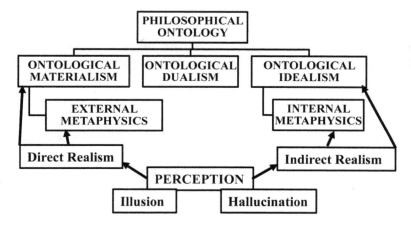

3.4 Dual Existence or Hybrid of Material and Mental Worlds

Figure 7 displays an ontological spectrum with materialism at one end and idealism at the other end. Towards the centre of the spectrum is the meeting point of materialism and idealism, referred to as ontological dualism. Hence, ontological dualism is a shared trait of materialism and idealism (Sayers, 1983). It represents a notion in an ontology that combines both materialism and idealism in the same research pursuit. In addition, an ontological spectrum displays, at the extreme ends, direct realism and indirect realism.

Figure 7. Ontological spectrum of materialism and idealism with philosophical perception

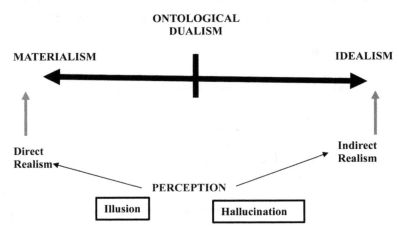

A hybrid of materialism and idealism is dualism. It fuses two distinct ontological stances. It becomes the meeting point of the material and mental worlds' existence. Therefore, materialism and idealism exist side by side.

According to Locke, ideas are purely subjective, private, mental entities, distinct from the objective, material world, which exists independently of consciousness. Locke's philosophy thus involves a sharp metaphysical dualism between ideas and things, between the mental and the material realms. Dualism is also a feature of his theory of knowledge, which involves a rigid distinction between subjective appearances and the objective reality of things (Sayers, 1983, p. 17).

Ontological materialism operates on the side of direct realism [with external metaphysics] and ontological idealism functions on the side of indirect realism [with internal metaphysics].

3.5 External Metaphysics: What Is Behind the Material Existence?

Under external metaphysics, the notion is that there is a single reality, which means that the truth is the same everywhere. Researchers wish to see reality just as God sees it; this notion is called "God's eye perspective" from the human point of view. Sankey (2003) has argued in two ways for the positive use of God's eye perspective in realism. External metaphysics considers reality without the use of any language or concept (Verhaegh, 2017). It further separates the knower from the known;

hence, the reality is observer-independent. In this manner, the reality is objective, implying no influence of the knower on the known. Objectivism is, therefore, value-free and operates in a value-neutral manner in which the researcher does not influence the research results. Hence, if it is a perception study using empiricism as an epistemology and materialism as an ontology based on external metaphysics, then these points hold.

3.6 Internal Metaphysics: What Is Behind the Mental Existence or Being?

Under internal metaphysics, a knower internalises reality (Verhaegh, 2017). Hence, as many knowers as possible, so multiple realities are there. Therefore, there is the notion of multiple realities under internal metaphysics. In this case, there is no separation between the knower and the known, as they are the same. This makes reality under internal metaphysics subjective; therefore, subjective reality is value-laden. In addition, subjective reality is human mind-dependent.

4. PHILOSOPHICAL AXIOLOGY

The term axiology comes from two Greek words: "axios" which means worth and "logia [logos]" referring to science, theory, or study (Hart, 1971). Hence, axiology is a science; it is a science of values; and, it is an inquiry into goodness in doing science (Bahm, 1993). Skowronski (2018, pp 251) uses terms such as "philosophy of value, axiology, and value inquiry" as alternative expressions. Viega (2016) discusses ethics and aesthetics as two fundamental values in axiology. Elsewhere, axiology is divided into three types: ethics, aesthetics, and social and political philosophy.

4.1 Research Ethics

From the European Union (2010), ethics deals with the values of the researcher and the values of the research participants. In this context, a researcher's values affect the several choices made in research. Such choices include research topic philosophy, data collection methods, data collection tools, data analysis techniques, and ethical considerations in research. In addition, the values of the research participants affect the responses provided. General normative ethics applied normative ethics, and non-normative ethics are the branches of ethics. General normative ethics is the discourse on morality in research. It is a choice between right and wrong, as well as good and bad behaviour in research. It is prescriptive and it tells a researcher what to do or not to do. In addition, general normative ethics include moral laws and principles in research. Another term for it is a normative theory, which implies the character traits of a researcher along the paths of good or bad, altruistic or destructive, and helpful or harmful. Another name is a moral theory, which is a choice between morally right and morally wrong issues and attitudes involved in research. Some types of general normative ethics include virtue, consequentialism, deontological ethics, utilitarianism, Kantianism, and ethical intuitionism. The second type of ethics applied to normative ethics is an application of general normative ethics in deciding which side of the debate on certain issues is right to argue for in the case of abortion, euthanasia, and the legalization of marijuana in Ghana. Finally, non-normative ethics is meta-ethics, and it is about the nature of ethics. Hence, it is not ethical choices but the facts underpinning certain issues or cases, for example, paternalism.

4.2 Aesthetics

Aesthetics is a philosophical discourse on beauty, sometimes; including art, taste, and the sublime (Cole & Sweeney, 2022). The focus of aesthetic philosophy is art and nature, beauty and taste, and art and the artist (Cole & Sweeney, 2022). According to Dewey (2005), social and political philosophy is the discourse on society and politics and social life: from the individual, and family through nation-states to international systems. It claims that mere chance, magic, or accident cannot explain human behaviour. Hence, science should include government, laws, authority, and, universals.

5. LINKAGE BETWEEN METHODOLOGY AND PHILOSOPHY

Research methodology discourse circles around quantitative, qualitative, and, q-square approaches. Researchers who use quantitative methods alone are quantitative purists (the philosophy is a positivist approach) as qualitative purists use only qualitative methods (the philosophy is interpretivism or constructivism). The q-square approach refers to research, which uses quantitative and qualitative methods in tandem (the philosophy is pragmatism, critical paradigm). Research involves four types of data analysis. These include descriptive (what happened?), diagnostic (why did it happen?), predictive (what is likely to happen in the future?), and, prescriptive (what is the best course of action to be taken?) data analyses (Stevens, 2021). Variables are either independent or dependent, exogenous or endogenous, respectively though loosely so (Kline, R. B. (1998). Variables could also be latent or observed (Sauro, J. (2016).

5.1 Quantitative Methods

Quantitative methods handle data analysis by testing causal linkages between two or more variables (Maria et al., 2019). According to Babbie (2010) and Muijs (2010), quantitative methods include the use of objective measurements, statistics, mathematics, and, numerical analysis. It subjects data to statistical analyses using computational techniques, software or manual statistical methods, and, statistical tables. Such quantitative data collection methods are polls, questionnaire administration, surveys, and already existing secondary statistical data. The quantitative methods stress reliability, objectivity, precision, generalizability, and, rigour (Babbie, 2010; Muijs, 2010).

5.1.1 Qualitative Methods

Qualitative methods explore, discover, and, understand by collecting and analyzing non-numerical data (Bhandari, 2020). Qualitative methods involve several approaches such as grounded theory, ethnography, action research, phenomenological research, and, narrative research ((Bhandari, 2020). Qualitative methods of data collection include focus group discussions, key informant interviews, and document analysis (Kawulich, 2005).

5.1.2 Mixed Methods

The q-square approach is a mixture of quantitative and qualitative methods (Legowo et al., 2020). Another name is mixed methods. Mixed methods combine quantitative and qualitative data to integrate their strengths and interpret the combined output (Creswell, 2014). According to Creswell (2014), there are three types of mixed methods: convergent design combines quantitative and qualitative data in tandem, the explanatory sequential design analyses quantitative data first and uses qualitative data to explain the quantitative findings; and, exploratory sequential design uses qualitative data first and quantitative data to supplement.

6. TYPES OR FORMS OF PHILOSOPHICAL PERCEPTION

Often, the literature discusses three types of perception. These are perceived of [simple perception], perceive to be and perceive that (Audi, 1998); or, simple seeing, perceiving as, and, perceiving that respectively (O'Brien, 2022). Simple perception uses the five senses in obtaining experiences: seeing [visual experience], hearing [auditory experience], touch [tactual experience], smell [olfactory experience] and taste [gustatory experience] (Audi, 1998). The sense provides the perceiver with perceptual experience. Therefore, perceptual experience is a source of knowledge from the external world out there and a justification for true belief (Roessier, 2009). For the content of perceptual experience read McDowell, (1994), Schellenberg, (2010), Roessier, (2009), and Sahoo, (2016).

6.2 Means or Methods of Philosophical Perception

Table 1 displays the major types of perceptual experience [perception] as direct and indirect realism. Direct realism indicates that the five senses capture direct and instant objective reality from the external world out there (Sayers, 1983). It implies that perception rather imposes itself on the perceiver; in a way that the perceiver plays no active role in perception; and, thus, there is no mediation between the perceiver and the external world out there, which is perceived [object of immediate perception] (Sfetcu, 2022).

Table 1. Major types of perception

Philosophical Perception	
Direct Realism	**Indirect Realism**
We perceive physical objects	We perceive the ideas
Sensory experience through the five senses (feeling, smelling, seeing, tasting, and hearing)	Perceived by the mind
Perceived indirectly	Perceived directly
Illusion = you see something not as it is. (scepticism's attack on direct realism)	Hallucination = you see something which does not exist. (scepticism's attack on indirect realism)
Common sense realism	Phenomenology/phenomenalism
Naïve realism/ veridical realism	Representational realism
EMPIRICISM = realist fully	RATIONALISM = realist to a point

6.3 Problems of Philosophical Perception

Perception is about a perceiver perceiving an object in the external world out there, if the object of perception is not available, there cannot be a perceptual experience of it, hence, no knowledge is generated rather illusion, hallucination, or, maybe a dream (Sahoo, 2016). Illusion and hallucination are classified as problems of perception; and, that if these two problems are possible then there cannot be perception or perception cannot be what it claims to be (Crane & French, 2016; Sahoo, 2016). "For we think of an illusion as 'any perceptual situation in which a physical object is actually perceived, but in which that object perceptually appears other than it really is' Smith (2002: 23)" (Crane & French, 2016, p.6). Illusion affects direct realism. Hallucination is associated with indirect realism in which the perceptual object is non-existent (Crane & French, 2016). For example a mirage. This type of hallucination has nothing to a medical condition. The perceiver perceives objects, which are not in existence at all. Hence, for perception to be a source of knowledge and justification of true belief, it has to be perception minus illusion and hallucination.

7. CONCLUSION

Philosophy of the social sciences offers researchers the opportunity to ground research in philosophy. Hence, researchers particularly those who have had the opportunity to study at the Master of Philosophy and Doctor of Philosophy levels should grasp the philosophy and this must reflect either overtly or covertly in their research. Therefore, researchers may openly state their stands in epistemology, ontology, and, axiology, and, match them to the methodology. The other way is equally good whereby researchers would not declare their philosophical positions by using the appropriate terminologies but rather argue out the research in the philosophical language of the various stands. In the latter case, a researcher does not state the study's position on epistemology, ontology, axiology, and methodology. However, the research write-up brings out clearly to the fore these philosophical positions in the arguments raised. Therefore, in perception studies as well, researchers are to go by one of these two ways. Figure 8 shows a diagrammatic summary of epistemology [empiricism, rationalism, or both], ontology [materialism, idealism, or dualism], axiology [ethics, aesthetics, social and political philosophy], and methodology [quantitative, qualitative, or q-square].

These philosophical choices of perspectives include positivism, post-positivism, interpretivism, and critical paradigm. Whereas, positivism advocates for the use of purely natural science methods in the social sciences and hinges on statistics and content analysis to uncover the truth, post-positivism is very critical about using the right scientific methods to get closer to the truth, even though the truth is unknown. In both cases, realism is the stand; positivists are realists and post-positivists are critical realists. However, interpretivism rejects both positivism and post-positivism and the tenets thereof and rather advocates for the interpretation of the truth, the meaning of the truth, and above all construction of the truth. The interpretivists are relativists for the truth is relative to various societies and ethnography could help bring this out or relative to individuals and phenomenology could reveal the differences and similarities. The critical paradigm is critical of positivism, post-positivism, and interpretivism. It considers these standpoints as traditional theories. The critical paradigm regards the traditional theory as enslaving; hence, the advocacy to overthrow the status quo. The critical paradigm reveals the weaknesses inherent in positivism, post-positivism, and interpretivism. It shows the actions essential to affect the required changes. By so doing, the critical paradigm deconstructs positivists, post-positivists, and interpretivists' orthodoxies, and re-constructs that is, co-produces 'new' knowledge.

Figure 8. Philosophy of the social sciences and methodology

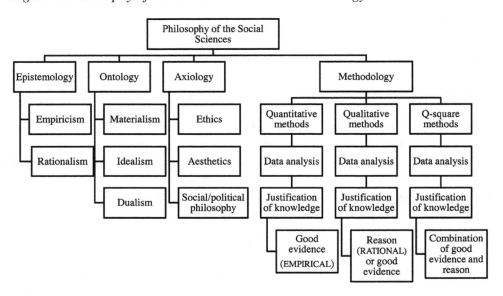

REFERENCES

Ahwaz, Aidje, Ajbird, Ajdecon, Alansohn, et al., (n.d.). *Philosophy of Science.* Stanford University. https://web.stanford.edu/class/symsys130/Philosophy%20 of%20science.pdf

Aliyu, A. A., Singhry, I. M., Adamu, H. A. R. U. N. A., & AbuBakar, M. A. M. (2015, December). Ontology, epistemology and axiology in quantitative and qualitative research: Elucidation of the research philosophical misconception. In *Proceedings of the Academic Conference: Mediterranean Publications & Research International on New Direction and Uncommon* (Vol. 2, No. 1).

Asghar, J. (2013). Critical paradigm: A preamble for novice researchers. *Life Science Journal, 10*(4), 3121–3127.

Audi, R. (1998). *Epistemology - A Contemporary Introduction to the theory of knowledge*. Routledge.

Babbie, E. R. (2010). *The Practice of Social Research* (12th ed.). Wadsworth Cengage.

Bahm, A. J. (1993). *Axiology: the science of values* (Vol. 2). Rodopi. doi:10.1163/9789004463615

Baima, N. R. (2015). Truth, Knowledge, and the Value of False Belief in Plato. *Arts & Sciences, Electronic Theses and Dissertations.* https://openscholarship.wustl.edu/art_sci_etds_/484

Barnett, B. C. (n. d.). The Analysis of Knowledge. In C. Hendricks, *Introduction to Philosophy: Epistemology*. PressBook. https://press.rebus.community/intro-to-phil-epistemology/chapter/the-analysis-of-knowledge/

Bhandari, P. (2020). *What is Qualitative Research? Methods & Examples*. Scribbr. https://www.scribbr.com/methodology/qualitative-research/

Brown, H. I. (1992). Direct Realism, Indirect Realism and Epistemology. *Philosophy and Phenomenological Research, 52*(2), 341–363. doi:10.2307/2107939

Bryman, A. (2004). *Social Science Research Methods* (2nd ed.). Oxford University Press Inc.

Cole, D., & Sweeney, M. (2022). Aesthetics Philosophy. *Study.com.* https://study.com/academy/lesson/what-is-aesthetics-in-philosophy-definition-history-quiz.html

Comte, A. (1975). *Auguste Comte and positivism: The essential writings*. Transaction Publishers.

Coolican, H. (2004). *Research Methods and Statistics in Psychology*. Hodder.

Crane, T., & French, C. (2016). The problem of perception. In E. N. Zalta (ed.), The Stanford Encyclopaedia of Philosophy, 1-12. Stanford Press.

Creswell, J. W. (2014). A concise introduction to mixed methods research. SAGE. https://plato.stanford.edu/archives/spr2016/entries/perception-problem/

Dudovskiy, (n. d.) *Research Methodology*. Business Research Methodology. https://research-methodology.net/research-philosophy/ontology/

European Union (2010). *European Textbook on Ethics in Research._Research and innovation*. European Commission (europa.eu).

Fenstermacher, G. D. (1994). The Knower and the Known: The Nature of Knowledge in Research on Teaching. *Review of Research in Education*, *20*, 3–56. doi:10.2307/1167381

Gerring, J. (2001). *Social science methodology: A criterial framework*. Cambridge University Press. doi:10.1017/CBO9780511815492

Giddings, L. S. (2006). Mixed-methods research: Positivism dressed in drag? *Journal of Research in Nursing*, *11*(3), 195–203. doi:10.1177/1744987106064635

Guarino, N., Oberle, D., & Staab, S. (2009). What Is an Ontology? In S. Staab & R. Studer (Eds.), *Handbook on Ontologies. International Handbooks on Information Systems.* Springer., doi:10.1007/978-3-540-92673-3_0

Hart, S. L. (1971). Axiology theory of values. *Philosophy and Phenomenological Research*, *32*(1), 29–41. doi:10.2307/2105883

Herlitz, G. N. (1994). The meaning of the term prima facie. *Louisiana Law Review*, *55*, 391.

Jenkins, J., & Steup, M. (2017). The Analysis of Knowledge. *Stanford Encyclopaedia of Philosophy*. Stanford Press. https://plato.stanford.edu/entries/knowledge-analysis/

Kaboub, F. (2008). Positivist Paradigm. *Leong (Encyc)*, *2*(2), 343.

Kawulich, B. B. (2005). Participant Observation as a Data Collection Method. *Qualitative Research, 6*(2). 43. https://www.qualitative-research.net/index.php/fqs/article/view/466/996

Kirkby, J., O'Keefe, P., & Howorth, C. (2001). Introduction: Rethinking Environment and Development in Africa and Asia. *Land Degradation & Development*, *12*(3), 195–203. doi:10.1002/ldr.431

Kivunja, C., & Kuyini, A. B. (2017). Understanding and Applying Research Paradigms in Educational Contexts. *International Journal of Higher Education*, *6*(5), 26–41. doi:10.5430/ijhe.v6n5p26

Kline, R. B. (1998). *Principles and Practice of Structural Equation Modeling*. Guilford Press. https://faculty.chass.ncsu.edu/garson/pa765/kline.htm

L'Amour, L. (n.d.). *Epistemology: How do you know that you know what you know?* 2022 Farnam Street Media Inc. https://fs.blog/epistemology-know-know-know/

Leach, M., & Mearns, R. (1996). Environmental change and policy. *The lie of the land: Challenging received wisdom on the African environment*, 1-33.

Legowo, M. B., Subanidja, S., & Sorongan, F. A. (2020, September). Model of Sustainable Development Based on FinTech in Financial and Banking Industry: A Mixed-Method Research. In *2020 3rd International Conference on Computer and Informatics Engineering (IC2IE)* (pp. 194-199). IEEE. 10.1109/IC2IE50715.2020.9274605

Maria, S., Darma, D. C., Amalia, S., Hakim, Y. P., & Pusriadi, T. (2019). Readiness to face industry 4.0. *International Journal of Scientific & Technology Research*, *8*(9), 2363–2368.

Markie, P. (2004). Rationalism vs. Empiricism. *Stanford Encyclopedia of Philosophy*. Stanford Press. https://plato.stanford.edu/entries/rationalism-empiricism/

Mastin, L. (2009, January). *Existence and Consciousness*. The Basics of Philosophy. https://www.philosophybasics.com/branch_metaphysics.html

McDowell, J. (1994). The Content of Perceptual Experience. *The Philosophical Quarterly*, *44*(175), 190–205. doi:10.2307/2219740

Mclaughlin, J. (n. d.). *Bertrand Russell – On Truth and Falsehood, In The Originals: Classic Readings In Western Philosophy*, PressBook. https://pressbooks.bccampus.ca/classicreadings/chapter/bertrand-russell-on-truth-and-falsehood/

MegaEssays.Com. (n.d.). *Critical theory approach to communication*. MegaEssays. https://www.megaessays.com

Moon, K., & Blackman, D. (2014). A Guide to Understanding Social Science Research for Natural Scientists. *Conservation Biology*, *28*(5), 1167–1177. https://onlinelibrary.wiley.com/doi/10.1111/cobi.12326/full. doi:10.1111/cobi.12326 PMID:24962114

Muijs, D. (2010). *Doing Quantitative Research in Education with SPSS* (2nd ed.). SAGE Publications.

Neuhaus, F. (2017). On the Definition of 'Ontology'. *FOUST Paper*, *2050*, 1–11.

O'Brien, D. (2022). *The Epistemology of Perception*. Internet Encyclopaedia of Philosophy. https://iep.utm.edu/epis-per/

Pelto, P. J. (2015). What is so new about mixed methods? *Qualitative Health Research*, *25*(6), 734–745. doi:10.1177/1049732315573209 PMID:25721718

Peperzak, A. T. (2007). Ontology and Ethics from the Perspective of Religion. *Archivio Di Filosofia*, *75*(1/2), 369–379.

Peprah, K. (2017). Trends in global development paradigms and the ramifications in Ghana (1950–2015). *Ghana Journal of Geography*, *9*(2), 40–67.

Pojman, L. P. (2001). *What can we know? An introduction to the theory of knowledge* (2nd ed.). Wadsworth.

Putnam, H. (2020). The many faces of realism. In *Pragmatism* (pp. 163–181). Routledge. doi:10.4324/9781003061502-12

Rigo-Lemini, M., & Martinez-Navarro, B. (2017). Epistemic States of Convincement. A Conceptualization from the Practice of Mathematicians and Neurobiology. In U. X. Eligio (Edt) Understanding Emotions in Mathematical Thinking and Learning. (pp. 451-457). Elsevier. doi:10.1016/C2014-0-02036-9

Roessier, J. (2009). Perceptual Experience and Perceptual Knowledge. *Mind*, *118*(472), 901–1216. https://www.researchgate.net/publication/249258749. doi:10.1093/mind/fzp131

Rose, D., & Brown, D. (2015). Idealism and materialism in perception. *Perception*, *44*(4), 423–435. doi:10.1068/p7927 PMID:26492727

Rutten. E. (n. d.). *Epistemological Aspects of Management and Organization*. SlidePlayer. https://slideplayer.com/slide/4884113/

Sahoo, J. (2016). The Problem of Perception. *Journal of the All Orissa Philosophy Association*, *II*(I), 126–131. https://www.researchgate.net/publication/292145607_The_Problem_of_Perception

Sandberg, J. (2005). How Do We Justify Knowledge Produced Within Interpretive Approaches? *Organizational Research Methods*, 8(1), 41–68. doi:10.1177/1094428104272000

Sankey, H. (2003). Scientific Realism and the God's Eye Point of View. *PhilSci*. 1-17. http://philsci-archive.pitt.edu

Saunders, M. N. K. (2009). *Understanding research philosophy and approaches to theory development*. Pearson Education. https://www.researchgate.net/publication/309102603

Sauro, J. (2016). *The Difference between Observed and Latent Variables*. MeasuringU. https://measuringu.com/latent-variables/

Sayers, S. (1983). Materialism, Realism and the Reflection Theory. *Radical Philosophy*, *33*(33), 16–26.

Schalley, A. C. (2019). Ontologies and ontological methods in linguistics, *Language and Linguistics, Wiley* 13:e12356. 1-19.

Schellenberg, S. (2010). The particularity and phenomenology of perceptual experience. *Philosophical Studies*, *149*(1), 19–48. doi:10.100711098-010-9540-1

Sfetcu, N. (2022). *Direct Realism and Indirect Realism. In Knowledge, Mind, Reality* MultiMedia Newsletter, https://www.telework.ro/en/direct-realism-and-indirect-realism/

Shahin, S. (2016). A Critical Axiology for Big Data Studies. *Palabra Clave (La Plata)*, *19*(4), 972–996. doi:10.5294/pacla.2016.19.4.2

Skowronski, K. P. (2018). Does the Pragmatist Reflection on the Ethical and Aesthetic Values need the Kantian Axiology for its (Pragmatist) Future Developments? *Pragmatist Kant*, 251.

Snare, F. (1974). The definition of prima facie duties. *The Philosophical Quarterly (1950-)*, *24*(96), 235-244.

Steup, M., & Neta, R. (2020). Epistemology. *Stanford Encyclopedia of Philosophy*. Stanford Press. https://plato.stanford.edu/entries/epistemology/

Stevens, E. (2021). What Are the Different Types of Data Analysis? *Career Foundry*. https://careerfoundry.com/en/blog/data-analytics/different-types-of-data-analysis/

Trochim, W. M. K. (2006). *Positivism and Post-Positivism*. Conjointly. https://conjointly.com/kb/positivism-and-post-positivism/

Truncellito, D. A. (n. d.). *Epistemology*. Internet Encyclopaedia of Philosophy. https://iep.utm.edu/epistemo/

Tuli, F. (2010). The Basis of Distinction between Qualitative and Quantitative Research in Social Science: Reflection on Ontological, Epistemological and Methodological Perspectives. *Ethiop. J. Educ. & Sc. 6*(1), 1 97-108. https://www.ajol.info/index.php/ejesc/article/download/65384/53078

Uddin, M. N., & Hamiduzzaman, M. (2009)... *The Philosophy of Science in Social Research The Journal of International Social Research.*, 2(6), 654–664.

Varghese, B. (n. d.). *Comte's Positivism*. ShCollege. https://www.shcollege.ac.in

Verhaegh, S. (2017). Blurring Boundaries: Carnap, Quine, and the Internal–External Distinction. *Erkenn*, *82*(4), 873–890. doi:10.100710670-016-9848-0

Viega, M. (2016). Science as art: Axiology as a central component in methodology and evaluation of arts-based research (ABR). *Music Therapy Perspectives*, *34*(1), 4–13. doi:10.1093/mtp/miv043

Von Hildebrand, D., & Seifert, J. (1960). *What is philosophy?* Routledge.

Weber, R. (2004). The Rhetoric of Positivism versus Interpretivism: A Personal View. *Management Information Systems Quarterly*, *28*(1), iii–xii. doi:10.2307/25148621

Wiesing, L., & Roth, N. A. (2014). *The Philosophy of Perception – Phenomenology and Image Theory*. Bloomsbury Publishing.

Section 2
Research Methods and Literature Review

Chapter 6
Research Design

Krishantha Wisenthige

(iD) https://orcid.org/0000-0001-8334-6434

Sri Lanka Institute of Information Technology, Sri Lanka

ABSTRACT

The framework of methods and techniques that the researcher has chosen to conduct the research is described as research design. In social science research, it is required to collect evidence relevant to the research problem, especially evidence required to evaluate a problem, to test the theory, or to describe a phenomenon. Successful research designs should be able to provide research insights that are accurate and unbiased. This chapter covers the type of research designs, and names key characteristics of a good research design; neutrality, reliability, validity, and ability for generalization as well as qualitative, quantitative, mix method research, and fix and flexible research designs.

1. INTRODUCTION

The framework of methods and techniques that the researcher has chosen to conduct the research described as Research design. The term "research" describes collection of data, evidence based on the research problem, analyzing, and coming to conclusions based on the findings taking research methodologies into consideration. It ensures the researcher that evinces obtained from the research effectively address research problem by minimaxing the ambiguously as possible. In the social science research, it is required to collect evidence relevant to the research problem, specially evidences required to evaluate a problem, to test the theory or describe a phenomenon. Successful research design should be able to provide research insights that are accurate and unbiased. This chapter covers the type of research designs, key characteristics of a

DOI: 10.4018/978-1-6684-6859-3.ch006

good research design; neutrality, reliability, validity, and ability for generalization as well as qualitative, quantitative & mix method research and fix & flexible research designs. Chapter also discuss the types of research design by grouping, benefit of research design and role of researcher.

2. RESEARCH METHODOLOGY

The research onion framework proposed by Saunders et al. (2012), explains the different aspects of the research to be considered to come up with a sound research design while Saliya's (2021) 7Ps model suggests integrated approach for conducting research (Figure 1). The research onion provides guidance to the researchers about essential steps that need to be taken when developing a research methodology for research. The research onion was divided the into three levels of decisions (Saunders et al., 2019) as first two outer rings, i.e., (i) Research philosophy and (ii) Research approach; Research design which constitutes (a) methodological choices, (b) research strategy and (c) time horizon; and (iii) tactics, i.e., the inner core of the research onion, which includes data collection and analysis aspects. Contrarily, Saliya's (2021) 7Ps provide seven pillars of the research process as an integrated flexible approach.

Figure 1. Integrated-flexible vs onion
Sources: Saunders et al. (2019) and Saliya (2021)

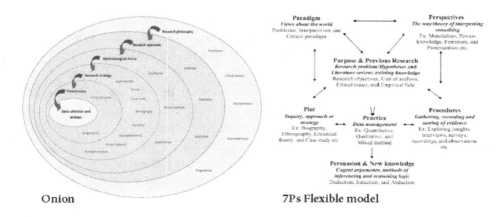

Onion   7Ps Flexible model

Research Philosophy, research approach, research strategy, methodological choices, time horizon and data collection & analysis are the six main layers of research onion proposed by Saunders et al. (2019) as a tool which helps to organize your research and develop research design.

3. RESEARCH DESIGN

Research design should provide a complete framework for research activities, provide researcher systematic pathway pursue in to unknow territory. Important feature of a good research design is the flexibility to incorporate midway changes during the research process. Researchers consider research design as the blueprint of conducting research and Data collection, measurements and analysis are the key element of any research design, and it is used as steppingstone to make critical decisions regarding what, where, how much, when, and steps for research design to be undertaken. It follows a unique structure that yield success from research and imperative to include elements that help solve the problem quickly.

The research design can be considered as a kind of a large plant (a collection of small machines/ processes) which can produce numerous types of output (designs) according to the input (the choices of methods/strategies) (Saliya, 2022). Those numerous kinds of designs are classified into various groups based on different perspectives such as:

1. Purpose: Descriptive, Explanatory, Experimental, Explorative, Diagnostic, Experimental and Correlational (Saliya, 2022); (Mukherjee, 2020).
2. Approach: Quantitative, Quantitative and Mixed methods (Mukherjee, 2020).
3. Strategy: Biography, Ethnography, Phenomenology, Case study, Survey, Aesthetic and Grounded theory etc. (Saunders et al.,2019)
4. Technology: Academic research, Market research and Development research
5. Time horizon: Cross sectional, Cross sequential, time series and Longitudinal (Saunders et al.,2019)
6. Complexity: Single-simple, Comparative and Multi-level

3.1. Essential Components of a Research Design

Developing a research design keeping in view the objectives of research and the expected outcome and subsequently implementing the design and modifying the same during research, whenever found necessary, are the most crucial aspects of a research process. Research design should be following the research problem, objectives and expected outcomes and resources availability, resource deployments, other possible implementation issues should be taken into the consideration.

Figure 2. Component of Research Designed (circled) within the 10Ps model of Integrated-flexible research methodology model
Source: Saliya (2022)

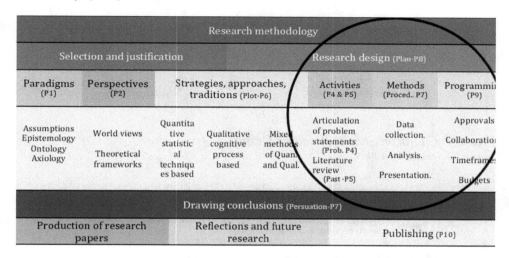

There is a tendency among some researchers to begin their investigations without proper planning and comprehensive idea about what data & information are required to be collected to answer the research question without addressing the design issues beforehand. It will lead to arriving weaker conclusions in the absence of strong empirical evidence and methodological approach that is unconvincing and, consequently, failing to adequately address the overall research problem.

Research Design can be either qualitative, quantitative or mix method approach. Researchers have freedom choose between different types of research methods and sub-types of research methods namely experimental design, defining research problems, descriptive studies, element of data collection, measurement of data and analysis of data. As a rule of thumb, research problem that researcher has identified will decide the determining factors of research design to be employed instead of the other way around. Purpose statement, research techniques, research setting, objectives, research methodology, types of measurements, analytical methods and time line are the key elements of research design (Figure 03).

3.2. Characteristics of Research Design

A proper research design sets your study up for success and provide insights that are accurate and unbiased results. You need to create a design that meets all of the main characteristics of a design.

Figure 3. Elements of Research Design
Source: Developed by Author

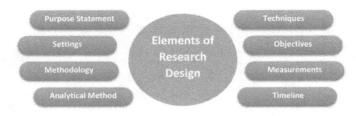

Figure 4. Characteristics of Research Design
Source: Developed by Author

Reliability	Produce similar results very time
Validity	Leverage on right measuring tools to gauge the accuracy and check whether the results align with the research objectives
Neutrality	Ensures that assumptions made by researcher free of bias and neutral
Generalizability	The degree of generalizability terms of the replicability and reproducibility of the findings despite different measures and settings respectively

4. QUANTITATIVE, QUALITATIVE OR MIXED RESEARCH DESIGNS

Researchers used research design to collect data for their research by employing research techniques and procedures. Many different types of research methods can be identified and each has its' own strengths and weaknesses. It is up to the researcher to select the appropriate method based on the research question to be addressed. The question being asked, and the nature of the data are the decisive criteria for selecting most appropriate research method for a particular study. Although different types of research methods are available, all of them have one common goal to provide information that can be used to solve problems, improve understanding and come to conclusions. Sanders et al. (2019) categorized research designs into three types: (i) quantitative research design; (ii) qualitative research design; and (iii) mixed methods research design.

4.1. Quantitative Research Designs

Qualitative Research is a research designs focused on exploring the research problem under investigation in depth. Qualitative research can be used to in the

Figure 5. Quantitative, qualitative or mixed methods research designs
Source: Developed by Author

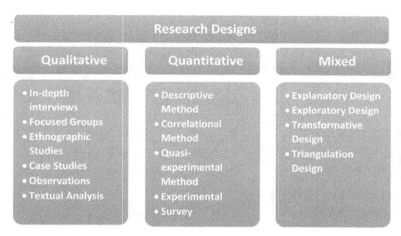

domains of social, cultural, individual as well as some scientific areas. Qualitative research design can be varied depending upon the method used; in-depth interviews, participant observations, focus groups are some methods which may be considered during qualitative research design. Qualitative methodologies are diverse in nature but there are also commonalities can also be observed between them.

The main reason for carrying out qualitative research is to gain a richly detailed understanding of a particular topic or issue based on first-hand experience. This is achieved by having a relatively small but focused sample base because collecting the data can be rather time consuming; qualitative data is concerned with depth as opposed to quantity of findings. A qualitative research design is concerned with establishing answers to the *why* and *how* questions in research.

Due to the fact, qualitative research is often defined as being subjective (not objective), and findings are gathered in a written format as opposed to numerical. This means that the data collected from a piece of qualitative research cannot usually be analysed in a quantifiable ways using statistical techniques because there may not be commonalities between the various collected findings. However, a process of coding can be implemented if common categories can be identified during analysis.

Although the questions/observations in qualitative research are not managed to gain a particular response the ability to code findings occurs more often than you may originally think. This is because the researcher 'steers' the research in a particular direction whilst encouraging the respondent to expand and go into greater detail on certain points raised (in an interview/ focus group), or actions carried out (participant observation).

Figure 6. Qualitative Research Design
Source: Author based on Saunders et al. (2019)

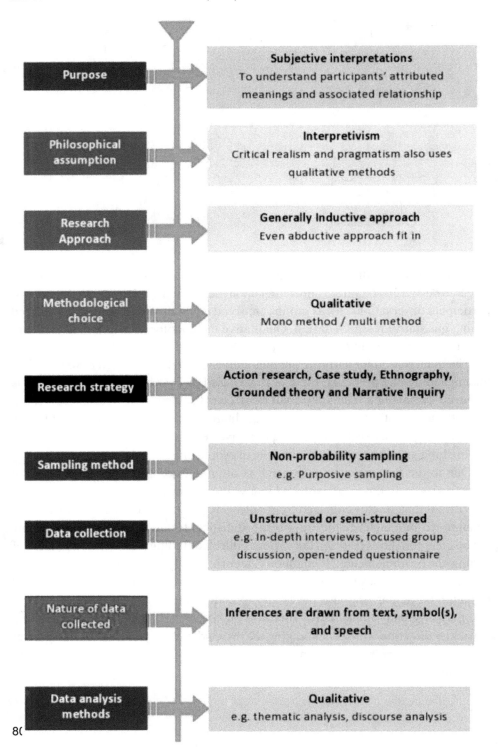

Qualitative research design should also not only account for what is said or done, but also the way something is spoken or carried out by a participant. Sometimes these mannerisms can hold answers to questions in themselves and body language and the tone of voice used by respondents are key considerations.

Figure 7. Quantitative Research Design
Source: Author based on Saunders et al. (2019)

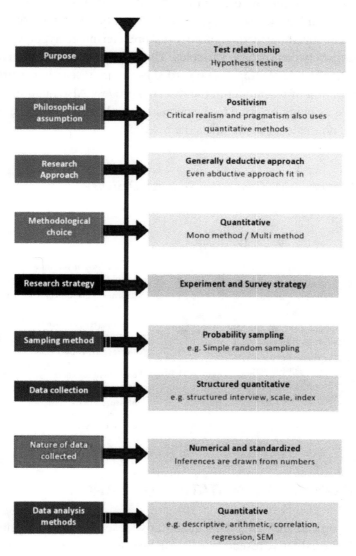

4.2. Quantitative Research Designs

Quantitative Research method is a way of collecting and analyzing data that uses mathematics and statistics. Quantitative researchers use statistical methods to analyze data, including sampling techniques, different types of statistical analysis based on the research. Quantitative researchers also use mathematical models to understand how different factors influence each other. The techniques used in quantitative research include random selection of research participants / observations from the study population in an unbiased manner, the standardized questionnaire or intervention they receive, and statistical methods used to test predetermined hypotheses regarding the relationship between specific variables. The researcher in quantitative research, unlike in the qualitative paradigm, is regarded as a great research instrument due to active participation of researcher in the research process Also quantitative designs are considered as being external to the actual research, and results are expected to be replicable, no matter who conducts the research.

Figure 8. Quantitative vs. Qualitative Research Designs
Source: Developed by Author

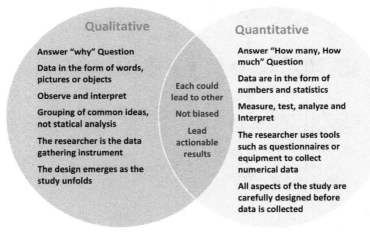

QUALITATIVE VS. QUANTITATIVE RESEARCH

When collecting and analyzing data, quantitative research deals with numbers and statistics, while qualitative research deals with words and meaning. One type of data is objective, to the point, and conclusive. The other type is subjective, interpretive, and exploratory. However, the right time to use either method or use both together, can vary depending on your research goals and needs. Basic difference between qualitative and quantitative designs are provided in figure 08.

The concept of predispositions in this context is used to refer to the acquired characteristics of both qualitative and quantitative research methods. Table 1 represents the predispositions of the qualitative and quantitative modes of inquiry. It further sums up how each of these research approaches operates and each of the predispositions is explained below.

With regard to the assumptions, the quantitative paradigm assumes that social facts have an objective reality and the researcher does not identify with the researched phenomenon. The qualitative paradigm, on the other hand, assumes that reality is socially constructed and the researcher's point of view matters because researcher identifies with the phenomenon being studied. The purpose of quantitative research is to predict, explain and generalize the outcomes of the research, whereas the purpose of qualitative research is to contextualize, interpret and understand the perspective of the actors.

Table 1. Quantitative Vs Qualitative

Quantitative	Qualitative
Assumptions	
• Social facts have an objective reality • Primacy of method • Variables can be identified, and relationships can be measured • **Etic (outsider 's point of view)**	• Reality is socially constructed • Primacy of subject matter • Variables are complex, interwoven, and difficult to measure • Emic (insider's point of view)
Purpose	
• Generalizability • Prediction • **Causal explanations**	• Contextualization • Interpretation • Understanding actors' perspectives
Approach	
• Begins with hypotheses and theories • Manipulation and control • Uses formal instruments • Experimentation • Deductive • Component analysis • Seeks consensus, the norm • Reduces data to numerical indices • **Abstract language in write-up**	• Ends with hypotheses and grounded theory • Emergence and portrayal • Researcher as instrument • Naturalistic • Inductive • Searches for patterns • Seeks pluralism, complexity • Makes minor use of numerical indices • Descriptive write-up
Researcher Role	
• Detachment and impartiality • **Objective portrayal**	Personal involvement and partiality Empathic understanding

Source: Developed by Author

Figure 9. Mix Method Research Designs
Source: Developed by Author

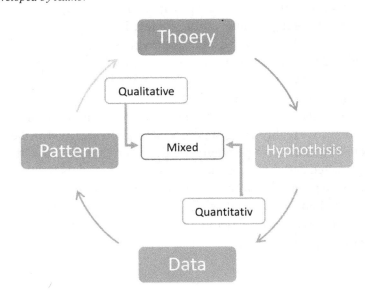

4.3. Mixed Methods Research Designs

Mixed research method is a type of research methodology that uses both qualitative and quantitative techniques facilitating researchers in investigating diverse perspectives and discovering relationships between the complex layers of sophisticated research questions. This approach can be used to collect data from a variety of sources, and then to analyze that data using both qualitative and quantitative methods. This approach can be useful in studying complex problems that cannot be studied using only one type of research methodology. Mixed research method can also provide a more complete picture of a problem than could be gained from using only one type of research methodology.

Mixed methods research involves an integration of approaches to data collection, data analysis, and elucidation of the evidence. The term 'mixed' signifies that data association or assimilation at an appropriate stage during the research process is essential to the mixed methods approach.

Rationale for Using Mixed Methods

- Obtain different, multiple perspectives: validation
- Build comprehensive understanding
- Explain statistical results in more depth
- Have better contextualized measures

- Track the process of program or intervention
- Study patient-centered outcomes and stakeholder engagement

Mixed methods research allows a research question to be studied comprehensively as it involves applying a precise and pre-determined research design that combines qualitative and quantitative elements to generate an integrated set of evidence addressing a single research question. Using mixed methods research allows the limitations of one approach to be compensated by the strengths of another approach. For example, the qualitative approach can provide deep insights about a trend discovered through quantitative research while the quantitative approach can validate a behavioral pattern disclosed by qualitative research. This type of research also encourages the development of conceptual models and the creation of new instruments to interpret the significance of outcomes of a study.

Five important characteristics of mixed methods designs are:

- **Triangulation**: This design allows the use of multiple methods to collect data on the same topic. It seeks convergence and validation of results from different methods.
- **Complementarity**: The results of one method are elaborated, enhanced, illustrated, and clarified with the results of another method.
- **Initiation**: Newly obtained insights help in the stimulation of new research questions.
- **Development**: The results of one method are used to build another method.
- **Expansion**: The research breadth and range are expanded using different methods for different areas of investigation

The need for mixed methods research stems from the complexity of research problems and researchers' desire for deep and broad understanding, both of which can be attained by combining qualitative and quantitative data. Further, this research method can produce firm and rich analyses and conclusions for various research problems. It also helps in generating deep and meaningful insights about a problem and its solutions.

5. COMMON TYPES OF RESEARCH DESIGNS

There are various ways to categorize research design depending on the purpose of research. Positivist and interpretivist are the two categories of research depending on the goal of the research. Interpretive designs are used for theory building research whereas positivist design are mainly used in theory testing research. Positivist designs seek generalized patterns based on an objective view of reality, while interpretive designs seek subjective interpretations of social phenomena from the perspectives of the subjects involved. Field experiment, field surveys, laboratory experiments, case research and secondary data analysis research used positivist designs whereas phenomenology, case research and ethnographic studies used interpretive designs. It is important to note that case research used for theory testing as well as theory building, but not at the same time.

5.1. Descriptive Design

Descriptive designs used for collecting and generating information to systematically describe population, situation, or phenomenon. This design answer what, where, when how questions regarding the research problem to be addressed rather than why. In descriptive research, many kinds of research methods can be used to investigate the variable in the research question. Qualitative techniques are mainly used in descriptive studies although qualitative methodologies are also used in some instances. In descriptive research, researcher do not control or manipulate any variables instead researcher only identify variables, observe, and measure. Some distinctive characteristics of descriptive research are:

Quantitative

Employ quantitative research methods to collect quantifiable information to be used in statistical analysis to infer the sample date to describe the population of study.

Uncontrolled Variables

The nature of the variables or their behavior is not in the hands of researcher since it uses observational methods to conduct research

Cross-Sectional

In nature, descriptive research are generally a cross-sectional where different dimensions belonging to the same population are studied.

Basis for Further Research

For further research based on descriptive research findings, different data collection and analysis techniques can be used and in subsequent researches. Data can also help point towards the types of research methods.

Multiple methods of data collection, fast and cost-effective, quantitative and qualitative research in amalgamation and high external validity are considered as main advantages of descriptive research

5.2. Experimental Design

Experimental research design testing or attempting to test the relationship among variables in a way of scientific research where one or more independent variables are manipulated and applied to one or more dependent variables to measure their effect attempting to prove a hypothesis by way of experimentation. Researchers can used experimental research design when they need to collect quantifiable information to be used in statistical analysis in order to infer sample data to describe population of study.

The effect of the independent variables on the dependent variables is usually observed and recorded over some time, to aid researchers in drawing a reasonable conclusion regarding the relationship between these 2 variable types. Experimental designs are carried out in a control environment over the time which enable researcher to form a corroborated conclusion about the two variables. Researcher collect data to support or reject hypothesis so that experimental research also called as hypothesis testing or a deductive research.

Experimental research is also used in social research to determining a causal relationships among variables. Experimental group to apply treatments and the control group should be selected where selection of subjects in this this group is simply by randomization. Through the process researcher will be able to control certain variables that may affect the experiment since the subject are selected simply by chance. After applying the treatment, the effects of the treatment on the experimental group can then be compared to the control group. The independent variables that cause the effects on the dependent variable can then be determined holding other extraneous variables constant.

There are three subtypes of research one can implement under the experimental research designs based on the way the researcher assigns subjects to different conditions and groups.

Pre-Experimental Research Design

This research design is implemented when it is required to determine whether further investigation is required to for group under study. A group or several groups are entailed to be observed after factors of cause and effects implemented. Pre-experimental design is considered as the simplest form of experimental research design and is treated with no control group.

Quasi-Experimental Research Design

When the randomization is impossible or impractical, this is the best research design researchers can used in experimental research. Quasi-experimental approach is mainly used in educational research where administrators are unwilling to allow the random selection of students for experimental samples.

True Experimental Research Design

The true experimental research design relies on statistical analysis to accept or reject a hypothesis. It is the most accurate type of experimental design that can establish a cause-effect relationships. The control group won't be subject to any changes where treatment is only applied to experiment group. Randomize Control Trails (RCT) are now increasingly used in the field of social sciences

5.3. Correlational Research Design

In order to establish a statistically corresponding relationship among two variables with the help of statistical analysis, correlational research method can be used as a type of non-experimental research method. The aim of correlational research is to identify variables that have some sort of relationship do the extent that a change in one creates some change in the other. This type of research is descriptive, unlike experimental research that relies entirely on scientific methodology and hypothesis.

Correlational research design is mainly used in all kinds of quantitative data sets, but it is commonly used within market research. For example, correlational research may reveal the statistical relationship between high-income earners and relocation; that is, the more people earn, the more likely they are to relocate or not. There are three types of correlational research as positive correlational research, negative correlational research and zero correlational research.

Positive correlational research involve two variables that are statistically corresponding where an increase or decrease in one variable creates a like change in the other where as negative correlational research involve two variables that are statistically opposite where an increase in one of the variables creates an alternate effect or decrease. Zero correlational research involves two variables that are not necessarily statistically connected each other and, a change in one of the variables may not trigger a corresponding or alternate change in the other variable

Once two variables are measured, then researchers can calculate statistical measure called correlation coefficient to identify how two factors or variable are correlated each other as well as strength and direction of the relationship that ranges from -1 to + 1 as per figure 02. Based on data collection methods, correlational

Figure 10. Ranges of Correlation Coefficient
Source: Developed by Author

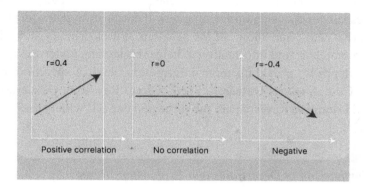

research can also be classified as Naturalistic observation research, survey research and archival research.

5.4. Diagnostic Research Design

Research design that tries to investigate the underlying cause of a certain condition or phenomena is called diagnostic research design. Diagnostic design can assist researchers to examine cause specific challenges faced. The research design is comprised of three phases as problem inception phase, problem diagnosis phase, and the problem solution phase.

Inception (Phase One): When did the issue arise? In what situations is the issue more evident?

Diagnosis (Phase Two): What is the underlying cause of the issue? What is influencing the issue to worsen?

Solution (Phase Two): What is working in curing the issue? Under what situations does the problem seem to become less evident

5.5. Explanatory Research Design

To understand different reasons, causes, and effects by connecting different ideas to attempt to find the answer to the question why. Mostly research studies start from exploratory research, then descriptive research and again exploratory research used to validate findings. This can serve as a starting point of more in-depth studies and learning about this type of research can help you understand how to determine the root cause of a certain situation and fill gaps in missing information.

Exploratory research explore questions without arriving definite conclusions and it also examine the extend of cause and effect relationship. Explanatory research design used in a researches focusing on forming new theories or hypothesis by providing insights on the "why" and "how" of the problem. It uses primary and primary and secondary research to find information to helps researchers understand a particular problem in depth by providing more information about a specific topic. Depth Interviews, Case Analysis Research, Focus Group Research, Observations, Pilot Studies, and Literature Research are the some popular and widely used exploratory research tools.

Table 2. Comparison of Descriptive and Exploratory Research

	Exploratory Research	**Descriptive Research**
Meaning	Formulate a problem for a clearer investigation.	Explore and explain an individual, group, or situation.
Objective	Discovery of ideas and concepts.	Explain characteristics and functions.
Overall Design	Flexible	Rigid
Statistical Design	No pre-planned design for analysis.	Pre-planned design for analysis.
Sampling	Non-probability sampling	Probability sampling

Source: Developed by Author

6. RESEARCH STRATEGY

The research strategy describes how the researcher aims to carry out the work (Saunders et al. 2019). There are several research strategies, viz., Experimental design, Survey design, Archival research, Case study, Ethnography, Action research, Grounded theory and Narrative inquiry (Saunders et al. 2012). Here we can include other research strategies appropriate to our study.

7. TYPES OF RESEARCH-TIME HORIZON

Depending on the time horizon, there are two types of research, i.e., Longitudinal research and cross-sectional. Research in which a researcher wants to study samples at a certain time is called cross-sectional research. Longitudinal research studies samples over a period of time. In longitudinal research, the period can range from short-term to long-term.

Figure 11. Research Strategies
Source: Developed Author

Experimental Design	To study the cause-effect relationship between two or more variables systematically manipulating the independent variable to study the corresponding changes in the dependent variable
Survey Design	To answers for 'what', 'who', 'where', 'how much' and 'how many' types of research questions, data is collected and analyzed from a sample of individuals
Case Study	To seek answers for 'how' and 'why' questions through empirical inquiry of an individual social unit
Action Research	To address real-life practical problems through a systematic inquiry by finding practical solutions for problems through participation and collaboration with members of a social unit.
Grounded Theory	To develop a theory by systematic inductive method for conducting qualitative research
Ethnography	To explore cultures and societies by collecting data through direct interaction and involvement so as to gain firsthand information from research subjects
Archival research	To systematic inquiry wherein primary sources held in archives studied for evidence collection or deep understanding

7.1. Cross-Sectional Research

A cross sectional study is a type of observational study in which a researcher collects data from many different individuals at a specific point in time. Researchers can use these studies to analyze several characteristics, such as income, gender, age, at once. Moreover, they give a glimpse into the prevailing characteristics in a population and can provide information about what is currently happening in the population. Therefore, cross sectional studies can provide a snapshot of a population or society at a specific moment. In fact, cross sectional studies are the opposite of longitudinal studies. Although cross sectional studies are used to analyze the characteristics in a society or community, they cannot analyze cause-and-effect relationship between variables. They also help to gather preliminary data for further research.

7.2. Longitudinal Research

Longitudinal study involves repeatedly examining the same subjects to detect changes that may occur over a period of time. This time period may be as short as a few weeks or as long as several decades. This is a type of observational research where the researcher does not interfere with the subjects. Since the research extends beyond a single moment in time, the researcher can identify changes or developments in the target population, at both group and individual levels, and establish sequences of events. They are a type of correlational studies. Moreover, there are three main types of longitudinal studies as panel study, cohort study and retrospective study.

- **Panel Study** – a study that provides longitudinal data on a group of people
- **Cohort Study** – a longitudinal study in which the sample share a defining characteristic such as birth year, geographical area, etc.
- **Retrospective Study** – a study that involves observing past events by analyzing historical information such as medical records.

Figure 12. Research Strategies
Source: Developed Author

Cross-Sectional Research	Longitudinal Research
Data collected at a specific point of time	Data collected over a period of time
Focuses on point of time	Focuses on period of time
Different samples chosen each time	Same samples participate in data collection
Interested in studying samples at macro-level, such as societal changes	Interested in studying samples at micro-level, such as changes in individual behavior
Consumes lesser time	Consumes more time

8. BENEFIT OF RESEARCH DESIGN TO RESEARCHER

Researchers used research design as a systematic procedure to implement different tasks of the research study. It is prerequisite to know the research design for the researcher to carry out the research in a systematic and proper way. It makes the research as efficient as possible by giving maximum information with minimal expenditure of effort, time and money. Proper research design or plan prior to data collection is needed to systematically collect and analysis the data and arrive acceptable findings and conclusions. Preparation of research design should be done carefully as even a minute error might ruin the purpose of the entire research. The design helps the researcher to organize the ideas, which helps to identify and correct his/her flaws, if any. In a good research design, all the components with each other or go together with each other in a coherent manner. The theoretical and conceptual framework must with the research goals and purposes. Likewise, the data collection strategy must fit with the research purposes, conceptual and theoretical framework and approach to data analysis. Research design provides firm foundation to the endeavor, reduces inaccuracy, helps to get maximum efficiency & reliability, it eliminates bias & marginal errors, minimizes wastage of time, reduce uncertainty, confusion &

practical haphazard related to the research problem, helpful for collecting research materials, helpful for testing of hypothesis. It also gives an idea regarding the type of resources required in terms of money, manpower, time, and efforts as well as guides the research in the right direction in the way of smooth & efficient sailing.

REFERENCES

Melnikovas, A. (2018). Towards an Explicit Research Methodology: Adapting Research Onion Model for *Futures Studies*. *Journal of Futures Studies*, *23*(2), 29–44. doi:10.6531/JFS.201812_23(2).0003

Mukherjee, S. P. (2020). *A Guide to Research Methodology: An Overview of Research Problems, Tasks and Methods* (1st ed.). Taylor & Francis.

Saliya, C. A. (2017), Doing Qualitative Case Study Research in Business Management, *International Journal of Case Studies*, *6*(12), 96–111.

Saliya, C. A. (2021). Conducting Case Study Research: A Concise Practical Guidance for Management Students. *International Journal of KIU*, *2*(1), 1-13. doi:10.37966/ijkiu20210127.

Saliya, C. A. (2022). *Doing Social Research: A Guide to Non-native English Speakers*. Springer. doi:10.1007/978-981-19-3780-4

Saunders, M., Lewis, P., & Thornhill, A. (2019). *Research methods for business students* (8th ed.). Pearson Education Limited.

Seakran, U. (2003). *Research Methods for Business*. John Wiley and Sons. https://iaear.weebly.com/uploads/2/6/2/5/26257106/research_methods_entiree_book_umasekaram-pdf-130527124352-phpapp02.pd

Chapter 7
Research Design and Methods in Social Sciences Research

Kavita Gupta
The Maharaja Sayajirao University of Baroda, India

ABSTRACT

A research design is a deliberate, well-organized technique that a researcher follows when conducting a scientific study. It is the coexistence of previously identified elements with any additional knowledge or data that leads to a reasonable end result. In simpler terms, research design is a glue that keeps the research endeavor together. The present chapter focuses on quantitative research design, qualitative research design and mixed method design. This chapter will help the budding researcher to have a deeper understanding of research designs therein enabling the researcher to utilize them for their purpose of research.

INTRODUCTION

A research design is a deliberate, well-organized technique that a researcher follows when conducting a scientific study. It is the coexistence of previously identified elements with any additional knowledge or data that leads to a reasonable end result. In simpler terms, Research design is a glue that keeps the research endeavor together. RESEARCH DESIGN is a term that relates to the research plan, conceptual framework, and strategy—the blueprint that guides the research process by logically connecting components. It includes the sequence of measures taken ahead of time to ensure that relevant data will be collected in a way that allows objective examination of alternative hypotheses formulated with respect to the research challenges. Further, it can be used as a framework or guidance for the study's planning, implementation,

DOI: 10.4018/978-1-6684-6859-3.ch007

and analysis by explaining how a researcher could use their chosen research design or approach to answer a specific research issue. Therefore, it is apt to say that a Research Design is a set of decisions about what, where, when, how much, and how to conduct an inquiry or research project.

In the present chapter, the three types of research designs, that is, quantitative, qualitative and mixed method with respect to menstrual health are being discussed in detail. In order to achieve Sustainable development goals, maintenance of menstrual health is essential. Research in this area is very important in understanding menstrual experiences, and their intersections with physical, mental, and social health. Given the multifaceted nature of menstrual health, good effective research designs are required for action and research.

DEFINITIONS

A research design is the arrangement of the conditions for collection and analysis of data in a manner that aims to combine relevance to the research purpose with economy in procedure (Selltiz, Deutsch and Cook, 1962, p. 50).

A research design is a plan, structure and strategy of investigation... to obtain answers to research questions or problems. It includes an outline of what the investigator will do from writing the hypotheses ...to the final analysis of data. (Kerlinger & Lein, 1986, p. 279)

Research Approach

Frequently, the terms "research approach" and "research designs" are used interchangeably. The term "research approach" refers to the strategy for investigating the topic under investigation using either structured (quantitative) or unstructured (qualitative) approaches, or a combination of both. It aids in determining the existence or lack of manipulation and control over variables, as well as group comparisons. Various instruments, strategies, procedures, or processes are used to acquire or review data or information in a research approach.

CHARACTERISTICS OF RESEARCH DESIGN

1. It is a plan that specifies the sources and types of information relevant to the research problem.

2. It is a strategy specifying which approach will be used for gathering and analyzing the data.
3. It includes the balancing of the research scope with time and cost-budget parameters.

RESEARCH DESIGN

Minimum Essentials

1. Clear statement of the problem:
    a. To Identify, Explore, describe, explain, evaluate, and understand a real-world problem related to human attitude, behavior, opinion, perception, values, emotions, Knowledge, social structure and relationships, culturally shared meaning, environmental contexts, processes and systems.
    b. To develop knowledge and theory
    c. To create an intervention program
    d. To contribute to a larger study
2. Techniques and approach to be used for gathering information:
    a. Quantitative: Cross-sectional, correlational, longitudinal
    b. Qualitative: Phenomenology, Ethnography, Grounded theory, Case study, Narrative analysis
    c. Mixed method: Convergent or Concurrent Parallel Design, Explanatory Sequential Design, Exploratory Sequential Design, Embedded Design, Transformative Design, Multiphase Design
    d. Sampling technique: Census, snowball, Purposive, Quota, Convenience, Random, systematic.
3. The population to be studied:
    a. Eligibility criteria
    b. Clients, Stakeholders, Dissertation committee, Scholars, Researchers, academicians, Funders.
    c. Number of sites
4. Methods to be used in processing and analysing data:
    a. Between groups comparison, Within groups comparison
    b. Data collection methods: self-report inventories, Participant observation, in-depth interviews, Focus group discussion.

NEED FOR RESEARCH DESIGN

1. To facilitate the smooth sailing of the various research operations.
2. To make research as efficient as possible that can yield maximal information with minimal expenditure of effort, time and money.
3. For advance planning of the methods to be adopted for collecting the relevant data and the techniques.
4. To prevent blind searching that can help in decision making.

FEATURES OF GOOD RESEARCH DESIGN

1. It should be capable of reducing bias and increase the consistency of data collected and processed.
2. It should yield the least amount of experimental error.
3. It should allow a researcher to consider a variety of various elements of a situation.
4. It should be the most cost-effective, appropriate, and effective design.

IMPORTANT CONCEPTS RELATING TO RESEARCH DESIGN

1. **Dependent and independent variables**: If one variable depends upon or is a consequence of the other variable, it is termed as a **dependent variable**. The variable which is independent of other variables but on which other variables depend is termed as an **independent variable**.
2. **Extraneous variables**: Independent variables that are not related to the purpose of the study, but may affect the dependent variable are termed as extraneous variables.
3. **Experimental units**: The pre-determined plots or the blocks, where different treatments are used, are known as experimental units.
4. **Confounded relationship**: When the dependent variable is not free from the influence of extraneous variable(s), the relationship between the dependent and independent variable is said to be confounded by an extraneous variable(s).
5. **Research Hypothesis**: When a prediction or a hypothesized relationship is to be tested by scientific methods, it is termed as research hypothesis.
6. **Experiment**: a procedure carried out under controlled conditions in order to test Hypothesis.
7. **Experimental and control groups**: In experimental hypothesis-testing research when a group is exposed to usual conditions, it is termed a '*control group*', but

when the group is exposed to some novel or special condition, it is termed an *'experimental group'*.

8.   **Treatment**: The different conditions under which experimental and control groups are put are usually referred to as 'treatments'.

9.   **Experimental and non-experimental hypothesis-testing research**: Research in which the independent variable is manipulated is termed 'experimental hypothesis-testing research'. Research in which an independent variable is not manipulated is called 'non-experimental hypothesis-testing research'.

Figure 1. Types of Research Design

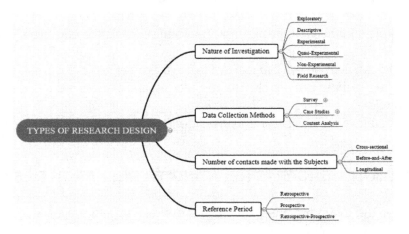

- There are different types of research design.
- Which one is the best for your study, depends on the purpose and scope of your study.
- While taking decisions on the research design, a number of factors have to be taken into consideration.
- These include:
  ○ Nature of investigation,
  ○ Data collection methods,
  ○ Number of contacts made with the subjects, and
  ○ The Period of reference of study.

Figure 2. Approaches to Research Design

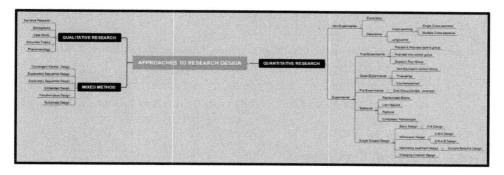

QUANTITATIVE RESEARCH

Quantitative research is a formal, objective, and systematic method of obtaining information about the world through the use of numerical data. It is the use of statistical, mathematical, or computational techniques to conduct a systematic empirical investigation of observable events. From the start, the research design is predetermined and stable. The data gathering questions are systematic and uniform for all participants.

Characteristics

Large sample size; structured data gathering questionnaire

TYPES OF NON-EXPERIMENTAL RESEARCH DESIGN

Non-Experimental Designs are research methods that look at social phenomena without altering the conditions that the individuals are in. There is also no chance of participants being assigned to different groups at random. Non-experimental research is characterized by the absence of an independent variable. Instead, the researcher observes and examines the circumstances in which the phenomena occur to acquire knowledge. The two types of Non-experimental designs are Exploratory and Descriptive research.

- **Exploratory research** is a type of study that is used to look into a topic that isn't well defined or understood. It answers questions like "what," "where," and "how" to help researchers gain a better understanding of a study problem.

- ○ **Example:** "An Exploratory Survey to Assess the Menstrual Characteristics and Prevalence of Dysmenorrhea in College Going Girls" (Dalal and Saini, 2015).
- **Descriptive research** is concerned with learning more about **"what"** the phenomenon is rather than **"why"** or **"how"** it occurs.
  - ○ **Example:** "A descriptive study of menstrual hygiene practices among women at the rural area of Haryana" (Sheoran, Kaur, Sadhanu and Sarin, 2020)

Cross-sectional Designs

- Ensure that information from every given sample of population items is only collected once.
- There is just one sample of respondents in single cross-sectional designs, and information is received from this sample only once.
- There are two or more samples of respondents in various cross-sectional designs, and information from each sample is acquired only once. Frequently, data from various samples is gathered at different periods.

Example: "A cross-sectional Study on Menstrual Hygiene among Rural Adolescent Girls of West Bengal" (Boral, Burman, & Sembiah, 2020).

Longitudinal Design

- The same variables are assessed repeatedly on a fixed sample (or samples) of population elements. The sample or samples in a longitudinal design remain the same over time, unlike in a cross-sectional design.
- "Menstrual characteristics, menstrual anxiety and school attendance among adolescents in Uganda: a longitudinal study" (Tanton et al., 2021).

Cohort Analysis

The cohort serves as the basic unit of analysis in a series of surveys completed at appropriate time intervals. A cohort is a group of people who have all had the same experience at the same time.

Example: "Menstrual Cycle Length and Patterns in a Global Cohort of Women Using a Mobile Phone App: Retrospective Cohort Study" (Grieger & Norman, 2020).

Study Designs Based on the Reference Period

1.   **Retrospective**: Investigating a phenomenon that has happened in past.

Example: Enquiring about Premenstrual symptoms.

2.   **Prospective**: Likely preference in of a phenomena or outcome in the future.

Example: Confirming about Premenstrual Distress symptoms from Diary method which the participants used to fill every day at a particular time.

3.   **Retrospective-Prospective:** Studying past trends on a phenomenon and predicting future.

Example: Diagnosis of Premenstrual Dysphoric Disorder (PMDD).

TYPES OF EXPERIMENTAL RESEARCH DESIGN

The Experimental design involves manipulating one variable to determine if changes in one variable cause changes in another variable. This method relies on controlled methods, random assignment and the manipulation of variables to test a hypothesis.

- Most scientifically sophisticated research method.
- Empirical research method used to examine a hypothesized causal relationship between dependent and independent variables.

EFFECTIVE RESEARCH DESIGN IN EXPERIMENT

The MAXMINCON Principle of Variance

The aim of a researcher is to determine the change that can be attributed to the independent variable, s/he need to design their study to ensure that the independent variable has the maximum opportunity to have its full effect on the dependent variable, while the effects that are attributed to extraneous and chance variables are minimized (if possible) or quantified or eliminated.

This is what Kerlinger and Lein (1986: 286) calls the **maxmincon** principle of variance.

1. **MAXimize Systematic Variance**: Produced in the dependent variables by the manipulation of the independent variables.
2. **MINimize Error Variance**: By increasing Reliability and Validity of measurement instruments.
3. **CONtrol Extraneous Variables**: Technique of elimination, Balancing, Counter balancing, Randomization.

True- Experimental Designs

Post-test Only Control Group Design

Two Group Design: Post-test Only Control Group Design
- In this design two groups or areas (test area and control area) are selected and the treatment is introduced into the test area only.
- The dependent variable is then measured in both the areas at the same time.
- Treatment impact is assessed by subtracting the value of the dependent variable in the control area from its value in the test area.

Example: "A study to assess the effectiveness of Jacobson muscle relaxation therapy on premenstrual syndrome among adolescent girls in C.S.I. Girls Higher Secondary School at Madurai" (Gayathri, 2018).

Pre-test Post-test Control Group Design

Two Group Design: Pre-Post test Control Group Design
- In this design two areas are selected and the dependent variable is measured in both the areas for an identical time-period before the treatment. The treatment is then introduced into the test area only, and the dependent variable is measured in both for an identical time-period after the introduction of the treatment.
- The treatment effect is determined by subtracting the change in the dependent variable in the control area from the change in the dependent variable in test area.

Example: "A Quasi Experimental Study to Assess the Effectiveness of Ginger Powder on Dysmenorrhea among Nursing Students in Selected Nursing Colleges, Hoshiarpur, Punjab" (Satyajit & Kaur, 2017).

Solomon Four Group Design

- Simple & Robust design
- Uses Pre-test and Post-test
- In use since 1949
- Two Experimental and Two Control Groups
- Random assignment to the four groups
- Only 1 experimental and 1 control group receive the pretest.
- Treatment/Intervention for both experimental groups.
- Post-test to all the four groups.

Example: "Menstruation and the Cycle of Poverty: A Cluster Quasi-Randomised Control Trial of Sanitary Pad and Puberty Education Provision in Uganda" (Montgomery et al., 2016).

Quasi Experimental Research Design

Quasi-experimental research involves the manipulation of an independent variable without the random assignment of participants to conditions or orders of conditions.

Quasi-experimental research is similar to experimental research in that there is manipulation of an independent variable. It differs from experimental research because either there is no control group, no random selection, no random assignment, and/or no active manipulation.

Non-equivalent Control Group Design

Also called nonequivalent comparison-group design, a nonequivalent groups design, then, is a between-subjects design in which participants have not been randomly assigned to conditions.

Example: "Effectiveness of Structured Teaching Programme on Knowledge, Attitude and Practice regarding Physical Problems of Menstruation among Adolescent Girls" (Maheswari, 2011).

Time-series Design

A Quasi-experimental design that involves the observation of units (e.g., people, countries) over a defined (long) time period. In this design, the experimenter would continue to administer the treatment and measure the effects a number of times during the course of experiment.

Example: "The forecasting of menstruation based on a state-space modeling of basal body temperature time series" (Fukaya et al., 2017).

TYPES OF PRE- EXPERIMENTAL RESEARCH DESIGN

Pre-Experimental design is a variation of experimental design that lacks the rigor of experiments and is often used before a true experiment is conducted.

Single-Group Design

- No Randomization and Control Group.
- In such a design a single test group or area is selected and the dependent variable is measured before the introduction of the treatment.
- The treatment is then introduced and the dependent variable is measured again after the treatment has been introduced.
- The effect of the treatment would be equal to the level of the phenomenon after the treatment minus the level of the phenomenon before the treatment.

Example: "A Pre-Experimental Study To Assess The Effectiveness Of Structured Teaching Programme On Knowledge Regarding Menstrual Hygiene Among Fmphw Ist Year Students At Ramzaan Institute Of Paramedical Sciences Nowgam Srinagar" (Mushtaq & Mir, 2019).

TYPES OF STATISTICAL RESEARCH DESIGN

Statistical designs offer relatively more control and use precise statistical procedures for analysis.

Randomized Block Design

Subjects are assigned to blocks, based on gender. Then, within each block, subjects are randomly assigned to treatments (either a placebo or a treatment).

It is an improvement over the C.R. design. In the R.B. design the principle of local control can be applied along with the other two principles of experimental designs. In the R.B. design, subjects are first divided into groups, known as blocks, such that within each group the subjects are relatively homogeneous in respect to some selected variable.

Completely Randomized Design

It involves only two principles viz., the principle of replication and the principle of randomization of experimental designs. The essential characteristic of the design is that subjects are randomly assigned to experimental treatments. A completely randomized design (CRD) is one where the treatments are assigned completely at random so that each experimental unit has the same chance of receiving any one treatment.

Latin Square Design

It is an experimental design very frequently used in agricultural research. The conditions under which agricultural investigations are carried out are different from those in other studies for nature plays an important role in agriculture. In such a case the varying fertility of the soil in different blocks in which the experiment has to be performed must be taken into consideration. A Sudoku grid is a special kind of Latin square where n×n matrices that are filled with n symbols in such a way that the same symbol never appears twice in the same row or column.

Factorial Group Design

Researcher manipulates two or more independent variables simultaneously to observe their effects on the dependent variables. This design is useful when there are more than two independent variables, called as factors to be tested.

Single-Subject Designs

- A research design where data is gathered from a few individuals.
- Here, data are collected and analyzed for only one subject at a time.
- It consists of 3 components:

Repeated Measurement

Prior to starting and during the intervention the subject's status on the target problem (Dependent variable) is measured at regular time intervals.

Baseline Phase (A)

An initial measurement of a condition that is taken at an early time point and used for comparison over time to look for changes. For example, the size of a tumor will be measured before treatment (preintervention) and then afterwards to see if the treatment had an effect.

- **Treatment phase (B)**: The time period during which the intervention is implemented.
- **Basic Design (A-B)**: It represents a baseline phase followed by a treatment phase.
- **Withdrawal Design**:
  ○ **The A-B-A Design**: In this design, a baseline is established during the first A phase, a treatment is introduced during phase B, and a second baseline is recorded after the withdrawal of the treatment.
  ○ **The A-B-A-B Design**: The design has four phases denoted by A_1, B_1, A_2, and B_2. In each phase, repeated measurements of the participant's behavior are obtained. Hence, the participant serves as his or her own control. The first phase, A_1, is used to establish a baseline for the behavior. The intervention phase, B_1, is introduced after a stable baseline has been established. In the third phase, A_2, the intervention is withdrawn, and the baseline condition is reinstated. After baseline stability has been reestablished, the intervention is presented a second time, the B_2 phase.

Examples

Basic Design (A-B)

Two parents who are having problems with one of their children. Meeting with their counselor, they complain that, over the last month, their 15-year-old daughter has been squabbling constantly with her brother and being rude and sarcastic with her parents. The counselor suggests that the parents use a point system, with points being accrued for poor behavior. Once a certain number of points are attained, the child will begin to lose certain privileges. To test the intervention, the parents are instructed to count and record every 3 days over a 15-day period the number of instances of sibling arguments begun by the child and the number of rude and sarcastic comments. The intervention begins on the 16th day, with the parents explaining how the child might get negative points and face the consequences of accumulating points.

The A-B-A Design

For example, Kirsten Ferguson and Margaret Rodway (1994) explored the effectiveness of cognitive-behavioral treatment on perfectionism by applying an A-B-A design to nine clients. They used two standardized scales to measure perfectionist thoughts and a nonstandardized client rating of perfectionist behaviors. In the baseline stage, clients completed the measurement twice a week (once a week at the beginning of an assessment with the practitioner and once a week at home 3 days after the session). Data were collected over 4 weeks. The intervention stage lasted 8 weeks, with assessment prior to each counseling session; but only one follow-up measure was obtained, 3 weeks after the last counseling session.

The A-B-A-B Design

Kam-Fong Monit Cheung (1999) used an A-B-A-B design to evaluate the effectiveness of a combination of massage therapy and social work treatment on six residents in three nursing homes. Measurements included an assessment of activities of daily living and the amount of assistance received. Each phase took 7 weeks, with the massage therapy applied in Weeks 8 through 14 and Weeks 22 through 28. In the first 7 weeks (the A phase), residents received their usual social work services; in the second 7 weeks (the B phase), residents received massage therapy and social work services. In the third 7-week period (the second A phase), residents received just social work services; and in the fourth 7-week period (the second B phase), massage therapy resumed.

Multiple Baseline

Multiple measures are used to obtain data over two or more baselines. As its name implies, in this design several baselines are simultaneously established prior to the administration of treatment. The researcher here takes several compatible behaviors that is, the behaviour that occurs simultaneously in the individual. He establishes baselines for each behaviour. Subsequently, a treatment is introduced for one target behaviour. If the researcher begins rewarding tooth brushing, face washing, hand washing and hair combing all at the same time, it is possible that the presence of the experimenter, the attention received, or a spontaneous decision was responsible for the change. The researcher, however, could begin rewarding only tooth brushing the first week, tooth brushing and face washing the second week and so forth until after four weeks, all behaviors were being rewarded. This sequence would make it possible to see whether the increase in behaviour coincided with the reward.

Changing Criterion Design

Best suited for evaluating effects of instructional techniques on stepwise changes in rate, frequency, accuracy, duration, or latency of single target behavior. Frequently used when reinforcement and punishment contingencies are in effect. For example, a researcher studying the effectiveness of money in reducing caffeine consumption may use a changing-criterion design with four treatment phases, each gradually decreasing the amount below which participants must maintain their caffeine intake.

SUMMARY OF EXPERIMENTAL DESIGNS

See Figure 3.

Figure 3. Summary of Experimental Research designs

Design	Group	Actions
True-Experimental Designs		
Pretest–posttest control group design	Two groups randomly assigned	Both groups pretest, one group experimental intervention, both groups posttest
Post-test-only control-group design	Two groups randomly assigned	One group experimental intervention, posttest, One group posttest only
Solomon four-group design	Four groups randomly assigned	• One group pretest, experimental intervention, posttest • One group pretest and posttest • One group experimental intervention and posttest One group posttest only
Quasi-Experimental Designs		
Non-equivalent control-group design	Two groups	One group pretest, experimental intervention, posttest, one group pretest and posttest only
Time-series experiment	Single/Two groups	Measures taken over time, experimental intervention, measures taken
Pre-Experimental Designs		
One-group pre-test–post-test design	Single group	Pre-test, experimental intervention, post-test
Single-Subject Designs		
Single-subject	One individual/ few individuals	Record multiple observations to determine baseline and then introduce the experimental intervention and record multiple observations

QUALITATIVE RESEARCH

Qualitative research is a method for describing and giving meaning to life experiences that is systematic, participatory, and subjective. In several situational features, the research design provides for some flexibility. The data gathering questions are unique to each participant and are determined by their responses.

- **Characteristics**: Data is collected via an unstructured questionnaire with a small sample size.

Narrative Research

The concentration is on recounting and inscribing the stories of others, and it covers the history of life, for example, descriptions of great life achievements.

Steps of Narrative Research

The first step is to determine the events in a person's life that will be chronologically organized into different stages of life. Through interviews, the researcher gets concrete contextual information. He collects tales. The stories are arranged according to several themes. The themes represent significant occurrences in an individual's life, and the researcher delves into the meaning of these tales. Therefore, Narrative research is a qualitative research design that is defined as a spoken or written text that gives a chronologically related narrative of an event or series of events or acts.

Example: "The Red Closet: Narrative Concept of Menstruation in Indian Advertisement" (Samaddar, 2015).

Types

1. **Biographical study**: The researcher writes and records the experiences of another person's life.
2. **Autobiography study**: This is written and recorded by the individuals who are subject of the study.
3. **Life history/Personal experience story**: It portrays an individual's entire life while personal experience story is a narrative study of an individual's personal experience found in single or multiple episodes, private situations.
4. **Oral history**: It consists of gathering personal reflections of events and their causes and effects from one individual or several individuals.

Case Study

The Case study focuses on a detailed examination of a unit or case. The nature of a case inquiry is exploratory. It entails gathering thorough, in-depth information from a variety of sources about all relevant facets of a case. Observations, interviews, audio-visual materials, documents, records, and other sources are examples of multiple sources. A case is to be investigated in a certain context, i.e., the case is to be studied in its environment. It aids a researcher in comprehending the complexity of an event or occurrences in context and developing insight into the nature and process characteristics of the events under investigation.

Steps of Case Study

The case to be researched, or a group of instances to be investigated, is identified as unique. The researcher delimits what is to be investigated within the scope of enquiry by considering various contexts and viewpoints on the subject. The researcher then seeks for various techniques for acquiring various types of evidence from various sources. The current status of the case is assessed through direct observation or record after the case and content have been identified. Data is gathered, and then it is analyzed. Themes or issues are used to make interpretations.

Example: "The Role of Menstruation – a Case Study amongst Women from Nakwa Village in Tanzania" (Danielsson, 2017).

Grounded Theory

Grounded theory gives the researcher a path to follow, directing them to develop new ideas or revise old ones. The primary goals of grounded theory are as follows: It guarantees the output of a "valid theory" because evidence is collected from numerous sources. The grounded theory approach focuses on the process of evaluating the theory. The quality of the theory is determined by this. Formulating hypotheses based on conceptual notions is one of the goals of a grounded theory.

Steps of Grounded Theory

1. **Memos:** Memos are a type of brief note that the researcher creates and writes.
2. **Sorting:** After the short notes or memoranda have been generated, the collected information is sorted to put them in the right order.
3. **Writing:** After sorting the memos, the next step in theory preparation is "writing." The ground theorist organises, connects, and verbalises the gathered data, giving it shape and significance.

Example: 'Making of a Strong Woman': a constructivist grounded theory of the experiences of young women around menarche in Papua New Guinea (Gumbaketi et al., 2021).

Phenomenological Study

The emphasis is still on articulating the meaning of multiple individuals' living experiences with a notion or occurrence. The researcher is stated to examine the structures of consciousness in human experiences using a phenomenological approach. Here, depending on memory picture and meaning, experiences include both the outside appearance and internal consciousness.

Steps of Phenomenological Study

1. To understand the phenomenon through the words of various experienced people, the researcher must first realize his or her own preconceived beliefs about it.
2. Second, he creates research questions that go deeper into the significance of the experience for different people.
3. Finally, the researcher gathers information from people who have witnessed the occurrence under examination. Typically, data is acquired through lengthy interviews with 5 to 25 experienced individuals.
4. Statements and units are used to analyze data. The units are then turned into meaning clusters. Finally, such an analysis is connected to a broad description of experiences that includes both what was experienced and how it was experienced.

Example: "A Qualitative Study Exploring Menstruation Experiences and Practices among Adolescent Girls Living in the Nakivale Refugee Settlement, Uganda" (Kemigisha et al., 2020).

Ethnography

The study's focus is on evaluating a group's patterns of behavior, habits, and ways of living. This method entails a protracted period of observation during which the researcher becomes a part of the people's daily lives.

Steps of Ethnography Study

1. **Selection**: The researcher chooses the culture/community/population that interests him.
2. **Literature Review**: The researcher next goes over the literature on the culture in order to gain a quick overview and historical sketch of the culture being studied.
3. **Identifying variables**: The researcher next determines which variables should be investigated.
4. **Entry**: The ethnographer now attempts to enter the culture and obtain approval from its members.
5. **Cultural Immersion**: Ethnographers spend months or even years immersed in the culture they are studying.

6. **Data Collection**: After winning the respondents' trust, the researcher collects data in the form of observational transcripts, interview recordings, and tape recordings.
7. **Theoretical development**: After examining the data, the researcher develops a theory based on the interpretation of the findings and reports.

Example: "Peer Ethnographic Study on Menstrual Health and Hygiene Management in Nepal" (Singh et al., 2017).

Contrasting Characteristics of Five Qualitative Approaches

See Figure 4.

Figure 4. Characteristics of Qualitative Approaches

Characteristics	Narrative Research	Case Study	Grounded Theory	Phenomenology	Ethnography
Type of Problem best suited for design	When detailed stories help understand the problem	When researcher has a case bounded by time or place that can inform a problem	When no theory exists or existing theories are inadequate	When the researcher seeks to understand the lived experiences of persons about a phenomenon	Description and interpretation of a cultural or social group or system
Unit of analysis	One or more individuals	An event, program, activity, or more than one individual	A process, action, or interaction involving many individuals	Several individuals who have shared the experience	One to one interviews with the members of group corroborated with participant observation
Data collection forms	Interviews, documents	Multiple forms: interviews, observations, documents, artifacts	Primarily interviews	Primarily interviews, although documents, observations.	Interviews and Participant observation

MIXED METHOD RESEARCH

The term "mixed methods" refers to the "combination" of quantitative and qualitative data inside a single investigation or long-term research project. The use of mixed methods research to combine quantitative and qualitative data has the ability to improve the rigor and enrich the analysis and findings of any study.

Six Major Mixed Method Research Designs

1. **Convergent or Concurrent Parallel Design:** In this design, Quantitative and Qualitative data are collected simultaneously & the data are brought together and merged & then compared.
2. **Explanatory Sequential Design:** In this design, Quantitative method is followed by Qualitative method in order to explain the Quantitative findings.
3. **Exploratory Sequential Design:** In this design, a topic is explored with a Qualitative method & use the findings to develop & implement a Quantitative instrument.
4. **Embedded Design:** In this design, one data set provides a supportive, secondary role in a study based primarily on the other data type where qualitative or quantitative data needs to be included to answer a research question within a largely quantitative or qualitative study.
5. **Transformative Design:** In this design, qualitative and quantitative methods are employed within a single phase, sequential phases, or concurrently.
6. **Multiphase Design:** This design is often used in program evaluation where quantitative and qualitative approaches are used over time to support the development, adaptation, and evaluation of specific programs.

CONCLUSION

The menstrual cycle is fundamentally a within-person process as females differ in their cyclical changes and non-cyclical background symptoms. For this reason, the research design approach should be valid to uncover the areas stated in problem statement of the research. Although the menstrual cycle and its effects on the physiological and psychological functioning of females have been studied for years, there is a lack of gold standard approach to select appropriate study design, collection and characterization of study samples, menstrual cycle phases tracking, followed by hypothesis testing. The present chapter highlights some research designs that could be helpful in designing research in a precise and coherent manner in the field of menstrual health. Therefore, we cannot conclude because Research is constantly evolving and being a Researcher, we possess a free mind which is always learning and never concluding!!! Thus, it could be a BLENDED approach.

REFERENCES

Ary, D., Jacobs, L., & Sorenson, C. Asghar. (2006). Introduction to Research in Education. (8th edition). Wadsworth Cengage Learning .

Boral, K., Burman, J., & Sembiah, S. M. (2020). A cross-sectional study on menstrual hygiene among rural adolescent girls of West Bengal. *International Journal of Contemporary Medical Research*, 7(10), J10–J14.

Brough, P. (2019). *Advanced Research Methods for Applied Psychology (Design, Analysis and Reporting)* (1st ed.). Routledge, Taylor & Francis.

Christensen, L. B., Johnson, R. B., & Turner, L. A. (2014). *Research Methods, Design, and Analysis* (12th ed.). Pearson.

Creswell, J. W. (2014). *Research Design: Qualitative, Quantitative and Mixed Method Approaches* (4th ed.). Sage.

Dalal, M., & Saini, P. (2015). An Exploratory Survey to Assess the Menstrual Characteristics and Prevalence of Dysmenorrhea in College Going Girls. *International Journal of Scientific Research*, 6(4), 754–757.

Edmonds, W. A., & Kennedy, T. D. (2017). *An Applied Guide to Research Designs Quantitative, Qualitative, and Mixed Methods* (2nd ed.). Sage. doi:10.4135/9781071802779

Grbich, C. (2013). *Qualitative Data Analysis- An Introduction* (2nd ed.). Sage. doi:10.4135/9781529799606

Kemigisha, E., Rai, M., Mlahagwa, W., Nyakato, V. N., & Ivanova, O. (2020). A Qualitative Study Exploring Menstruation Experiences and Practices among Adolescent Girls Living in the Nakivale Refugee Settlement, Uganda. *International Journal of Environmental Research and Public Health*, 17(18), 6613. doi:10.3390/ijerph17186613 PMID:32932817

Kerlinger, P., & Lein, M. R. (1986). Differences in winter range among age-sex classes of Snowy Owls Nyctea scandiaca in North America. *Ornis Scandinavica*, 1–7.

Kothari, C. R. (2008). *Research Methodology, Methods and Techniques* (2nd ed.). New Age International Publication.

Leavy, P. (2017). *Research Design- Quantitative, Qualitative, Mixed Methods, Arts based, and Community based Participatory research approaches* (1st ed.). The Guilford Press.

Marczyk, G., DeMatteo, D., & Festinger, D. (2005). *Essentials of Research Design and Methodology* (1st ed.). John Wiley & Sons, Inc.

Maulingin-Gumbaketi, E., Larkins, S., Gunnarsson, R., Rembeck, G., Whittaker, M., & Redman-MacLaren, M. (2021). 'Making of a Strong Woman': A constructivist grounded theory of the experiences of young women around menarche in Papua New Guinea. *BMC Women's Health*, *21*(1), 144. doi:10.118612905-021-01229-0 PMID:33832465

Montgomery, P., Hennegan, J., Dolan, C., Wu, M., Steinfield, L., & Scott, L. (2016). Menstruation and the Cycle of Poverty: A Cluster Quasi-Randomised Control Trial of Sanitary Pad and Puberty Education Provision in Uganda. *PLoS One*, *11*(12), e0166122. doi:10.1371/journal.pone.0166122 PMID:28002415

Mushtaq, B., & Mir, J.A. (2019). A Pre Experimental Study To Assess The Effectiveness Of Structured Teaching Programme On Knowledge Regarding Menstrual Hygiene Among Fmphw Ist Year Students At Ramzaan Institute Of Paramedical Sciences Nowgam Srinagar. *Indian Journal of Applied Research, 9* (7).

Samaddar, R. (2015). The Red Closet: Narrative Concept of Menstruation in Indian Advertisement. Thesis for: Masters in Mass Communication Journalism.

Satyajit, & Kaur, I. (2017). A Quasi Experimental Study to Assess the Effectiveness of Ginger Powder on Dysmenorrhea among Nursing Students in Selected Nursing Colleges, Hoshiarpur, Punjab. *International Journal of Innovative Research in Medical Science, 2* (8), 1204-1210.

Sheoran, P., Kaur, S., Sadhanu, H., & Sarin, J. (2020). A descriptive study of menstrual hygiene practices among women at the rural area of Haryana. *Journal of Nursing and Midwifery Sciences*, *7*(4), 269. doi:10.4103/JNMS.JNMS_18_20

Singh, A. K. (2006). *Tests, Measurements and Research Methods in Behavioral Sciences* (5th ed.). Bharati Bhawan.

Singh, G., Bartaula, S., Dhakal, N., Gurung, Y., Shrestha, S. K., Basnet, M., Poudel, M., & Sherpa, L. Y. (2017, December 15).. . *BMC Women's Health*, *21*, 410. doi:10.118612905-021-01544-6

KEY TERMS AND DEFINITIONS

Mixed Method Research Design: This design aims at providing in-depth findings by combining quantitative and qualitative approaches in a single research study.

Qualitative Research: Qualitative research focuses on non-numerical subjective data obtained through analysis of concepts, opinions or experiences of responses gathered from small sample sizes.

Quantitative Research: Quantitative research focuses on numerical objective data obtained through statistics of quantity of responses gathered from large sample sizes.

Research Design: A well-planned conceptual framework that enables the researcher to collect high-quality relevant unbiased data by using authentic and credible sources thereby to achieve valid conclusions.

Chapter 8
Writing a Literature Review

Thulitha Wickrama
University of Nebraska, Lincoln, USA

Michael J. Merten
University of Nebraska, Lincoln, USA

Nuwanthi Tharaka Perera
Girne American University, Cyprus

ABSTRACT

A literature review is a summary of existing literature on topics of interest to the study. It provides proof of a gap in the literature that must be filled by the current study. Having a thorough literature review is the first step in planning a new research project. There are several critical reasons for writing a literature review. First, it is to identify the practical problem. Second, it is to identify the theoretical problem. The researcher should examine the literature about the problem area; both the theoretical literature and research literature. This helps to identify specific research purposes, questions, or testable hypotheses. Published research often makes specific suggestions for future research in the last section of their articles. This chapter on the literature review will provide a step-by-step method to write an effective literature review.

INTRODUCTION

Writing an Abstract

An abstract is an overall summary of the whole document. It stands as a briefing section of the whole document providing the essential information regarding the

DOI: 10.4018/978-1-6684-6859-3.ch008

content of the document. Abstracts are a required part of submissions to all journals. It is written immediately after the title. While the abstract is written at the beginning of the document, it is in practice written last after all information is known about the study at the study's conclusion. The information in the abstract must be reflective of the information in the document. Information not in the document itself must not be included in the abstract.

It is important to remember that not everyone that reads the abstract will read the entire document, instead most will only get the essential information of the study from the abstract. The abstract should not be more than 250 words in most types of academic writing such as scientific journal articles. It should be written concisely, in a clear manner so that the reader is not confused and doubtless about the topic, findings, and conclusions of the document they would read in detail if they wished. The population of interest and the sample provide in the abstract will highlight the information regarding the individuals the study belongs to. The goals which may be stated in the abstract for the study will clearly inform the reader about the direction of the investigation. The implications will allow the reader to understand the contribution the study has made to the scientific body of literature and the practical implications of the study. Overall, the abstract will convey the direction, significance, and contribution of a study to the reader. Thereafter, the reader can decide the relevance of the study for in depth reading of the entire document.

Important Parts of an Abstract

1. introduction or background
2. research questions or hypotheses
3. methodology including the population of interest
4. sampling strategy
5. analytical strategy
6. results and conclusions
7. briefly on implications of the study.

Objective of Writing an Abstract

The objective of writing an abstract is to summarize the major aspects of the proposal or paper. It helps the reader decide whether they want to read the rest of the paper. A writer must first catch the reader's attention with an intriguing title, then further lure them in with an abstract that interests them. The establishment of those two things will increase the chances that a person will read the entire paper/proposal.

Order of an Abstract

The abstract should be kept to a 200- 300 word limit. Hence, limit your statements concerning each segment of the paper/proposal to two or three sentences. An outline to follow when writing the abstract is as follows.

1.   In the first or second sentence of the abstract, state clearly the research questions you intent to investigate.
2.   The study design and the method to be used should be articulated with a few sentences.
3.   Describe the basic design of the study, describe the methodology without too much details, and describe briefly the techniques of the study.
4.   Indicate the results of the study briefly.
5.   The quantitative findings, statistical trends, changes in data, differences between comparison groups, and other major analytical findings with relevance to the hypotheses should be stated.
6.   It should include an interpretation of the discussions and conclusions with implications.

Figure 1.

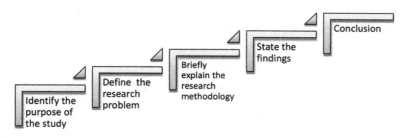

What Is a Structured Abstract?

The structured abstract should be fact specific without opinions or subjectivity, free of acronyms, excluding excessive background information, briefly mentioning the purpose and introduction, giving more emphasis to the methods and results, summarizing in just a couple of sentences with a conclusion and a link back to the introduction, while staying to the point staying within the subtopics. Certain types of studies such as review articles and case reports do not require structured abstracts as they do not follow such steps in their studies. Thus, these articles use unstructured abstracts.

- A structured abstract has five formal sections which are the essential components of an abstract requested by scientific journals:
  - ◦ introduction
  - ◦ objective
  - ◦ methods
  - ◦ results
  - ◦ conclusions.

STRUCTURED ABSTRACT EXAMPLE

- **Background and Objectives:** Women in Sri Lanka have been uniquely exposed to a complex and protracted set of stressors stemming from a civil war conflict spanning over 25 years and the tsunami which struck Southeast Asia in 2004. This study investigates coping strategies and their association with trauma-related symptoms of tsunami-exposed mothers in Sri Lanka at two time points.
- **Design:** Data for this study come from surveys administered in two waves of data collection to investigate both mothers' and adolescent children's post-tsunami mental health in early 2005, three months after the tsunami struck, and again in 2008, three years later.
- **Methods:** Latent-variable structural equation modeling was used to test the study hypotheses among 160 tsunami-affected mothers in the Polhena village, Matara district, Sri Lanka.
- **Results:** Among the various coping strategies examined, the use of cultural rituals as well as inner psychological strength was associated with lower levels of posttraumatic stress symptoms. In contrast, passive religious beliefs were associated with greater posttraumatic stress levels.
- **Conclusions:** The results of this study reveal the differential associations of various coping strategies including rituals used by mothers exposed to the tsunami in Sri Lanka and their posttraumatic stress symptom levels." (Wickrama, Wickrama, Banford, & Lambert, 2017, pp. 415)

UNSTRUCTURED ABSTRACT EXAMPLE

"Using a sample of 20,000 adolescents (Add Health data), this study examined the influences of community poverty and race/ethnicity on adolescent obesity. Multilevel analyses revealed strong evidence for the unique influences of community poverty and race/ethnicity on adolescent obesity net of family characteristics. The prevalence of obesity is significantly higher in poor communities than in affluent communities; and it is higher among African Americans, Hispanics and Native Americans than among Whites. The interaction between race/ethnicity and community poverty indicates that race/ethnicity moderates the influence of community poverty on the prevalence of obesity. Although the prevalence of obesity is higher among minorities than among Whites, the influence of community poverty is stronger for Whites than for minorities, suggesting that unlike Whites, most minority groups may not accrue benefits of structural community advantages. The state of being overweight as the outcome variable provided essentially the same findings. The practical implications are discussed." (Wickrama, Wickrama, & Bryant, 2006, pp. 647)

SELECTING KEY WORDS

Key words are the set of words which give a brief idea about the entire research. Through key words the researcher can denote what the entire research is about. It helps other researches to find research articles relevant to their field more easily.

Important facts to be considered when selecting keywords:

- Keywords should be directly related to the research.
- At least 3 words should be included.
- Scientific names can be used as a keyword.
- 5 -10 keywords can be used.

Example Keywords:

1. Community Poverty, Race/Ethnicity, Adolescent Obesity
2. Tsunami, PTSD, Culture, Coping, Religious, Sri Lanka

SELECTING A TITLE

A title conveys what the research is about. It is the first thing the reader pays attention. Hence, it should be meaningful and easily understood. It is difficult to decide a title at the beginning of a research. Thus, a title can be decided after the research is fully completed.

Important facts to be considered when selecting a title:

- The title should be easily understood by the reader.
- It must not be too long or too short.

•   Use a simple language.

Example Titles:

1.   "Community influence on adolescent obesity: Race/ethnic differences" (Wickrama, Wickrama, & Bryant, 2006, pp. 647)
2.   "PTSD symptoms among tsunami exposed mothers in Sri Lanka: the role of disaster exposure, culturally specific coping strategies, and recovery efforts" (Wickrama, Wickrama, Banford, & Lambert, 2017, pp. 415)

WRITING AN INTRODUCTION

An introduction is the beginning of the scientific document. It provides a background to the topic giving information about reasons to undertake a study in the relevant topic. In varying journals the introduction may also be referred as the background. A simple format can be followed when writing an introduction. Most introductions for journal articles can be written in one to two pages. First two paragraphs should provide the background information (classical documents and vital statistics should be cited). The research questions should be brought up during these early paragraphs. The next paragraphs should emphasize the significance of the problem for a particular group of people (the prevailing unresolved problems should be mentioned along with that). Finally, the subsequent paragraphs should contain the rational including the justification, urgency, and the importance of committing to such a study.

Figure 2.

Background information	Research Question	Past attempts to solve the problem	Objective of the study	Common factors to consider when writing an introduction
*Give specific details regarding the study.	*Highlight the significance of the problem. *State who will benefit from solving the problem?	*Include clear, robust information about the past experiments.	*State how will the study bridge the gap between what is known and unknown	*Use a simple language *Arouse interest while encouraging the reader. *Do not repeat the same idea. *Always stick to the problem.

Figure 3.

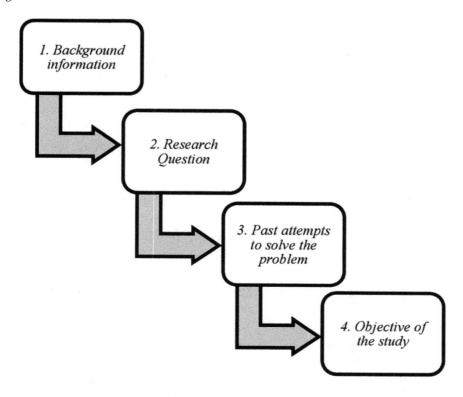

EXAMPLE INTRODUCTION

"Obesity is a major public health problem in the United States (Bouchard, 2000). A critical period for the development of obesity in adolescence is the period during which pubertal growth spurts occur (Garrow, 1999). In the United States, more than 25% of adolescents are overweight and more than 11% of them are obese (Wang, 2001). Adolescent obesity poses both contemporaneous and long-term physical and mental health consequences. This increases the heterogeneity in health status in later life (Ferraro and Kelly-Moore, 2003). Research shows that obesity has been found to co-occur with several physical and mental health problems (Blazer et al., 2002). Obese adolescents are at high risk for physical and mental health problems such as lower-body disability, diabetes, hypertension, heart disease, as well as orthopedic, endocrine, and psychological disorders such as depression (Black, 2002; Wadden et al., 2001). Adolescent obesity poses long-term health consequences through the accumulation of various health risk factors over the life course.

Current obesity is in part, socially structured (Young and Nestle, 2002). Recent research has shown that individual factors such as gender, race/ethnicity, and family and community socioeconomic conditions influence adolescent obesity (Cristol, 2003; Karlsen and Nazroo, 2002; Sanjay, 2000; Wang, 2001). More importantly, a growing body of community research suggests that community socioeconomic characteristics uniquely influence youth health outcomes (Wickrama and Bryant, 2003). Only a handful of studies show that community characteristics contribute to obesity independent of family characteristics and race/ethnicity (e.g., Sanjay, 2000; Armstrong et al., 2003). As part of this study, we will examine the influence of community poverty on obesity independent of family and individual characteristics.

The prevalence rate of obesity among minorities is higher than among Whites. The prevalence of obesity among African American and Hispanic American adolescents has increased by more than 10% during the last decade (Ogden et al., 2002). This has contributed to greater health problems among minority adolescents than among Whites. For example, the high prevalence of diabetes among Hispanic and African American adolescents is associated with high prevalence of obesity (Acton et al., 2002; Tucker and Odilia, 2000). Long-term health consequences of adolescent obesity create racial disparities in adult health over time (Chief Surgeon's Report on American health, 2000).

To our knowledge no study has examined both additive and multiplicative influences of community and race/ethnicity on adolescent obesity. Using a sample of 20,000 adolescents, derived from the National Longitudinal Study of Adolescent Health, this study examines (1) the additive influences of community poverty and race/ethnicity on adolescent obesity net of the influences of family poverty and (2) the multiplicative influence between community poverty and race/ethnicity on adolescent obesity. In other words, it examines the moderating influence of race/ethnicity on the relationship between community poverty and obesity. In addition, this study also examines the influence of the aforementioned factors (race/ethnicity, community poverty) on adolescents characterized as overweight. We define obesity and being overweight using age and gender specific Body Mass Index (BMI) charts provided by the Centers for Disease Control." (Wickrama, Wickrama, & Bryant, 2006, pp. 647)

Reasons to Have a Justification for a Study

- The reasons you provide as justification may be to advance further knowledge in the field of study, intellectual merit in further studying the topic to deepen scientific knowledge.

- May be your topic of study has a great need to be studied in order to solve a problem in the community. Therefore, the findings are of utmost importance to address prevailing problems in the particular community.
- May be to build on existing literature and address scientific questions raised by previous literature. Thus, building on past findings to expand the knowledge of the subject as well as to expand the paradigm of the field.

Importance of Statistics

- Statistical justification is important for showing the pressing nature of the problem in society and the population of interest. Such statistics can show the current news of the issue.
- These data can be found at government statistics department reports, reputed organizational reports, and current publications.
- These prevalence statistics provide justification for undertaking the study with great time, energy, resources, and commitment by academics.
- Indicating statistics within an introduction and other related literature should be accurately cited.

WRITING A LITERATURE REVIEW

A literature review is a summary of the existing knowledge in the field regarding the topic. There are several critical reasons for writing a literature review. First, it is to identify the practical problem. Second, it is to identify the theoretical problem. The researcher should examine the literature about the problem area: the theoretical literature and research literature. This helps to identify specific research purposes, questions, or testable hypotheses. Published research often make specific suggestions for future research in the last section of their articles. It also provides proof of a gap in the literature that must be filled by the current study. Having a thorough literature review is the first step in planning a new research project.

There are several implications for research as a result of a thorough literature review. The proposed study may result in being a strict replication of a former study. It may try to mimic an important study to test for same results that have important implications to validate the original. The new study may be a modified replication. A replication with some major modifications such as examining a new population or using an improved measurement or analytical technique. The proposed study may be a new design to resolve a conflict in literature. The proposed study may investigate unique research questions that delve deeper into a topic, create new knowledge about a topic, expand the paradigms of research in the area, or test existing and new theories. The new study could also be a creative idea that is not a direct extension of existing research.

The common types of literature reviews are given below:

1. Annotated bibliographies
2. Scoping reviews
3. Narrative or traditional literature reviews
4. Critically Appraised Topic (CAT)
5. Systematic literature reviews

Why should we review the literature?

1. To recognize the progress in the selected field of study.
2. To study the weaknesses/ strengths and limitations of a selected topic (identifying successful measuring tools (instruments), identifying flawed instruments to avoid)
3. To identify the specific research methodologies used by others and to find whether there are any errors
4. Identifying and avoiding dead ends (ideas for research already investigated enough and not fruitful! (e.g. failed treatments)
5. Getting ideas on how to organize and write research papers and reports by learning the styles of research and locating your research within the literature map.

Important facts to consider when writing a literature review:

Do not include any direct quotations from the authors you cited. Writing a series of summaries of individual articles is not an effective way of writing a literature review. Make sure the literature review is a critical one to generate intellectual justification for the study. Write a broad and then a detailed outline prior to writing your literature review. Such an outline should have the heading, subheading, citations, literature points, transitions, arguments, theoretical points, and many more which you will follow step by step when writing the literature review. The articles you have chosen must be equally rigorous in their science. Even a published article with conclusions can be shown to be incorrect in subsequent studies. Different articles will show evidence toward different aspects of a research question and topic. Then they can be taken together to synthesize summaries.

Writing a literature synthesis per sub topic allows us to summarize past findings accurately. It tells us what we know, what we need to know, how different findings come together to form a broad picture of knowledge, where our study fits in within this landscape and what gaps our study fills in knowledge. These synthesized summaries must flow from one sub section to another. Moreover, they must flow within a sub section with logic and good writing skills using good paragraph formation and transitions. Throughout the writing it is very important to remember to cite multiple times within each sentence if necessary indicating where parts or all ideas within a sentence came from. Common themes between articles can be pointed out as well as differences between the findings across articles. Within each sub section, you can argue for the gaps that exist in knowledge and what you will do with you study to fill such gaps. Throughout the writing of sub topics, hypotheses should be made after the critical writing, syntheses, and arguments. Once the subtopics and topics have been exhausted, a summary of the overall literature review should be written. Subsequent to that, list out your hypotheses.

STEPS OF A LITERATURE REVIEW

1. State the topic and its significance.
2. Indicate the prevailing problems and their impact on the population of interest.
3. Define major terms and key concepts before going further in depth.
4. Start citing multiple sources for the statements you make.
5. Cite using the appropriate citation format for your specific discipline. (You can use American Psychological Association (APA) style, Harvard Style, American Medical Association Style (AMA), or any other).
6. Write what scientists have found about the topic.
   a. This should follow a format of having major headings for broad areas of literature and subheading within these sections for minor sub topics within the larger topics.
   b. Within these sub topics, their relevant literature must be summarized. This must not be summaries of individual articles. Instead, information from several articles must be combined in different ways to summarize the information within a subtopic

Figure 4. Steps of literature review

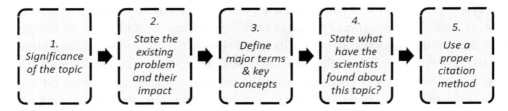

EXAMPLE LITERATURE REVIEW

"Community Poverty Previous research has demonstrated that community disadvantage contributes to adverse physical health outcomes of adolescents. These health outcomes include health risk behaviors such as substance use and several chronic diseases (Auchincloss and Hadden, 2002). Community level processes that influence these adverse adolescent health outcomes (over and above the influence of individual and family factors) should also influence adolescent obesity (Armstrong et al., 2003; Sanjay et al., 2000).

There appears to be several adverse community processes that may contribute to obesity. First, the influence of community poverty on adolescent obesity may operate through several structural constraints that limit availability of health resources in the community (Sorensen et al., 1998). For example, poor communities are unable to meet their residents' dietary-health needs (Kaplan, 1995). For example, unaffordable prices can limit access to proper food in poor communities, and poor communities have a greater number of unhealthy fast food restaurants than do higher income communities (Morland et al., 2002). In addition, lack of recreational activities, lack of community safety for physical activities (Ross and Mirowsky, 2001), and lack of availability and accessibility of health care services in disadvantaged communities may also contribute to the higher prevalence of adolescent obesity (Surgeon General Report, 2001).

Second, community poverty may influence adolescent obesity through the erosion of community norms and values (Wickrama and Bryant, 2003). Previous norms and values in poor communities may not exert social control over improper body management practices and unhealthy dietary practices. These community norms and values do not have adequate power to enforce healthy dietary practices and weight management. Instead, the emergence of "health-related subcultures" in disadvantaged communities increases the community level tolerance for risky lifestyles, obesity, and being overweight (Browning and Cagney, 2004; Kowaleski-Jones, 2000; LaCory, 2000). We contend that the reduced importance of local norms and emergence of "health-related subcultures' regarding being both over-weight and obese in poor communities can adversely influence the motivation for adolescents to properly manage their weight.

Third, community influence may operate through adolescent learning, emulating, and cognitive processes. Adolescents who live in poor communities are less likely to find positive role models that support and promote healthy activities among youth (Kowaleski-Jones, 2000). Instead, they may often find negative role models that exert negative influences on adolescent health behaviors. This influence can be explained by both the social learning theory (Bandura, 1977), and the 'Prototype' perspective, in which social imagery relates to body image and lifestyle. Consistent with social learning theory, adolescents who are exposed to community members who engage in unhealthy behaviors related to obesity may model or emulate them through social learning (Wickrama et al., 1999). Consistent with the risk and 'Prototype' perception perspective, adolescents may operate with favorable attitudes and perceptions (cognitions) of obesity and therefore engage in behaviors that promote obesity (Thornton et al., 2002). This willingness to engage in such behaviors is a result of opportunities presented at the community level— not of the individual level.

Finally, community poverty contributes to the erosion of social trust and social cohesion among residents, which in turn, results in lower collective efficacy to acquire health promoting and preventive services. Collective efficacy is distinct from social support in that it emphasizes the willingness to engage in (and the capacity to take collective action towards) community goals regardless of pre-existing Community Influence on Adolescent Obesity: Race/Ethnic Differences 649 social ties (Browning and Cagney, 2004; Sampson et al., 1997). Communities with low levels of collective efficacy may not have the ability to develop health services or programs needed to control health-damaging behaviors (Browning and Cagney, 2004; Kawachi and Berkman, 2000; Sampson et al., 1997)." (Wickrama, Wickrama, & Bryant, 2006, pp. 648-9)

EXAMPLE HYPOTHESES

"Specific hypotheses based on the literature review presented, we developed the following hypotheses.

1. The higher the level of community poverty, the higher will be the prevalence of adolescent obesity after controlling for race/ethnicity and family poverty.
2. Minority status will positively influence adolescent obesity. That is, the prevalence rate of obesity is higher among minority adolescents than among White adolescents.

3. The influence of community poverty on adolescent obesity will be stronger for White adolescents than for minority adolescents. 4. We hypothesize similar influences of community and race/ethnicity on adolescents being overweight." (Wickrama, Wickrama, & Bryant, 2006, pp. 649-50)

"Specific hypotheses:

1. Higher levels of tsunami exposure at time 1 (Wave I of data collection three months post tsunami) will associate positively with PTSD symptoms at time 2 (Wave II of data collection three years post tsunami).
2. Higher exposure to recovery efforts at time 1(Wave I of data collection three months post tsunami) will associate with lower PTSD symptoms at time 2 (Wave II of data collection three years post tsunami).
3. Higher levels of coping strategy use (except karma beliefs) will associate with lower PTSD symptoms at time 2 (Wave II of data collection three months post tsunami).
4. The associations between tsunami exposure and recovery effort at time 1 (Wave I of data collection three months post tsunami) and PTSD symptoms at time 2 (Wave II of data collection three years post tsunami) will vary by the use of coping strategies." (Wickrama, Wickrama, Banford, & Lambert, 2017, pp. 419)

CONCEPTUAL/THEORETICAL STUDY MODEL

Depending on how much information previous research gives us for anticipating what will happen, based on our reasoning, with prior information, we have: research questions (if we only know basic information) or hypotheses (if we know a lot of information) that something will happen in a certain direction and magnitude. These research question and hypotheses in the broader context of our study gives rise to our unique conceptual or theoretical study models.

SEARCHING FOR LITERATURE

Literature is sought for writing the literature review, inclusive of past studies on the topic and theoretical background. This literature will mostly be found in peer reviewed scientific journals, textbooks, reputed publications, classical works, and government records and reports. Journal articles are found through academic paid search engines such as PsychInfo, Socabstracts, and Ebscohost and open access

Figure 5. Example conceptual or theoretical study model
(Wickrama & Wickrama, 2011)

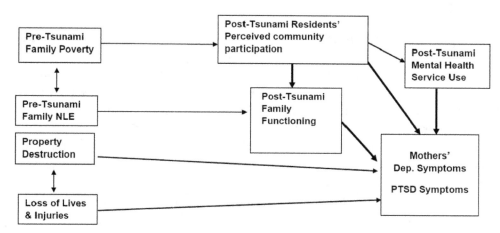

(no cost) academic search engines such as Google Scholar, PubMed, Eric, and others. These sites will allow you to search only abstracts or full text articles. You can specify to search by key words, phrases, title, by author, journal name, years of publication, and many other factors. You must consider these factors carefully to be particular to your topic of study. While most literature is gathered through such journal databases, important information can also be found in textbooks, reputed subject specific books, and government publications.

Key Considerations in Literature Selection

1. Consider the accuracy of information- whether the given information is reliable and based on proven evidence.
2. Pay attention to the published date and whether the given information is accurate at present or outdated.
3. Make sure to get information only from published academic journals, books, reputed websites, and well-cited articles.
4. Avoid using blogs/articles with ambiguous information (blogs which are on the internet can contain false as well as misleading facts.).
5. Select documents which are error-free and published by a well-qualified author (check whether the author is qualified enough to publish such an article).
6. Check whether the selected information is relevant to the purpose of the proposed study (Read carefully whether those details are suitable or not for your topic).

CHAPTER SUMMARY

This chapter gives information regarding how to write an abstract, an introduction, and a literature review respectively. The aforementioned parts play an important role in a journal. The main objective of this chapter is to illustrate the proper way of writing a literature review. By reading this chapter, a student has obtained a thorough knowledge of the literature review process. Hence, attention should be paid when writing as well as selecting primary/secondary resources for the literature review.

An abstract depicts the summary of the content of the entire journal. Under the main topic of how to write an abstract, sub-topics such as what is an abstract, important parts, objectives, and order of writing an abstract are given. The introduction states the background information regarding the topic and the specific reasons for undertaking the study in that area. What is an introduction, format of writing an introduction, justification, and the importance of statistics are the sub-topics discussed under the main heading "writing an introduction."

A literature review gives an accurate picture of the study by analyzing the summary of the prevailing knowledge in the relevant field. What is a literature review, significance, why do we need a literature review, how to select resources for the literature review, format, important facts to consider when writing a literature review, critical analysis, conceptual and theoretical models, and designing of the study is the particular set of sub-topics examined under "writing a literature review". Whenever selecting resources for the literature review, make sure that the given information is reliable and accurate. It is advised to use published articles, books, and renowned websites when getting information for the study. Try to avoid articles from various blogs because the given details might not be reliable. Prioritize information that is up to date. Make sure to use resources that are error-free and published by qualified authors. Paying attention to these details is highly crucial, otherwise the quality of the research will get reduced.

Common mistakes such as language errors, plagiarism, repetition of the same facts, and disorganized content are highly discouraged when writing a journal. Always stick to the central idea by proving it through evidence taken from published research articles, books, and renowned websites. Priority should be given to credible information only. A suitable citation method must be properly used throughout the journal. Using simple, clear language to convince ideas is also important. All these facts should be considered when writing a research article. Also, be attentive when selecting primary/secondary resources to get information. The usage of inaccurate information can directly affect the standard.

Conducting research according to high standards is difficult. A student will have to face numerous challenges when doing research. The majority of students find it very difficult to conduct literature review properly since they are unaware of the factors such as how to select reliable resources with accurate information, how to use referencing properly (e.g. APA, AMA, Harvard), and how to find up-to-date information. As the authors of this chapter, we tried to make the process of writing a literature review look easy for the students to the best of our ability. Hope this chapter helps you to clarify any doubts you face while writing the literature review.

REFERENCES

Branson, R. D. (2004). Anatomy of a Research Paper. *Respiratory Care*, *49*, 10. PMID:15447807

Krathwohl, D. R. (2009). Methods of Education and Social Science Research: An Integrated Approach (2nd ed). Waveland Press, Inc. Long Grove, Il.

Libguides. (2022). Research Guides, Literature Review - Finding the Resources: Evaluating Sources. (2022). *Libguides*. https://libguides.library.cityu.edu.hk/litreview/evaluating-sources/

McNally, K. (2022). Library Guides: Literature Review: Types of literature reviews. *Libguides*.csu.edu.au. https://libguides.csu.edu.au/review/Types

Patten, M. L., & Newhart, M. (2018). Understanding Research Methods; An Overview of the Essentials (10th ed.). Routledge, Taylor & Francis Group. New York and London.

Shah, J. N. (2015). How to write "introduction" in scientific journal article. *Journal of Patan Academy of Health Sciences*, *2*(1), 1–2. doi:10.3126/jpahs.v2i1.20331

Wickrama, K. A. S., & Wickrama, T. (2011). Perceived community participation in tsunami recovery efforts and the mental health of tsunami affected mothers: Findings from a study in rural Sri Lanka. *The International Journal of Social Psychiatry*, *57*(5), 518–527. doi:10.1177/0020764010374426 PMID:20603268

Wickrama, K. A. T., Wickrama, K. A. S., & Bryant, C. M. (2016). Community Influence on Adolescent Obesity: Race/Ethnic Differences. *Journal of Youth and Adolescence*, *35*(4), 647–657.

Wickrama, T., Wickrama, K. A. S., Banford, A., & Lambert, J. (2017). PTSD symptoms among tsunami exposed mothers in Sri Lanka: The role of disaster exposure, culturally specific coping strategies, and recovery efforts. *Anxiety, Stress, and Coping*, *30*(4), 415–427. doi:10.1080/10615806.2016.1271121 PMID:27960534

Chapter 9

The Acceptable R–Square in Empirical Modelling for Social Science Research

Peterson K. Ozili

https://orcid.org/0000-0001-6292-1161
Central Bank of Nigeria, Nigeria

ABSTRACT

This chapter examines the acceptable R-square in social science empirical modelling with particular focus on why a low R-square model is acceptable in empirical social science research. The paper shows that a low R-square model is not necessarily bad. This is because the goal of most social science research modelling is not to predict human behaviour. Rather, the goal is often to assess whether specific predictors or explanatory variables have a significant effect on the dependent variable. Therefore, a low R-square of at least 0.1 (or 10 percent) is acceptable on the condition that some or most of the predictors or explanatory variables are statistically significant. If this condition is not met, the low R-square model cannot be accepted. A high R-square model is also acceptable provided that there is no spurious causation in the model and there is no multi-collinearity among the explanatory variables.

1. INTRODUCTION

This paper examines the acceptable R-square in empirical social science research. It focuses on why a low R-square model is acceptable in empirical social science research.

DOI: 10.4018/978-1-6684-6859-3.ch009

As a general principle, an econometric model is considered to have a high predictive power if the model has a high R-square or adjusted R-square (Gujarati, Porter, & Gunasekar, 2012). This general principle often gives the scientist some confidence that the explanatory variables in the model are good predictors of the dependent variable (Hill, Griffiths, & Lim, 2018).

Many social scientists, who follow this principle, are often excited when their models report a high R-square and they get worried when their models report a very low R-square. Their worry is further amplified when they learn that statisticians and scientists in the pure sciences will dismiss a model as "weak", "unreliable" and "lacking a predictive power" if the reported R-square of the model is below 0.6 (or 60 percent when expressed in percentage). In this paper, I address this issue and show that empirical modelling in social science has a different purpose compared to empirical modelling in the pure science.

The rest of the paper is structured as follows. Section 2 discuss the imperfect nature of social science. Section 3 highlights the different range of R-square. Section 4 presents the conclusion.

2. LITERATURE REVIEW

There is adequate literature about the R-squared. The literature about R-squared shows some of its applications. Miles (2005) showed that the R-squared and the adjusted R-squared statistics are derived from analyses based on the general linear model (e.g., regression, ANOVA), and they represent the proportion of variance in the outcome variable which is explained by the predictor variables in the sample (R-squared) and an estimate in the population (adjusted R-squared). Hagle and Mitchell (1992) suggest a refinement to the R-squared called the pseudo R-squared. They suggest that the corrected Aldrich-Nelson pseudo R-squared is a good estimate of the R-squared of a regression model because of its smaller standard deviations and range of errors, and its smaller error of regression. They also point out that the Aldrich-Nelson correction to the R-squared is more robust when the assumption of normality is violated. However, they cautioned that the pseudo R-squared should be used with caution because even a good summary measure can be misinterpreted; therefore, it was suggested that the pseudo R-squared should be used in conjunction with other measures of model performance. Chicco et al (2021) suggested that the use of the R-squared statistic as a standard metric to evaluate regression analyses is popular in any scientific domain. This is because the coefficient of determination (or R-squared) is more informative and truthful than other goodness of fit measures. Cameron and Windmeijer (1997) show that R-squared type goodness-of-fit summary statistics have been constructed for linear models using a variety of methods. They propose an R-squared measure of goodness of fit for the class of exponential family regression models, which includes logit, probit, Poisson, geometric, gamma, and exponential. They defined the R-squared as the proportionate reduction in uncertainty, measured by Kullback-Leibler divergence, due to the inclusion of regressors. They also show that, under further conditions concerning the conditional mean function, the R-squared can also be interpreted as the fraction of uncertainty explained by the fitted model. Gelman et al (2019) argued that the usual definition of the R-squared statistic (variance of the predicted values divided by the variance of the data) has a problem for Bayesian fits, as the numerator can be larger than the denominator. They proposed an alternative definition similar to one that has appeared in the survival analysis literature. The definition they propose defined the R-squared as the variance of the predicted values divided by the variance of predicted values plus the expected variance of the errors.

Hagquist and Stenbeck (1998) examined the importance of the R-square as a measure of goodness of fit in regression analysis. They argued that the utility of goodness of fit measures depends on whether the analysis focuses on explaining the outcome (model orientation) or explaining the effect(s) of some regressor(s) on the outcome (factor orientation). They further argued that in some situations a decisive goodness of fit test statistic exists and is a central tool in the analysis. In other situations, where the goodness of fit measure is not a test statistic but a descriptive measure, it can be used as a heuristic device along with other evidence whenever appropriate. They also argued that the availability of goodness of fit test statistics depends on whether the variability in the observations is restricted, as in table analysis, or whether it is unrestricted, as in OLS and logistic regression on individual data.

Some scholars consider the R-squared to be of limited importance (e.g. King, 1986; King, 1990). Others consider the R-squared to be very useful (Lewis-Beck, and Lweis-Beck, 2015). Lewis-Beck and Skalaban (1990) sounded a word of caution about using R-squared. They argued that a researcher should be careful to recognize the limitations of the R-squared as a measure of goodness of fit, and that one must be extremely cautious in interpreting the R-squared value for an estimation and particularly in comparing R-squared values for models that have been estimated with different data sets. They also argued that the R-squared measures nothing of serious importance because it measures nothing of importance in most practical political science situations and the interpretation of the R-square adds little meaning to political analyses.

Onyutha (2020) criticized the R-squared, and argued that the most extensively applied goodness-of-fit measure for assessing performance of regression models is the R-squared or coefficient of determination. The author showed that although a high R-squared tends to be associated with an efficient model, the R-squared has been cited to have no importance in the classical model of regression because it does not give any information on the model residuals. The author also argued that a very poor model fit can yield a high R-squared, and more importantly, regressing X on Y yields an R-squared which is the same as that if Y is regressed on X, thereby invalidating its use as a coefficient of determination. Figueiredo Filho et al (2011) argued that no substantive meaning can be drawn from the R-squared statistic. They argued that the R-squared cannot help us to make causal claims about the relationship between the independent variables and the dependent variable, and that the R-squared does not assist us regarding omitted variable bias. They further argued that the R-squared does not inform us if X1 is strongly correlated with X2 (collinearity problems in the data). Maydeu-Olivares and Garcia-Forero (2010) argued that the goodness of fit of many models cannot be assessed using summary statistics such as proportions or covariance. They argued that, in the context of linear regression and related models, the R-square is sometimes described as a goodness of fit statistic, but if a linear regression model can fit the data perfectly, the R-squared will be zero if the slope is zero. Ijomah (2019) showed that the R-squared is the single most extensively used measure of goodness of fit for regression models, and it measures the proportion of variation in the dependent variable explained by the predictors included in the model. But it is widely misused as the square of correlation coefficient, and this has led to poor interpretation of research reports in regression model. CSCU (2005) argued that one pitfall of R-squared is that it can only increase as predictors are added to the regression model. This increase is artificial when predictors are not actually improving the model's fit. They show that to remedy this problem, the adjusted R-squared incorporates the model's degrees of freedom. They show that the adjusted R- squared will decrease as predictors are added if the increase in model fit does not make up for the loss of degrees of freedom; likewise, it will increase as predictors are added if the increase in model fit is worthwhile. Reisinger (1997) found that the R-squared gets smaller as the sample size increases and the number of regressors decreases in a study. The author also found that time-series studies achieve higher values for R-squared than cross-sectional studies. The author further found that studies with secondary data achieve higher values for R-squared than studies with primary data. Cornell and Berger (1987) argued that the R-squared is one of the most widely used statistics and it is determined by calculating the proportion of the total variation in goodness-of-fit of the equation. However, they pointed out that the R-squared value is affected by several factors, some of which are associated more closely with the data collection scheme or the experimental design than with how close the regression equation actually fits the observations. They argued that the design factors are: the range of values of the independent variable (X), the arrangement of X values within the range, the number of replicate observations (Y), and the variation among the Y values at each value of X. Ferligoj and Kramberger (1995) showed that, even though scholars usually question the use of R-squared as a measure of goodness of fit in ordinary least square regression, there is no great danger in using R-squared in ordinary least squares regression. Spiess and Neumeyer (2010) argued that the R-squared is inappropriate when used for assessing model performance in certain nonlinear models especially in pharmacological and biochemical scientific research.

3. THE IMPERFECT NATURE OF SOCIAL SCIENCE

In the pure science, models should have a high predictive power or a high R-squared. This is because researchers in the pure sciences deal with molecules, materials, objects or atoms whose properties are known and whose behaviour are predictable and do not change over time. As a result, it is reasonable to expect a high R-squared in the models used in the pure science. In contrast, the social sciences deal with human behaviour or human relationship that is subject to change from time to time. Human behaviour may change due to individual self-interest, group dynamics, feelings and other factors. For this reason, it is difficult to accurately predict human behaviour in the social sciences; therefore, the modelling of human behaviour will be an imperfect science and it will be difficult for a single model to capture all the factors that predict human behaviour at a given time. And even if it is possible to include all the explanatory variables that explain human behaviour into the model, some of the included explanatory variables may have a weak or non-linear relationship with the dependent variable thereby weakening the R-squared goodness-of-fit of the model.

4. R-SQUARED CATEGORIES

4.1. Negative R-Squared

In social science empirical modelling, a univariate linear model that reports a negative R-squared should be rejected. Similarly, a multivariate linear model that reports a negative adjusted R-squared should be rejected. The reason is because the model shows that the explanatory variables do not predict the changes in the dependent variable.

A negative R-squared or negative adjusted R-squared value means that the reported predictive power of the model is less accurate than the average value of the data set over time. It also means that the model is predicting worse than the mean of the data set. The implication is that the explanatory variables do not predict the specific human behaviour or social norm being estimated. For example, assume the profit-before-tax (PBT) of a firm depends on its cost ratio (COST), the prevailing rate of inflation (INFLATION) and the revenue ratio (REVENUE). Estimating the multivariate regression model using the data set below and using the ordinary least square regression method would yield a negative R-squared and a negative adjusted R-squared.

Table 1. Hypothetical data

Year	PBT (%)	Cost (%)	Inflation (%)	Revenue (%)	Taxes (%)
2001	16	25	2	54	15
2002	14	22	2	38	15
2003	12	34	3	47	14.5
2004	17	27	4	49	16
2005	16.5	28	3	51	15
2006	18	30	2.5	50	20
2007	14.5	31	4.5	49	21
2008	11	34	3.8	54	10
2009	19	35.6	2.9	37	14
2010	15	29	3.4	50	15

4.2. R-squared Between 0 and 0.09

A R-squared between 0 and 0.09 (or between 0% to 9%) is too low for an empirical model in social science research. This range of R-squared is not acceptable. It should be rejected. A social science researcher who is faced with a low R-squared within this range can increase the R-squared by doing one of these: (i) replace the explanatory variables with a new set of explanatory variables, (ii) introduce additional explanatory variables together with the existing explanatory variables in the model, (iii) change the entire dataset, (iv) change the model estimation method, (v) change the dependent variable, (vi) change the structural form of the model, (vii) remove the highly correlated explanatory variables, or (viii) combine the highly correlated variables.

4.3. R-squared Between 0.10 and 0.50

A R-squared that is between 0.10 and 0.50 (or between 10 percent and 50 percent when expressed in percentage) is acceptable in social science research only when some or most of the explanatory variables are statistically significant. For example, assume the profit-before-tax (PBT) of a firm depends on its cost ratio (COST), the prevailing rate of inflation (INFLATION), and the tax rate (TAX). Estimating the multivariate regression model using the data set below and using the ordinary least square regression method yields an of R-squared of 0.106. A model with a R-squared that is between 0.10 and 0.50 is good provided that some or most of the explanatory variables are statistically significant. In table 3, the COST and TAX variables are statistically significant at the 10% and 5% level. However, a model with a R-squared that is between 0.10 and 0.50 must be rejected if all the explanatory variables in the model are statistically insignificant.

Table 2. OLS Result for Negative R^2 and adjusted R^2

Dependent Variable: PBT
Method: Least Squares
Date: 11/17/22 Time: 12:21
Sample: 2001 2010
Included observations: 10

Variable	Coefficient	Std. Error	t-Statistic	Prob.
COST	0.317369	0.239697	1.324042	0.2271
INFLATION	-0.912513	1.666351	-0.547612	0.6010
REVENUE	0.179281	0.136803	1.310501	0.2314
R-squared	-0.556121	Mean dependent var		15.30000
Adjusted R-squared	-1.000726	S.D. dependent var		2.529822
S.E. of regression	3.578358	Akaike info criterion		5.631010
Sum squared resid	89.63254	Schwarz criterion		5.721786
Log likelihood	-25.15505	Hannan-Quinn criter.		5.531430
Durbin-Watson stat	2.886551			

4.4. R-squared Between 0.51 and 0.99

A R-squared between 0.50 to 0.99 is acceptable in social science research especially when most of the explanatory variables are statistically significant. The only caveat to this is that the high R-squared should not be caused by spurious causation or multi-collinearity among the explanatory variables.

Table 3. OLS Result for Negative R^2 between 0.1 and 0.5

Dependent Variable: PBT Method: Least Squares Date: 11/17/22 Time: 12:51 Sample: 2001 2010 Included observations: 10				
Variable	**Coefficient**	**Std. Error**	**t-Statistic**	**Prob.**
COST	0.297996	0.154547	1.928190	0.0952
INFLATION	-1.182598	1.249790	-0.946237	0.3755
TAX	0.647678	0.226518	2.859280	0.0244
R-squared	0.106101	Mean dependent var		15.30000
Adjusted R-squared	-0.149298	S.D. dependent var		2.529822
S.E. of regression	2.712104	Akaike info criterion		5.076652
Sum squared resid	51.48857	Schwarz criterion		5.167427
Log likelihood	-22.38326	Hannan-Quinn criter.		4.977071
Durbin-Watson stat	2.110080			

5. CONCLUSION

This paper examined the acceptable R-squared in empirical modelling in social science research with particular focus on whether a low R-squared is acceptable. Assuming the R-squared is the only decision rule being considered, the paper argued that a low R-squared of at least 0.10 is acceptable in social science empirical modelling provided that some or most of the explanatory variables are statistically significant. This means that regression models that have a low R-squared are good models if some of the explanatory variables are statistically significant. Therefore, a regression model in social science research should not be discarded solely because it has a low R-squared. The decision on whether the model is good or not should take into account the statistical significance of the explanatory variables in the model. It is hoped that this commentary article will guide young researchers who are beginners in social science empirical research. I wrote this piece specifically for them.

REFERENCES

Cameron, A. C., & Windmeijer, F. A. (1997). An R-squared measure of goodness of fit for some common nonlinear regression models. *Journal of Econometrics*, 77(2), 329–342. doi:10.1016/S0304-4076(96)01818-0

Chicco, D., Warrens, M. J., & Jurman, G. (2021). The coefficient of determination R-squared is more informative than SMAPE, MAE, MAPE, MSE and RMSE in regression analysis evaluation. *PeerJ. Computer Science*, *7*, e623. doi:10.7717/peerj-cs.623 PMID:34307865

Cornell, J. A., & Berger, R. D. (1987). Factors that influence the value of the coefficient of determination in simple linear and nonlinear regression models. *Phytopathology*, *77*(1), 63–70. doi:10.1094/Phyto-77-63

CSCU. (2005). *Assessing the Fit of Regression Models*. The Cornell Statistical Consulting Unit.

Ferligoj, A., & Kramberger, A. (1995). Some Properties of R 2 in Ordinary Least Squares Regression.

Figueiredo Filho, D. B., Júnior, J. A. S., & Rocha, E. C. (2011). What is R2 all about? *Leviathan (São Paulo)*, (3), 60–68. doi:10.11606/issn.2237-4485.lev.2011.132282

Gelman, A., Goodrich, B., Gabry, J., & Vehtari, A. (2019). R-squared for Bayesian regression models. *The American Statistician*, *73*(3), 307–309. doi:10.1080/0003 1305.2018.1549100

Gujarati, D. N., Porter, D. C., & Gunasekar, S. (2012). *Basic econometrics*. Tata Mcgraw-Hill Education.

Hagle, T. M., & Mitchell, G. E. (1992). Goodness-of-fit measures for probit and logit. *American Journal of Political Science*, *36*(3), 762–784. doi:10.2307/2111590

Hagquist, C., & Stenbeck, M. (1998). Goodness of fit in regression analysis–R 2 and G 2 reconsidered. *Quality & Quantity*, *32*(3), 229–245. doi:10.1023/A:1004328601205

Hill, R. C., Griffiths, W. E., & Lim, G. C. (2018). *Principles of econometrics*. John Wiley & Sons.

Ijomah, M. A. (2019). On the Misconception of R-square for R-square in a Regression Model. [IJRSI]. *International Journal of Research and Scientific Innovation*, *6*(12), 71–76.

King, G. (1986). How not to lie with statistics: Avoiding common mistakes in quantitative political science. *American Journal of Political Science*, *30*(3), 666–687. doi:10.2307/2111095

King, G. (1990). Stochastic Variation: A Comment on Lewis-Beck and Skalaban's "The R-Squared". *Political Analysis*, *2*, 185–200. doi:10.1093/pan/2.1.185

Lewis-Beck, C., & Lewis-Beck, M. (2015). *Applied regression: An introduction* (Vol. 22). Sage publications.

Lewis-Beck, M. S., & Skalaban, A. (1990). The R-squared: Some straight talk. *Political Analysis, 2*, 153–171. doi:10.1093/pan/2.1.153

Maydeu-Olivares, A., & Garcia-Forero, C. (2010). Goodness-of-fit testing. *International encyclopedia of education, 7*(1), 190-196.

Miles, J. (2005). *R-squared, adjusted R-squared.* Encyclopedia of statistics in behavioral science.

Onyutha, C. (2020). From R-squared to coefficient of model accuracy for assessing" goodness-of-fits." *Geoscientific Model Development Discussions*, 1-25.

Reisinger, H. (1997). The impact of research designs on R2 in linear regression models: An exploratory meta-analysis. *Journal of Empirical Generalisations in Marketing Science, 2*(1).

Spiess, A. N., & Neumeyer, N. (2010). An evaluation of R2 as an inadequate measure for nonlinear models in pharmacological and biochemical research: A Monte Carlo approach. *BMC Pharmacology, 10*(1), 1–11. doi:10.1186/1471-2210-10-6 PMID:20529254

Section 3

Quantitative Research Strategies

Chapter 10

An Overview of Structural Equation Modeling and Its Application in Social Sciences Research

Sai Priyanka Pagadala
Indian Agricultural Research Institute, New Delhi, India

Sangeetha V.
Indian Agricultural Research Institute, New Delhi, India

Venkatesh P.
Indian Agricultural Research Institute, New Delhi, India

Girish Kumar Jha
Indian Agricultural Research Institute, New Delhi, India

ABSTRACT

Social science research deals with the highly complex phenomenon guided by various latent and interrelated constructs. As these constructs are invisible and not directly measurable, social scientists employ highly sophisticated multivariate analytical techniques that can simplify a complex data pattern to derive meaningful conclusions. Structural equation modeling (SEM) is a methodology used to represent, estimate, and test a network of relationships among variables. It is an integrated model for hypothesis testing and constructs' validity. This chapter deals with the various aspects of the SEM methodology, starting from describing the statistical algorithms used, the role of theory, measurement and structural model, stages in testing model validity, etc., meticulously explained in simple terms to provide with a basic understanding of this intricate technique.

DOI: 10.4018/978-1-6684-6859-3.ch010

INTRODUCTION

Structural equation modeling (SEM) is considered as a broad statistical approach for testing hypotheses of relations among and between both kinds of variables, observed and latent (Hoyle, 1995). It is a family of statistical techniques permitting researchers to test complex research questions of multivariate models. The goal of SEM and factor analysis is alike; that is, to provide a brief summary of all possible interrelationships between latent psychological variables (Kahn, 2006). Path analysis and SEM are similar in that each permits testing hypothesized relationships between constructs. This way SEM can be regarded as a hybrid of factor analysis and path analysis. Like in multiple regression models, where researchers freely conduct several combinations to find a suitable model, SEM also identifies and removes weaknesses in the model and refines to present a model similar to one originally hypothesized. Hence, it can be regarded as integrated model for hypothesis testing and constructs' validity. SEM analysis goal is to determine the range whether obtained sample data support the hypothesized theoretical model. If data supports more complex models may be hypothesized; if not supported original model is to be modified, or other theoretical models need to be developed. In doing so, SEM can help us assess the measurement properties and test the proposed theoretical relationships specified by using a single technique. Compared with other general linear models, where constructs may be represented with only one measure and measurement error is not modeled. Still, SEM involves complex, multi-faceted constructs that are measured with error i.e., the use of multiple measures to represent constructs and address the issue of measure-specific error. Here advantage of SEM is its ability to incorporate both quantitative and qualitative data (in coded form) for analysis. This framework is an integration that combines Measurement Theory from Psychology, Factor analysis from Psychology and statistics, Path analysis from biology (epidemiology), Regression modeling from statistics and Simultaneous equations from Econometrics. Therefore in existing literature SEMs are also known as Covariance structure analysis, Analysis of Moment Structures (AMOS), Analysis of Linear Structural Relationships (LISREL), and Causal modelling.

BACKGROUND

SEM is an old statistical technique that has undergone progress over years, yet is not completely explored by researchers. The history of this technique started with the work of Spearman (1904) by introducing factor analysis method which forms basis for measurement of latent variables. Later with Wright (1918) path analysis approach of correlations were applied to determine relationships between parameters to estimate direct, indirect and total effects. With time, psychometrics research utilized theory testing through proposed hypothesis among abstract constructs (Tarka, 2018). Hence, theoretical assumptions are essential for analysis rather than theory building.

Role of Theory in SEM

To set ne should not go with gut feeling about relationships between variables, specification of parameters, etc. For this, a sound theory is essential. Theory can be thought of as a set of relationships providing consistency and comprehensive explanations of the actual phenomenon. This theory can also be published in the literature, previously developed models and established relations from various studies. A theory serves as a conceptual scheme based on foundational statements assumed to be valid for developing a model. It is very important that the SEM model be based on a theory because all the relationships must be specified before can be estimated. Therefore, theory is needed to determine measurement and structural models, for modifications to the proposed relationships, and many other aspects of evaluating a model. Theory also helps in establishing causation.

SEM vs. Multivariate Techniques

1. In SEM, constructs can be represented as unobservant or latent factors independent relationships.
2. Allows estimation of multiple and interrelated dependence relationships incorporated in an integrated model
3. Provides an explanation of the covariance among the observed variables.
4. Pursues to signify hypotheses regarding structural parameters about the variance, mean and covariance of observed data as the hypothesized model.
5. In other approaches, direct and indirect effects based on pre-assumed relations are tested, but this is unlikely in SEM.

Path Analysis

A path model is a diagrammatic representation of a theoretical model using a standardized notion. Regression models, simultaneous regression equations, multivariate models, more and more complex problems can be addressed with the help of path models. D represents Disturbance and is defined as the error with latent dependent variables. Observed variables are exclusively specified in the path model. Apart from this, it also allows flexibility in representing multiple independent and dependent observed variables, and if latent variables are shown, it becomes SEM. If it is with latent variables, it is nothing but SEM. In path analysis latent variables are represented by elliptical-shaped variables and are measured with one or more rectangular-shaped observed variables. Every observed variable is measured along with an associated error term indicated in a circle shape. Within the model, covariance, direct effects, and or indirect (mediated) effects are the different types of relationships expressed among latent variables. Covariance represented by double-headed arrows are equivalent to correlations and are described as relationships among independent latent variables which are non-directional. The direct effects relationship represented by single-directional arrows is similar to multiple regressions and ANOVA among measured and latent variables. An indirect or mediated effect is a relationship between an independent and a latent dependent variable that is mediated by one or more factors (Baron & Kenny, 1986). Mediation may be complete or partial. Total effects include both direct and indirect effects together.

Let us understand path analysis notations with the help of the following hypothetical example of path model diagram. Here three latent variables are used namely grades (G), intelligence (I) and problem solving skills (PSS). Each of these three variables is measured with three indicators along with their associated error terms with fixed loadings. PSS is the endogenous variable in the example. G and I have a directionless association and are depicted with covariance with double-headed arrow, when G and I are taken as exogenous variables. Direct effect, $\beta 1$ is path coefficient of G on PSS. If we suppose I and PSS are also endgenous variables with only G as exogenous variables, then path coefficients of G's on I and that of I's on PSS are $\beta 2$ and $\beta 3$ respectively. We can say that G has indirect effect on I and D1 would be disturbance term of I and D2 is for PSS. Hence, the total effect of G on PSS would be calculated as $\beta 1 * (\beta 2 + \beta 3)$.

Figure 1. Hypothetical example of path diagram

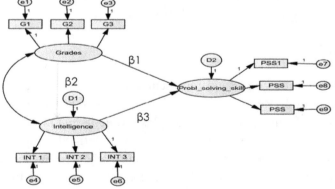

Exploratory Factor Analysis (EFA)

- It can be regarded as an 'unrestricted' factor analysis.
- It finds factor loadings that best reproduce correlations between observed variables.
- Here, factors are determined by variables (no. of factors = no. of observed variables).
- All the variables are related to all factors, meaning all the variables show factor loading for each factor.
- For SEM, we retain only those factors that are less than latent factors that explain a satisfactory amount of observed variance (60%).
- Based on pattern matrix showing item (observed variables) loadings on their hypothesized factors.
- EFA follows an inductive, atheoretical approach. We first collect data and later check for appropriate theory. Hence, Data > Theory.
- In most cases, directly CFA is performed for SEM, skipping EFA.

Confirmatory Factor Analysis (CFA)

- It is regarded as 'restricted factor model' with no cross-loading of variables.
- It consists of observed variables that are hypothesized to measure latent variables (independent or dependent).
- Here the researcher's measurement theory will be tested for validity.
- The confirmatory factor analysis tests whether indicators load on specific latent variables as the theory proposed.
- All standard rules and procedures that produce valid descriptive research apply (missing data, multivariate normality, sample size).

Assumptions of SEM

- Multivariate normality
- No systematic missing data
- Sufficiently large sample size
- Linear relationship of variables
- Correct model specification

Measurement Theory Validation With CFA (Construct Validity)

1. **Face Validity: (content validity)** it is the subjective but systematic evaluation of how well the content of a scale represents the measurement task at hand. Given its subjective measure, it alone is not sufficient measure of validity.

2. **Convergent Validity:** When indicators measuring a construct share high amount of common variance it is known as convergent validity.
   a. Factor loading: It is the simple correlation between item and factor. The size (>0.5 or >0.7) and significance of factor loading indicates convergent validity.

3. **Average variance extracts (AVE):** It is calculated as mean variance extracted for the items loading on a construct and is summary indicator of convergence. AVE value of above 0.5 indicates convergent validity.

4. **Composite reliability (CR):** Reliability is also an indicator of validity. It is computed from the squared sum of factor loadings for each construct and the sum of error variance terms for a construct. CR value of above 0.7 indicates convergent validity.

5. **Discriminant Validity:** It is the level to which a construct is actually different from other constructs. It can be tested by comparing the AVEs with squared inter constructs correlation. If AVEs are greater than squared inter construct correlation, and then the analysis indicates discriminant validity.

6. **Nomological Validity:** It is the extent to which the construct relates to other constructs in a predictable manner. It tests by examining whether the correlations among the constructs in measurement model make sense.

Only when the CFA satisfies the criterions as mentioned above, then only we can say model has sufficient construct validity.

Model Diagnostics

CFA's goal is to see whether a given measurement model is valid. It also suggests modification for either addressing unresolved problems or improving the model's test of measurement theory. Some areas that can be used to identify problems with measures are:

Standardized Residuals: Research can use the residual values to identify item pairs for which the specified measurement model does not accurately predict the observed covariance between these two items. Generally, standardized residuals of less than 2.5 do not suggest any problem. Anything above 4.0 indicates problem and it might lead to dropping of such variables.

Measurement and Structural Models

Thinking of SEM as a combination of factor analysis and path analysis sets the researcher up for thinking about SEM's two primary components: the measurement model and the structural model. Measurement model usually represents the theory. It specifies how the measured variables in the study combine to represent the theory. In the measurement model of SEM researcher is allowed to assess how well his or her observed measured variables come together to find causal hypothesized constructs. This model is tested using confirmatory factor analysis. Structural model signifies the theory in which it illustrates how the constructs are related to one another. Relationships specified in structural part of model indicate hypothesized relationships between latent variables. Path analysis is used for relationships among latent variables are described as covariance, direct effects, or indirect (mediated) effects. Covariance are analogous to correlations in that they are defined as non-directional relationships among independent latent variables. When the measurement model and the structural model are considered together, the model may be called the *composite or full structural equation model.*

Example: Figure 2 represents composite or full structural equation mode. From Fig. 2, it can be explained that there are three Measurement models like A, B, and C; and one structural model describing the relationships among the three variables.

Figure 2. Full Structural Equation Model
(Tanya & Claudio, 2010)

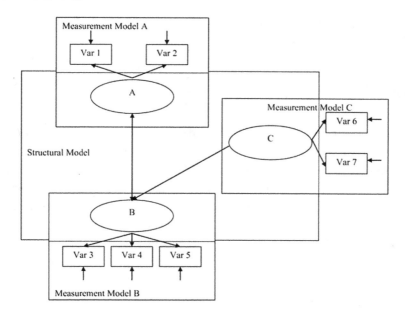

Stages in SEM

The following diagram represents the process of SEM in 6 stages, wherein the first 4 stages are related to Measurement model and last stages are those of Structural Model.

Figure 3. Stages in SEM

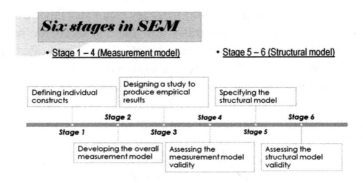

Steps in SEM

1. Model Specification
2. Model Identification
3. Model Estimation
4. Data issues & corrections
5. Model Testing
6. Model Modification

1. Model Specification

In this step, all variable relationships and parameters present in the model need to be specified properly by the researcher. A given model is properly specified when the true population model is deemed consistent with the implied theoretical model being tested—that is, the sample covariance matrix S is sufficiently reproduced by the implied theoretical model. Model is said to be *misspecified* if true model and implied model are not consistent. Hence, model specification forms the important first step to specify parameters in three ways such as covariance, variance and directional effects. Directional effects describe relationships between latent variables and indicators (called factor loadings) and relationships between latent variables and other latent variables (called path coefficients). One of SEM's advantages over other methods is its capacity to accommodate estimates of variance for both the variables and their associated error terms. Loadings of error terms on the dependent variables to 1.0 (the default on some software programs) or can standardize the error term and estimate parameters. Covariances are non-directional associations that are established when researchers sets that there is an association between two latent variables but a causal relationship doesn't exist. Parameter relationships are set to zero and not estimated, these are not included in the model. Another parameter relationship is set to non-zero (mostly 1.0) and not estimated. Lastly parameters are left free to estimate, these are what we actually measure.

2. Model Identification

After model specification parameters are designated as free, fixed and constrained. As discussed above here we have to consider free parameters to estimate values. A fixed parameter is a parameter that is not free, but is fixed to a specified value, typically either 0 or 1. On the other hand constrained parameters are usually unknown and constrained as one. Then parameters are combined to calculate å (model variance – covariance matrix). Hence, ascertaining the model identification involves determining the number of degrees of freedom (Dof) by subtracting number of parameters to be estimated from number of correlations in covariance matrix. Instead of that, following formula (Rebecca & Paul, 2006) can be used

Dof = (no. observed variables [no. observed variables +1])/2.

Based on model identification, three types of models will be seen, these are:

1. A model is *under-identified* (or not identified) if one or more parameters may not be uniquely determined because there is not enough information in the matrix S.
2. A model is *just-identified* if all of the parameters are uniquely determined because there is just enough information in the matrix S.
3. A model is *over-identified* when there is more than one way of estimating a parameter (or parameters) because there is more than enough information in the matrix S.
    ◦   If a model is either just- or over-identified, then only the model is considered as identified.

3. Model Estimation

This step involves determining those unknown parameters left behind in previous step along with error of estimated value. As in regression, researchers include both unstandardized and standardized parameter values, and coefficients, as output. Unstandardized coefficients are B weight equivalent in regression, and is divided by standard error to give z value similar to t value of regression weights. The standardized coefficient is analogous to β in regression. Standardized estimates are only mentioned in Path diagram but only after we determine the significance by examining the unstandardized portion of the output.

Critical factor (z) = B/SE (i.e., z^3 1.96 for p £ .05)

Techniques like maximum likelihood (ML) estimation, least squares (LS) – weighted or generalized, etc., are available for estimation of models. Among those ML is the default for many model-fitting programs. After model estimation, researchers examine factor loadings to determine whether any indicators do not load as expected. Two approaches of estimation needs a mention here. One is Anderson and Gerbing (1988), in which they follow CFA to test measurement model later estimate full structural model. Other is Mulaik and Millsap (2000) four-phase alternative, of which first phase is the equivalent of estimating an exploratory factor analysis, with paths from each latent variable to all observed variables. CFA test is second phase and simultaneous measurement and structural model testing in third phase. Fourth phase is a priori hypothesis testing which uniquely address need for alternative models.

4. Data Related Issues and Corrections

Before the data collection, ideally model has to be specified and identified. Then, sample size and other data related issues can be addressed properly in this step.

- **Sample size:** Most researchers prefer 200 to 400 sample size with 10 to 15 indicators; thumb rule: 10 to 20 times as many cases as variables
  - Not raw data but variance/covariance matrix of observed variable is analyzed.
    - **Multicollinearity:** is a situation in which the measured variables are highly related among themselves, so basically are to be laid off.
  - Screening bivariate correlation can avoid multicollinearity. When two observed variables are highly correlated (r=.85), one solution is to remove one of the redundant variables

- **Outliers:** or influential data points that are extreme or a typical on either the independent (X variables) or dependent (Y variables) variables or both.
  - ○ Univariate outliers can be transformed/ changed, whereas multivariate outliers have to be recoded/ removed.
    - **Normality:** Multivariate normal distribution is assumed mostly while using SEM. Violating this assumption can be problematic because non-normality will affect the accuracy of statistical tests. Since it's not possible to screen normality of multiple variables, we can examine the distribution of each observed variable.
  - ○ If normality is not observed data transformations can be an option.
    - **Missing data:** Missing data can be described in three categories such as completely missing data at random, missing at random, or not missing at random (NMAR) as according to Rubin (1976).
  - ○ These can be corrected by replacing values, Maximum Likelihood, GLS etc., techniques.

Model Fit and Interpretation

Once estimated, the model's fit to the data must be evaluated. The objective is to determine whether the associations among measured and latent variables in the researcher are estimated. In Social Sciences research, exact fit and approximate fit values of model can be used for analysis. In model fit we compare the two covariance matrices. Model fit is assessed by significance of estimated parameters, variance explained by variables and overall model fit. Although addressing the first two criteria is a fairly straightforward task, there exists considerable disagreement over what constitutes acceptable values for global fit indices. A loading of at least 0.5 is satisfactory and 0.7 is desirable in path loadings. Variances should not have negative values and correlations should not exceed 1. There are multiple model fit indices for evaluation, among those the following are widely considered by researchers. Absolute fit indices like Goodness of fit index (GFI) (Joreskog & Sorbom, 1981) and Chi-square test χ^2 (Satorra & Bentler, 1994) sensitive to sample size. CFI an incremental index with value near 1.0 is best fit. Root mean square error of approximation (RMSEA) (Steiger, 1990; Steiger & Lind, 1980) – this index corrects for a model's complexity, and standardized root mean square residual (SRMR) index both having values of .00 indicates exact fit. Guidelines for acceptable fit include a non-significant χ^2, CFI greater than .90 (Hu & Bentler, 1995), RMSEA less than .10 with a maximum upper bound of the 90% CI of .10 (Browne & Cudek, 1993), and SRMR less than .10 (Bentler, 1995).

5. Model Testing

Testing is done by comparing models of similar complexity, yet representing varying theoretical relationships. Alternative model testing is often overlooked which requires attention. The fit of the alternative model is compared with that of the proposed model in three ways:

1. significance evaluation of parameter estimates,
2. consider the change in explained variance, and
3. Test significant improvement in model fit with a chi-square difference test and improvement in other fit indices.

Nested models (A= B + parameter restrictions), i.e., one model (B) subset of original model (A) but with certain parameter restrictions, can also be used to test the fit of better model.

6. Model Modification

Rarely is a proposed model the best-fitting model. Consequently, modifications (re-specification) are needed. Modifications include freeing or setting parameters. However, problems are more, when researchers -

1. use small samples,
2. do not limit modifications to those that are theoretically acceptable, and
3. Severely misspecify the initial model (Green et al., 1998).
   a. Standardized residuals < 2.5 is suggested and >4.0 indicates problem and leads to drop variables as solution.
   b. *Specification search:* to alter the original model in the search for a model that is better fitting in some sense and yields parameters having practical significance and substantive meaning. Lagrange multiplier test, Wald test, modification indices can be used for model modification purpose.

Issues of SEM

- The popularity of structural equation modeling has led to the creation of a scholarly journal "Structural Equation Modeling" devoted specifically for publication of structural equation modeling related articles.
- SEMNET a popular electronic discussion list focuses mainly on SEM and its related issues.

- There exist many software programs which allow flexible and sophisticated modeling.
  - LISREL (Linear Structural Relationships) the original
  - EQS (Equations)
  - AMOS (Analysis of Moment Structures) integrated with SPSS
  - MPlus, Python Package (sempoy) and R Packages (sem, lavaan, Mplus, EQS, LISREL)
  - CALIS, LISCOMP, RAMONA, SEPATH and others

Limitations in SEM

- The confirmatory technique used in SEM requires a preliminary knowledge of all the relationships to be specified in the model.
- SEM is a fairly technical, complex procedure and requires sound statistical knowledge.
- It is a large sample technique and comparative studies are hard to measure.
- Problems in making generalizations, as variables may behave differently over time.
- As there is no consensus on model fit indices, criteria differ from case to case.

Applications of SEM

SEM can be applied with complex relationships including multiple constructs in certain broad areas such as

- Psychology
- Social Sciences Research
- Marketing Research
- Ecological Research
- Educational Research
- Medical research (Psychiatry)

Applications include the examination of growth trajectory over time through the analysis of repeated measures, comparison of multiple groups to test for factorial invariance, and analysis of hierarchical data with multilevel modeling.

Social Science Research and SEM

Multiple indicator variables are required for measuring latent constructs in social science research. Behavioral studies, a sub-category in social science research use psychological variables which show differential effects and often behaviors are formed with influence of many such variables. Certain abstract constructs like attitudes, intelligence, motivation, satisfaction, involve multifaceted aspects which cannot be measured nothing like age or net income, etc. and complex phenomenon are difficult to analyze thus application of SEM becomes ideal that allows in testing multiple relationships and develop a model to replicate in similar situations along with theory testing.

UNEXPLORED TYPES OF SEM

1. Longitudinal Growth Curve Modeling

There may be potential danger that the variables themselves may behave differently over the time. So, longitudinal studies in this area could help in understanding the causality and interrelationship among variables. Longitudinal growth curve models are used in such a case to ascertain the changes that occur over time. In this model provided with the intercept and slope, we can constraint the paths coefficients and measure the subject trajectories of latent variables over time. Halil and Petek (2013) had applied this technique of latent growth model with longitudinal data to assess gender difference and problem solving skills of programming knowledge.

2. Partial Least Square – Path Modeling (PLS – PM)

This method can be used when there is little theoretical base of relationships among variables. It is more of exploration rather than confirmatory. However, small sample size is another advantage of this model. Variance based relationship is used in PLS model in contrast to covariance matrix approach in conventional SEM (Fan, et. al, 2016). Reliability and validity are more for this model, provided that the composite based models ensure better outcomes.

Bayesian modeling, Hierarchical modeling, etc. also form important types but discussion here is limited to those which are more suitable for social science research. To understand better all the above mentioned set of rules and methodological procedures in detail, the following studies help in depth learning and ease of application of the technique.

Case Study – 1

Abrahim et al. (2019) conducted a study in Japan on 385 students with the objective to design a structural equation model and test confirmatory factor analysis system in order to explain how students now-a-days can utilize social media networks such as Facebook for their educational purposes. Facebook model exclusively consist of three latent variable indicators (benefit, purpose and social media usage of Facebook) and 14 observable variables. Hypothetical model in SPSS AMOS is conceptualized based on published literature to investigate diffusion, benefit and acceptance of Facebook by undergraduate, graduate and research students at the University of Toyama. Benefit was an exogenous (independent) latent variable; Users' purposes and Social media usage of Facebook were Endogenous (dependent) latent variable for this model. The findings of this study were like this, total variance experienced by the model was 71%. R2 for Benefit on Purpose was 74% and Purpose on Usage was 65%. Among all purposes studied social media (Facebook) usage for resource and material sharing was one of the most vital factor. Usage has a positive relationship with its observed variables and all the observed variables have almost equal distributions, that means students are willing to accept Facebook as one of the study tools. The model was specified as a good one or even better based on values from the analysis and all the 14 hypotheses based on the study are verified and accepted.

Case Study – 2

Sivakumar et al, (2014) conducted a study on 299 KVK extension personnel from Odisha and Tamil Nadu with the purpose to develop a Computer Utilization Model for extension professionals by integrating the perceptual and organizational variables to explain the extent of computer use in extension organizations based on theory of Technology Acceptance Model (TAM) variables. Structural model is specified using SPSS AMOS with system usage as endogenous variable, organizational support and task uncertainty as exogenous variables, Perceived usefulness and perceived ease of use are moderating variables. EFA retained 6 factors but only one variable was loaded on factor six, it was not included in the model and these factors are subjected to CFA for improving convergent validity. The final Confirmatory Factor Analysis model along with estimated regression coefficients is displayed after assessing through standardized loadings, composite reliabilities and variance extracted by each latent factor. The results of the Structural Model Analysis showed that most of the goodness-of-fit indicators are close to the recommended level, indicating adequate model fit and hypotheses H1 to H5 were tested by measuring the significance of the path coefficients. They found that organizational support has great influence on computer utilization in organizations and with small indirect effect on Perceived use. This indicates providing financial and technical support to purchase computers, training employees in computer use, maintenance of computers and networking are necessary prerequisites for effective computer use. Computer Utilization Model developed through this study can serve as a valuable management tool for extension managers. This model was developed with a large sample of respondents using rigorous psychometric procedures that are customized for Indian conditions. It is a diagnostic tool that can help extension managers to identify the perceptual problems of their staff (inadequate computer skills and negative perceptions of computers) and organizational deficiencies (inadequate computers and maintenance).

Case Study – 3

Rebecca and Paul (2006) conducted an experimental study on undergraduate college students who participated in a vocational psychology research project. From that available data they made a hypothetical review example of SEM, with each of the four latent variables represented by three measured variables Self Efficacy Beliefs, Outcome Expectations, Interests and Occupational Considerations. They hypothesize self-efficacy beliefs to have a direct effect on interests and an indirect effect on interests through outcome expectations. Outcome expectations variable partially mediates self-efficacy beliefs impact on interest with both the direct and indirect effects. In contrast, the impact of self-efficacy beliefs on occupational considerations is fully mediated (by interests) because only an indirect effect is specified. After testing the model was found to be significantly good fit meeting all the criteria of fit indices and construct validity. But, the alternative model also was tested to be significantly better fit over the hypothesized model. The former fully mediated model is more restricted than the alternative partially mediated model because the dashed paths from self-efficacy beliefs and outcome expectations to occupational considerations are set to zero and not estimated. Thus the alternative partially mediated model is nested within restricted full mediated model as the two paths remain free to be estimated.

CONCLUSION

Social research studies have complex relationships wherein the same dependent variables at times acts as independent variables in other phenomenon. This lands in a complicated situation where sophisticated statistical technique is needed. SEM is a powerful multivariate analysis tool that has great potential to satisfy estimation of multiple parameter effects with factor loadings and analyzing different relationships among variables through path coefficients alongside testing of alternate models. The technique finds use in psychometrics, behavioral science, business, and marketing research with feasibility of application. Many easy-to-use software programs have increased the accessibility of this quantitative method. However those interested in understanding SEM, try not to attempt to master any static set of decision rules.

Instead, should emphasize the need to continue to seek out information on the appropriate application of this technique.

REFERENCES

Abrahim, S., Mir, B. A., Suhara, H., Mohamed, F. A., & Sato, M. (2019). Structural equation modeling and confirmatory factor analysis of social media use and education. *International Journal of Education Technology and Higher Education.*, *16*(1), 32. doi:10.118641239-019-0157-y

Anderson, J. C., & Gerbing, D. C. (1988). Structural equation modeling in practice: A review and recommended two-step approach. *Psychological Bulletin*, *103*(3), 411–423. doi:10.1037/0033-2909.103.3.411

Baron, R. M., & Kenny, D. A. (1986). The moderator-mediator variable distinction in social psychological research: Conceptual, strategic, and statistical considerations. *Journal of Personality and Social Psychology*, *51*(6), 1173–1182. doi:10.1037/0022-3514.51.6.1173 PMID:3806354

Bentler, P. M. (1995). *EQS structural equations program manual*. Multivariate Software.

Browne, M. W., & Cudek, R. (1993). Alternative ways of assessing model fit. In K. A. Bollen & J. S. Long (Eds.), *Testing structural equation models* (pp. 136–162). Sage.

Fan, Y., Chen, J., Shirkey, G., John, R., Wu, S. R., Park, H., & Shao, C. (2016). Applications of structural equation modeling (SEM) in ecological studies: An updated review. *Ecological Processes*, *5*(1), 19. doi:10.118613717-016-0063-3

Green, S. B., Thompson, M. S., & Babyak, M. A. (1998). A Monte Carlo investigation of methods for controlling Type I errors with specification searches in structural equation modeling. *Multivariate Behavioral Research*, *33*(3), 365–383. doi:10.120715327906mbr3303_3 PMID:26782719

Halil, Y., & Petek, A. (2013). Learning programming, problem solving and gender: A longitudinal study. *Procedia: Social and Behavioral Sciences*, *83*, 605–610. doi:10.1016/j.sbspro.2013.06.115

Hoyle, RH. (1995). *Structural equation modeling: concepts, issues, and applications*. Sage, Thousand Oak.

Hu, L. T., & Bentler, P. M. (1995). Evaluating model fit. In R. H. Hoyle (Ed.), *Structural equation modeling: Concepts, issues and applications* (pp. 76–99). Sage.

Jöreskog, K. G., & Sörbom, D. (1981). *Analysis of linear structural relationships by maximum likelihood and least squares methods* (Research Report No. 81-8). Uppsala, Sweden: University of Sweden.

Kahn, J. H. (2006). Factor analysis in counseling psychology research, training, and practice: Principles, advances, and applications. *The Counseling Psychologist, 34*(5), 684–718. doi:10.1177/0011000006286347

Mulaik, S. A., & Millsap, R. E. (2000). Doing the four-step right. *Structural Equation Modeling, 7*(1), 36–73. doi:10.1207/S15328007SEM0701_02

Rebecca, W., & Paul, A. G. (2006). A Brief Guide to Structural Equation Modeling. *The Counseling Psychologist, 34*(5), 719–751. doi:10.1177/0011000006286345

Rubin, D. B. (1976). Inference and missing data. *Biometrika, 61*(3), 581–592. doi:10.1093/biomet/63.3.581

Satorra, A., & Bentler, P. (1994). Corrections to test statistics and standard errors on covariance structure analysis. In A. Von Eye & C. C. Clogg (Eds.), *Latent variables analysis* (pp. 399–419). Sage.

Sivakumar, P. S., Bibudha, P., Raghu, N. D., & Anantharaman, M. (2014). Determinants of computer utilization by extension personnel: A structural equations approach. *Journal of Agricultural Education and Extension, 20*(2), 191–212. doi:1 0.1080/1389224X.2013.803986

Spearman, C. (1904). General Intelligence: Objectively determined and measured. *The American Journal of Psychology, 5*(2), 201–293. doi:10.2307/1412107

Steiger, J. H. (1990). Structural model evaluation and modification: An internal estimation approach. *Multivariate Behavioral Research, 25*(2), 173–180. doi:10.120715327906mbr2502_4 PMID:26794479

Steiger, J. H., & Lind, J. C. (1980). *Statistically based tests for the number of common factors.* Paper presented at the annual meeting of the Psychometric Society, Iowa City, IA.

Tanya, N. B., & Claudio, V. (2010). Structural equation modeling in medical research: A primer. *BMC Research Notes, 3*, 26. PMID:20969789

Tarka, P. (2018). An overview of structural equation modeling: Its beginnings, historical development, usefulness and controversies in the social sciences. *Quality & Quantity, 52*(1), 313–354. doi:10.100711135-017-0469-8 PMID:29416184

Wright, S. (1918). On the nature of size factors. *Genetics*, *3*(4), 367–374. doi:10.1093/genetics/3.4.367 PMID:17245910

KEY TERMS AND DEFINITIONS

Construct: A concept with additional meaning evolved for scientific purposes.

Endogenous Variables: These are latent, a multi-item equivalent of a dependent variable that is determined by constructs or variables within the model.

Exogenous Variables: These are latent, a multi-item equivalent of an independent variable that is determined by factors outside of the model.

Latent Variables: These are the variables that are not directly measured or observed; a set of observed variables are used to define or infer the latent variable or construct (e.g., intelligence). Variables either if they are observed or latent, they can be defined as independent variables or dependent variables based on researchers' interest.

Model: This is a statistical statement, expressed with equations or a diagram, about the hypothesized relationships among variables based on theory and research. In short, a model is the representation of theory.

Observed Variables: These are the variables that are measured directly, or also indicator variables; that is we actually measure these by using tests, surveys, and so on (e.g., grades).

Chapter 11
Analytical Hierarchical Process in Decision Making

Sanath Jayawardena
Sri Lanka Institute of Information Technology, Sri Lanka

R. A. R. C. Gopura
Department of Mechanical Engineering, University of Moratuwa, Sri Lanka

ABSTRACT

In the introduction, what decision making is and the significance of the decision making was introduced. Few popular decision-making techniques were listed out and three rational techniques were discussed in a nutshell. Then Professor Saaty's seminal work, Analytical Hierarchical Process (AHP) was described, starting with the evolution of AHP and moving towards its practice through a four-step process. The AHP generates weights on a relative ratio scale with an input of measurements on a standard scale and due to the normalization process linearity of the results was destroyed. Finally, the four-step analytical hierarchical process was illustrated through an example of the selection of a job. During the progression, outcomes of the key theoretical aspects have been touched on without providing proof.

INTRODUCTION

Decision-Making and Its Significance

Decision-making is a fact-based judgmental process made to select one among many alternatives after careful evaluation of each of them and it is rarely a choice between right and wrong. The decision-making process is generally a managerial function

DOI: 10.4018/978-1-6684-6859-3.ch011

though it is imperative everywhere. Decision-making has only a significant impact in certain contexts, but it inevitably becomes crucial and critical in other scenarios. On one hand, decisions have an enormous impact on success or failure, while in another way it can be seen as a creative task. The complexity of the decision-making process varies from a simple binomial decision to a complex hierarchical structural decision underlined with multi-decision criteria.

Decision-Making Techniques

Ample numbers of decision-making methods could be found in the literature and only a few mile-stone decision-making processes would be briefed under this section. The techniques such as Nominal Group Technique, Delphi technique, Brain-storming, Multi-voting, Step Ladder technique, SWOT analysis, and Pareto analysis are a few famous practical techniques used, however, some of them are not based on solid mathematical background and hence lack in deductive nature. Most of the techniques are subjective, and heuristic in nature but very much useful in a practical context. The nutshell of the three objective criteria is outlined in the following paragraphs.

The decision tree evolved as a rational means of taking decisions. Based on the potential outcomes, the probabilities of such potential outcomes, and their associated costs, the consequences of a complex decision are evaluated in the decision tree analysis technique. The tree approach is particularly useful in the analysis of quantitative data and its usage is limited due to the amount of information required as well as the existence of such information may not be quite obvious in nature. However, with the advent of machine learning algorithms, the decision tree approach was transformed into a type of supervised machine learning technique used to categorize or make predictions.

The Decision Matrix is one of the most popular Multiple-Criteria Decision Analysis (MCDA) techniques. It is used to select the best option based on weighted criteria with their importance (Salmerona & Smarandacheb, 2010). In the Decision Matrix approach, the list of options/choices available is used as rows on a table, while the factors/criteria need to be considered as columns with factors/criteria ratings. Then fill the element of the matrix with the weights of each option based on each factor/criterion. Then calculate the overall score for each option by taking the sum of the product of factors/criteria and weights (relative importance of the factor). Based on the overall scores, decisions are made.

In 1970, a rigorous form of multi-criteria decision analysis tool termed as Analytic Hierarchy Process (AHP) was added to the scientific knowledge base. The Analytic Hierarchy Process (AHP) is a structured technique for organizing and analyzing complex decisions, using mathematics and psychology. It allows making decisions in complex environments in which many variables or criteria are considered in the prioritization and selection of alternatives. Based on the final score for each alternative under different criteria under consideration, the best option is selected. Hereafter the remaining part of the book chapter is devoted to explaining and illustrating the AHP.

ANALYTIC HIERARCHICAL PROCESS

The analytical hierarchical process (AHP) was first coined by Thomas L. Saaty, a Distinguished University Professor at the University of Pittsburgh in his book titled "The Analytic Hierarchy Process" (Saaty, 1980). However, mathematical proof behind the evolution of AHP has put forward in his paper "A scaling method for priorities in hierarchical structures" in 1977 (Saaty, 1977). Subsequently, a large number of papers were published explaining and illustrating the analytic hierarchical process and only a few ground-breaking papers were cited (Saaty, 1988; Saaty, 1987).). Then the AHP concept was so appealing to many types of research, that researchers started to use it intensively in their research. Professor Saaty's seminal scholarly publication in 1988 (Saaty, 1988) was cited in more than 84,400 scholarly articles and book chapters providing a good indicator of the extensive use of AHP in research. Subsequently, an extension of the classical analytical hierarchical process, the fuzzy analytical hierarchical process was evolved and used extensively in the research field.

The AHP is widely used and not limited to cost-benefit analysis, strategic planning, research and development priority setting and selection, technology choice, investment priority, priority for development criteria, evaluation of telecommunication service, and other evaluation of alternatives.

The Analytic Hierarchy Process (AHP) is a theoretical framework that starts from the relative measurement of intangible criteria known as pairwise comparison measurements to derive a scale of priorities. It involves both subjective human judgments and objective evaluation such as Eigenvector (weights) and also examines the consistency of the evaluation by Eigenvalues.

AHP can also be considered a rational and comprehensive framework for structuring a decision problem, representing and quantifying its elements, relating the said elements to overall goals, and evaluating alternative solutions. The AHP can be explained in four steps.

Step 1: Decompose the decision-making problem into a hierarchy
Step 2: Make a pairwise comparison and establish priorities among the elements in the hierarchy

Step3: Synthesize judgments or more specifically derive the overall scale rating
for each alternative

Step 4: Evaluate and check the consistency of judgments

Step 1: Decompose the decision-making problem into a hierarchy

In the hierarchy, the top level is the goal, the second level is the criteria/factors used
for evaluation and the third level is the alternatives/choices.

Figure 1. Hierarchical structure

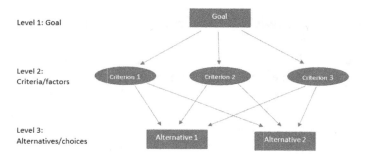

For instance, it is required to select a car. The goal is to select a car. The criteria
would be safety, fuel economy, number of passengers, and the initial cost. The
alternative or choices may be Toyota, Benz, Mitsubishi etc. and only 3 were selected
based on personal preference. So, it can be put in a hierarchical structure as follows.

Figure 2. Hierarchy - selection of car

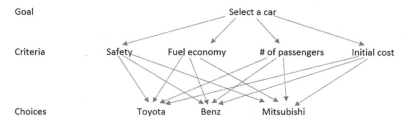

If a person wants to select a job under multi-decision criteria, it can be represented in a hierarchical structure. An example, the different layers of a hierarchical structure could be given in the following way.

Table 1. Hierarchical elements at different levels in the selection of a job

Hierarchical Position	Description	Elements in Each Level
Level 1	Goal	To select a job
Level 2	Factors to consider	Salary, security, growth, workload
Level 3	Job choices	University, research institute, company, own business

Step 2: Make a Pairwise Comparison and Establish Priorities

Once the hierarchy is developed as in step 1, the next step is to systematically evaluate its various elements by comparing them to one another, two at a time and it is termed a pairwise comparison with respect to the impact on an element of the developed hierarchy. For pairwise comparison, a 9-point scale was introduced by Saaty (Saaty, 1980; Saaty, 1988).

Table 2. Pairwise comparison for AHP (Saaty, 1988)

Intensity of Importance	Definition	Explanation
1	Equal importance	Two activities contributed equally to the objective
3	moderate importance one over the another	Experience and judgment slightly favour one activity over the another
5	Essential or strong importance	Experience and judgment strongly favour one activity over the another
7	Very strong importance	An activity is favoured very strongly over another, its dominance demonstrated in practice
9	Extreme importance	The evidence favouring one activity over another is of the highest possible order of affirmation
2,4,6,8	Immediate values between the two adjacent judgment	--
Reciprocals	If activity i has one of the above numbers assigned to it, when compared with activity j, then j has the reciprocal value when compared with i	--
Rationals	Ratio arising from the table	If consistency were to be forced by obtaining n numerical values to span the matrix

Pairwise comparisons are made with ratings ranging from 1 to 9 (rationales) and 1 to 1/9 (reciprocals). For instance, if attribute A is more important than attribute B then it is rated as a rational rating as per table 2 while reciprocal ratings are used if attribute A is less important than attribute B. This is a linear scale used for pairwise ratings and other ratings also

In making the comparisons, absolute data, as well as ordinal data such as rank, can be used. It is the essence of AHP where human judgments as well as underlying information can be used in performing evaluations.

Consider the example of selecting a job among the four alternatives as given in Table 1 and this constitutes level 3.

A1: University
A2: Research institute
A3: Company
A4: Own business

Selection of job is given at level 1. Level 2 comprises the criteria that contribute to selecting a job and it can be summarized as follows.

C1: Salary
C2: Security
C3: Workload
C4: Growth

Since there are four criteria under consideration, six pairwise judgments are to be made. Mathematically, if n criteria are under consideration, then $n(n-1)/2$ pairwise judgments are to be made. In this example, the following six pairwise decisions are to be made.

(C1/C2) =(7/1), (C1/C3)=(1/1), (C1/C4)=(7/1), (C2/C3)=(1/5), (C2/C4)=(2/1), (C3/C4)=(5/1)

Once the upper triangular matrix is constructed, the remaining lower triangle elements can be calculated by taking the reciprocal of the corresponding element and such matrix is mathematically called reciprocal matrix.

$$\left(Cj \, / \, Ci\right) = \frac{1}{(Ci \, / \, Cj)} \tag{1}$$

In general, a reciprocal pairwise comparison matrix can be constructed as in Fig. 3, and specifically for the above example, the reciprocal pairwise comparison matrix can be found in Fig. 4.

Figure 3. Generic reciprocal pairwise comparison matrix

	C1	C2	C3	C4
C1	1	C1/C2	C1/C3	C1/C4
C2	C2/C1	1	C2/C3	C2/C3
C3	C3/C1	C3/C2	1	C3/C4
C4	C4/C1	C4/C2	C4/C3	1

Figure 4. Reciprocal pairwise comparison matrix for different criteria in the example of job selection

	A	B	C	D	E	F
1			C1	C2	C3	C4
2	=1/D2	C1	1.00	7.00	1.00	7.00
3		C2	0.14	1.00	0.20	2.00
4	=1/E2	C3	1.00	5.00	1.00	5.00
5		C4	0.14	0.50	0.20	1.00
6	=1/F2					
7						
8			=1/F3			

Similarly, for the car selection problem, a pairwise comparison between the criteria of selecting the car namely safety, fuel economy, number of passengers, and initial cost can be done. However, the construction of the pairwise comparison matrix for the car selection problem was not included here as the logical progression of one example (i.e., job selection example) is required to be illustrated for the convenience of the reader.

Against each criterion C1-Salary, C2-Security, C3-Workload, and C4-Growth, a pairwise comparison of alternatives related to the job selection example namely A1-University, A2-Research institute, A3-Company, and A4-Own business has been made and the reciprocal pairwise comparison matrices are constructed similarly. Such constructed matrices are given in Fig.5.

Figure 5. Reciprocal pairwise comparison matrices of alternatives for each criterion

Salary	A1	A2	A3	A4		Security	A1	A2	A3	A4
A1	1.00	0.33	0.20	0.14		A1	1.00	7.00	3.00	7.00
A2	3.00	1.00	0.50	0.20		A2	0.14	1.00	0.50	1.00
A3	5.00	2.00	1.00	0.33		A3	0.33	2.00	1.00	2.00
A4	7.00	5.00	3.00	1.00		A4	0.14	1.00	0.50	1.00

Workload	A1	A2	A3	A4		Growth	A1	A2	A3	A4
A1	1.00	5.00	2.00	1.00		A1	1.00	1.00	0.33	0.20
A2	0.20	1.00	0.25	0.14		A2	1.00	1.00	0.33	0.25
A3	0.50	4.00	1.00	0.50		A3	3.00	3.00	1.00	0.50
A4	1.00	7.00	2.00	1.00		A4	5.00	4.00	2.00	1.00

Step 3: Synthesize Judgments to Derive the Overall Scale Rating for Each Alternative

In step 2, AHP converts the pairwise comparison into numerical values of the reciprocal pairwise comparison matrix that can be processed in step 3 to derive a numerical weight or priority deserved for each branch of the hierarchical structure (arrows indicating branching). Therefore, AHP allows contradicting and often incomparable elements to be compared to one another in a rational and consistent way.

The corresponding normalized reciprocal pairwise comparison matrix can be calculated by dividing each element in the column by the respective column sums. The weights for each criterion can be calculated by taking the arithmetic mean of each row of the normalized reciprocal pairwise comparison matrix.

For the given example on job selection, weights for four criteria, C1-Salary, C2-Security, C3-Workload, and C4-Growth can be calculated in the following way using Microsoft excel and the necessary formulae are illustrated.

Figure 6. Calculation of weight vector for criteria

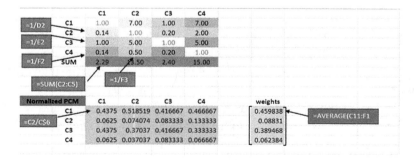

Similarly, the relative contribution among four jobs on the four criteria is computed as follows.

Figure 7. Calculation of weight vector of alternative jobs under salary and workload criteria

Salary	A1	A2	A3	A4
A1	1.00	0.33	0.20	0.14
A2	3.00	1.00	0.50	0.20
A3	5.00	2.00	1.00	0.33
A4	7.00	5.00	3.00	1.00
SUM	16.00	8.33	4.70	1.67

Norm_Sal	A1	A2	A3	A4	Weights	C1
A1	0.0625	0.039616	0.042553	0.083832	0.057125	
A2	0.1875	0.120048	0.106383	0.11976	0.133423	
A3	0.3125	0.240096	0.212766	0.197605	0.240742	
A4	0.4375	0.60024	0.638298	0.598802	0.56871	

Workload	A1	A2	A3	A4
A1	1.00	5.00	2.00	1.00
A2	0.20	1.00	0.25	0.14
A3	0.50	4.00	1.00	0.50
A4	1.00	7.00	2.00	1.00
SUM	2.70	17.00	5.25	2.64

Norm_WL	A1	A2	A3	A4	Weights	C3
A1	0.37037	0.294118	0.380952	0.378788	0.356057	
A2	0.074074	0.058824	0.047619	0.05303	0.058387	
A3	0.185185	0.235294	0.190476	0.189394	0.200087	
A4	0.37037	0.411765	0.380952	0.378788	0.385469	

The relative contribution matrix of all alternatives (four jobs: A1-University, A2-Research institute, A3-Company, and A4-Own business) with respect to four criteria (C1-Salary, C2- Security, C3- Workload, and C4-Growth) can be constructed by taking alternatives in rows and criteria in columns. The entries of the matrix could be filled with the weight vectors of each criterion as columns under the corresponding criteria. The derived contribution matrix of four jobs (alternatives) and weights for each criterion as the last column prior to nomenclature is given in Fig. 9.

The AHP generates weights on a relative ratio scale. The measurements of a set of objects on a standard scale can be converted to a relative measurement scale through normalization. Because, for normalization, a separate set of numbers are used and thus destroys the linear relationship among them.

Figure 8. Calculation of weight vector of alternative jobs under job security and growth criteria

Security	A1	A2	A3	A4
A1	1.00	7.00	3.00	7.00
A2	0.14	1.00	0.50	1.00
A3	0.33	2.00	1.00	2.00
A4	0.14	1.00	0.50	1.00
SUM	1.61	11.00	5.00	11.00

Norm_Sec	A1	A2	A3	A4	Weights	C2
A1	0.620018	0.636364	0.6	0.636363636	0.623186	
A2	0.088574	0.090909	0.1	0.090909091	0.092598	
A3	0.204606	0.181818	0.2	0.181818182	0.192061	
A4	0.086802	0.090909	0.1	0.090909091	0.092155	

Growth	A1	A2	A3	A4
A1	1.00	1.00	0.33	0.20
A2	1.00	1.00	0.33	0.25
A3	3.00	3.00	1.00	0.50
A4	5.00	4.00	2.00	1.00
SUM	10.00	9.00	3.66	1.95

Norm_GRW	A1	A2	A3	A4	Weights	C4
A1	0.1	0.111111	0.090164	0.102564103	0.10096	
A2	0.1	0.111111	0.090164	0.128205128	0.10737	
A3	0.3	0.333333	0.273224	0.256410256	0.290742	
A4	0.5	0.444444	0.546448	0.512820513	0.500928	

Figure 9. Contribution matrix of four jobs

	C1	C2	C3	C4
A1	0.057125	0.623186	0.356057	0.10096
A2	0.133423	0.092598	0.058387	0.10737
A3	0.240742	0.192061	0.200087	0.290742
A4	0.56871	0.092155	0.385469	0.500928
Weights	0.459838	0.08831	0.389468	0.062384

A1	University	C1	Salary
A2	Research institute	C2	Security
A3	Company	C3	Workload
A4	Own business	C4	Growth

The calculated weights can be represented in the hierarchical structure as in Fig. 10. Suppose that the goal is G to select a job and the weight of criteria C1 to goal G is 0.459838. Similarly, C2 to G= 0.08831, C3 to G= 0.389468 and C4 to G= 0.062384. Similarly, the relative weight of A1 to C1 is equal to 0.057125343 which is approximated to 0.06 when rounded to the second decimal place as in Fig. 10. Other corresponding weights are also given in Fig. 10.

Figure 10. Illustration of relative weights in a hierarchical structure in the selection of job

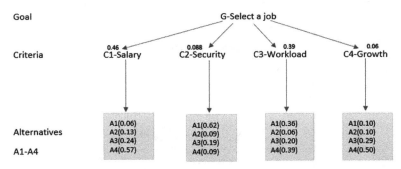

The final stage is to compute the contribution of each alternative (overall score of alternatives) to the overall goal of the selection of a job. The contribution of each alternative to the overall goal can be computed by aggregating the resulting weights computed in all vertical branches directed to each alternative from the goal. The resulting weight of a vertical branch can be calculated by multiplying the weights along the corresponding vertical branch. The details of the computation for the selection of a job could be found in Fig. 11.

Figure 11. Computation of contribution score of each alternative to the final goal

Alternative	Score for alternative
A1	0.226273
A2	0.098968
A3	0.223728
A4	0.45103

=SUMPRODUCT(B52:E52,B$56:E$56)

According to the alternative for each score, A4 (own business) has the highest value, then A1 (University). A3 (company) and A2 (research institute) have subsequent scores in descending order. So, the ranking of alternatives can be given as in Fig. 12.

Figure 12. Ranking of alternatives

Alternative	Score	Rank
A1	0.226273	2
A2	0.098968	4
A3	0.223728	3
A4	0.45103	1

Step 4: Evaluate and Check the Consistency of Judgments

The essence of AHP comprised human judgments and subsequent deductive calculations as proved mathematically by Saaty (1977). So, it is imperative to check the consistencies of the original preference rating made based on human judgment. So, the next step is to the analysis of the consistency of the reciprocal pairwise comparison matrix at each stage. This can be determined by the calculation of the consistency ratio.

The consistency ratio can be derived in two steps.

1. Calculate the consistency index (CI)

$$CI = \frac{\lambda_{max} - n}{n - 1}$$

Where λ_{max} is the maximum eigenvalue of the reciprocal pairwise comparison matrix, and n is the dimension of the matrix.

2. Calculate the consistency ratio (CR)

CR=CI/RI

Where RI is the random index. This can be found in Table 3

Table 3. Random Index (RI) (source: (Saaty, 1980))

N	1	2	3	4	5	6	7	8	9	10
Random Consistency Index (RI)	0	0	0.58	0.90	1.12	1.24	1.32	1.41	1.45	1.49

If the consistency ratio is less than 0.1, Saaty argued that the judgments are within the limit of consistency (Saaty, 1980). If CR>0.1, then the judgments are inconsistent. Any higher value for CR warrants re-examining and revising the pairwise comparison. For perfect consistency, the maximum eigenvalue equals n (Saaty, 1988) and thus consistency index becomes zero.

The matrix given in Fig. 3 should have the following condition to be satisfied for perfect consistency

$$(Ci \ / \ Ck) * \left(Ck \ / \ Cj\right) = \left(Ci \ / \ Cj\right) \tag{2}$$

The necessary condition for consistency is that the reciprocal pairwise comparison matrix should be a reciprocal matrix. However, this condition is not sufficient to hold the consistency, and hence additionally the consistency condition given in equation (2) should also be satisfied for perfect consistency (Saaty, 1988). A higher value (greater than 10%) for consistency ratio compels revisiting and adjusting the values of the reciprocal pairwise comparison matrix. In the construction of the pairwise comparison matrix, it must be a reciprocal matrix, and thus meeting the necessary condition for consistency is mandatory. However, a greater deviation from the sufficient condition should be observed, and adjust its value through pairwise comparison to make the human observations consistent.

At this stage, the consistency of each comparison matrix used for calculation is tested. For the calculation of the consistency ratio, the maximum eigenvalue needs to be calculated. Though Microsoft Excel has the facilities to calculate eigenvalues through the Goal Seek function and Solver (without using add-ins), the eigenvalue yield may vary with the starting point from which iterations are started. So obtaining the maximum eigenvalue is not guaranteed in the process. Hence, GNU Octave, an open source counterpart for MATLAB is used for calculating the eigenvalues so that the maximum could be selected conveniently. The consistency ratio is also calculated using GNU Octave as illustrated in Fig.13 for reciprocal pairwise comparison matrix for criteria.

Figure 13. Calculation of consistency ratio for pairwise comparison matrix for criteria

```
>> criteria=[1.00      7.00      1.00      7.00
0.14      1.00      0.20      2.00
1.00      5.00      1.00      5.00
0.14      0.50      0.20      1.00
]
criteria =

    1.0000    7.0000    1.0000    7.0000
    0.1400    1.0000    0.2000    2.0000
    1.0000    5.0000    1.0000    5.0000
    0.1400    0.5000    0.2000    1.0000

>> eig(criteria)
ans =

    4.0655 +         0i
   -0.0483 +         0i
   -0.0086 + 0.5525i
   -0.0086 - 0.5525i

>> max_lamda=ans(1)
max_lamda = 4.0655
>> n=4;
>> CI=(max_lamda-n)/(n-1)
CI = 0.021824
>> RI=0.90
RI = 0.9000
>> CR=CI/RI
CR = 0.024249
```

The consistency ratio yields 0.024249 which is less than 0.1 or 10%. It can be concluded that the reciprocal pairwise comparison matrix for criteria is consistent in making a human judgment in comparison. Similarly, the same set of calculations was repeated to obtain a consistency ratio for other all pairwise comparison matrices constructed for alternatives under different criteria and tabulated in Table 4.

Based on the above confidence ratios, there is no requirement of revisiting and adjusting none of the reciprocal pairwise matrices constructed.

Table 4. Consistency ratio of alternatives under different conditions

Criteria	Consistency Ratio (CR)
C1-Salary	0.024540 (< 0.1)
C2- Security	0.0034777 (< 0.1)
C3- Workload	0.0064177(< 0.1)
C4- Growth	0.0040212(< 0.1)

AHP in Nutshell

Analytical Hierarchy Process (AHP) can be considered one of the best ways for making complex decisions structured at different decision levels. However, the AHP should essentially follow one-way hierarchical relationship among decision levels in a structure. The inter-relationship and interdependencies among the hierarchical levels could not be dealt with AHP. An analytic network process (ANP) was developed to identify decision-making priorities of multiple variables without establishing a one-way hierarchical relationship among decision levels. However, detailing ANP is beyond the scope of this chapter.

Further, decisions in certain applications mimic stochastic nature and are incorporated with fuzzy behavior. Cater to such applications, a fuzzy AHP was evolved as a synthetic extension of the classical AHP method when the fuzziness of the decision makers is considered. The fuzzy analytic hierarchy process is the integration method of qualitative and quantitative methods.

AHP involves both subjective human judgments and objective evaluation. The subjective judgement is made in pairwise comparison and the consistency of making subjective judgment is measured through the consistency ratio. The consistency ration is kept within 10% to ensure yielding a reasonably good decision through the objective evaluation done by eigen value calculations.

REFERENCES

Saaty, R. W. (1987). The analytic hierarchy process—what it is and how it is used. *Mathematical Modelling, 9*(3–5), 161-176.

Saaty, T. L. (1977). A scaling method for priorities in hierarchical structures. *Journal of Mathematical Psychology, 15*(3), 234–281. doi:10.1016/0022-2496(77)90033-5

Saaty, T. L. (1980). *The Analytic Hierarchy Process*. McGraw-Hill.

Saaty, T. L. (1987). Rank generation, preservation, and reversal in the analytic hierarchy decision process. *Decision Sciences, 18*(2), 157–177. doi:10.1111/j.1540-5915.1987.tb01514.x

Saaty, T. L. (1988). What is the analytic hierarchy process? In *Mathematical models for decision support* (pp. 109–121). Springer. doi:10.1007/978-3-642-83555-1_5

Saaty, T. L. (1988). *What is the Analytic Hierarchy Process*. Springer. doi:10.1007/978-3-642-83555-1_5

Saaty, T. L. (2001). *Decision making for leaders: the analytic hierarchy process for decisions in a complex world*. RWS publications.

Salmerona, J. L., & Smarandacheb, F. (2010). Redesigning Decision Matrix Method with an indeterminacy-based inference process. Multispace and Multistructure. Neutrosophic Transdisciplinarity. *100 Collected Papers of Sciences, 4*, 151.

Chapter 12
Analytical Network Process in Decision Making

Thantirige Sanath Siroshana Jayawardena
Sri Lanka Institute of Information Technology, Sri Lanka

Chandimal Sanjeewa Jayawardena
Sri Lanka Institute of Information Technology, Sri Lanka

ABSTRACT

Analytic Network Process (ANP) is a generalized form of the Analytical Hierarchical Process (AHP). AHP is an objective theory of deriving the decision makings on absolute scale values starting from subjective relative measurements perhaps on tangible or intangible or a mix of both rated by the experts. A consistency measure of the relative ratings is verified with a consistency ratio to assure the ratings of the experts are consistent. The clustering of criteria/sub-criteria with inner and outer dependencies as well as feedback is taken into account in ANP. In ANP rather than a hierarchical process, a network structure is assumed and all nodes in the network are treated equally with interaction between nodes and grouping into clusters. A super-matrix is constructed, then normalized it to get weighted super matrix and raised it to a sufficient power to converge this into a unique eigen vector representing the final weights in limit super-matrix. Step by step iterations of ANP was demonstrated with a selection of car example.

INTRODUCTION TO THE DECISION-MAKING PROCESS

Decision-making is a process of selecting a single alternative from a set of alternatives in a systematic and logical way. The basic underlying step-by-step process involved

DOI: 10.4018/978-1-6684-6859-3.ch012

in decision-making is called a decision-making process. The Decision-making process can also be defined as a reasoning process that identifies and chooses one alternative among many based on the values, preferences, and beliefs of the decision-maker (Simon, 1977)

Decision-making is a criterion-based or criteria-based process and many decision models have been accommodated. However, the generic decision-making process can be explained with the following block diagram.

Figure 1. Generic block diagram of the decision-making process

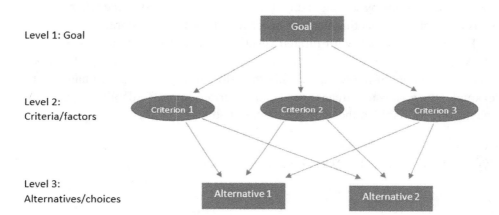

The block diagram given in Fig. 1 accepts the decision problem as an input and generates the best alternative as an output. However, in certain cases such as shortlisting of alternatives, instead of a single alternative (best alternative) a set of good suitable alternatives are generated.

Hierarchical Structure and Decision-Making Models

In general, people are poor at assimilating large quantities of information on problems and attempt to deal with cognitive overloading through the application of heuristics or meta-heuristics that simplifies the problem or reach a solution without getting into the details of the problem (use of meta-heuristic black-box models such as neural networks). Such a solution lacks analytical aspects and also leads to sub-optimal solutions.

As a remedial strategy and for a better understanding of a problem, the problem breaks down into smaller constituent parts and constructs a hierarchical model. Relevant and enough details are included at the different levels of the hierarchy and arranging the levels in the appropriate order are the basic steps in a hierarchical model. So the goal is at the top level and the criteria/sub-criteria are included in subsequent layers while alternatives are included at the bottom layer.

Decision-making models can be categorized as single-criterion decision-making models and multi-criteria decision-making models with and without interaction among decision criteria. Sometimes, sub-decision criteria may be presented in group form with interaction among groups.

In single decision-making models, the overall goal is dependent on a single criterion, as illustrated in Fig.2. The interaction among criteria is not applicable in this model and this is the simplest type of model in decision-making. Decision-making can be done by scoring methods for alternatives based on the criterion under consideration and selecting the best alternative based on the score.

For instance, a man with limited cash in hand wants to select a meal among many meals available at a shop and he is not interested in the taste, preference, or wholesome value of the food, but only the affordability with cash in hand. In this example, the goal is to purchase food and the criterion is affordability. Types of set menu-food available in the shop are the alternatives.

Figure 2. Single criterion Decision-making model

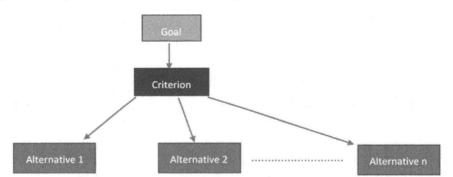

In multi-criteria decision-making models, the goal is depending on two or more than two criteria as in "the selection of job example" illustrated in the previous chapter titled AHP in decision making. If no interaction between the criteria exists, the decision maker can effectively apply Advance Hierarchical Process (AHP) with promising accuracy. However, interaction among criteria (feedback), hanging a set of criteria as a group (for instance, sub-criteria related to the main criterion), or interaction among a group of alternatives may cause it to deviate from its accuracy.

As a solution, a novel approach Analytical Network Process was invented by Prof Saaty in 1996 (Saaty, 1996).

Figure 3. Multi-Criteria Decision-making models with criteria interaction and hangs as a group

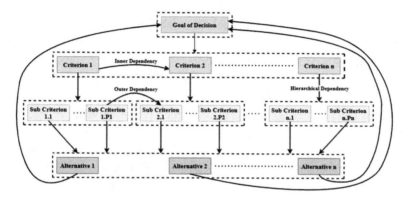

In Fig.3, a cluster is formed as the main criteria which span over multiple sub-criteria with hierarchical dependency. However, in addition to feedback from alternatives to criteria/sub-criteria or goal, intra-dependency within clusters termed inner dependencies and interdependency between clusters termed outer dependencies are taken into consideration in modeling.

On the contrary, Analytical Hierarchical Process (AHP) was discussed in the previous chapter (refer to AHP in decision making chapter for details) and considered only the un-directional hierarchical relationship among decision levels. Though AHP is deemed to be a rational tool/framework which can be dealt with complex multi-criteria decision-making (MCDM), it is less effective when applied to problems involving multi-layer criteria or hierarchy-dependence relationships (Saaty, 1980). This is due to the following underlying assumptions of AHP.

1.   Criteria do not affect alternatives
2.   Criteria do not depend on each other
3.   Alternatives do not depend on each other

ANALYTICAL NETWORK PROCESS (ANP)

AHP suffers from a serious limitation in assuming independence among the decision-making criteria as well as the absence of feedback between layers. In real-world decision-making problems especially in complex decisions, cross-dependency among criteria and alternatives as well as feedback is inevitable. This circumstance paved the way for the development of a much more generic framework by Prof. Saaty in 1996 (Saaty, 1996) and it is called Analytical Network Process (ANP). In ANP, the multilayered structure can view much as a network structure rather than a hierarchy when modeling due to interdependencies of higher-level elements from lower-level elements, and also of the elements within the same level. Hence the name was derived as Analytical Network Process. ANP also allows the inclusion of all the relevant criteria (tangible or intangible, objective or subjective, etc.) including clustered sub-criteria that can help in arriving at an optimal decision (Saaty, 2001).

Both ANP and AHP derive ratio scale priorities through pairwise comparison of elements on common property or criteria. In the ANP framework, the spirit of AHP is preserved and AHP becomes a subset of the process. The interactions among the elements of a system form a network structure via a super-matrix approach. The historical use of ANP found in a plethora of literature is inevitably a lengthy list, but the selected initial pure use of ANP can be given in Table 1. Subsequently, fuzzy logic was incorporated into ANP and much fuzzy ANP evolved.

Table 1. Initial use of ANP

Authors	Year	Usage	Citation
Lee and Kim	2000	To select an information system project	(Lee & Kim, 2000)
Cheng and Li	2004	To select a contractor	(Cheng & Li, 2004)
Poonikom et al.	2004	University selection decisions	(Poonikom et al., 2004)
Jharkharia and Shankar	2007	To select logistics service providers	(Jharkharia & Shankar, 2007)
Pi-Fang Hsu, Min-Hua Kuo	2011	To select best advertising agency	(Hsu & Kuo, 2011)
Hsu	2009	To select advertising spokespersons	(Hsu, 2009)
Hsu	2010	Selection of independent media agencies	(Hsu, 2010)
Coulter and Sarkis	2005	Media selction	(Coulter & Sarkis, 2005)

The process of ANP can be explained by the following four major steps.

Step 1: Model construction and problem structuring
Step 2: Pairwise comparison matrices and priority vectors
Step 3: Formation of super-matrix
Step 4: Selection of the best alternative

Step 1: Model Construction and Problem Structuring

In this step, the decision-making problem should be clearly stated and decomposed into a rational structure such as a network. In addition to hierarchical dependencies, all inter and intra-layer dependencies should be marked to convert the hierarchical structure into a fully-fledged network framework. This framework can be determined based on decision-maker opinion through brainstorming or other appropriate methods. The basic procedure under step 1 can be stated as follows

- First clearly define the decision-making problem
- Identify decision criteria and sub-criteria of relevance and deemed to be important
- Arrange the decision criteria and sub-criteria if available into clusters
- Identify interdependencies (feedback, inner and outer dependencies) among decision criteria and sub-criteria

The selection of a car described in "AHP in decision making chapter" is taken as an example. The selection of a car is the objective or goal of the decision-making problem. Fuel economy, safety, number of passengers, and initial cost are selected as control criteria of relevance and importance. These control criteria can further be decomposed to the lower levels, called sub-criteria. Table 2 shows the most important three sub-criteria under consideration for each criterion. The cars from the Toyota, Benz, and Mistubishi brands are selected as potential alternatives for selection (this is a selection of three brands based on the choice of the decision maker on situational grounds).

Table 2. Most relevant and important three sub-criteria for each criterion

Fuel Economy	Safety	Number of Passengers	Initial Cost
Injector technology	No. of airbags	Car size	Technology used
Engine capacity	ABS	Number of doors	Brand name
Road condition	Road grip/hold	Maximum load	Features

In this example, the interdependencies between the criteria exist. For instance, safety depends on the number of airbags used, the availability of the Antilock Brake System (ABS), and the deployment of road grip technology. All features and technologies used for safety in turn, affect the initial cost. So inner dependency exists between criteria safety and initial cost.

The number of passengers determines the size of the car and it is commensurate with the maximum load in turn depends on the engine capacity which indirectly affects the fuel economy. Fuel economy directly depends on safety features such as road grip technology. Similarly fuel economy depends on the technology used and it affects the initial cost.

In addition to interdependencies among criteria, there exist sub-criteria connected to each criterion and among sub-criteria also interdependencies do exist. Further, the brand name also plays a psychological effect on the selection of the car. For instance, the Benz brand is well known for safety and comfort.

The inner and outer dependencies with feedback constitute a network structure, about which decision-making could be done with ANP. This network is subjective as it can be expanded or reduced based on the importance of criteria as well as the options interested to the decision maker and also it may vary according to the situation for the same decision maker. Each variable can be measured with its quantifiable directly attributed characteristics or using a standard defined scale, but we do not intend to discuss the operationalization details of research here.

Figure 4. A network model in the selection of a car

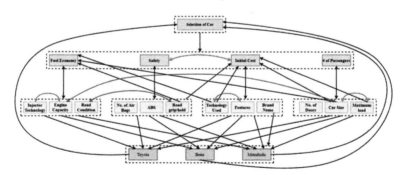

Step 2: Pairwise Comparison Matrices and Priority Vectors

Contrary to AHP described in the previous chapter where hierarchical connection spans from goal to control criteria, then to sub-criteria down to alternatives, ANP has control criteria, sub-criteria, and alternatives which are arranged in equally treated nodes and such nodes can be grouped into clusters. The control criteria to sub-criteria in ANP nodes might be grouped in clusters. For instance, the control criteria named fuel economy in the example depends on the sub-criteria injector technology, engine capacity, as well as road condition and such sub-criteria hang as a cluster.

In ANP each node might be compared to any other node if there is a relationship exists between them. In other words, the ranking of alternatives not only depends on the weight of criteria to the goal but also on the given alternatives as well as other criteria can influence the ranking of criteria. In the example taken for illustration, each control criterion has an influence on the goal (i.e. selection of a car), and specifically, the control criterion – the initial cost depends on other control criterion safety as well as the alternatives namely brands of the car.

In order to create an unweighted super-matrix that is required in step 3, the pairwise comparison is to be carried out at node level and cluster level in order to determine the local priorities of one node to a set of other nodes, as well as cluster priorities. In pairwise comparison, Saaty's fundamental scale of absolute numbers (Saaty, 2008) is used in order to make the comparison matrix a reciprocal matrix. (refer to the previous chapter on AHP in decision making). In the construction of a reciprocal matrix, the reciprocal value is assigned to the inverse comparison. i.e. a_{ij} $=1 / a_{ij}$ where a_{ij} denotes the importance of the ith element of the matrix as compared to the jth element).

As the reciprocal matrix of pairwise comparison is generated by the division of scale values, it can be proved that the following relationship exists (Hsu & Kuo, 2011).

$$Aw = \lambda_{max} w \tag{1}$$

Where A denotes the matrix of pair-wise comparison, w represents the eigenvector, and λ_{max} is the largest eigenvalue of matrix A. In case, the perfect consistency of the comparison matrix A is followed, it can be proved that the value of λ_{max} is equal to n.

If matrix A is known, λ_{max} can be calculated and the weighting factor w in the application can be determined by obtaining the solution to X in the following equation and normalizing it.

$$\left(A - \lambda_{max} I\right) X = 0 \tag{2}$$

So w can be given by

$$w = X / \sum x_i \tag{3}$$

The consistency index, CI is defined by Saaty (Saaty, 1980) as

$$CI = \frac{\left(\lambda_{max} - n\right)}{\left(n - 1\right)} \tag{4}$$

Where n is the size of the matrix A.

The consistency ratio is the compensated consistency index based on the size of the matric and it is calculated by taking the ratio of consistency index, CI to random index RI (Saaty, 1980).

$$CR = CI / RI \tag{4}$$

Refer to Table 3 for the random index.

Table 3. Random Index (RI) (source: (Saaty, 1980))

N	1	2	3	4	5	6	7	8	9	10
Random Consistency index (RI)	0	0	0.58	0.90	1.12	1.24	1.32	1.41	1.45	1.49

If the consistency ratio is less than 0.1, Saaty argued that the judgments are within the limit of consistency (Saaty, 1980). If CR>0.1, then the judgments are inconsistent and solicited to revise the comparison matrix until CR < 0.1.

The pairwise comparison between the control criteria has been made and assigned relative scores by an individual who is interested in making a personal decision for him for illustration purposes.

However, this decision is made for a company/organization, the average score of the pairwise comparison comparisons made by individuals who are involved in strategic decision-making should be used instead of an individual score to get a collective view in decision-making. In the calculation of eigenvector and eigenvalues as of equations (2) and (1) respectively, Octave software is used subsequently. Alternatively, the arithmetic means approach can also be utilized as explained in the previous chapter named AHP. The consistency ratio is calculated using equations (3) and (4) and checked whether it is less than the benchmark value of 0.1 to make sure that the comparison made by the person is consistent enough to proceed with the decision-making. The same procedure is followed for other pairwise comparisons required to generate the super-matrix. The results of pairwise comparison matrices at different levels and consistency for each hierarchical level are given in Table 4 and Table 5

Table 4. Pairwise comparison matrix for control criteria at level 2

Criteria	C1	C2	C3	C4	Eigenvector
Fuel Economy (C1)	1	5	7	3	0.5899
Safety (C2)	0.20	1	1.5	1	0.1374
Initial cost (C3)	0.142857	0.666667	1	0.666667	0.0929
No. of passengers (C4)	0.5	1	1.5	1	0.1797

λ_{max} =4.1814, CI=0.0600467, CR=0.067185 < 0.1

Table 5a. Pairwise comparison matrix for sub-criteria at level 3

Fuel Economy (C1)	S1	S2	S3	Eigenvector
Injector technology (S1)	1	1/5	1/3	0.1095
Engine capacity (S2)	5	1	2	0.5816
Road condition (S3)	3	1/2	1	0.3090

λ_{max} =3.0037, CI=0.00185, CR=0.00319 < 0.1

Table 5b. Pairwise comparison matrix for sub-criteria at level 3

Safety (C2)	S4	S5	S6	Eigenvector
No. of airbags (S4)	1	1/7	1/3	0.087946
ABS (S5)	7	1	3	0.669417
Road grip/hold (S6)	3	1/3	1	0.242637

λ_{max} =3.007, CI=0.0035, CR=0.006034 < 0.1

189

Table 5c. Pairwise comparison matrix for sub-criteria at level 3

Initial Cost (C3)	S7	S8	S9	Eigenvector
Technology used (S7)	1	2	7	0.615253
Features (S8)	1/2	1	3	0.292219
Brand name(S9)	1/7	1/3	1	0.092528
λ_{max} =3.0026, CI=0.0013, CR=0.002241 < 0.1				

Table 5d. Pairwise comparison matrix for sub-criteria at level 3

No. of Passengers (C4)	S10	S11	S12	Eigenvector
No. of doors (S10)	1	2	2	0.4934
Car size (S11)	1/2	1	2	0.3108
Maximum load (S12)	1/2	1/2	1	0.1958
λ_{max} =3.0536, CI=0.0268, CR=0.046207 < 0.1				

The next step is to establish the interdependencies between the second-level control criteria and the third-level sub-criteria. A pairwise comparison is made to determine interdependency weights between criteria and sub-criteria are made and it is given in table 6.

Table 6a. Pairwise comparison matrix for interdependent weights between control criteria

Fuel Economy (C1)	C2	C3	C4	Eigenvector
Safety (C2)	1	1/7	2	0.131221
Initial cost (C3)	7	1	9	0.792757
No. of passengers (C4)	1/2	1/9	1	0.076021
λ_{max} =3.0217, CI=0.01085, CR=0.018707 < 0.1				

Table 6b. Pairwise comparison matrix for interdependent weights between control criteria

Safety (C2)	C1	C3	C4	Eigenvector
Fuel Economy (C1)	1	3	2	0.5396
Initial cost (C3)	1/3	1	1/2	0.1634
No. of passengers (C4)	1/2	2	1	0.2970
λ_{max} =3.0092, CI=0.0046, CR=0.007931 < 0.1				

Table 6c. Pairwise comparison matrix for interdependent weights between control criteria

Initial Cost (C3)	C1	C2	C4	Eigenvector
Fuel Economy (C1)	1	7	3	0.6817
Safety (C2)	1/7	1	1/2	0.1025
No. of passengers (C4)	1/3	2	1	0.2158
λ_{max} =3.0026, CI=0.0013, CR=0.002241 < 0.1				

Table 6d. Pairwise comparison matrix for interdependent weights between control criteria

No. of Passengers (C4)	C1	C2	C3	Eigenvector
Fuel Economy (C1)	1	3	5	0.6483
Safety (C2)	1/3	1	2	0.2297
Initial cost (C3)	1/5	1/2	1	0.1220
λ_{max} =3.0037, CI=0.00185, CR=0.00319 < 0.1				

   With respect to a particular sub-criterion, a pairwise comparison is made between the remaining sub-criteria and consistency check is carried out by calculating the consistency ratio and verified that it is below 0.1. Then normalized eigenvector is calculated to this particular sub-criterion and tabulated under corresponding row and column with zero entries as the diagonal elements. Table 7 is constructed according to the procedure described above and it gives the interdependence matrix of sub-criteria which lists the interdependent weights between sub-criteria.

Table 7. Interdependence matrix of sub-criteria

Between sub criteria	S1	S2	S3	S4	S5	S6	S7	S8	S9	S10	S11	S12
Injector technology (S1)	0.0000	0.0205	0.0000	0.0790	0.0600	0.1154	0.0006	0.0000	0.0005	0.1623	0.0395	0.0820
Engine capacity (S2)	0.1463	0.0000	0.0000	0.0566	0.2087	0.0363	0.0000	0.0000	0.1779	0.0411	0.2199	0.0104
Road condition (S3)	0.0000	0.0000	0.0000	0.0000	0.0000	0.2101	0.1167	0.0000	0.1958	0.2042	0.1289	0.1665
No. of airbags (S4)	0.0962	0.0912	0.0000	0.0000	0.0130	0.0963	0.1210	0.0857	0.1422	0.1515	0.0627	0.0674
ABS (S5)	0.1907	0.1351	0.0000	0.0078	0.0000	0.1198	0.0667	0.1562	0.0405	0.0512	0.1030	0.0557
Road grip/hold (S6)	0.1709	0.0082	0.3753	0.1530	0.1922	0.0000	0.1915	0.2665	0.0355	0.0157	0.0314	0.0557
Technology used (S7)	0.2214	0.0000	0.1058	0.1405	0.0776	0.1503	0.0000	0.2833	0.1431	0.0737	0.0157	0.0444
Features (S8)	0.0000	0.0000	0.0473	0.0790	0.1676	0.1752	0.2332	0.0000	0.1607	0.0000	0.0000	0.0850
Brand name(S9)	0.0005	0.1652	0.0944	0.1912	0.0459	0.0288	0.1509	0.2083	0.0000	0.1170	0.0653	0.0854
No. of doors (S10)	0.0081	0.0663	0.0000	0.1625	0.0556	0.0109	0.0719	0.0000	0.0939	0.0000	0.0749	0.1179
Car size (S11)	0.0572	0.3724	0.2057	0.0787	0.1269	0.0292	0.0136	0.0000	0.0038	0.0803	0.0000	0.3146
Maximum load (S12)	0.1087	0.1410	0.1715	0.0518	0.0526	0.0276	0.0338	0.0000	0.0061	0.1030	0.2587	0.0000

The pairwise comparison was done for three alternatives namely Toyota, Benz and Mitsubishi with respect to each sub criteria and results were tabulated in Table 8.

This completes all the pairwise comparisons required to form the unweighted super-matrix. The eigenvectors calculated from pairwise comparison matrices are used in columns in the formation of unweighted super-matrix and the color code used may be helpful in the identification of corresponding eigenvectors.

Table 8. Pairwise comparison among alternatives with respect to each sub criterion

Injector technology -S1	A1	A2	A3	E-vector	
Toyota (A1)	1	5	2	0.5949	
Benz (A2)	0.2	1	0.5	0.1285	
Mitsubishi (A3)	0.5	2	1	0.2766	
				CR=	0.0047

Engine capacity-S2	A1	A2	A3	E-vector	
Toyota (A1)	1	0.25	1	0.1750	
Benz (A2)	4	1	3	0.6332	
Mitsubishi (A3)	1	0.33	1	0.1918	
				CR=	0.0047

Road condition-S3	A1	A2	A3	E-vector	
Toyota (A1)	1	0.14286	2	0.1429	
Benz (A2)	7	1	7	0.7671	
Mitsubishi (A3)	0.5	0.14286	1	0.0900	
				CR=	0.0462

# air bags-S4	A1	A2	A3	E-vector	
Toyota (A1)	1	0.5	3	0.3092	
Benz (A2)	2	1	5	0.5813	
Mitsubishi (A3)	0.33333	0.2	1	0.1096	
				CR=	0.0032

ABS-S5	A1	A2	A3	E-vector	
Toyota (A1)	1	0.33333	2	0.2299	
Benz (A2)	3	1	5	0.6479	
Mitsubishi (A3)	0.5	0.2	1	0.1222	
				CR=	0.0032

Brand name -S9	A1	A2	A3	E-vector	
Toyota (A1)	1	0.11111	0.33333	0.0769	
Benz (A2)	9	1	3	0.6923	
Mitsubishi (A3)	3	0.33333	1	0.2308	
				CR=	0.0000

No of doors-S10	A1	A2	A3	E-vector	
Toyota (A1)	1	0.5	1	0.2611	
Benz (A2)	2	1	1	0.4111	
Mitsubishi (A3)	1	1	1	0.3278	
				CR=	0.0462

Car size -S11	A1	A2	A3	E-vector	
Toyota (A1)	1	0.5	1	0.2500	
Benz (A2)	2	1	2	0.5000	
Mitsubishi (A3)	1	0.5	1	0.2500	
				CR=	0.0000

Maximum load-S12	A1	A2	A3	E-vector	
Toyota (A1)	1	0.5	1	0.2500	
Benz (A2)	2	1	2	0.5000	
Mitsubishi (A3)	1	0.5	1	0.2500	
				CR=	0.0000

Road grip-S6	A1	A2	A3	E-vector	
Toyota (A1)	1	0.33333	2	0.2160	
Benz (A2)	3	1	7	0.6814	
Mitsubishi (A3)	0.5	0.14286	1	0.1026	
				CR=	0.0022

Technology used-S7	A1	A2	A3	E-vector	
Toyota (A1)	1	0.2	2	0.1676	
Benz (A2)	5	1	7	0.7380	
Mitsubishi (A3)	0.5	0.14286	1	0.0944	
				CR=	0.0122

Features-S8	A1	A2	A3	E-vector	
Toyota (A1)	1	0.33333	1	0.2000	
Benz (A2)	3	1	3	0.6000	
Mitsubishi (A3)	1	0.33333	1	0.2000	
				CR=	0.0000

Step 3: Formation of Super-Matrix

The network of the ANP can be represented as a matrix that is composed of listing all nodes horizontally and vertically. So it becomes essentially a square matrix and it is called a super-matrix. Super-matrix resolves the interdependencies (inner dependencies- interaction within clusters and outer dependencies-interaction between clusters) between the nodes of the network.

In AHP, the local priorities are derived from the Eigenvector of the comparison matrix, and these priorities are then arranged as column vectors in the super-matrix. After all, comparisons are incorporated into the super-matrix, an "Unweighted Super Matrix" (generally referred to as super-matrix) could be obtained.

Each non-zero element of the matrix represents the connection from the node in the column header to another node with a row header and the number represents the weight between the nodes. In other words, an unweighted super-matrix is a partitioned square matrix in which each criterion comprises the vectors determined from the pairwise comparison covering all nodes in the network. Further super-matrix includes the interaction within clusters namely intra-cluster inner dependencies.

Step 4: Selection of the Best Alternative

Then the matrix is normalized such that sum of all columns scaled to one and it is called weighted super-matrix. The weighted super-matrix is transformed the values in unweighted super-matrix into a set of stochastic values. When the column stochastic super-matrix is then raised to a sufficiently large power, convergence of the matrix occurs (Saaty, 1996),(Meade & Sarkis, 1998) and it is called the final limit matrix.

Table 9 gives the unweighted super matrix and weighted super matrix formed such that column sums are scaled to 1 is given in Table 10.

Table 9. Unweighted super matrix

| | Goal: Select a car | Criteria | | | | Sub-criteria | | | | | | | | | | | | Alternatives | | |
		C1	C2	C3	C4	S1	S2	S3	S4	S5	S6	S7	S8	S9	S10	S11	S12	A1	A2	A3
Goal: Select a car	0	0	0	0	0	0	0	0	0	0	0	0	0	0	0	0	0	0	0	0
Fuel Economy (C1)	0.5299	0	0.5396	0.6817	0.6483	0	0	0	0	0	0	0	0	0	0	0	0	0	0	0
Safety (C2)	0.1374	0.531221	0	0.1025	0.2297	0	0	0	0	0	0	0	0	0	0	0	0	0	0	0
Initial cost (C3)	0.0929	0.792767	0.1634	0	0.122	0	0	0	0	0	0	0	0	0	0	0	0	0	0	0
No. of passengers (C4)	0.1797	0.076021	0.297	0.2158	0	0	0	0	0	0	0	0	0	0	0	0	0	0	0	0
Injector technology (S1)	0	0.1095	0	0	0	0.0000	0.0025	0.0000	0.0790	0.0600	0.1154	0.0006	0.0000	0.0005	0.1621	0.0595	0.0820	0	0	0
Engine capacity (S2)	0	0.5816	0	0	0	0.1463	0.0000	0.0000	0.0566	0.2087	0.0363	0.0000	0.0000	0.1779	0.0411	0.2199	0.0104	0	0	0
Road condition (S3)	0	0.309	0	0	0	0.0000	0.0000	0.0000	0.0000	0.0000	0.2101	0.1167	0.0000	0.1958	0.2042	0.1289	0.1605	0	0	0
No. of airbags (S4)	0	0	0.087946	0	0	0.0962	0.0912	0.0000	0.0000	0.0130	0.0963	0.1210	0.0857	0.1422	0.1515	0.0627	0.0674	0	0	0
ABS (S5)	0	0	0.669417	0	0	0.1907	0.1351	0.0000	0.0078	0.0000	0.1198	0.0667	0.1562	0.0405	0.0512	0.1030	0.0557	0	0	0
Road grip/hold (S6)	0	0	0.242637	0	0	0.1709	0.0082	0.3753	0.1530	0.3922	0.0000	0.1915	0.2665	0.0157	0.0314	0.0557	0	0	0	0
Technology used (S7)	0	0	0	0.615253	0	0.2214	0.0000	0.1058	0.1405	0.0776	0.1503	0.0000	0.2833	0.1431	0.0737	0.0157	0.0444	0	0	0
Features (S8)	0	0	0	0.292258	0	0.0000	0.0000	0.0473	0.0790	0.1676	0.1752	0.2332	0.0000	0.1607	0.0000	0.0000	0.0000	0	0	0
Brand name (S9)	0	0	0	0.091528	0	0.0005	0.1652	0.0944	0.1912	0.0459	0.0258	0.1509	0.2083	0.0000	0.1170	0.0663	0.0854	0	0	0
No of doors (S10)	0	0	0	0	0.4934	0.0081	0.0663	0.0000	0.1625	0.2056	0.0109	0.0719	0.0000	0.0989	0.0000	0.0749	0.1179	0	0	0
Car size (S11)	0	0	0	0	0.3108	0.0572	0.3724	0.2057	0.8787	0.1269	0.0292	0.0136	0.0000	0.0038	0.0803	0.0000	0.3146	0	0	0
Maximum load (S12)	0	0	0	0	0.1958	0.1087	0.1410	0.1715	0.0518	0.0526	0.0338	0.0000	0.0061	0.1090	0.2587	0.0000	0	0	0	0
Toyota (A1)	0	0	0	0	0	0.3949	0.1750	0.1429	0.3092	0.2299	0.2180	0.1676	0.2000	0.0769	0.2611	0.2500	0.2500	1	0	0
Benz (A2)	0	0	0	0	0	0.1285	0.6332	0.7671	0.5813	0.0479	0.6614	0.7380	0.6000	0.6923	0.4113	0.5000	0.5000	0	1	0
Mitsubishi (A3)	0	0	0	0	0	0.2766	0.1918	0.0900	0.1096	0.1222	0.1026	0.0944	0.2000	0.2308	0.3278	0.2500	0.2500	0	0	1

Table 10. Weighted super matrix

			Criteria						Sub-criteria										Alternatives		
		Goal: Select a car	C1	C2	C3	C4	S1	S2	S3	S4	S5	S6	S7	S8	S9	S10	S11	S12	A1	A2	A3
	Goal: Select a car	0.0000	0.0000	0.0000	0.0000	0.0000	0.0000	0.0000	0.0000	0.0000	0.0000	0.0000	0.0000	0.0000	0.0000	0.0000	0.0000	0.0000	0.0000	0.0000	0.0000
Criteria	Fuel Economy (C1)	0.5900	0.0000	0.2696	0.3409	0.3242	0.0000	0.0000	0.0000	0.0000	0.0000	0.0000	0.0000	0.0000	0.0000	0.0000	0.0000	0.0000	0.0000	0.0000	0.0000
	Safety (C2)	0.1374	0.0656	0.0000	0.0513	0.1149	0.0000	0.0000	0.0000	0.0000	0.0000	0.0000	0.0000	0.0000	0.0000	0.0000	0.0000	0.0000	0.0000	0.0000	0.0000
	Initial cost (C3)	0.0925	0.3964	0.0817	0.0000	0.0610	0.0000	0.0000	0.0000	0.0000	0.0000	0.0000	0.0000	0.0000	0.0000	0.0000	0.0000	0.0000	0.0000	0.0000	0.0000
	No. of passengers (C4)	0.1797	0.0380	0.1485	0.1079	0.0000	0.0000	0.0000	0.0000	0.0000	0.0000	0.0000	0.0000	0.0000	0.0000	0.0000	0.0000	0.0000	0.0000	0.0000	0.0000
	Injector technology (S1)	0.0000	0.0547	0.0000	0.0000	0.0000	0.0000	0.0102	0.0000	0.0995	0.0300	0.0577	0.0063	0.0000	0.0002	0.0812	0.0197	0.0410	0.0000	0.0000	0.0000
Sub-criteria	Engine capacity (S2)	0.0000	0.2808	0.0000	0.0000	0.0000	0.0731	0.0000	0.0000	0.0283	0.1043	0.0182	0.0000	0.0000	0.0890	0.0205	0.1100	0.0052	0.0000	0.0000	0.0000
	Road condition (S3)	0.0000	0.1345	0.0000	0.0000	0.0000	0.0000	0.0000	0.0000	0.0000	0.1080	0.0584	0.0000	0.9979	0.1021	0.0644	0.0833	0.0000	0.0000	0.0000	0.0000
	No. of airbags (S4)	0.0000	0.0000	0.0440	0.0000	0.0000	0.0481	0.0456	0.0000	0.0000	0.0005	0.0482	0.0605	0.0428	0.0711	0.0757	0.0314	0.0337	0.0000	0.0000	0.0000
	ABS (S5)	0.0000	0.0000	0.3947	0.0000	0.0000	0.0953	0.0676	0.0000	0.0039	0.0000	0.0599	0.0934	0.0761	0.0202	0.0256	0.0313	0.0279	0.0000	0.0000	0.0000
	Road grip/hold (S6)	0.0000	0.0000	0.1213	0.0000	0.0000	0.0854	0.0041	0.1876	0.0765	0.0961	0.0000	0.0958	0.1333	0.0178	0.0078	0.0157	0.0279	0.0000	0.0000	0.0000
	Technology used (S7)	0.0000	0.0000	0.0000	0.3076	0.0000	0.1107	0.0000	0.0529	0.0702	0.0388	0.0751	0.0000	0.1417	0.6716	0.0968	0.0079	0.0222	0.0000	0.0000	0.0000
	Features (S8)	0.0000	0.0000	0.0000	0.1461	0.0000	0.0000	0.0000	0.0236	0.0895	0.0838	0.0876	0.1166	0.0000	0.0803	0.0000	0.0000	0.0000	0.0000	0.0000	0.0000
	Brand name (S9)	0.0000	0.0000	0.0000	0.0463	0.0000	0.0003	0.0826	0.0472	0.0956	0.0229	0.0144	0.0755	0.1042	0.0000	0.0585	0.0827	0.0427	0.0000	0.0000	0.0000
	No of doors (S10)	0.0000	0.0000	0.0000	0.0000	0.2467	0.0001	0.0532	0.0000	0.0813	0.0278	0.0054	0.0380	0.0000	0.0469	0.0000	0.0376	0.0590	0.0000	0.0000	0.0000
	Car size (S11)	0.0000	0.0000	0.0000	0.0000	0.1354	0.0289	0.1802	0.1028	0.0393	0.0634	0.0146	0.0068	0.0000	0.0019	0.0402	0.0000	0.1573	0.0000	0.0000	0.0000
	Maximum load (S12)	0.0000	0.0000	0.0000	0.0000	0.0979	0.0844	0.0705	0.0858	0.0289	0.0283	0.0188	0.0189	0.0000	0.0031	0.0515	0.1293	0.0000	0.0000	0.0000	0.0000
Alternatives	Toyota (A1)	0.0000	0.0000	0.0000	0.0000	0.0000	0.2574	0.0875	0.0715	0.1546	0.1345	0.1080	0.0838	0.1000	0.0383	0.1306	0.1250	0.1250	1.0000	0.0000	0.0000
	Benz (A2)	0.0000	0.0000	0.0000	0.0000	0.0000	0.0643	0.3166	0.3836	0.2908	0.3240	0.3407	0.3690	0.3000	0.3462	0.2056	0.2500	0.2500	0.0000	1.0000	0.0000
	Mitsubishi (A3)	0.0000	0.0000	0.0000	0.0000	0.0000	0.1383	0.0959	0.0450	0.0548	0.0611	0.0513	0.0472	0.1000	0.1154	0.1639	0.1250	0.1250	0.0000	0.0000	1.0000

When the weighted super matrix is raised to its sufficiently large power it converges, stabilized to certain set of non-zero values to attain a unique eigenvector in the alternative rows while other elements become zero and such matrix is called limit super matrix. The limit super matrix derived for the given example is given in Table 11.

Table 11. Limit super matrix

Limit super matrix		Goal: Select a car	C1	C2	C3	C4	S1	S2	S3	S4	S5	S6	S7	S8	S9	S10	S11	S12	A1	A2	A3
Criteria	Goal: Select a car	0.0000	0.0000	0.0000	0.0000	0.0000	0.0000	0.0000	0.0000	0.0000	0.0000	0.0000	0.0000	0.0000	0.0000	0.0000	0.0000	0.0000	0.0000	0.0000	0.0000
	Fuel Economy (C1)	0.0000	0.0000	0.0000	0.0000	0.0000	0.0000	0.0000	0.0000	0.0000	0.0000	0.0000	0.0000	0.0000	0.0000	0.0000	0.0000	0.0000	0.0000	0.0000	0.0000
	Safety (C2)	0.0000	0.0000	0.0000	0.0000	0.0000	0.0000	0.0000	0.0000	0.0000	0.0000	0.0000	0.0000	0.0000	0.0000	0.0000	0.0000	0.0000	0.0000	0.0000	0.0000
	Initial cost (C3)	0.0000	0.0000	0.0000	0.0000	0.0000	0.0000	0.0000	0.0000	0.0000	0.0000	0.0000	0.0000	0.0000	0.0000	0.0000	0.0000	0.0000	0.0000	0.0000	0.0000
	No. of passengers (C4)	0.0000	0.0000	0.0000	0.0000	0.0000	0.0000	0.0000	0.0000	0.0000	0.0000	0.0000	0.0000	0.0000	0.0000	0.0000	0.0000	0.0000	0.0000	0.0000	0.0000
Sub-criteria	Injector technology (S1)	0.0000	0.0000	0.0000	0.0000	0.0000	0.0000	0.0000	0.0000	0.0000	0.0000	0.0000	0.0000	0.0000	0.0000	0.0000	0.0000	0.0000	0.0000	0.0000	0.0000
	Engine capacity (S2)	0.0000	0.0000	0.0000	0.0000	0.0000	0.0000	0.0000	0.0000	0.0000	0.0000	0.0000	0.0000	0.0000	0.0000	0.0000	0.0000	0.0000	0.0000	0.0000	0.0000
	Road condition (S3)	0.0000	0.0000	0.0000	0.0000	0.0000	0.0000	0.0000	0.0000	0.0000	0.0000	0.0000	0.0000	0.0000	0.0000	0.0000	0.0000	0.0000	0.0000	0.0000	0.0000
	No. of airbags (S4)	0.0000	0.0000	0.0000	0.0000	0.0000	0.0000	0.0000	0.0000	0.0000	0.0000	0.0000	0.0000	0.0000	0.0000	0.0000	0.0000	0.0000	0.0000	0.0000	0.0000
	ABS (S5)	0.0000	0.0000	0.0000	0.0000	0.0000	0.0000	0.0000	0.0000	0.0000	0.0000	0.0000	0.0000	0.0000	0.0000	0.0000	0.0000	0.0000	0.0000	0.0000	0.0000
	Road grip/hold (S6)	0.0000	0.0000	0.0000	0.0000	0.0000	0.0000	0.0000	0.0000	0.0000	0.0000	0.0000	0.0000	0.0000	0.0000	0.0000	0.0000	0.0000	0.0000	0.0000	0.0000
	Technology used (S7)	0.0000	0.0000	0.0000	0.0000	0.0000	0.0000	0.0000	0.0000	0.0000	0.0000	0.0000	0.0000	0.0000	0.0000	0.0000	0.0000	0.0000	0.0000	0.0000	0.0000
	Features (S8)	0.0000	0.0000	0.0000	0.0000	0.0000	0.0000	0.0000	0.0000	0.0000	0.0000	0.0000	0.0000	0.0000	0.0000	0.0000	0.0000	0.0000	0.0000	0.0000	0.0000
	Brand name (S9)	0.0000	0.0000	0.0000	0.0000	0.0000	0.0000	0.0000	0.0000	0.0000	0.0000	0.0000	0.0000	0.0000	0.0000	0.0000	0.0000	0.0000	0.0000	0.0000	0.0000
	No of doors (S10)	0.0000	0.0000	0.0000	0.0000	0.0000	0.0000	0.0000	0.0000	0.0000	0.0000	0.0000	0.0000	0.0000	0.0000	0.0000	0.0000	0.0000	0.0000	0.0000	0.0000
	Car size (S11)	0.0000	0.0000	0.0000	0.0000	0.0000	0.0000	0.0000	0.0000	0.0000	0.0000	0.0000	0.0000	0.0000	0.0000	0.0000	0.0000	0.0000	0.0000	0.0000	0.0000
	Maximum load (S12)	0.0000	0.0000	0.0000	0.0000	0.0000	0.0000	0.0000	0.0000	0.0000	0.0000	0.0000	0.0000	0.0000	0.0000	0.0000	0.0000	0.0000	0.0000	0.0000	0.0000
Alternatives	Toyota (A1)	0.2155	0.212	0.2223	0.2022	0.2274	0.4073	0.2014	0.1748	0.2867	0.227	0.2223	0.1883	0.2008	0.1041	0.2541	0.2371	0.3416	1.0000	0.0000	0.0000
	Benz (A2)	0.6071	0.6141	0.6128	0.6328	0.5677	0.3728	0.6018	0.6682	0.585	0.6196	0.644	0.681	0.6242	0.6079	0.4567	0.5433	0.5338	0.0000	1.0000	0.0000
	Mitsubishi (A3)	0.1767	0.1735	0.1644	0.1648	0.203	0.2199	0.197	0.132	0.1498	0.1531	0.1335	0.1117	0.1755	0.1985	0.2022	0.2196	0.2196	0.0000	0.0000	1.0000

The limit matrix is column-stochastic, and represents the final eigenvector. The rankings of the three makes of the cars (Toyota, Benz and Mitsubishi are selected as alternatives) in selection of car can be given as Toyota (0.2125), Benz (0.6071) and Mitsubishi (0.1767). So the best selection would be the Benz car.

SPECIAL CIRCUMSTANCES AND POPULAR SOFTWARE USED FOR ANP

For instance, if a particular control criterion does not possess any sub-criteria, still ANP can be applied and the column vector of that criterion corresponding to sub-criteria rows becomes a zero vector in the super-matrix. Further, if many zero elements are in the super-matrix (if the super-matrix is a sparse matrix), it converges early to limit the super-matrix before raising to a significantly higher power (say less than ten).

The Octave software was used to calculate eigenvectors, eigenvalues, and raise the power of weighted super-matrix to calculate limit super-matrix for illustrative purposes. However, it may not be convenient for the user especially in the case of multiple responses to enter to take a collective decision. So software on ANP has been developed to use even for a novice researcher without going into the detailed calculations of ANP. Three such popular software named Super Decisions (www.superdecisions.com) Expert Choice (www.expertchoice.com) and Decision Lens (www.decisionlens.com) are available for convenient calculation of super-matrix and limit super matrix where pairwise comparison can be given as an input.

REFERENCES

Cheng, E. W. L., & Li, H. (2004). Contractor selection using the analytic network process. *Construction Management and Economics*, 22(10), 1021–1032. doi:10.1080/0144619042000202852

Coulter, K., & Sarkis, J. (2005). Development of a media selection model using the analytic network process. *International Journal of Advertising*, 24(2), 193–215. do i:10.1080/02650487.2005.11072914

Hsu, P. F. (2009). Evaluating advertising spokespersons via the ANP-GRA selection model. *Journal of Grey System*, 21(1), 35–48.

Hsu, P.F. (2010). Selection model based on ANP and GRA for independent media agencies. Quality & Quantity). doi:10.1007/s11135-010-9323-y

Hsu, P.-F., & Kuo, M.-H. (2011). Applying the ANP model for selecting the optimal full-service advertising agency. *International Journal of Operations Research*, 8(4), 48–58.

Hsu, P.-F., & Kuo, M.-H. (2011). Applying the ANP Model for Selecting the Optimal Full-service Advertising Agency. *International Journal of Operations Research*, *8*(4), 48–58.

Jharkharia, S., & Shankar, R. (2007). Selection of logistics service provider: An analytic network process (ANP) approach. *Omega*, *35*(3), 274–289. doi:10.1016/j.omega.2005.06.005

Lee, J. W., & Kim, S. H. (2000). Using analytic network process and goal programming for interdependent information system project selection. *Computers & Operations Research*, *27*(4), 367–382. doi:10.1016/S0305-0548(99)00057-X

Meade, L. M., & Sarkis, J. (1998). Strategic analysis of logistics and supply chain management systems using the analytic network process. *Transportation Research Part E, Logistics and Transportation Review*, *34*(3), 201–215. doi:10.1016/S1366-5545(98)00012-X

Poonikom, K., O' Brien, C., & Chansangavej, C. (2004). An application of the analytic network process (ANP) for university selection decisions. *Science Asia*, *30*(4), 317–326. doi:10.2306cienceasia1513-1874.2004.30.317

Saaty, T. L. (1980). *The Analytic Hierarchy Process*. McGraw-Hill, Inc.

Saaty, T. L. (1980). *The Analytic Hierarchy Process*. McGraw-Hill.

Saaty, T. L. (1996). *Decision Making with Dependence and Feedback: The Analytic Network Process*. RWS Publications.

Saaty, T. L. (2001). *Decision Making with Dependence and Feedback: the Analytic Network Process* (2nd ed.). RWS Publications.

Saaty, T. L. (2008). Decision making with the analytic hierarchy process. *International Journal of Services Sciences*, *1*(1), 83–98. doi:10.1504/IJSSCI.2008.017590

Simon, H. A. (1977). *The New Science of Management Decision*. Prentice-Hall.

Chapter 13
Estimating Latent Growth Curve Models:
An Introduction

K. A. S. Wickrama
ⓘ https://orcid.org/0000-0002-9239-1648
The University of Georgia, USA

ABSTRACT

Although LGC modeling is gaining popularity in some disciplines, it has not been widely employed in social-epidemiological studies. This paper presents an introduction to the latent growth curve (LGC) technique within a structural equation modelling (SEM) framework as a powerful tool to analyze change in individual attributes over time (e.g., behaviors, attitudes, beliefs, and health) and potential correlates of such changes. The rationale for LGC analysis and subsequent elaboration of this statistical approach are discussed. For illustrations, Mplus (version 8, Muthén & Muthén, 2012) software and depressive symptoms as the individual outcomes attribute are used. The limitations of traditional analytical methods are also addressed. Particularly, the chapter considers socio-contextual factors as correlates of change in the outcomes variable, and examines the dynamic systematic relationship with the socioeconomic factors (however, these correlates can also be factors other than social-context).

INTRODUCTION

Although LGC modeling is gaining popularity in some disciplines, it has not been widely employed in social-epidemiological studies. This paper presents an introduction to the latent growth curve (LGC) technique within a structural equation modelling

DOI: 10.4018/978-1-6684-6859-3.ch013

(SEM) framework as a powerful tool to analyze change in individual attributes over time (e.g., behaviors, attitudes, beliefs, and health) and potential correlates of such changes. The rationale for LGC analysis and subsequent elaboration of this statistical approach are discussed. For illustrations, Mplus (version 8, Muthén & Muthén, 2012) software and depressive symptoms as the individual outcomes attribute are used. The limitations of traditional analytical methods are also addressed. Particularly, the paper considers socio-contextual factors as correlates of change in the outcomes variable, and examines the dynamic systematic relationship with the socioeconomic factors (However, these correlates can also be factors other than social-context). It is assumed that reader of this chapter already has a basic understanding of structural equation modeling (SEM).

THE LIMITATIONS OF TRADITIONAL ANALYTICAL APPROACHES

Traditional analytical approaches often used in social behavioral research are insensitive to within-individual changes of individual attributes over time. In particular, regression methods, mean comparisons, and repeated measures Manova are not sensitive to within-individual changes over time and, consequently, entail several related limitations. First, the non-dynamic nature of traditional analytical approaches views an individual attribute (e.g., depressive symptoms) which will be used for illustrations in this paper) as a status rather than a process that unfolds over time. Second, when individual change follows a non-linear trajectory, regression methods are unlikely to reveal intricacies of such change. Moreover, 'Ignoring the continuous nature of change process, traditional methods prevent empirical researchers from entertaining a richer, broader spectrum of research questions, questions that deal with the nature of individual development' (Willet, 1988, p. 347). Moreover, this change process may be systematically associated with socio contexual and other developmental processes.

THE NEED TO INVESTIGATE DIFFERENT GROWTH PARAMETERS

Change entails different facets. Individual-specific growth parameters can capture different facets of change. These parameters include not only the intensity or severity (*level*) and but also the amount of growth or decline (*rate of change or slope*) in an outcome over time. Traditional methods are not sensitive enough to capture this difference and to distinguish the difference between these two courses of development, although these courses may have different sequelae and also different antecedents (Willet & Sawyer, 1994; Wickrama et al., 2016). For example, development of depressive disorder may not simply correspond to the severe end of a continuum of depressive symptoms. 'The causal structure for initiation, prolongation, and exacerbation (of prodromal build-up of symptoms) are not well understood' (Eaton et al., 1995). The lack of focus on within-individual changes could result in incomplete and/or potentially inaccurate conclusions concerning changes in psychosocial, behavioral or health attributes, but also their antecedents and sequelae (Wickrama et al., 2003; 2016). Since growth curve analysis explicitly estimates within-individual changes with multiple facets and their inter-individual variations and then examine potential correlates of change, it addresses most of the limitations of traditional analytical approaches.

Estimating Univariate Latent Growth Curve Models (LGCM)

The process of estimating the growth curves for each individual p (p = 1, 2 . . . n), is done by writing and then estimating equations linking the observed scores (DEP) at each time point in time (DEP1, DEP2, and DEP3.) to time (t1, t2, and t3). This includes two parameters, an intercept (level) $\pi0$ and a slope (rate of change) $\pi1$ as expressed in these equations. That is, conceptually, latent growth curve modeling is done by fitting a regression line (a growth curve) linking the outcome variable (e.g., measurements of depressive symptoms, DEP) to time t for each individual P (individual trajectory of DEP) as follows.

For time t $DEP_p = 1 * \pi0_p + t * \pi1_p + E$ (E=residual error)

Figure 1. Individual Trajectories of depressive symptoms, DEP for three individuals

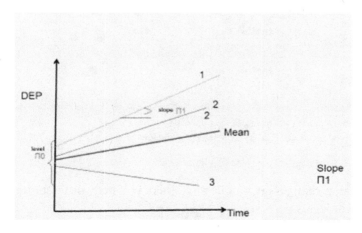

As depicted in Figure 1, similar regression equations can be written for three individuals (1, 2 and 3). It shows fitting regression lines for each person with growth parameters (change is systematically related to the passages of time).

Fitting regression lines for each person with growth parameters – Change is Systematically related to the passage of time

If the focus is within-individual change, for individual P, equations ror time point t1, t2 and t3 are as follows:

$$DEP1p = 1 * \pi 0p + t1 * \pi 1p + E11 \tag{1a}$$

$$DEP2p = 1 * \pi 0p + t2 * \pi 1p + E22 \tag{1b}$$

$$DEP3p = 1 * \pi 0p + t3 * \pi 1p + E33 \tag{1c}$$

In the above equations E11, E22, and E33 are the residuals at each point in time and are assumed to be normally distributed with zero means. These three regression equations (1a, 1b and 1c) for individual P correspond to a SEM model with two latent construct with observed multiple indicators/measurements are shown in Figure 2 (t1=0, t2=1 and t3=2).

Figure 2. Translating Individual trajectory into a Latent Growth Curve Model

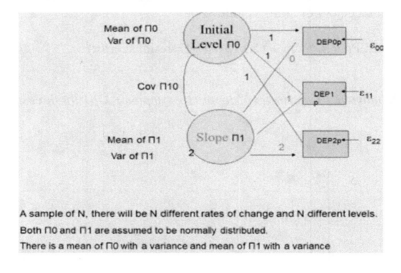

A sample of N, there will be N different rates of change and N different levels.
Both Π0 and Π1 are assumed to be normally distributed.
There is a mean of Π0 with a variance and mean of Π1 with a variance

Summarizing change – A sample of N, there will be N different rates of change and N different levels.

Both η_0 and η_1 are assumed to be normally distributed.

There is a mean of η_0 with a variance and mean of η_1 with a variance.

In the structural equation framework (figure 2), $\pi0$ and $\pi1$ can be considered as two latent variables measured by three observed indicators DEP1, DEP2, and DEP3. The coefficients of $\pi0$ in three equations (these are always 1) are equal to factor loadings of three indicators (measurements) for 'level' latent variable. The coefficients of $\pi1$ for three equations (t1, t2, and t3,) are equal to factor loadings of three measurements for 'rate of change' latent variables. If t1, t2, and t3 are 0, 1 and 2 respectively, change would be a linear increase across three time points and the level (intercept) is defined by measurement of DEP at first time point, the point at which factor loading is equal to 0. The individual growth parameters (the intercept/ level $\pi0$ and slope $\pi1$) can then be summarized to obtain an average intercept and average slope of depressive symptoms for all individuals. Mplus syntax for univariate growth curve with four time points is given in figure 3.

(If time intervals are not equal, appropriate factor loading should be given proportionate to unequal time intervals). Mplus syntax for the above growth curve with four time points is given in figure 3 (Y=DEP).

Figure 3. Mplus syntax for univariate growth curve with four time points

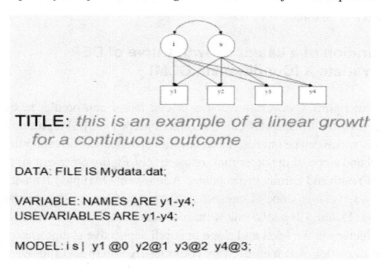

```
TITLE: this is an example of a linear growth
       for a continuous outcome

DATA: FILE IS Mydata.dat;

VARIABLE: NAMES ARE y1-y4;
USEVARIABLES ARE y1-y4;

MODEL: i s | y1 @0 y2@1 y3@2 y4@3;
```

An example of a linear growth model for a continuous outcome –

Variable names: $y^1 - y^4$; Usevariables are: $y^1 - y^4$

Model: i s | $y^1@^0$ $y^2@^1$ $y^3@^2$ $y^4@^3$

The form of change may not always be linear; it may be quadratic, or otherwise. Then appropriate loadings for slope (rate of change $\pi1$) would be different. For example, appropriate loadings for a quadratic term with four time points would be 0, 1, 4, and 9. Individual trajectories (level and rate of change) are expected to be different from individual to individual. That is, Although the trajectories for each individual vary in initial level and rate of change, these can be aggregated to create mean and variance values for the initial level and slope. A significant variance in a change parameter implies different rates of change among individuals in the sample. For a sample of n individuals, there will be as many as n different rates of change over time and n different levels of symptoms. Although each individual trajectory varies in level and rate of change, they can be aggregated so that, for the whole sample, there is an average level (mean of $\pi0$) with a variance, and an average rate of change (mean of $\pi1$), also with a variance. The mean and variance of the level parameter identify the overall average of the individual-specific levels and variability of levels (dispersion) across individuals. The mean for Slope $\pi1$ Level $\pi0$ are shown in figure 2. The goal is then to use theoretically driven covariates (X) to explain why some individuals have higher initial levels of depressive symptoms (intercepts) than others, and why some have greater rates of change (steeper slopes) in depressive symptoms .

An Illustration of a Latent Growth Curve of DEP With Covariate X (Conditional LGCM)

As shown in figure 4, covariate such as social factor can predict or explain the variabilities of growth parameters, the level and slope. $\beta01$ and $\beta11$ represent regression coefficients which can be interpreted ad one unit change in x corresponding changes in the level and slope of the outcomes, respectively. Figure 5 present an Illustration using Iowa Youth and Family Project data;. Adolescent Disrupted Transition (ADT) predicts the Level and slope of depressive symptoms Trajectories, unstandardized coefficients .25 and .12 (p <.05) show that one unit change in ADT results in .25 and .12 units changes in the level and slope in youth depressive symptoms trajectories. Disrupted transition was measured by counting five disrupted life events (school drop-out, early leaving home, early sexual activities, teenage pregnancy &early marriages).

Figure 4. Explaining and predicting growth parameters

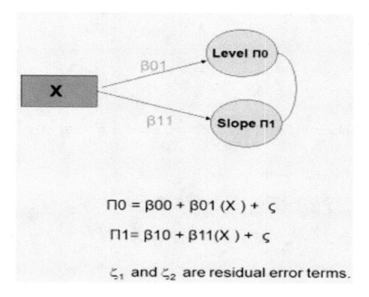

$$\Pi0 = \beta00 + \beta01\,(X\,) + \varsigma$$

$$\Pi1 = \beta10 + \beta11(X\,) + \varsigma$$

ς_1 and ς_2 are residual error terms.

Figure 5. An Illustration. Adolescent Disrupted Transition predicts the Level and slope of depressive symptoms Trajectories

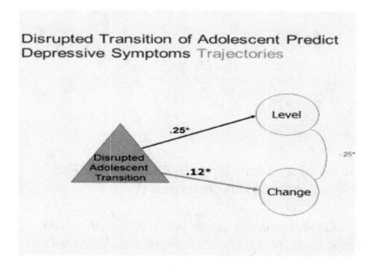

Figure 6. Mplus syntax: Covariate X explain the variablities I or predict the level $\pi 0$ and slope $\pi 1$

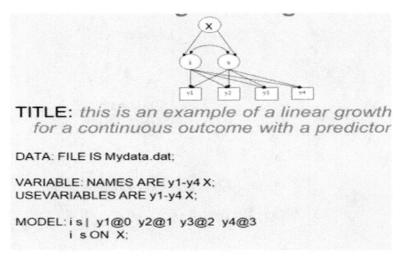

TITLE: *this is an example of a linear growth for a continuous outcome with a predictor*

DATA: FILE IS Mydata.dat;

VARIABLE: NAMES ARE y1-y4 X;
USEVARIABLES ARE y1-y4 X;

MODEL: i s| y1@0 y2@1 y3@2 y4@3
i s ON X;

Covariate X explain the variablities I or predict the level $\pi 0$ and slope $\pi 1$.

Figure 6 presents Mplus syntax for an conditional LGCM with covariate X and four time points of the outcomes variable.

Covariate X explain the variablities I or predict the level $\pi 0$ and slope $\pi 1$

An example of a linear growth curve model for a continuous outcome –

Variable names: $y^1 - y^4$ X; Usevariables are: $y^1 - y^4$ X;

Model: i s | $y^1@^0$ $y^2@^1$ $y^3@^2$ $y^4@^3$

i s ON X:

An Illustration of a Latent Growth Curve of DEP and Covariate X and Distal Outcome U

The beauty of LGCM approach is that, as shown in figure 6, growth parameters (the level and slope) can also be used as predictors of distal outcomes U (sequelaes) the same analytical framework. That is, it allows to examine independent influences of different facets of change (the level and slope) on distal outcomes. Figure 7 presents corresponding regression equations predicting distal outcomes U with regression coefficients βs.

Figure 7. LGCM with predtictors and seqeulaes

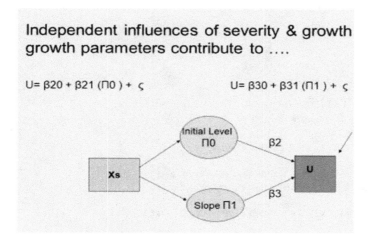

Figure 8. An emirical illustration for LGCM with preditors and seqeulaes.

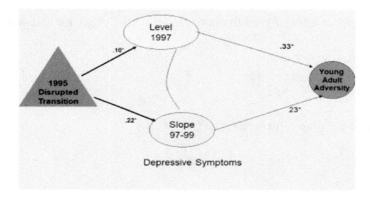

Examining sequelae of change – GC as predictors – (Independent influences of severity & growth –Which growth paramters contribute to which…)

Figure 8 presents an emprical illustration with Iowa Youth and Family project data.

In this model, adolescent disrupted transition influences the level and slope of dpressive symptoms trajectories which in turn influence young adult socioeconomic adversity.

Young adult socioeconomic adversity was measured by counting sressful socioeconomic conditions in young adulthood (Wickrama et al., 2008). This type of longitudianl models using prospective data elucidate life course processes stemming from early life laeding to socioeconmic outcomes in adulthood. Figure 7 presetn Mplus syntax and corresponding regresion eqautuons for this model.

Figure 9. Mplus syntax for LGCM with a predictor Z and sequelae U

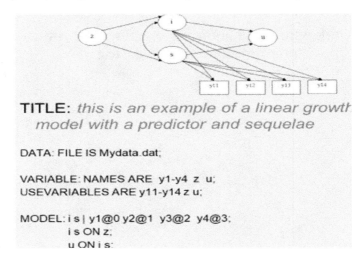

TITLE: *this is an example of a linear growth model with a predictor and sequelae*

DATA: FILE IS Mydata.dat;

VARIABLE: NAMES ARE y1-y4 z u;
USEVARIABLES ARE y11-y14 z u;

MODEL: i s | y1@0 y2@1 y3@2 y4@3;
i s ON z;
u ON i s;

Disrupted transition, depressive symotoms trajectories and young adult adversity
An example of a linear growth curve model with a predictor and sequelae –

Variable names: $y^1 - y^4$ z u;

Usevariables are: $y^1 - y^4$ z u;

Model: i s | $y^1@^0 \; y^2@^1 \; y^3@^2 \; y^4@^3$

i s ON z:

u ON i s

Examining Model Fit of LGCM: Model Fit Indices and Cut Points

One of the primary concerns researchers have when assessing GC models is the overall fit of the model to the data. In evaluating the goodness-of-fit of a LGCM, several model fit statistics are used. Most model fit statistics are derived from the chi-square goodness-of-fit statistic. Often used model fit indices are listed below (Wickram et al., 2016) (Mplus output provide these indices):

1.   The most often used model fit index is the chi-square statistic ($\chi 2$), which is based on maximum likelihood model estimation is calculated as: $\chi 2$ = FML(sample

size-1) where FML represents the F-value reflecting minimization of the maximum likelihood criterion. The $\chi 2$ value is associated with df (degrees of freedom) and is used to test the conventional null hypothesis for the goodness of model fit. If the discrepancy between the covariances implied by the model and the observed sample covariances is large (as expressed by $\chi 2$), then the model is not supported. However, the chi-square statistic is sensitive to sample size. Models based on small sample sizes are not easily rejected, whereas models based on large sample sizes are easily rejected. In order to take into account the effect of sample size as well as model complexity, several alternative model fit indices have been developed.

2. The standardized root mean residual (SRMR). This value is the standardized discrepancy between observed and predicted correlations. The SRMR ranges from 0.0 to 1.0 with smaller SRMR values indicating better model fit.

3. The root mean square error of approximation (RMSEA) . The RMSEA is calculated as: RMSEA = SQRT (d/df) (2.18) where d = $\chi 2$ —df / (sample size − 1) and df = the degrees of freedom (df) available in the hypothesized model. The RMSEA is relatively insensitive to sample size. RMSEA values of 0 indicate perfect model fit to the data.

4. The comparative fit index (CFI) evaluates the fit of a hypothesized model compared to a reduced nested model (known as the restricted model).
    The CFI has a range of possible values from 0.0 to 1.0, with values closer to 1.0 indicating a good model fit.

5. The Tucker-Lewis index (TLI) (Tucker & Lewis, 1973) is another model fit index that takes model complexity into account. The TLI also compares the hypothesized model with a reduced/constrained model. Similar to the CFI, TLI values approaching 1.0 indicate a good model fit.

In summary, to evaluate model fit of LGCM, the chi-square () statistic is typically examined. A with a significant *p*-value indicates that the hypothesized LGCM is a poor fit to the data. However, the statistic is sensitive to sample size and is commonly significant when the sample size is large (Wickrama et al., 2016). Alternatively, other fit indices can be examined, such as the Comparative Fit Index (CFI, [3] 0.90 acceptable fit., >.95 a good git and Root Mean Square Error of approximation (RMSEA, £ 0.08 acceptable fit, <.06 a good fit; Little, 2013).

CONCLUSION

This chapter provides an overview of latent growth curve modeling (LGCM), and demonstrates the strengths of this approach via a practical illustration with Mplus software. A LGCM estimation can be considered as two different processes capturing intra- and inter- change. First, a latent initial level and a latent slope (i.e., the growth factors) are estimated based on each individual's trajectory (known as intra-individual changes; Second, growth factors estimate the *average* trajectory and *variation* across individuals' trajectories (known as inter-individual variation). Therefore, a LGM allows researchers to examine individual trajectories over time and their inter-individual variations simultaneously and to investigate how these trajectories are associated with predictors and distal outcomes. We hope our illustrations serve as a guide for researchers and prompt increased interest in the use of LGCM as we believe this approach is a useful tool for examining research questions centered on life course development.

REFERENCES

Eaton, W. W., Badawa, M., & Melton, B. (1995). Prodromes and precursors: Epidemiological data for primary prevention of disorders with slow onset. *The American Journal of Psychiatry, 152*(7), 967–972. doi:10.1176/ajp.152.7.967 PMID:7793466

Little, T. D. (2013). *Longitudinal structural equation modeling.* Guilford Press.

Muthén, L. K., & Muthén, B. O. (2012). *Mplus user's guide* (7th ed.). Authors.

Wickrama, K. A. S., Conger, R. D., & Abraham, W. T. (2008). Early family adversity, youth depressive symptoms trajectories, and young adult socioeconomic attainment: A latent trajectory class analysis. *Advances in Life Course Research, 13*, 161–192. doi:10.1016/S1040-2608(08)00007-5

Wickrama, K. A. S., Lee, T. K., O'Neal, C. W., & Lorenz, F. O. (2016). *Higher-order growth curves and mixture modeling with Mplus: A practical guide.* Routledge/Taylor & Francis Group.

Willet, J. B. (1988). Questions and answers in the measurement of change. In E. Z. Rothkpf (Ed.), *Review of Research in Education* (Vol. 15, pp. 345–422). American Educational Research Association. doi:10.2307/1167368

Willet, J. B., & Sayer, A. G. (1994). Using covariance structure analysis to detect correlates and predictors of individual change over time. *Psychological Bulletin, 116*(2), 363–381. doi:10.1037/0033-2909.116.2.363

Chapter 14

Simple Guide to Conduct Qualitative Research Using Grounded Theory Method

Ranasinghe M. W. Amaradasa
The University of Fiji, Fiji

ABSTRACT

Conducting qualitative research is an art. A skilled artist produces a high-quality piece of artwork using experience, tools, and intrinsic attributes developed over the years. In the same manner, a qualitative researcher produces a high-quality piece of research. Novice researchers need to gradually develop understanding and practice the fundamentals of qualitative research. In this context, the current chapter provides guided practical sessions, and research problems for experimentation and to improve their research capabilities. Conceptual sessions address interview technologies, recording tools, transcribing standards, coding, memoing, categorizing, and development of themes, which are the fundamentals in the grounded theory approach. The guided practical sessions that are selected carefully to make the targeted research group more comfortable and familiar with the coding process focus on the application of grounded theory approach for researchers to get a better understanding of concepts while clearing potential doubts in applications.

INTRODUCTION

The term "grounded" means the lowest possible level. Conventional research is conducted to describe research problems with the help of existing theoretical framework. Although such attempts may contribute to extend the existing knowledge,

DOI: 10.4018/978-1-6684-6859-3.ch014

the finding may show unavoidable shortcomings due to confirmation to assumptions of the existing theoretical framework.

The "Grounded Theory" approach minimizes such shortages. It advocates the use of any theoretical framework other than methods followed in the process of building a new concept. The concept is established using original data gathered from original primary sources.

BACKGROUND

The foundation for using the grounded theory approach is data gathered from qualitative research. Typically, it can be from surveys and interviews. If you wish to conduct high quality research using the grounded theory approach, surveys and interviews should be designed very carefully to capture the original data while maintaining neutrality to avoid any bias (Macdonald, & Birdi, 2019). The author does not intend to describe survey design and interview design in this chapter, but it is important to note the criticality of their designs to conduct quality qualitative research (Morgan., 2015). However, in order to provide an indication, author emphasize that well-designed open-ended questions and semi-structured interviews are recommended.

"Grounded Theory" method in qualitative research falls under interplay of "Inductive approach" and "Deductive approach". That means, the observations and textual data are processed to search for patterns and then to develop an explanation which ultimately ends up with a theory or new knowledge inductive and deductive approaches. Findings from the grounded theory approach are always subject to criticism as the process of coding and categorizing will have subjective element of bias and the quality of researchers who conduct analysis. Hence, researchers are always advised to maintain neutrality and use a triangulation mechanism where findings are telling the similar pattern when you deal with other related analysis such as quantitative analysis. Case studies can be used to strengthen more cohesion of the findings (Chenail et al., 2011). Such mechanisms will generate strong arguments for and against the findings from qualitative research.

MAIN FOCUS OF THE CHAPTER

The purpose of this chapter is to give novice career researchers an introduction to understanding the Grounded Theory Method in a simple way and use it in their qualitative research approaches. The examples given in the chapter allow the reader to gather a better coverage, including interviews, transcribing, coding process, achieving of saturation level, use of snow ball sampling, code book, grouping, and finally conceptualizing. The author believes that although a few examples are described in the chapter, ideas and methods of Grounded Theory are adequately covered.

The term "categories" and "groups" are used interchangeably in this chapter. If the same topic is looked at by a different researcher, he/she may use different "codes" for transcribed interview notes. It is similar to drawing by different individuals when they asked to draw a "face of a pretty woman". Out of many drawings, many observers will agree with one drawing as the "Best". To draw a better drawing, you need to practice more and more while adhering to basics as the foundation. This is true for many areas such as sports. Quality comes from practice. The readers are advised to conduct their own research using Grounded Theory Method and improve the quality of your qualitative research.

To facilitate the early career researchers to take-off, the author decided to design a set of semi structured interview questions for one of the above research topics, which a given in the annexure

ISSUES, CONTROVERSIES, PROBLEMS

1. Interviews

In relation to conducting semi-structured interviews in qualitative research, the following guidelines will be useful for all novice researchers:

- Limit the number of interview questions to cover key points only. Less interview questions are recommended.
- Conduct a few pilot scale interviews to develop your competency to conduct interviews.
- Interviews should not be too short or too long. Less than one hour is recommended.
- Record your interview (obtain permission to record before you start recording).
- Be punctual in your appointments and make sure the environment does not interfere.
- Build rapport with your interviewee before beginning the interview, and then continue your chat for few more minutes even after completing your interview questions and recording.
- Transcribe your recorded interview within 24 hours.
- Prepare a memo describing everything about the interview. These memos will assist you to pick up some points that you may have misses out in

the interview design. For example, interviewee may describe many things more freely and with relaxed mood once the recording has concluded. Such behavior and your observations are very useful input for research work.

- Let the interviewee talk freely (for example stories). No attempt should be made to divert attention unless the responses have come to a stop. At the analysis stage, these stories may provide unexpected insight for your research.

2. Transcribing

As mentioned above, the researcher should be serious about when the interview should be transcribed. Typically, the research can use A4 paper (or an Excel sheet) with two columns where you keep first column blank (for coding) and the second column to write word by word questions and responses. Transcribed notes for each interview should be given a serial number and each question can be numbered. See Julia Bailey (2008) for more details.

3. Coding Process

The process of "**Open coding**" is described by Strauss & Corbin (1998) as "to open up the text and expose the thoughts, ideas, and meanings contained therein. They are closely examined, and compared for similarities and differences". Codes can be developed deductively or inductively. Deductive codes come from prior studies and published knowledge. For example, if one research article has identified that the consumption of alcohol by a male partner contribute to home violence, the researcher may be able to develop a deductive code when a respondent makes any statement on a similar pattern. Inductive codes may be developed using researcher's prior reading (not necessarily published academic papers) and his experience or exposure to the subject. For example, when a respondent talks about any event related to aggressive behavior of a driver, the researcher's experience on aggressiveness enables the researcher to use it as a inductive code. This is an important first step as the rest of the analysis that follows could not occur without it. Further, Strauss & Corbin (1998) has conceptualized an advanced set of selective coding and axial coding process as analytical tools that can be used at the next level of analysis when dealing with categories and sub-categories. We will look into a couple of examples to understand the coding process.

4. Categorizing (Grouping)/Themes

Categorizing is a process where you try to group several codes together and give a higher order name. This tool, while heavily dependent on the earlier coding process, may lead to different interpretations by different researchers. For example, a set of four wooden sticks, attached to a plate of wooden sheet can be interpreted as a "chair" by one person, and can be viewed as a "stand" by another. Some other person can interpret that as a "stool". Similarly, the same codes developed through the careful coding process can be interpreted differently. To make you analyse and interpret more precisely, the researcher may use micro-analysis as a tool. In this context, the memos the research used will give a deep insight into the analysis. Once a category is identified, the researcher should be able to abstract the category and explain in terms of responding to the questions such as when, where, why, how, and so on.

5. Conceptualizing

During the process of grouping you may come up with a few numbers of themes or groups where you can analyse them further to see whether you can develop one or two key groups. We call it a conceptualization process which can become the major finding of your research. When the researcher becomes more experienced on qualitative research, it becomes more comfortable to develop such core categories.

Figure 1. Process of Grounded Theory method

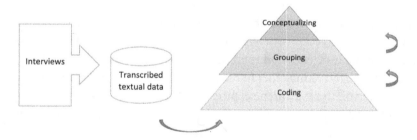

6. Example One

Suppose a researcher wishes to conduct research with the aim of finding out factors that contribute to increased number of road accidents caused by the bus commuters in a country. The researcher can use a mix-method in his/her research design to address this question.

In relation to qualitative method, the researcher may design his research to conduct interviews (semi-structured interviews are recommended) with different stakeholders including bus drivers, passengers, general public, regulatory bodies, officers in organizations related to road networks, and the Police Department. Out of them, the researcher can categorize the interviewees as respondents and some of them as gate keepers, such as officers in regulatory bodies and the "Police". Similarities and conflicting opinions by those categories are useful inputs for the analysis.

The semi structured interviews can have only few questions. In this case, the sample interview questions can be as follows;

Question One: What is your opinion on how bus drivers are responsible for increased number of road accidents?

Question Two: What do you think about passengers or commuters and how they might be responsible?

Question three: What do you think about road conditions and maintenance?

Question four: What is your opinion on regulatory bodies?

Question five (as sub-question to question four): How can those regulatory bodies can make a difference?

It is important to remember that even the interview questions should be neutral not giving any inducement to response. The interview questions for interviews with gatekeepers can be slightly different to extract the point of view. For example, the interview questions can be modified using the opinion received from other respondents. Probably, you may need to take in to account the role of a passenger or the bus driver when conducting the interview. For example, you can add a question to inquire about their vigilance about the increasing road accidents and steps taken by them to reduce such accidents. A possible question may be "What have you done to enhance public awareness on road safety"? Around this main question, you can continue dialogue by asking other related questions such as "What kind of challenges do you face during these awareness programs"?

As mentioned earlier, it is always good to conduct a set of pilot interviews to get used to flaw of interview questions and prepare for possible distractions, and design your own strategies to overcome those distractions.

A typical response from passengers related to your interview question on drivers (**Question one**) can be as follows;

"Respondent One: Nowadays bus drivers are very careless. They are in competition for more passengers. No care about road disciplines. Probably, they should be properly trained. Those who are victims should go through a rehabilitation process.

"Respondent two: These days, getting driving license is quite easy. Once they get it, they may feel they know everything and road is theirs"

The early career researchers can adopt different strategies in the process of coding. You may use line-by-line coding or analyzing the whole sentence or paragraph of the transcribed textual data. It is always advisable to start with line-by-line coding to practice and experience the coding process. Of course, when you master the coding process you may even use more than a paragraph for coding.

Now, both responses in the above example are analysed as a whole sentence or paragraph. You can see that the respondents talk about behavior of drivers where they are required to go through a proper training process. Hence, the possible codes can be "Carelessness" and "Education & Training".

When you conduct several interviews, many respondents may raise similar issues that can be coded under the above both codes and one of the codes. However, after conducting few interviews, you may find some new data coming from respondents.

Respondent 5: "Some drivers seems to have health issues such as not having proper eye sight, fatigueless, poor visibility in the dark that may contribute to accidents".

Here, you can generate a code on fitness to drive. Similarly, as you move on, several additional codes will evolve. Once all codes are generated using all transcribed textual data, you need to generate a code book to include all codes.

Now let us look at another interview question which is related to issues on passengers (**Question two**). The responses can be as follows;

Respondent One: "We need to be careful about road signs and obey them. Should not cross-roads from dangerous places. Nobody knows when the "killer" arrives. Some people use mobile phone while walking & crossing. They cannot see or hear. Especially, the teenagers and students are victims. Sometimes, people are not careful when they get-in and get-down from the bus. Drives may not see them properly".

Respondent Two: "Public awareness on road accidents is not adequate. Authorities may us TV channel to highlight potential hazards. My grandfather also died from a road accident. While crossing. It seems he managed to cross to the other side safely but the vehicle overtook the other vehicle lost control when the driver shows "Grandpa" crossing and then, hit him at the edge of the road. It was an on the spot death".

In this case, you may be able to generate codes as you have done earlier. The possible additional code can be "public awareness", "vigilance", and "distractions" due to the use of mobile phones. Further, you may observe that during the interviews, the Respondent Two may tend to talk about his past experience as a story. The qualitative researcher should be able to listen to those stories and extract (deductive approach) an appropriate code and make it inclusive. The possible deductive code that can evolve may be "avoidance of danger". Also, when the researcher come across such a story from a respondent, he needs to remember to express empathy towards the respondent and then encourage participation in the research.

With respect to question about road conditions & maintenance (Question three) the possible responses are as follows;

Respondent One: "Road conditions are pathetic. After heavy rain season, you will see many pot halls on the road. Temporary measures to use gravel make it worst. Road development companies make money out of it".

Respondent Two: "We are paying road tax. I do not know where this money goes. It is responsibility of the authorities to use tax payer's money maintain roads".

Respondent Three: Roads are becoming more and busier in urban areas. Certain time you get heavy traffic. You need to use advanced technology to maintain proper movement of traffic. I know road conditions in rural areas also becoming better, but I am not sure whether such upgrading is in line with the demand expected by citizens. There may be financial issues".

In this case, Respondent One expresses his "disappointment in maintenance". Respondent Two talks about "return on tax money" and "role of relevant authorities". Both of them indicate "poor maintenance". On the same note, Respondent Three brings a new dimension about the use of "modern practices" in traffic control while agreeing with "poor maintenance" in rural areas.

Also, it is possible that some respondents will talk about unethical practices such as "Bribery" and "Under hand dealings" between responsible authorities and road development companies. They may talk about such things related to vehicle fitness tests, issuing driving licenses etc.

In this Chapter, the above few selected questions and sample responses are used to describe the rest of the procedures related to use of grounded theory method. It is important to remember that the number of questions can be decided by the researcher depending of the research question he wants to address. Also, the number of respondents can be decided using "the Saturation" concept.

7. Interviews With "Gate Keepers"

Interviewing "Gate keepers" usually follow the rest of the respondents. The issues raised by drivers, commuters, and the public can be used to design interview questions as mentioned above. These interviews and analysis will help you to do micro-analysis to provide a better picture on the issue and in most cases bring your findings into a upper level inviting attention of policy makers. By doing so, your research can become better appropriated and applicable in the context of today.

For example, the owners of a "bus company" may mention about the difficulty in retaining good drivers in the company due to compensation issues. They need to use newcomers frequently and provide adequate induction, and training can be disorganized due to rapid changes of personnel. They may look to increasing the price of bus tickets or other means of incentives to accommodate the increase of wages to drivers. They may not reveal technical problems, if any, to do with their buses. Sometimes, they may talk about tax issues in relation to importation of spare parts. All these textual data are useful for your micro-analysis to make your findings more useful.

On the same note, an interview with a police officer may open up a different perspective based on the police records and investigations. He may reveal different types of illegal and unethical instances with examples, while discussing issues which are of public knowledge. Those critical incidences may be again useful in your micro-analysis and final discussions in your research. For example, the police officer may talk about driving by an unauthorized individual, and accidents dues to drunkenness (both drivers and commuters). They may hardly talk about technical faults due to inadequate road signs and road maintenance issues. Knowing that such kind of responses from such "Gate keepers", it is the quality of researcher to become vigilant and design interview questions in a pro-design manner.

8. Effect of Saturation

Saturation is a tool that can be used to decide about sample size of respondents. For example, when you continue your interviews, transcribing and coding, you may see that when the number of respondents is increasing after some number there is hardly any "New code" that can be generated. There is no point in continuing more interviews, unless you see that you can explore and integrate a new perspective into your research. Such change is discussed in **Example Two**. When you see any new code has not evolved from your interviews, you can terminate interviews and decide it as the saturation point.

9. Code Book

Code book is a useful tool to capture the overall picture of your textual data. It can be prepared as a matrix that basically summarizes all your textual data in to a table. A sample code book for the above example can look like as follows.

10. Grouping/Categorizing

When you analyze the above code book, you may see that certain codes can be grouped together. For example, Carelessness, public awareness, vigilance, avoidance of danger & distraction can be group as "behavioral changes". Similarly, Bribery, Underhand dealings, & Fitness to drive can be grouped under "Code of conduct". Probably, Education & training can also be included based on the micro- analysis. Certain codes such as "return on tax" and "disappointment on maintenance" can be grouped as a "Transparency" issue. Also, you may develop a group on "Modernization" where you can group code on "modern traffic control systems" with any other code

Table 1. Development of a code book based on the above example

Code	Respondent	Inductive/ Deductive	Inclusive	Exclusive
Carelessness	One	Inductive	Drivers negligence	Does not talk about commuters
Education & Training	One & Two	Inductive	Programmes for all relevant stake holders	None active stakeholders such as kids and others who are not actively engaged in
Fitness to drive	Five	Inductive	Drivers' health conditions & regular health check ups	Legal requirements such as appropriate category of license
Public awareness	One & Two	Inductive	Programmes to enhance the awareness of public on "Road Safety"	Paid courses and academic programmes
Vigilance	One	Inductive	Sense for potential accidents by commuters	Drivers' point of view
Distraction	One	Inductive	Distraction caused by not having attention	Traffic and any other purposeful social distractions
Avoidance of danger	Two	Deductive	Public awareness on potential accidents to avoid them through media	Special education & training for drivers
Disappointment on Road Maintenance	One, two & three	Inductive	Perception by commuters (possibly drivers too)	Maintenance of vehicle condition (unless drivers claim about negligence by bus owners)
Return on Tax	Two	Inductive	Road tax	Other related administrative payments, fines etc
Modern traffic controls systems	Three	Deductive	Systems that can be used in urban areas	Sophisticated systems seen in other developed countries
Bribery	Any	Inductive	Any mode of unethical practice using money to get things done compared to standard process	Friendship, Assisting with none monetary gain,
Underhand dealings	Any	Inductive	Movements between two parties bypassing standards processes expecting some kind of return.	Internal processes without expecting any kind of return

developed from transcribed textual data. A possible code can be modernization of fitness tests where human interface has very limited engagement. Also, people are now aware of the modern speed control systems applied in countries like Singapore where no human interaction when the vehicle exceed the speed limit, but the fine is automatically generated. During this grouping process, it is useful and essential to re-visit your memos and previous studies to derive any possible deductive codes which can strengthen inclusivity and exclusivity of your category. However, the derivation of deductive codes has to be done with an extra precaution. If the researcher does not capture the inclusivity and exclusivity, the deductive code might reflect a different picture. For example, in a research on home violence, the female respondent may say (about her husband), "He does not care about me. All problems start because of that". If the researcher has read a lot about "After marriage affairs", he may derive a deductive code related to such affairs. But the woman may be talking about her husband's heavy engagement with his employment or social activities, and neglect home affairs. Hence, the issue of inclusivity and exclusivity plays a role, especially in derivation of deductive codes.

Further, during the analysis & micro-analysis for categories, you may find it is useful to develop sub-categories that can be used later to find connections between categories. Strauss & Corbin (1998) has explained this process as "**Axial Coding**". For example, category on "Behavioral Change" can be sub-categories as "Customer Care", and category on "Code of Conduct" may have a sub-category on "Customer Safety". The "Inclusivity" and "Exclusivity" in the code book can be used as the base for sub-categories. These two sub-categories can become the link that connect two categories on "Behavioral Change" and "Code of Conduct". Similarly, the category on "Education & Training" may have many sub-categories connecting almost all other categories. As Strauss & Corbin (1998) has stated, sub-categories assist the researcher to better explain & describe the questions on the different components of the "Concept" that you develop out of research.

When we move from codes to categories, we get involve in interpreting categories to some degree. Although the codes are based on textual data where we use inductive approach, when we more upward (i.e. Categorizing and Conceptualizing), we may integrate more with deductive approach. This is where our data go alone with our reading, assumptions, literature that we carry in our heads, and all other intellectual inputs the researcher capture. Hence, you may see and interplay between inductive and deductive approach at this stage and above. You may see such nature of interplay between two approaches in the example two.

11. Diversion of Focus to a New Perspective

While you continue your coding and categorizing process as discussed above, you may find that your findings are diverting to a new unexpected direction. This sense of diversion will need special attention by researchers. For example, suppose you may be conducting a research on "Factors contributing to divorce from marriages". You may get many codes and categories related to social, behavioral, demographic and cultural factors. Among them you may see that there are few serial cases within a same family tree leading to divorces or near divorces. You may be able to interpret this using a possible genetic relationship where certain attitudes are displayed in common. When you see this new perspective, you should be able to redesign your interview questions and follow up with heavy focus on your new perspective. Once again, such approach is shown in example two.

12. Developing a Concept

Once the groups or the categorization is done, you may visualize them leading towards a concept, which is your final destination. Depending on the nature of categories you may develop and indicate interactive nature of relationships among categories even with a pictorial form. "Transparency" in the above example may have interactions with "Modernization" which can be described using micro-analysis coming from memos and interviews with "Gate keepers". Hence, it can be shown as a "Venn diagram" or any other diagram to show the interaction. The nature of interaction can be described separately. Similarly, "Code of conduct" and "Behavioral Changes" can show interactions through "education & training". The way you present and interpret your concept can become something new to the knowledge of the world. A possible integration is shown in Figure Two, where the three groups can be stirred through a "Education & Training funnel" to bring the concept of "Road Safety". You may see that the category of "Transparency" is standing alone. Now, you have an option to modernize your "Concept on Road Safety" to include "Transparency". To do this, you need to revisit all your textual data, memos and previous studies to see how you can capture "Transparency" into "Road safety". The author propose to use "Reliable Road Safety" as the concept, for the purpose simplicity. Please make a note that all these will depend on your data. Researchers are advised to visualize an innovative integration of different categories. Potential mapping of such integrations is given as examples below.

Figure 2. A sample pictorial presentation of development of categories and the concept using Example One

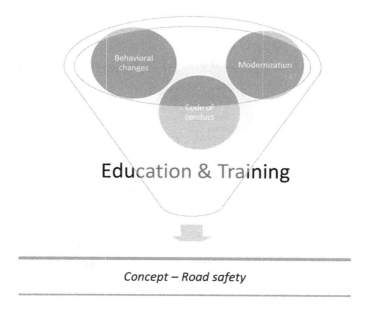

Concept – Road safety

13. Example Two (Source: "Enterprising Mothers in Fiji Need Comprehensive Support" by C.A. Saliya, The Qualitative Report in TQR)

The second example is from the above article where the research has attempted to conceptualize how Fijian working mothers are striving to promote equality and diversity in the work place, society, and family-life. The researcher has used the grounded theory method, semi-structured interviews, and the coding & categorizing process to generate core categories leading to major findings on working mothers' efforts to conquer gender inequality.

The author has originally generated 116 codes, and subsequently while grouping them had redesigned the interviews to capture responses from working mothers and incorporated new interview questions. Such accommodation of new interview questions can also be done at the early stage of interviews. For example, when you have finished eight interviews and have gone through the coding process, you may learn the necessity of adding new interview questions and explore another perspective related to you research problem. Such changes are viable in the grounded theory method. This brings to the notice the importance of transcribing and coding as earliest as possible once you finish an interview. Through the process of grouping codes (categorizing), the researcher has developed a core concept with four themes as the final outcome of the research. The readers are encouraged to read and study the process (Figure three) indicated in this article by Saliya, C.A (https://orcid.org/0000-0002-9239-1648), .

Figure 3. Process in the Grounded theory method described by Saliya (2022).

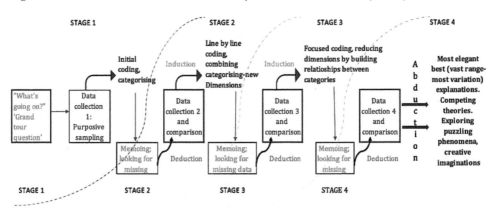

14. Example Three

Suppose a researcher wishes to conduct research on "The effect of the internet on the education of school children". You may see that the topic is very broad and probably needs to be narrowed down to a manageable scope, depending on the purpose of your research. Secondly, you need to read a lot about this subject, as there can be many similar researches already done. Those previous studies can be used for developing deductive codes.

Also, you should be careful about your target sample of respondents. If you limit your target sample to one type of respondents, you may miss out on the other sides. For example, the subject matter is about school children. Hence, engagement of school children in the research sample is also important. This will have ethical issues as you may find it unethical to ask certain questions from school children. Similarly, you may come across issues related to access to respondents. Even when you are interviewing the respondents, they may become biased in front of their parents and teachers. Otherwise, they might respond differently. In this context, the interview environment, any noticeable body languages and any interferences, and such are useful to note in your memos. These memos, as stated before, will give an insight to do micro-analysis.

It is recommended to have strata samples for interviews such as parents, teachers, and students or narrow it down your research questions to a specific perspective (for example parents' perspective). Also, the level of internet access may be different for different geographical locations. Hence, it is recommended to conduct interviews at two contrasting locations for comparative purposes. It may be affected by cultural and social attributes. The researcher may look into that aspect too, when deciding about respondents. Probably, any previous studies may assist you to develop your research problem accordingly. For example, if a previous study reveals that there is no influence by cultural factors, you may take it as it is, or challenge it in your research.

Based on your research problem, you can develop appropriate research questions to match your target group of respondents. Here you may see that there is high possibility to incorporate a mix-method in your research, which will be useful for cross tabulations. Once you design interview questions, you can conduct the interviewing, transcribing, memoing, and coding process as discussed in Example One. As the subject matter is a matter commonly discussed in the public domain, there is a high chance of diverting your attention a wider scope of the subject matter during data collection and analysis stages.

15. Proposed Exercises

At this stage, the author wishes to provide an opportunity for the readers to practice the lessons learnt in this chapter. Readers can design research questions, interview questions, and conduct pilot interviews on one or many of the topics at their choice.

1. Drug abuse
2. Increased crime rate
3. Home violence
4. Inequality at workplace

The above topics are given as they are common themes in the public space. You may identify respondents, as well as gate keepers, in all four cases, as you have seen in the Example One. You may identify different types of respondents for different topics. For example, you may not find voluntary respondents in some cases, such as research on home violence. The situation may be same in many other research areas such as studies on "cancer patients" and "abortions". In those cases, the researcher may have to adopt a different sampling technique such as "Snow Ball" samples. Furthermore, there can be situation where the respondent become very sensitive and emotional. As a researcher, you may not be qualified or not trained enough to handle such situations. Hence, you may need to think about it proactively, and take appropriate steps to manage such situations. Usually, accompanying a person who has counselling abilities can be opted.

16. Sample Interview Questions to Conduct a Research Study on "Inequality at Workplace"

Step 1: Spend few minutes to set the platform to commence your interviews. Explain the process of your research as well.

Step 2: Start with very comfortable, easy to understand question such as "Can you describe your workplace composition?'. This can be followed by any sub-question related to composition and their role.

Step 3: Follow with specific questions such as workload, performance expectations, compensation, benefits, opportunity for training and career growth.

e.g. If you wish to explore on equity against gender, you can ask a question on "What do you think about assigning employees from any gender to conduct (specific) work)"

Step 4: Get ready with few critical (and sometimes sensitive) questions such as staff departure, retention rate, and any critical incident you may capture during interviews.

e.g. you may ask a question about getting staff to work on late hours, weekends and night shifts

Step 5: Conclude the interview with a reassurance of confidentiality of the research data.

Step 6: Observe things that happen after the interview and recording.

It is recommended to revisit interview questions after conducting few initial (even after the first interview) and develop more appropriate set of questions.

RECOMMENDATIONS

As mentioned earlier, a researcher planning to use "Grounded Theory Method" need to prepare him/herself adequately to maintain neutrality and improve quality. The author believe that the readers gain adequate knowledge to conduct qualitative research using the examples and exercises described in this chapter. It is always a good practice to start with a pilot project and gain confidence in all aspects including interviewing and transcribing.

REFERENCES

Bailey, J. (2008, April). First steps in qualitative data analysis: Transcribing. *Family Practice*, *25*(2), 127–131. doi:10.1093/fampra/cmn003 PMID:18304975

Chenail, R. J., Duffy, M., St. George, S., & Wulff, D. (2011). Facilitating coherence across qualitative research papers. *Qualitative Report*, *16*(1), 263–275. http://www.nova.edu/ssss/QR/QR16-1/coherence.pdf

Demetri, L. M. (2015). Criticality in Qualitative Research. *Qualitative research: Bridging the conceptual, theoretical, and methodological.* Thousand Oaks. https://works.bepress.com/demetrilmorgan/11/

Macdonald, S., & Birdi, B. (2019). The concept of neutrality: A new approach. *The Journal of Documentation*, *76*(1), 333–353. doi:10.1108/JD-05-2019-0102

Saliya, C. A. (2022). *Doing Social Research: A Guide to Non-native English Speakers.* Springer., https://link.springer.com/book/10.1007/978-981-19-3780-4

Strauss, A. L., & Corbin, J. (1996). *Basics of Qualitative Research: Techniques and Procedures for Developing Grounded Theory.* Sage.

Chapter 15
Doctrinal Legal Research:
A Library–Based Research

Gaurav Shukla
University of the South Pacific, Fiji

ABSTRACT

This chapter is an attempt to provide a basic understanding to law researchers of doctrinal legal research. The chapter is drafted in such a manner that it will give a systematic approach to acquainted with the doctrinal legal research. It includes the brief historical background, purpose, and steps to conduct doctrinal legal research, tools that are used, advantages and limitations, and summing up with a conclusion. The author has tried his best effort to give all the relevant tools, however, there were limitations due to the huge expansion of information and technology, e.g. social media. These limitations restrain the author to stick to more traditional tools of research.

1. INTRODUCTION

According to H.L.A. Hart a prominent jurist of the positive school of jurisprudence, doctrinal research "takes an internal, participant-oriented epistemological approach to its object of study" (Paul, 2008, p. 30) Doctrinal research also known as library-based research or called as "black letter" methodology (Jerome Hall Law Library, 2019, para 3) is focused research on the letter of law instead of law in action. In this research methodology one doesn't have to work or collect data from the field rather the researcher composes a descriptive and detailed analysis of legal rules and regulations, case laws, juristic writings, etc from primary and secondary sources. Primary and secondary sources are discussed future in the later part of this chapter.

DOI: 10.4018/978-1-6684-6859-3.ch015

The doctrinal legal method revolves around gathering information, organizing them, and describing the law.

The chapter starts with the definitions of doctrinal legal research given by prominent jurists with an expression of concern about the relevance of these definitions in the digitalised world. Then after the author tested the historical background of doctrinal research.

Further, the chapter provides the readers with the tools that are traditional as well as contemporary for conducting doctrinal legal research. Its purpose and steps to conduct are elaborated in the later part of the chapter followed by the advantages and limitations of doctrinal legal research. This chapter will help the law researcher to explore the doctrinal legal research method which has been useful for attorneys, judges, etc, this method helps to examine legal theories and doctrines and provide the solution to legal problems with lesser time

2. BACKGROUND

The doctrinal legal research is like the Roman God Janus who has two faces one looking into the past and another in the future, doctrinal research has strong roots in the past, but now transitioning towards a digitalised single world (Hutchinson, 2015, p. 136). In the 1980s doctrinal legal research was the predominant form of research used for the assessments of law. The Australian Pearce Committee 1987 highlighted doctrinal legal research as the category in its research taxonomy ((Hutchinson, 2015, p. 131)

In 1987 The Australian Pearce Committee defined doctrinal legal research as "research that provides a systematic exposition of the rules governing a particular legal category, analyses the relationship between rules, explains areas of difficulty and, perhaps, predicts future developments" (Pearce, Campbell & Harding, 1987, p. 312). The definition was further expanded by The Council of Australian Law Deans stating, "Doctrinal research, at its best, involves rigorous analysis and creative synthesis, the making of connections between seemingly disparate doctrinal strands, and the challenge of extracting general principles from an inchoate mass of primary materials" (Council of Australian Law Deans, 2005, p. 3).

The Dean of Harvard Law School Martha Minow stated that doctrinal restatement is one of the essential contributors that legal researchers make to their research (Minow, 2013, p. 65). From the civil law countries' perspective, Rob van Gestel and H.-W. Micklitz defined doctrinal legal research as, "arguments are derived from authoritative sources, such as existing rules, principles, precedents, and scholarly publications" (Gestel & Micklitz, 2011, p. 26).

Prof. S. N. Jain defined doctrinal research as, "a research that involves analysis of case law, arranging, ordering and systematizing legal propositions and study of legal institutions through legal reasoning or rational deduction" (Jain, 2006, p. 68). The definition was further elaborated by Dr. S.R. Myneni, "A doctrinal research means a research that has been carried out on a legal proposition or propositions by way of analysing the existing statutory provisions and cases by applying the reasoning power" (Myneni, 2006, p.16). For Ian Dobinson and Francis Johns, "Doctrinal or theoretical legal research can be defined in simple terms as research which asks what the law is in a particular area. It is concerned with the analysis of the legal doctrine and how it has been developed and applied. This type of research is also known as pure theoretical research. It consists of either simple research directed at finding a specific statement of the law or a more complex and in-depth analysis of legal reasoning" (Ian Dobinson & Francis Johns, 2007, p.18-19). According to Prof. Ranbir Singh and G.S. Bajpai, "doctrinal legal research is research into legal doctrines through analysis of legal rules, principles or doctrines" (Singh & Bajpai, p.3)

2.1 Brief History of Doctrinal Research

Friedrich Karl von Savigny a German Jurist of legal understanding and his school of thought presented a different dimension once named "coming from another world" by Joachim Rückert. His texts do not provide specific text related to legal methods in their practical application. He focused on the study of law and its scientific analysis and creation of law (Rückert, 2006, 58). Savigny belongs to the German historical school of jurist or thought, however, doctrinal research finds its roots in the positivist or the analytical school of jurisprudence. The analytical or Positivist school of jurisprudence is founded on the legal maxim, 'Ubi civitas ibi lex' that signifies, "where there is state, there will not be anarchy", (Mittra, 2021, para 3) the foundation is based on the relation of law with that of a State. The analytical school was objective and value-free often more epistemologically oriented and didn't concern people or society. The doctrinal legal research method does not study law in its normative form. It rarely considers the human aspect of law and how it affects society (iPleaders, 2021, para 10).

In this method, the researcher is concerned about the black letter of the law in its present stage. Its emergence is the consistence of rising of common law principles in the 19th and 20th centuries (Hutchinson & Duncan 2012, p.85). The common law system is based on the doctrine of precedents and is developed by the efforts of jurists and the Court's decisions (Cornell Law School, 2021, para 1). All of these gave the researcher sufficient literature to discover the intent of lawmakers within the black letter. It started when judges and attorneys started investigating laws from different primary and secondary sources. At the same time, academicians started exploring the doctrinal research method when the law entered the academic field in Europe (Tiwary 2020, p.5). Due to this historical linkage, doctrinal research is also known as traditional research.

3. PURPOSE AND STEPS TO CONDUCT DOCTRINAL LEGAL RESEARCH

3.1 Purpose

Doctrinal legal research helps judges, attorneys, and academicians to do their research sitting in one place (Bhat, 2020, p.327). The main purpose of doctrinal legal research is to improve the substantial law rather than procedural law by means that could result in harboring the wider goals of law (Hutchinson, 2015 p. 136). Doctrinal legal research is a study carried out on legal issues by analysing the present law that is applicable and case laws related to that issue (National Law University, Delhi, 2015, p. 1).

3.2 Steps

Doctrinal legal research involves jurisprudential analysis of an issue, the issue is further analysed by applying the applicable statutes and analysing the statutes, examining the historical development of any legal doctrine or legal system, analysing the related case law and legal theories.

Table 1 shows an example of the steps.

Table 1. Steps

Issue	Steps
Tax Avoidance by MNEs through Treaty Shopping	Analysis of an issue of tax avoidance by MNEs through Treaty Shopping
Applicable law	Anti-Tax Avoidance Rules and Bilateral Tax Treaties
Analysis of the statutes	Anti-Tax Avoidance Rules and Bilateral Tax Treaties
Historical development of any legal doctrine or legal system	Westminster principle, Limitation of Benefit, Beneficial ownership, tax havens, etc.
Analysis of related case laws	Inland Revenue Commissioners v. Duke of Westminster [1936] A.C.1; 19 TC 490 (U.K. case), McDowell & Company Limited v. The Commercial Tax Office 1986 AIR 649 (Indian case) Vodafone International Holdings v. Union of India & Anr (2012) 6 SCC 613 (Indian case), Crown Forest Industries Ltd. v. Canada [1995] 2 SCR 802 (Canadian case)

3.2.1 Elaboration of Steps

1. **Introduction**: State a brief introduction of the topic/issue dealt with in the paper in a few paragraphs or pages depending on the issue. Draft it in such a way that the readers understand the in-hand issue/research problem. Include a brief trial of logical arguments and an analytical tone to place the issue and arguments.

2. **Conceptual Framework**: Conceptual framework consists of a detailed framework of the concepts, propositions, and doctrines in the proposed research. There should be a specific linkage between the issue and the concepts that will be examined.

This conceptualization should give an introduction to the general area of research of the paper.

3. **Statement of Research problem**: A clear statement of the problem is a must to take on the research. The statement should be precisely narrowed down to the addressable issue and try to make it neutral instead of showing biasness and conclusiveness. The statement or the narrative should clearly highlight the coverage of the investigation and the purview of the problem. The statement should mention the issue as well as sub-issues that are dealt with in the research. The problem statement should explain the issue in its theoretical and applied context of the concerned area of research.

4. **Review of Literature**: It provides a survey of scholarly writing on the given research problem. This not only includes research articles but also includes international and national reports, debates, text and reference books, case laws, working papers, etc.

There must be a systematic flow of literature in ascending order of year of publications. Inclusion of path-breaking research expressed through various writing. The literature review should have a clear link with the research problem.

5. **Aims or Objectives**: Categorically state the aims or objectives of the research undertaken. The number of aims or objectives depends on the nature of research and academic instructions of the institute, however, commonly three to five objectives are sufficient enough.

6. **Hypothesis/Research questions**: A brief statement linking it with the objectives entailing two or more variables stating the presumed relationship or influence on each other, e.g., *"tax evasion can be linked with different modes of doing money laundering"*. The validity of the hypothesis is unknown in the beginning and

it can be in the form statement or proposition. It is just a tentative assumption made to test its validity. At the end of the research, the researcher must either affirm or reject that, *"tax evasion can be linked with....."*

Designing of hypothesis is very crucial as it gives significant clues about the research method used for analysis. It narrows downs the research and keeps the researcher on track during the investigation. A hypothesis should be precise, specific, and clear. The hypothesis is good when the researcher has a good idea about the subject matter under investigation, if the researcher is early researcher research questions are a much better option.

Additionally or alternatively research questions addressing the research objective can also be framed. Research questions should be linked with research objectives and should be clear about the coverage and scope, that is duration or number of cases and nature of cases covered or geographical area, or any institution (like for example case study of the Enforcement Directorate in India), or any timeframe. Sampling is not needed in doctrinal legal research, however, all kinds of methods need some kind of data. This data is available in two sources, primary and secondary sources.

PRIMARY SOURCES

According to Vibute. "the sources that contain original information and observations are known as primary sources of information". (Vibhute & Filipos, 2009, p. 46) Such information can be gathered from the source from where it is generated or from any other sources where it is duplicated from the original source. That is why legal periodicals and journals are essential for doctrinal legal research. They contain enriched information and in-depth analysis. Reports from governmental or non-governmental institutions are also well informative and useful.

Primary legal sources are the actual law passed by the parliament, Constitution, case laws, statutes, bye-laws, and administrative rules and regulations. **Secondary Sources**: These sources drive the information from primary sources. Information is systematically organised. They include textbooks, treatises, commentary, abstracts, bibliographies, dictionaries, encyclopaedias, indexes, reviews, case comments, etc. Textbooks, legal treatises, and commentaries constitute significant secondary sources. These sources not only restate the law, but also discuss, analyse, describe, explain, or criticise as well. The authors tend to put up their viewpoints while discussing any legal provisions. These sources are used to help locate primary sources of law, define legal words, explain legal maxims, and are very useful for doctrinal legal research.

SEEING THE DIFFERENCE

The Indian Supreme Court decision of Kesavananda Bharti vs. State of Kerala AIR 1973 SC 1461 was a landmark judgement in which the 13 judges' bench of the Supreme Court gave the doctrine of basic structure. The actual case is a primary source. The book Commentary on the Constitution of India by Durga Das Basu discusses the case and its historical context, the book is a secondary legal source.

Article 21 of the Indian Constitution states that "Protection of life and personal liberty: No person shall be deprived of his life or personal liberty except according to procedure established by law" as this is taken directly from the Constitution and constitutes the primary source. The 2020 Piyashna Das article "Critical Analysis on Interpretation of Article 21 of the Constitution" in the International Journal of Law Management and Humanities, is a critical analysis and discussion of Article 21, which makes it a secondary legal source.

1. **Data Analysis Plan**: Data analysis could be done manually or electronically. The use of IBM, SPSS, and MegaStat (plugin of Excel) can be used to analyse the data collected in the non-doctrinal method, however, in the doctrinal legal method, there is no requirement to use these software for analysing data.
2. **Significance of the study**: The researcher should clearly state the significance of the study. Why the research is taken and what significance it will make to the present legal structure and society?

4. TOOLS

4.1 Statutory Materials

There are multiple sources where one can find required statutory materials. Laws or statutes are available in hard as well as soft copies. Now where days Government website provides soft copies for public use and awareness. Secondly, there are private databases like, Westlaw, Manupatra, LexisNexis, etc. that are available on payment, mostly Universities procure these for students. Along with statutes these databases also provide case laws, case briefs, case comments, research articles, etc. Statutes include Acts of Parliament including amendments, secondary and subordinate legislations in form of rules, regulations, orders, notification, bye-laws, etc. made thereunder. The case law refers to case reports that are verbatim that reproduced, sometimes in raw or edited form.

Statutes and case laws are the primary tools for doctrinal research, however, the researcher will need other secondary tools to accomplish the research. These secondary tools include research articles, text and reference books, online blogs, or any other information like newspapers, etc. References can also be taken from parliamentary debates and other government records or reports for discovering the intention of the legislators. Thus the list of basic tools of doctrinal legal research is inclusive and not exhaustive.

4.2 Case Law

In the common law justice system precedents are one of the major sources of law. Judgements of higher and the highest courts are published in case law reports, like All England Reporter (All ER) All India Reporter (AIR), Supreme Court Cases (SCC), etc by different publishers. These case laws are also available on legal databases like Manupatra for India, Westlaw International for Globe, Paclii for South Pacific, Austlii for Australia, and many more. Some of these databases are available on subscription and some are free. In case laws there is another resource that is very useful known as Case Digests. These digests refer to all the reported cases in a particular year or five years etc. These digests help in collecting cases on a particular subject/topic. In India, e.g., Yearly Digest, Five Yearly Digest, Fifteen Years Digest, etc, in the U.S. there are US Supreme Court Digest and American Digest System. These digests are more useful than text or reference books as they provide all the reported cases without any discretion, however, on the other hand in books authors may omit cases considered irrelevant.

These digests consist of experts' comments on the leading cases, some of these digests also provide 'Notes on Cases' wherein brief but pertinent comments/summary on leading cases are published. In addition to these Annual Survey is also published comprising of a summary of the most important cases and their impact on different branches of law. The researchers may get the idea of the development of laws that are relevant to their research.

4.3 Research Articles

In doctrinal legal research, papers published in journals are a good source of information and capture the view of others on the issue at hand. Reading these articles not only provides information but also helps the researcher to critically think about the subject matter. These papers are also helpful in developing a logical thread of argumentation that is the key to a good paper. New ideas may develop after reading these research papers/articles. Even the researcher may get new dimensions of the problem, and change the approach adopted by the researcher. It is important to refer to these articles as that will give confidence to the researcher that he has covered all the relevant aspects of the research and now can expand the research with their findings and suggestions. These readings will also enhance the drafting and communication skills. In one way these readings become an indispensable tool for doctrinal legal research.

5. ADVANTAGES AND LIMITATIONS OF DOCTRINAL LEGAL RESEARCH

5.1 Advantages

There are number of appreciable aspects of doctrinal research. In this research, the researcher analysis legal principles, theories, concepts, or doctrines and there is a logical and systematic organization of propositions that may be helpful in practice. The researcher in his continuous efforts can provide answers to the problem quickly due to the exposition and analysis of law and case law. It may provide a workable body of doctrine with the integration of legislative provisions and judgements. Doctrinal research in comparison to non-doctrinal (empirical) research takes less time to draw conclusions which is helpful for lawyers, judges, and others with limited time.

Kenneth Culp Davis observed in relation to this, that

--- [I]t may be a hundred or several hundred years before we get truly scientific answers to some of the questions I am trying to explore, and we need to make some judgments in the meantime. Some of the most useful thinking can be unscientific, impressionistic, intuitive based on inadequate observation or insufficient data or wild guesses or imagination. Scientific findings are obviously the long-term objective, but a good many judgments which fall far short of scientific findings are valuable, respectable and urgently needed (Davis, 1964-65, pp.151-152).

Another advantage of doctrinal research is that it allows one to do research on those topics where doing non-doctrinal research is next to impossible, the subject matter is too sensitive for humankind, or the collection of data is very difficult or dangerous. Take, for example, a researcher who wants to do research on Tax Avoidance by MNEs, the researcher can only have access to the estimated data from the Government and International Organisation, in no case MNEs will be disclosing the sophisticated structures used for tax avoidance or even accept that they are involved in tax avoidance practices.

Further doctrinal legal research expands the jurisprudence on a subject matter. The researcher tests the logical relativity, consistency, and technical eligibility of a legal proposition or doctrine. Sound reasoning and logical outflow of arguments may lead to the development of the law. The detailed analysis in a scientific manner contributes to the understanding of the law, its concepts, and the explanation of the legal process in a better way. This deep analysis not only helps in understanding law but also helps to find out drawbacks in form of inconsistency and uncertainty.

Furthermore, the systematic analysis in a scientific manner with logical inference exposes the loopholes, gaps, or ambiguities in the substantive law or any legal principle or doctrine added through case laws in the substantial law. One of the most recent e.g. is the OECD Base Erosion and Profit Shifting (BEPS) report that exposed the loopholes in tax treaties as well as in domestic income tax laws. The report gives the option to incorporate Limitations of Benefit (LOB) in Tax Treaties or General Anti-Avoidance Rule (GAAR) in domestic law or both by the countries to curtail tax avoidance practices. Many countries have amended their tax treaties through protocols as well as domestic laws by incorporating Limitations of Benefit in treaties and General Anti Avoidance rules in domestic law. Doctrinal legal research helps in the development or improvement of the law. If the researcher is involved in the comparative study of different jurisdictions having a common law legal system further impetus to improve the law, legal concepts, or doctrines, as well as helps other researchers to gather information about other jurisdictions. Doctrinal research not only develops the law or legal principles or doctrines but may also generate new principles or doctrines which may in due course of time gain recognition.

The systematic analysis of legal principles in the light of judicial pronouncements may determine the future path of the in-hand principle or concept of law. Doctrinal legal research creates a strong foundation for non-doctrinal legal research. Even if the researcher is embarking on non-doctrinal research one has to be through with the doctrinal legal research to lay down the theoretical aspect of the law. The researcher has to well establish the theory in form of legal provisions, case laws, and other literature before applying it to the practical scenario. Once a prominent jurist Upendra Baxi observed that "law-society research cannot thrive on a weak infrastructure base of doctrinal type analyses of the authoritative legal material", he further wrote that, it "provides not merely an assurance of sound understanding, but may also hold the promise of needed starting-points for sociological research" (Baxi, 1975, p. 648). The doctrinal legal research expands the knowledge base.

S N Jain once said that "It is naive to think that the task of a doctrinal researcher is merely mechanical - a simple application of a clear precedent or statutory provision to the problem in hand, or dry deductive logic to solve a new problem. He may look for his value premises in the statutory provisions, cases, history in his own rationality and meaning of justice. He knows that there are several alternative solutions to a problem (even this applies to a lawyer who is arguing a case before a court or an administrative authority) and that he has to adopt one which achieves the best interests of the society. The judges always unconsciously or without admitting think of the social utility of their decisions, --- (Verma & Wani, 2001, p.74)

In addition to the above merits, it is often traditionally taught that legal methods should be performed in the primitive stage of legal training, due to this most legal scholars will focus on the techniques used at the time, to fulfill graduate research components. For new graduates, there will be a good number of experts capable of training them (Ali, Yusoff, and Ayub, 2017, p. 493)

5.2 Limitations

Doctrinal legal research leaves the space for subjective interpretation and personal biasness. A personal view on the subject matter may dominate the mind of the researcher. Therefore, on the same subject matter, there can be totally opposite interpretations by two different researchers. Take for example the penal laws of domestic violence, the first impression after listening to this phrase of domestic violence gives the impression that it must be against women, however, in practise it can happen against a man also or against any other gender. Even some countries' law does not recognise domestic violence against any other gender except a woman. The person can be subjective biased as well as a personal bias which makes it one of the drawbacks of doctrinal research.

The results from doctrinal research can be unrealistic. It can be devoid of any support from social facts. The presumptions and assumptions can be far off from social reality. Doctrinal legal research rejects the factors that are outside the blanket of law, which might have an impact on the law, which creates a serious concern as law can act as an instrument of social transformation. Doctrinal legal research does not take into consideration the actual practice and attitudes of people who are responsible for enforcement and judicial system e.g, custodial deaths in India still remind the colonial mentality of the police.

Doctrinal legal research sometimes fails in presenting the true picture, it moves around the presumptions that are not real in practical life, this gives the wrong impression about the present state of law and the practical loopholes continues to deny the objective.

Doctrinal legal research is theoretical and technical, uncritical, conservative, trivial, and does not consider socio-economic-political factors. It must be noted that doctrinal legal research is narrow and choices of topics are limited and this limits the legal profession in the greater social context. Law operates in a particular context and how it links to the context is essential to be known, however, the jurisprudential methodology does not provide a sufficient framework to address the issue at hand. Doctrinal legal research assumes that the law exists in an ideal doctrinal framework without interacting with social factors, this makes its approach limited (Ali, Yusoff, and Ayub, 2017, p.493-4). Law and society interact in a very close periphery sometimes law shapes the society and sometimes society shapes the law (e.g. same-sex marriage) either can't be understood in the vacuum which is a drawback to doctrinal legal research.

6. CONCLUSION

Doctrinal legal research is an old traditional form of research. It has its own merits and demerits, though still widely used by legal scholars, judges, lawyers, etc. It does provide a solution in lesser time but it is a lengthy process that requires determination and dedication. As it does not involve any field work sometimes researchers lose interest, they have to motivate themselves. Doctrinal legal research is a good tool when the subject matter is difficult to be researched without danger or may be impossible to collect data. Reading between the lines for doing the interpretation is essential for doctrinal legal research.

REFERENCES

Ali, S. I., Yusoff, Z. M., & Ayub, Z. A. (2017). Legal Research of Doctrinal and Non-Doctrinal. *International Journal of Trend in Research and Development*, 4(1), 493–495. http://www.ijtrd.com/papers/IJTRD6653.pdf

Baxi, U. (1975). Socio-legal Research in India-A Programschrift, 416-449. Indian Council of Social Science Research (ICSSR).

Bhat, I. P. (2019). *Idea and Methods of Legal Research*. Oxford University Press.

Cornell Law School. Legal Information Institute, Stare decisis. Retrieved from https://www.law.cornell.edu/wex/stare_decisis

Council of Australian Law Deans. (2005) Statement on the Nature of Legal Research. CALD. https://cald.asn.au/wp-content/uploads/2017/11/cald-statement-on-the-nature-of-legal-research-20051.pdf

Davis, K. C. (1964-65). Behavioural Science and Administrative Law, 17. *Journal of Legal Education*, 137–148.

Dobinson, I., & Johns, F. (2007). Legal Research as Qualitative Research. In M. McConville & W. H. Chui (Eds.), *Research Methods For Law* (pp. 18–47). Edinburgh University Press.

(2006). Doctrinal And Non-Doctrinal Legal Research. In Verma, S. K., & Wani, M. A. (Eds.), *Legal Research And Methodology*. Indian Law Institute.

Gestel, R. V., & Micklitz, H. W. (2011). Revitalizing Doctrinal Legal Research in Europe: What About Methodology? *European University Institute Working Papers Law.*

Government of India. (n.d.). An MHRD Project under its National Mission on Education through ICT (NME-ICT) Pathshala. Government of India. http://epgp. inflibnet.ac.in/epgpdata/uploads/epgp_content/law/09._research_methodology/08. qualitativeanddoctrinalmethodsinresearch/et/8155etet.pd

Hart, H. L. A. (1961). The Concept Of Law. Clarendon Press, Oxford. Cited in Chynoweth Paul, (2008) Legal Research in the Built Environment: A Methodological Framework. In Andrew Knight & Les Ruddock (Eds.), Advanced Research Methods in the Built EnvironmentWiley-Blackwell.

Hutchinson, T. (2015). The Doctrinal Method: Incorporating Interdisciplinary Methods in Reforming the Law, *Erasmus. Law Review*, *3*, 130–138.

Hutchinson, T., & Duncan, N. (2012). Defining and Describing What We Do: Doctrinal Legal Research, *Deakin. Law Review*, *17*(1), 83–119. https://ojs.deakin. edu.au/index.php/dlr/article/view/70/75

Jain, S. N. (1982). Doctrinal and Non-Doctrinal Legal Research. *Journal of the Indian Law Institute*, *24*(2/3), 341–361.

Jerome Hall Law Library. (2019) *Legal Dissertation: Research and Writing Guide.* Maurer School of Law. https://law.indiana.libguides.com/dissertationguide#:~:text =Doctrinal,%2C%20statutes%2C%20or%20regulations)

Library Highline College. (2022) *Primary and Secondary Legal Sources.* Highline College. https://library.highline.edu/c.php?g=344547&p=2320319

Minow, M., M. (2013). Archetypal Legal Scholarship – A Field Guide. *Journal of Legal Education*, *63*(1), 65–73.

Mittra, A. (2021) Analytical School of Jurisprudence, *Lawcorner.in*. https://lawcorner. in/analytical-school-of-jurisprudence/

myneni. S.R. (Ed.). (2006) Legal Research Methodology, (1st ed.). Allahabad Law Agency.

National Law University. (n.d.). *Delhi, Handbook for Research Project Writing.* National Law University. https://nludelhi.ac.in/download/publication/2015/NLU%20 old.pdf

Pearce, D., Campbell, E., & Harding, D. (1987). *Australian Law Schools: A Discipline Assessment for the Commonwealth Tertiary Education Commission.* Australian Government Publishing Service.

Rückert, J. (2006) Friedrich Carl von Savigny, the Legal Method, and the Modernity of Law, *Juridica International XI.* https://www.juridicainternational.eu/public/pdf/ji_2006_1_55.pdf

Tiwary, S. (2020) Doctrinal and Non-Doctrinal. *Academia.* https://www.academia.edu/40656281/Doctrinal_and_Non_Doctrinal_Methods_of_Legal_Research

Vibute, K. I. & Filipos, A. (2009) *Legal Research Methods: Teaching Material, Justice and Legal System Research Institute.* Wordpress. chilot.wordpress.com

Section 4
Research Results

Chapter 16
Basics of Research Report Writing for Behavioural Science Students and Emerging Scholars

Bassey Asuquo Bassey
University of Calabar, Nigeria

Valentine Joseph Owan
 https://orcid.org/0000-0001-5715-3428
University of Calabar, Nigeria

ABSTRACT

This chapter is written with behavioural science students and emerging scholars in mind. Behavioural science in this context includes but is not limited to management sciences, social sciences, psychology, education, and any discipline that deals with human actions. The chapter is written to sharpen the knowledge and skills of students in these areas in writing a good quality research report (at advanced undergraduate level), thesis, or dissertation (at postgraduate level). The chapter has valuable hints that will guide behavioural science students and emerging scholars in writing good quality research reports, theses, or dissertations. The hints will also be helpful for supervisors and mentors in guiding and assessing their student's work. A research project, thesis, or dissertation is essential for graduation from tertiary institutions. The need, therefore, to write good quality research reports requires that students possess the necessary knowledge and skills in writing.

DOI: 10.4018/978-1-6684-6859-3.ch016

CHAPTER SUMMARY

This chapter was written primarily to guide emerging scholars, students, and early career researchers on the basic constituents of a research report for a thesis, projects, dissertation and other related documents. The chapter was organised to capture the basic elements in the preliminary pages of a research report, the sub-components of chapters 1, 2, 3. 4 and 5, as well as supplementary pages. The preliminary pages comprised the title page, declaration, certification, acknowledgement, abstract, tables of contents, list of tables and list of figures. Chapter one provides the basic idea or problem underlying the research, including a justification of its needs based on existing studies in the literature. Crucial research questions and/or hypotheses (for quantitative studies) underlying the study are posed in this chapter. In chapter two, an extensive and detailed review of relevant and related literature is reviewed. It is also in chapter two that all relevant gaps in methodology, evidence, theory, knowledge, and population are identified to enable the researcher to find a base for his/her study. In chapter three, the methods, materials, and procedures are presented to achieve the goals (broad and specific) earlier stated in chapter 1. Chapter four is concerned with the presentation and interpretation of results as well as the discussion of key findings. Chapter five presents the summary of the entire research process from chapters one to four. Conclusions reached based on the results in chapter four are mentioned in chapter five, including the study's theoretical, practical and research implications. Finally, suggestions for further research are made in chapter five based on the study's limitations.

INTRODUCTION

The theme of this chapter is twofold; hints that will guide behavioural science students in writing good-quality research projects, theses and dissertations. The hints will also be helpful for supervisors and mentors in guiding and assessing their students' work. Behavioural science in this paper includes but is not limited to management sciences (e.g., management, marketing, etc.), social sciences, education and any discipline that deals with human actions. The need to adopt best practices in research reports and supervise students' theses motivated the writing of this chapter.

Problems exist in every sphere of life, and knowledge is incomplete in every discipline. Many questions require answers to solve numerous problems in the world. Gaps in our knowledge and unresolved problems can be addressed by asking relevant questions and seeking answers through research (Swales & Feak, 2014). Research is a fundamental tool for decision-making in most fields of endeavours (Kerlinger, 2000). Therefore, researchers, including tertiary-level students, emerging scholars, supervisors, and academic mentors, must understand what to write and how to write and research the chosen topic in their fields for graduation.

The researcher who completes his/her research must present a written report using a good style and format. In writing a research report, the objectives should be evident in the researcher's mind. S/He should understand that his/her presentation should achieve these specific objectives (Isangedighi & Bassey, 2012).

1. Research reports are written to acquaint the reader with the research problem. Through reading the report, the reader should be clear about what the researcher had in mind regarding the problem, his conception, and what the problem implied. Such clarity will help the reader to orient himself properly while reading the work;

2. Reports are written to fully and comprehensively outline the research data. Such data should be presented to see the basis for results interpretation and conclusions. The data should be so precisely presented that anyone who wants to replicate the study is adequately armed. The data should be logically presented. This is seen in the precise description of the data gathered, their coding and utilisation in addressing each subset of the problem;

3. reports are written to show appropriate data interpretation and the implications of the data in solving the problem. This means that giving research data is not enough. The mind must be allowed to battle with the available data to bring out meaning. It is only when the mind inquiries into the innate meaning of the data so assembled that the problem is said to have been resolved.

It has, however, been observed that researchers, students and emerging scholars need to adopt better practices in research report writing. This agrees with the position of Ugodulunwa (2016) that there are common pitfalls in many thesis proposals for defence and manuscripts submitted for review in journals. These include a preliminary literature review; poorly written abstract; unclear introduction; ambiguous research questions and hypotheses; inadequate description of sample and sampling procedure; inappropriate methodology/use of wrong statistical techniques; inappropriate description of instruments for data collection; poor presentation of results, discussion and conclusion. They also indulge in over-generalisation of findings, and poor writing and citation styles, among others. This chapter is, therefore, motivated by the need to sharpen students' knowledge and skills in writing acceptable research reports for undergraduate projects, theses, and dissertations and to provide guidance for supervising students' research reports for graduation. This chapter is written to satisfy that need.

At the end of this chapter, readers should be able to:

1. define the term 'research';
2. explain the usefulness of research guidelines in the writing and supervision of scholarly works;
3. outline the basic features of a suitable research project format;
4. discuss the major areas in the research presentation format outlined in (iii) above;
5. write a good research proposal, project, and thesis following the format in this chapter.

FORMAT FOR UNDERGRADUATE PROJECT, THESIS OR DISSERTATION

This section focuses on the format for organising and presenting reports of students' research projects, theses and dissertations in management sciences, social sciences education, and humanities. Generally, the format of the reports serves as a guide to researchers/students. Different institutions and faculties adopt various formats, and any of them serves the same purpose as long as the fundamentals of research report details are included. Therefore, students and emerging scholars are advised to adhere strictly to the required format of their institution, funding agency or publication outlet as much as possible.

Research projects, theses or dissertation reports writing are usually structured or formatted into three parts, namely:

*   The Preliminary Pages (usually numbered in Roman Numerals)
*   The Main Body (consisting of five chapters)
*   The Ending Pages (usually numbered in Arabic Numerals)

The components of each section, including what the researcher or student is expected to say under each component, are given below:

PRELIMINARY PAGES (USUALLY NUMBERED IN ROMAN NUMERALS)

i. Cover Page

This is usually a softbound cover for the proposal and thesis before the defence. It is often transformed into a hardcover page ready for submission after a successful defence. The colour of the cover is determined by the institution, type of degree or student's department. It must contain the title of the thesis, the student's name, registration numbers, the department and the month and year of successful defence, depending on the institution's style.

ii. Title Page

The title page contains information on the project title, thesis or dissertation, students' name, degree in view, name of the institution, and the date (month and year) of submission of the report. An example of a cover page is shown in Figure 1; however, this might vary with institutions.

Figure 1.

CONFLICT MANAGEMENT STRATEGIES AND SECONDARY SCHOOL
TEACHERS' JOB EFFECTIVENESS IN OBUBRA LOCAL
GOVERNMENT AREA OF CROSS RIVER STATE,
NIGERIA.

A RESEARCH PROJECT

BY

OWAN, VALENTINE JOSEPH
MATRIC. NO. 15/063143057

SUBMITTED TO

DEPARTMENT OF EDUCATIONAL ADMINISTRATION
AND PLANNING, FACULTY OF EDUCATION
UNIVERSITY OF CALABAR
CALABAR, NIGERIA.

IN PARTIAL FULFILMENT OF THE REQUIREMENTS FOR THE AWARD
OF BACHELOR OF EDUCATION DEGREE (B.Ed.) IN EDUCATIONAL
ADMINISTRATION AND PLANNING.

SEPTEMBER, 2018.

iii. Declaration Page (by the Student)

Here, the student declares or attests that the research is an original work; appends his/her signatures with the date. The implication is that if it is discovered that there was plagiarism over time, the student becomes liable for committing academic fraud. An example of a declaration page is shown in Figure 2.

Figure 2.

DECLARATION

I Owan, Valentine Joseph an undergraduate student of the Department of Educational Administration and Planning, Faculty of Education, University of Calabar, Calabar, with Matriculation Number 15/063143057, declare that this research work on "Conflict Management Strategies and Secondary School Teachers' Job Effectiveness" is an original study carried out in Obubra Local Government Area of Cross River State in 2017/2018 academic session. I hereby also declare that the work has not been duplicated in parts or in full for any other Diploma or Degree programme.

_____   _____
Owan, Valentine Joseph   Date
(Student)
Department of Educational
Administration and Planning,
Faculty of Education,
University of Calabar, Calabar.

iv. Certification Page (by the Examiners)

Here, all the people that have the final say on the project, theses or dissertation certify by appending their signatures and date. This includes the supervisor (s), head of department, graduate school representative, and external examiner. Their signatures and dates give credence that having read and examined the work has met the requirements for awarding a degree in a specialised field of endeavour. An example of a certification page is presented in Figure 3.

Figure 3.

CERTIFICATION

This is to certify that this study on Conflict Management Strategies and Secondary School Teachers' Job Effectiveness in Obubra Local Government Area of Cross River State, is an original research work conducted by **Owan, Valentine Joseph** with Matriculation number 15/063143057 under my supervision. I hereby certify that this work has been approved as having met the requirements for the award of Bachelor of Education degree in the Department of Educational Administration and Planning, Faculty of Education, University of Calabar, Calabar.

Prof. Charles P. Akpan
(Supervisor)
Department of Educational
Administration and Planning,
University of Calabar, Calabar.

_____
Signature

_____
Date

v. Dedication PAGE (if Any)

A research project, thesis or dissertation report, just like a textbook, may be dedicated to a particular person or group of persons - a spouse, children, parents or other family members, a group of students, etc. The choice depends on the author. It is, however, not a requirement.

vi. Acknowledgments

In this section, the researcher formally expresses appreciation to various individuals or groups who have contributed in one way or the other to the successful completion of the study. Such contributions may have been intellectual, financial, moral or spiritual. Since the research is an academic exercise, acknowledgement or persons in the academic circle should be acknowledged first before considering others. The order of acknowledgement could be God first, supervisor(s), head of department, lecturers and other scholars, family members, etc. A sample of acknowledgement is presented in Figure 4.

Figure 4.

ACKNOWLEDGEMENTS

I am most grateful to the Lord Almighty for granting me life and good health throughout my academic duration, and for the uncommon strength he gave to successfully complete this research work. I am particularly grateful to my supervisor Prof. Charles P. Akpan for his diligence, guidance, and constructive corrections he offered to ensure that the product of the study was standardized. May God grant you more strength and wisdom.

Specifically, it will be unwise if I fail to acknowledge the efforts of Assoc. Prof. Barr. Arop, Festus O; Assoc. Prof. B. A. Bassey; Dr. (Mrs). Odigwe, Francisca N.; Mr. Offem O. Otu; Mrs. Ene, Egbula Ogar; Assoc. Prof. James E. Okon; Prof. (Mrs). Uchendu C. C.; Dr. (Mrs.) R. O. Osim; Prof. M. O. Nyong; Dr. Ebi Bassey; Dr. Peter Ubi; Assoc. Prof. Ovat, O. O.; Mr. Ekaette Samuel O.; Mrs. Nwannunu Blessing Iheoma; and Mr. Wonah Fidelis, all of whom have been like parental figures to me throughout my time in the university, and for imparting positive intellectual and moral skills to my person.

My heartfelt gratitude, utmost joy, and intense honour goes to my parents Mr. and Mrs. Owan, Joshua N.; and my siblings Tina, David, Augustine, and Ruth Owan for their doggedness, labour, hard work, financial and moral support, prayers, encouragement and for inconveniencing themselves just to make me relevant in life. I am sincerely grateful to the entire family of Rev. Dr. Steve Owan for their whole-hearted love, care, prayer and support throughout the duration of my study.

vii. Abstract

An abstract is a summary or a synopsis of the entire work, giving the reader a clear and precise idea of what was done. An abstract should briefly state the study's problems, the purpose of the study, the method of investigation, the significant findings are, as well as the major recommendations. An informative abstract of a research project, thesis or dissertation should be between 300-500 words or one and a half pages at most (Asim et al., 2017; Ndiyo, 2005). A sample of an abstract is presented in Figure 5.

Figure 5.

ABSTRACT

The study investigated conflict management strategies and secondary school teachers' job effectiveness in Obubra Local Government Area of Cross River State. Six null hypotheses were formulated to guide the study. The study adopted correlational and factorial research designs. Purposive sampling technique was used to select a sample of 222 teachers from a population of 352 secondary school teachers. Conflict Management Strategies Questionnaire (CMSQ) and Secondary School Teachers' Job Effectiveness Questionnaire (SSTJEQ) were used respectively, as instruments for data collection. The hypotheses were tested at .05 level of significance using Population t-test, Pearson Product Moment Correlation and Multiple Regression analyses. Findings revealed that, teachers' job effectiveness level in Obubra Local Government Area is significantly high. Findings also revealed that arbitration, dialogue, and effective communication strategies respectively, had a significant relationship with secondary school teachers' job effectiveness. Smoothing strategy had no significant relationship to secondary school teachers' job effectiveness. The findings also revealed among others that; the four conflict management strategies (arbitration, dialogue, effective communication and smoothing) had a joint significant influence on secondary school teachers' job effectiveness. Based on these findings, it was recommended among others that; secondary school principals should not rely totally on one conflict management strategy as the best for all situations, instead they should learn how to use various conflict management strategies, and apply them in any given conflict situation in their schools.

viii. Table of Contents

This contains the title/sub-titles of every section/sub-section of the report, indicating the specific pages where each section and subsection can be located in the body of the report. It consists of a list of preliminary information, chapters and titles, as well as a list of tables, list of figures, a list of abbreviations, references/bibliography and an appendix. A sample of a table of contents is displayed in Figure 6.

Figure 6.

TABLE OF CONTENTS

ix. List of Tables (if Any)

This constitutes all the tables produced during the study. They are serially and consecutively numbered and are listed according to their numbers, title, and the specific pages where they may be located in the report. An example of a list of tables is shown in Figure 7.

Figure 7.

LIST OF TABLES

x. List of Figures (if Any)

Where figures like graphs, maps, diagrams, photographs or plates have been produced during the study and reported in any work, they have to be listed, showing their titles and the pages where they can be located in the report.

xi. List of Abbreviations (if Any)

This is a list where abbreviations used in the study are listed and explained for clarity.

CHAPTER ONE: INTRODUCTION

Chapter one of the report deals with the "introduction" to the study. It is the gateway to the whole study (Isangedighi & Bassey, 2012). Chapter one is "an introduction to the whole research, which is reported from chapters two to five. Chapter one is a window to the whole work" (Asim et al., 2017, p.187). In quantitative research, chapter one usually gives information under the following subsections:

i. Background to the Study

The essence of this subsection is to provide the necessary background information that will show the readers the conditions, circumstances and factors that have given rise to the problem under investigation. Here, the researcher presents how deep-seated the problem under investigation is and, if not adequately addressed, may lead to more unpleasant consequences. It is also in the background of the study that both dependent and independent variables are explained and linked up correctly.

ii. Theoretical Framework

A theoretical framework is a group of related ideas that guides a research project (Asim et al., 2017). It establishes the perspective through which the researcher views the problem. It provides the rationale for research to investigate a particular problem (Mertler & Charles, 2008). It provides the theoretical base that supports the researcher's investigation and offers the reader a justification for the study. Here, the researcher is expected to identify a theory (or theories), mention who propounded it, the year it was propounded, state the tenets of the theory, and link the variables in the study with the tenets of the theory. The identified theory or theories must have relevance to the study's variables.

iii. Statement of the Problem

This is where the researcher should clearly express his intention of the study so well as to leave no reader in doubt about what the work is trying to address. In other words, the focus here is to present the actual problem to which one is trying to contribute a solution in clear terms and present the problem by elaborating, clarifying and delineating its scope. The statement of the problem can be stated in either a declarative or an interrogative form. In whichever form the problem is stated, it should be unambiguous and short (not exceeding a page of an A-4 paper).

iv. Purposes of the Study

Here, what the researcher intends to accomplish in the study is clearly stated or outlined. The purpose of the study should be stated in general and specific terms. In most cases, each purpose of the study is linked directly with a research question or hypothesis, where applicable.

v. Research Questions

Research questions refer to the major questions the researcher seeks to answer in the investigation. Good research questions would arouse and create sustained interest in the researcher to seek answers to such questions. Note that good research questions should be empirically answerable, not lend themselves to a yes or no answer, and be framed to guide the study's conduct. An example of a research question is *how much do males differ from females in their mathematics achievement mean scores?* Another example is *to what extent are school infrastructural facilities available in tertiary institutions?* Other examples of research questions can be found in Figure 8.

Figure 8.

    i.   What is the level of secondary school teachers' job effectiveness in Obubra Local Government Area?

    ii.   How does arbitration strategy relate to secondary school teachers' job effectiveness?

    iii.   How does dialogue strategy relate to secondary school teachers' job effectiveness?

    iv.   How does effective communication strategy relate to secondary school teachers' job effectiveness?

    v.   How does smoothing strategy relate to secondary school teachers' job effectiveness?

    vi.   How does arbitration, dialogue, effective communication, and smoothing strategies jointly influence secondary school teachers' job effectiveness?

vi. Statement of Hypotheses

Hypotheses refer to intelligent guesses or hunches that the researcher formulates to guide his research for a solution to the problem. Hypotheses reflect measurable variables. They should be stated in a measurable and testable form. They should be stated in declarative form and tested using an inferential statistical test. It is essential to point out that some types of research, for instance, a descriptive survey, may require research questions with no compulsion for testing hypotheses. Hypotheses may be stated in alternative form or null form. An example of an alternative hypothesis is that *there is a significant difference in the mean scores of males and females in mathematics.* In null form, the same hypothesis may be stated as *there is no significant difference in the mean scores of males and females in mathematics.*

vii. Significance of the Study

This subsection provides the justification or rationale for conducting the research. It tries to establish whether or not the study is of some value. It argues why your research matters, how it impacted your field, what it added to the body of knowledge, and how it will benefit others. The researcher should also explain the study's usefulness in advancing already-known theories, positions and results. The practical significance of the study should also be discussed. This implies that the researcher must identify all the stakeholders likely to benefit from the research outcome. In other words, the researcher should emphasise practical benefits derived from the study's findings by different stakeholders, one after the other. Thus, your research's significance, value, and contribution should be made clear to the reader in your academic writing.

viii. Assumptions of the Study

Assumptions in research are out of the researcher's control, but if they disappear, your findings will be invalid, or your study will become irrelevant (Simon, 2011). For example, if you are conducting an empirical study, you need to assume that the variables involved in the study are measurable. If you are choosing a sample, you need to assume that this sample is representative of the population you wish to make an inference. It has been submitted by Leedy and Ormrod (2010) that "assumptions are so basic that, without them, the research problem itself could not exist" (p.62). Every research (behavioural science research) is carried out with some basic assumptions that border principally on the variables and sample of the study. For the variable, the basic assumptions are that the variable is measurable and normally distributed. For the sample, the basic assumptions are that the sample selection must be free of bias (fair) and the sample should be representative of the population of the study.

ix. Scope of the Study (or Delimitation)

The scope/delimitation of the study refers to those characteristics that limit the coverage and define the boundaries of your study. The delimitations are in your control. The scope factors include the problem of the study, the choice of the objectives, the research questions/ hypotheses, variables of interest, theoretical perspectives to adopt and the population you choose to investigate. Here the researcher needs to set a boundary for his study correctly. Things to consider are the variables and substances of interest, the sample and the study area. When the scope of the study is appropriately delineated, it makes the discussion of findings and generalisation realistic and meaningful.

x. Limitations of the Study

Limitations of a study are potential weaknesses in your study. We find limitations in almost everything we do. Suppose you are using a sample of conveniences instead of a random sample; then, the results of your study cannot be generally applied to a larger population, only suggested. If you look at one aspect, achievement tests, the information is only as good as the test itself. Alternatively, if you use a questionnaire to collect information when the most appropriate data collection strategy would have been using an observational schedule, that is a limitation. Another limitation is time. A study conducted over a specific time interval is a snapshot dependent on conditions occurring during that time (Simon, 2011). In this subsection, you must explain how you intend to deal with the limitations you are aware of so as not to affect the study's outcome. Limitations of the study usually focus on weaknesses of design, method and procedure that will limit the validity and generalisation of findings.

CHAPTER TWO: LITERATURE REVIEW

This chapter reviews all literature about the research theme, usually organised under relevant subheadings based on research questions or hypotheses. No matter how innovative or novel a research study may appear, earlier researchers may have done something related to that research or in certain aspects of the research to which the new study attempts to contribute. A literature review relating to the field of interest is necessary to avoid any attempt to reinvent the wheel and waste precious resources (Asim et al., 2017). Here, the researcher is expected to do the following, among others (Ugodulunwa, 2016):

- Review variables in the research topic and problem as well as relevant theories and empirical studies
- Organise and present literature reviewed coherently by ensuring each sentence is linked to the following and paragraphs are linked to one another using link words or phrases.
- Critique the studies regarding their weaknesses in design, method and procedure.
- Comment on the implications of the literature reviewed for your study.
- Cite current literature in the review; and
- End with a summary of the literature reviewed and clearly show the gaps to be filled.

CHAPTER THREE: RESEARCH METHODOLOGY

This chapter deals with the investigation procedure and consists of different sub-sections, depending on the type of investigation (research). Generally, it describes the design, sampling techniques, data collection techniques, and data analysis strategies as follows:

i. Research Design

Here, the researcher is expected to relate the design to the general approach adopted in the study. The researcher should mention the design, describe it, and justify why and how it is adopted in the study. The research design chosen and adopted should be appropriate and have high internal or external validity.

ii. Area of the Study

Here, the researcher is expected to locate the study area in terms of latitudes and longitudes (geographically and sometimes with demographic descriptions). This could be stated in the country, state, education, political/administrative zone, local government area etc., as the case may be. The researcher is also expected to indicate the study area's geographical borders (regarding neighbours).

iii. Population of the Study

Here, the researcher should mention the population of the study and describe its characteristics and context. A population may be finite if all items or subjects that constitute it can be counted. It is infinite if the size (number) cannot be counted.

The population should be described explicitly in terms of geographical limits, demographic and sociological characteristics, the period covered, etc., as dictated by the problem of the study. The description should be such that it would leave no doubt in the readers' minds as to who is qualified or not qualified to be a member of the population under study. If possible, state the total members of the population.

iv. Sampling Techniques

Mention the sampling technique(s) to be adopted and describe it clearly. Describe how the sampling technique is applied in sample selection. Justify the choice of the sampling techniques and present the distribution of the population of the study in a table. Before drawing the sample, the researcher must define his unit of analysis or study. Who is being studied, and what constitutes the population from which the sample will be drawn? Other considerations that must be made when deciding on the sampling technique are the nature of the population, its characteristics, sub-groups and size. The researcher must also decide whether probability or non-probability sampling methods will be more suitable and justify the choice using literature support. The researcher must determine whether it is feasible to implement specific sampling strategies in selecting respondents based on factors such as the geographical spread of the population, access to the sample, available time, financial cost, etc. The type of research method pursued/adopted for the study is another determinant. Furthermore, the need to ensure unbiasedness in selecting participants must also be considered. For example, a researcher may use a proportionate stratified random technique for his study. The researcher may choose this method because he wants to give every member of the population an equal opportunity to participate (randomisation). Secondly, his population of interest contains males and females; thus, he stratifies it along gender lines. Thirdly, he wants to select his sample based on the proportion of individuals in both the male and female categories. Doing this will not only yield an unbiased sample but will promote fairness.

v. Sample

The sample (that portion of the population from which data were collected) is defined here as how it can be obtained. It may or may not be a representative part of the population. The proportion or percentage of the population selected as the study sample should be clearly stated, and the sample distribution should be presented in a table. Justify your decision to choose a particular sample size given your study's anticipated or desirable precision. When deciding on the sample size for a study, special attention must be given to the statistical power to be achieved/ required; the allowance for possible attrition, missing data or non-response, the number of variables in the study; the type of research pursued, the number of sub-groups in the population to avoid sample over- or under-representation; the method of statistical analysis to be used; the size of the population; the expected response rate; the research timeframe; the funds at the researchers' disposal; the expected impact or utility value of the study. For example, a researcher might decide to study an entire population if it is small or manageable. In another situation, a researcher may require a large sample size due to statistical analytic requirements such as structural equation modelling (SEM). In contrast, another researcher may recruit a small sample for his study because it is qualitative.

vi. Instrumentation

This involves a description of the instrument(s) used in collecting the data. Such a description should include how the instrument was developed and the major features of the instrument. If the instrument used is constructed by you, describe clearly, with accurate details, how the set of items used to elicit responses for each variable was constructed. If the items were adapted from an existing instrument, summarise the procedure used in its construction and measurement properties. If the instrument was adopted, say so. In behavioural sciences, different instruments can be used for data collection, such as questionnaires, interviews, observation, and tests.

vii. Validity and Reliability

The validity of the instrument(s) used for the study should be established. Mention the type of validity established (whether face, content, predictive or construct) and justify the validity choice. Describe clearly the procedure you adopted for establishing the validity, and present the results of validity analysis (where necessary). Ensure that the instrument measure what it is supposed to measure.

An instrument is reliable if it consistently gives the same or similar results. This also should be established for the instrument (s). Mention the type of reliability estimate (whether internal consistency, stability or equivalence) and justify your choice. Describe the procedure for establishing the instrument's reliability (split-half, test-retest, Cronbach Alpha, etc.). Mention the criteria or standards from the literature for judging the reliability level of the instrument.

viii. Procedure for Data Collection

Here, the researcher reports the steps to collect pertinent data for the study. This entails whether the researcher collected the data, with the help of field assistants, by mail, etc. The researcher should state how authorities sought permission to collect data from the population as the sample. Describe how research assistants (if any) were trained and used for data collection. Describe clearly how each instrument was administered. Mention the duration of data collection. Describe how data from each instrument were scored. In the case of an experimental study, the researcher should also describe pre-test administration, treatment package/ intervention/ programme, treatment given to the experimental group, package given to the control group and how sources of internal invalidity were controlled. Treatment should last for at least eight weeks for sufficient impact to be made (Ugodulunwa, 2016).

ix. Procedure for Data Preparation and Scoring

In research that generates an extensive mass of data, the researcher needs to state beforehand how he plans to process the data collected/ generated. Data processing involves transferring collected data into coded data for further processing through a data processing instrument, reliably through computer statistical software for data management and analysis (Owan & Bassey, 2018). The researcher also describes how he scored the participants' responses variable by variable. States how he coded or transformed the data in preparation for analyses.

x. Procedure for Data Analysis

The procedures for analysing collected data deal with the technical procedures needed for statistical or quantitative analysis. The student/ researcher should reflect on the statistical techniques appropriate for the research design. The most appropriate mode of statistics appropriate for the data collected must be used. Note that the choice of each technique depends on the nature of the data (nominal, ordinal, interval or ratio). Present data analysis techniques you used for each research question and/or hypothesis; describe how and why each technique is applied. If the data are not many, simple frequency count, for example, can be used, and statistical computation is done manually. The data analysis techniques may be the elementary application of measures of central tendency, variability, regression, correlation, time series, ANOVA, contingency analysis or more complicated techniques involving programming etc. Results from the data analysis should be presented appropriately in charts, graphs, etc., describe the method(s)/mode (s) used, or cite sources that do. Report the statistical analysis, including data sources and the name of any computer software packages used.

xi. Operational Definition of Research Variables

Here, the student or researcher should define only terms whose meanings or methods of obtaining measurement are subject to ambiguity in measurable terms. Critical variables in the research topic, research questions and hypotheses need to be operationally defined in how they are measured in the study. Definitions of terms should be either conceptual or operational.

xii. Ethical Considerations

Ethical concerns refer to the regulations that outline the appropriate and inappropriate actions for researchers to take when conducting their studies. While conducting your study, understanding the governing ethical principles is important to guide the research conduct. Therefore, researchers must indicate how relevant ethical principles were considered and followed in the research. In their text, Cohen et al. (2018) listed the following as some ethical issues that must be considered in behavioural research: informed consent; confidentiality and anonymity; identification and non-traceability; non-maleficence; beneficence and duty of care; responsibilities (for what and to whom); gaining access; overt and covert research; disclosure and public versus private knowledge; relationships and differential power relations; interest at stake in the interest; rights, permissions and protections; ownership and control of data; access to data and its archiving; the role and powers of research sponsors.

CHAPTER FOUR: RESULTS AND DISCUSSION

i. Results

This chapter embodies the results or findings and discussion of the study. Here, you present your research results in tables and/or graphs according to the research questions and/or hypotheses formulated for the study. Note that only the summaries of such analyses in the form of tables, figures and charts are presented in this chapter. Each table, figure or chart should have a title and number. The number should be in the Arabic numeral and not Roman. For tables, the number and title should appear on top of the table, while for figures, the number and title should appear below the figures. It is advisable to present the results according to the research questions or hypotheses to which they relate. The results so presented are duly interpreted. After statistical interpretations have been given to data analysis, there is a need to explain clearly what the statistical result means.

ii. Discussion of Findings

How the outcome/findings of the present study fit into previous research, as highlighted in the areas of literature review, becomes evident at this point. Here, the researcher tries to advance possible interpretations and explanations of his findings and relates these to previous research findings. Implications of the findings, that is, how the present findings relate to specific uses, theories, or practise, can also be discussed here. The limitations of generalising study findings should also be discussed, with good suggestions for future researchers.

CHAPTER FIVE: SUMMARY, CONCLUSION AND RECOMMENDATION

This chapter is a recapitulation of what the research set out to do and the outcome of the research undertaking. It has the following subsections:

i. Summary of the Study

This subsection has to do with a restatement of the purpose of the study, a brief explanation of the methodology adopted and an outline of significant findings. Summary of the study provides a snapshot of the entire research process, including the study's objectives, theories used, the hypotheses formulated, the methods used (including instruments, sampling methods, data collection methods etc.), and an overview of the results/findings reached.

ii. Conclusion

The conclusion is the inference that may be drawn from the study based on the major research findings. In conclusion, the research has to give some impact implications of the study's outcome regarding the original problem that necessitates the research. The research should be able to answer a question like: "giving these findings, what next?" (Isangedihi & Bassey, 2012). Thus, the conclusion does not restate the findings already highlighted in chapter four or elsewhere in this report. In other words, a conclusion is drawn based on the study's findings and is usually stated assertively. A reasonable conclusion should also clearly state the implications of the study's findings for policy and practical reforms.

iii. Recommendations

Suggested actions could be taken in light of findings to bring about improvements in the system or the discipline. The recommendations should be based on major research findings. Sometimes it may be necessary to direct such recommendations to different groups of beneficiaries or stakeholders of the research results, for example, policymakers, teachers, students, parents and society at large, depending on the research outcome.

iv. Suggestions for Further Research

Since research is a continuous process, it follows that the end of one study marks the beginning of another. To ensure this, it is necessary to make suggestions at the end of each study on areas on that future research could be based. Such suggestions might take care of the new areas/ideas that emerged during the research or the literature review. Suggestions could also be made for replication of the study, change of population or sample, the addition of study variables, etc.

ENDING PAGES

i. References

The references section lists all sources cited in the work, such as textbooks, journals, conference/seminar papers, theses, indexes, mimeographs, etc., used during the study. Therefore, all works cited in the body of the report should be listed in the references to enabling other researchers to identify and locate such sources. For references, it is important to consider very recent sources (works within the past five years) for empirical studies. However, for theories and methodology, seminal works are highly recommended; thus, old literature may be used for these sections. Only cite works that are very useful and related to the study at hand to provide a basis for your work. Before citing any source in your writing, ensure it has complete bibliographic information. Therefore, use such information to prepare proper referencing of the material before citing to avoid citation issues without corresponding references. The latest referencing style should be used for citation in-text and compilation of reference lists as per the requirement of the particular journal.

ii. Appendices

This subsection consists of supplementary materials, which in the researcher's opinion, need not be included in the body of the report but could be crucial to the reader. An appendix contains samples of an instrument(s) used for the study and detailed calculations made to arrive at the final results. The materials could be research instruments, correspondences made during the study, list(s) of units studied, etc. Appendix headings are in boldface, centred, at the top margin. Allow two block lines between the heading and first entries (Ndiyo, 2005). Appendices are labelled A, B, C or I, II, III etc. Different types of material should be in a separate annexe, and each type of material should be complete in and of itself. The appendices follow the reference list.

CONCLUSION

In research report writing, students or researchers make serious mistakes that could cause total rejection of their thesis during the proposal defence or even during the final oral defence. According to Kinash (n.d), these mistakes include frequent use of long quotations, too many typographical and spelling mistakes, grammatical errors, statements, and generalisations not supported by literature evidence, plagiarism, and improper citation in text and references. Other errors could be using secondary sources, writing off-topics, exceeding the specific word count or pages in some sections of the thesis, fabricating, falsifying and misrepresenting data, and non-adherence to acceptable style/format and thesis guidelines, generally. Students should, therefore, guard against these pitfalls in writing their research projects, theses or dissertations for graduation.

REFERENCES

Asim, A. E., Idaka, I. E., & Eni, E. I. (2017). *Research in education: Concepts and techniques*. University of Calabar Press.

Cohen, L., Manion, L., & Morission, K. (2018). *Research methods in education* (8th ed.). Routledge., doi:10.4324/9781315456539

Isangedighi, A. J., & Bassey, B. A. (2012). Research report writing. In A. J. Isangedighi (Ed.), *Essentials of research and statistics in education and social sciences* (pp. 287–292). Eti-Nwa Associates.

Kerlinger, F. N. (2000). *Foundations of behavioural research*. Holt, Rinehart and Wilson.

Kinash, S. (n.d.). Fatal mistakes in academic writing. [Internet source]. http://www. bong.edu.gu/prod_ext/groups/public@pub-tis-gen/documents/genericwedocument/ bd3_12330pdf

Leedy, P. D., & Ormrod, J. E. (2010). *Practical research: Planning and design* (9th ed.). Merril.

Mertler, C. A., & Charles, C. M. (2008). *Introduction to educational research*. Allyn and Bacon.

Ndiyo, N. A. (2005). *Fundamentals of research in behavioural sciences and humanities*. Wusen Publishers.

Nworgu, B. G. (2005). *Educational research: Basic issues and methodology*. Wisdom Publishers Limited.

Owan, V. J., & Bassey, B. A. (2018). Comparative study of manual and computerised software techniques of data management and analysis in educational research. [IJIEM]. *International Journal of Innovation in Educational Management, 2*(1), 35–46.

Simon, M. K. (2011). *Assumptions, limitations and delimitation*. [Excerpt from dissertation and scholarly research: Recipe for success. Seatle, W. A.] Dissertation Success, LLC.

Swales, J. M., & Feak, C. B. (2014). Commentary for academic writing for graduate students: Essential tasks and skills (5th ed.). University of Michigan Press/ESL.

Ugodulunwa, C. A. (2016). *Basics of academic writing: A guide for students*. Fab Anieh Nigeria Ltd.

ADDITIONAL READING

Beins, B. C. (2020). *APA style simplified: writing in psychology, education, nursing, and sociology*. John Wiley & Sons.

Bradley, L., Noble, N., & Hendricks, B. (2021). Mastering the new APA publication manual: Teaching techniques. *The Family Journal (Alexandria, Va.), 29*(1), 4–9. doi:10.1177/1066480720954207

Gill, S. L. (2020). Qualitative sampling methods. *Journal of Human Lactation, 36*(4), 579–581. doi:10.1177/0890334420949218 PMID:32813616

Heeringa, S. G., West, B. T., & Berglund, P. A. (2017). *Applied survey data analysis*. Chapman And Hall/CRC.

Kornuta, H. M., & Germaine, R. W. (2019). *A concise guide to writing a thesis or dissertation: Educational research and beyond*. Routledge. doi:10.4324/9780429056888

Owan, V. J. (2022). A data mining algorithm for accessing research literature in electronic databases: Boolean operators. In T. Masenya (Ed.), *Innovative technologies for enhancing knowledge access in academic libraries* (pp. 140–155). IGI Global. doi:10.4018/978-1-6684-3364-5.ch009

Privitera, G. J. (2022). *Research methods for the behavioral sciences*. Sage Publications.

Sarstedt, M., Bengart, P., Shaltoni, A. M., & Lehmann, S. (2018). The use of sampling methods in advertising research: A gap between theory and practice. *International Journal of Advertising*, *37*(4), 650–663. doi:10.1080/02650487.2017.1348329

Shirahatti, R. V., & Hegde-Shetiya, S. (2015). Review of research designs and statistical methods employed in dental postgraduate dissertations. *Indian Journal of Dental Research*, *26*(4), 427. doi:10.4103/0970-9290.167634 PMID:26481893

Tan, W. C. K. (2022). *Research methods: A practical guide for students and researchers*. World Scientific., doi:10.1142/12863

KEY TERMS AND DEFINITIONS

Citation: Citation simply refers to an acknowledgement given to an author or a source for using their work. The aim of citation is to let readers know the original source where a piece of information presented in a document has been derived.

Data: Data are raw facts that are gathered from the research awaiting processing for relevant meaning associated with them to be uncovered. When data are processed, meanings can be made from them for a thorough understanding of the event, phenomena or trait about which the data was collected.

Emerging Scholars: Emerging scholars are individuals undergoing training at a tertiary institution that are venturing or intending to venture into research, writing and publication. These can include undergraduates, postgraduates or doctoral students and graduates that have yet to become major authorities in their fields.

Research Methods: This is a generic term used to refers to a compendium of all the procedures, tools, approaches and materials used in pursuing a given research project. Basically, research methods can be classified into mono-methods and mixed methods.

Research Reporting: This is the last stage in the research process where researchers communicate the results of their studies to the wider community. Research reports can be prepared as journal articles, chapters in books, theses/dissertations, books, etc.

Research: Research is an action-oriented exercise and a systematic means of acquiring knowledge through the collection, preparation, analysis and interpretation of data to reach meaningful conclusions.

Sample: This is a portion of the population selected (using one or more acceptable strategy) for an investigation. A sample can be homogenous or heterogenous; it can be small or large; it can be representative or non-representative. However, the information derived from a sample about a phenomenon of interest can be generalised to the population.

Sampling: This is the process of selecting a sample for a research project. It can also be a collection of procedure followed in recruiting a sample for a study. Sampling procedures can be probability-based or non-probability-based, with each having their strengths, weaknesses and suitable situations.

Chapter 17
Scientific Publication Guide for Non-Native English-Speaking Researchers

Ltifi Moez

 https://orcid.org/0000-0003-3210-1845

College of Science and Humanities, Shaqra University, Saudi Arabia & Higher Business School, Sfax University, Tunisia

ABSTRACT

Scientific publication is an essential aspect of technical, medical, social, economic, and other progress. New advances in human knowledge in any field are communicated to the rest of the world through publications. Scientific research is universal, so it is essential that this communicated knowledge is accurate, valid, reproducible, and practically useful. Researchers and scientists dream of publishing their work in high impact journals. To make these dreams come true, it is essential to learn, follow, and know the basic principles of research methodology and scientific publication. In this chapter book on the basis of the author's experiences and knowledge, the author presents a personal opinion on how to publish a chapter book in a high impact journal. The author talks about how to carry out good research, the design of the manuscript preparation, the respect of the editorial policy of the journal, the likely results, and the reasons for failure or success. The author provides the competitive weapons of publication in the form of advice, recommendations, and explanations, in order to achieve scientific success.

DOI: 10.4018/978-1-6684-6859-3.ch017

INTRODUCTION

Impact factor journals are the best journals in the world. They are the guardians of scientific advancement. For this reason these journals aim to publish the best research with valid conclusions and solid contributions that will stand up to scrutiny. To enhance their scientific positions, impact journals always seek to publish a product that has a positive impact on science and society (Emad & El-Omar, 2014).

Competition is always present even in the field of scientific research. Knowing something means being more competitive than others. Today, knowledge management has an important interest in this area.

Knowledge is one of the most important strategic resources for the researcher and is valuable and inimitable. Replacing existing knowledge, implicit or explicit, which may be erroneous or insufficient, requires the acquisition of new knowledge from internal and external sources. This knowledge is useful for solving problems and barriers to scientific publications.

Knowledge management involves the identification and valorisation of the collective knowledge of researchers. It is about getting the right knowledge to the right people at the right time and enabling researchers to share and implement information to improve their scientific positions and add to scientific research. However, the most valuable knowledge lies in the human brain.

Knowledge sharing and knowledge management are the strategic elements that enable researchers to develop a competitive advantage, to exchange scientific knowledge and experience with each other.

The objective of this chapter is to help researchers produce a manuscript of high scientific quality in order to meet the requirements of the impacted journals and succeed in their publications. The scientific quality, experience, writing capacity ... vary from one researcher to another. Even the most experienced scientists sometimes forget the requirements of scientific research as well as the requirements of the journals, which generally results in a lower level of their productions. In this chapter book, I present the essential requirements and how to manage researchers' knowledge in order to achieve a solid publication with high impact (Balibar, 2014).

DESIGN OF THE MANUSCRIPT PREPARATION

The research method generally follows an orderly path from observation through a research problem, a research question, a hypothesis, a research objective and a method of resolution to the discussion of the scientific findings.

Importance of the Choice of Title

The research title is the first window through which readers (including the publisher of the targeted journal) can view your work. Therefore, choose a title that catches their attention, accurately describes the content of your manuscript, and catches people's attention to read more.

At the outset, it is important to stress that the title of a research paper need not be boring, long and tedious. It can even be interesting, fun and challenging. However, it doesn't have to be esoteric or silly either. It should inform and interest the potential reader. When reading it, the person should at least be able to recognize the subject matter or problem being discussed. This should be sufficiently precise to determine whether your work is of interest to him or her. The title may also refer to the main findings and indicate the angle of approach used. Technically, a title is usually less than 200 characters long (Martinsuo & Huemann, 2021).

Abstract

Usually, all research work is accompanied by a summary. This summary should help the reader to quickly get an accurate idea of the content. The structure of this summary is relatively standard. It generally begins with a sentence or two that situates the problem being studied.

This is followed by the main elements that led to the formulation of the objectives, questions or hypotheses formulated. These are announced very briefly. The research approach and the angle of approach to the research are then outlined. Finally, the summary concludes with the main findings and conclusions of the work, including proposed new avenues of research. The challenge is to manage to say all this in less than five hundred words and ideally even in less than two hundred words (Patriotta, 2017).

Key Words

A keyword is a term that will clearly and precisely designates a theme or notion, and translate the object of the research. It is generally presented in the singular, without any determinant. Several keywords may be necessary to translate all aspects of the research. Their combination thus makes it possible to formulate queries when querying a database (Hanna, 1989).

To translate concepts into keywords, use thesauri, lexicons and indexes: they help to remove ambiguities of meaning and spelling and to fine-tune terms. Five keywords characterising the search are usually placed immediately below the abstract.

These key words are chosen to evoke, according to their relevance, the subject, the sample, the method and the results.

Introduction

Research work is the construction of a scientific object. It allows the author to:

- Explore a phenomenon.
- Solve a problem.
- Question or refute the results provided in previous work.
- Experiment a new process, a new solution, a new theory.
- Apply a practice to a phenomenon.
- To describe a phenomenon.
- To explain a phenomenon.

The structure of the introduction is also quite similar from one research to another. It consists of two parts. The first part corresponds to the substance of the study. It is the main part of the introduction. It is devoted to the content of the study and usually begins by introducing the topic under study in a general way. Then this general theme is narrowed down around a particular social or scientific problem by presenting the concerns and motivations of the research. Then, the general objective of the research is specified in relation to this problem. Finally, the interest of studying this problem is underlined. The second part of the introduction deals with the form of the study. Relatively brief, it presents the structure of the text. This part is usually placed at the end of the introduction (Fortin 2006).

PROBLEM / OBJECTIVE / RESEARCH QUESTION

The Problem

A problematic is a question linked to a management problem in the broad sense. Establishing a problem is first of all a task of describing a situation or phenomenon that poses a scientific or social problem. This work is both conceptual and written (Tinke & Lowe, 1982).

On the conceptual level, the work consists of organising a description of the state of knowledge about the situation or phenomenon studied based on what is already known in the scientific literature. This work is more than a simple operation aimed at summarising. In fact, establishing the problem is the first step in the analysis, as the information is organised and grouped together in such a way as to make sense of it and lead to the definition and formulation of the problem and research question (Gauthier, 1992).

In terms of writing, establishing the problem consists in trying to formalise this organisation of data and known facts. Most of the time, this writing work is carried out in several iterations, by successive approximations, making it possible to produce a relatively clear and accessible synthesis of the state of the situation in relation to the subject that interests us. The final text must present all the known facts that lead to our research question. Reading it should make it possible to get to know the people involved, the milieus, the institutions and the environment in which the topic is situated. In this way, the conceptual work and the writing work are mutually oriented and clarified in the course of successive versions. The final text presenting the problematic is the fruit of this work of circular iterations between our ideas and their formalization in writing (Fovet-Rabot, (2018).

Present the General Objective of the Research

The research objective, at least the general objective, is directly derived from the formulation of the problem. Indeed, it is implicit, when presenting the problem that the objective of the research will be to contribute to solving it. But, beyond this obvious fact, the general objective defines the approach to the problem. Specifying the objective of the research means seeking to make explicit our intention to explore or contribute to a better understanding of a situation or phenomenon, or our intention to verify certain assumptions. Better understanding essentially means aiming to develop or improve an explanatory model of the interrelationships between the various components of the problem. It may also involve the development of explanatory hypotheses that may eventually be subject to verification. Exploring means identifying the elements that make it possible to account for an unknown situation. Finally, verifying refers to the testing of an assumed relationship between two elements, of the type if X, then B.

Specifying the general objective by delimiting from the outset a portion of the problem which will be more particularly deepened in the research and specified following the presentation of the theoretical framework. Following the presentation of the theoretical framework, the general objective will be broken down into specific sub-objectives related to specific elements of the problem. At this stage, there should be no hesitation to limit the study to only part of the problem identified. It is a matter of setting interesting, certainly, but above all realistic objectives within the timeframe already given and with the financial and other means at our disposal. It should be remembered that it is not the scope of the subject that will determine the quality of the study; it is its rigour, relevance and elegance (Fovet-Rabot, (2019).

Formulating the Research Question

The research question refers to the information that will be collected to achieve the objective. What will we seek to know to improve our understanding? What will we observe in order to report on a situation? What will we compare to verify our prediction? For example, if our research problem is the gap between the feminist discourse on the cooperative values associated with the exercise of power and the communication practices actually exercised by women in power, a research question in line with an objective of better understanding could be: How do women in power represent the exercise of power by women? An exploration question could be: What are the communication practices of women in power? Finally, a verification question could be: Do women in power really use different communication practices than men in power?

Thus, if the question begins with a "Do...", the question could be: "Do women in power really use different communication practices than men in power? "or with an "If... then...", the research approach and methodology is likely to be quantitative, as the underlying objective of this type of question is one of verification and generalisation. We want to know whether or not there is a significant relationship between A and B. If the question begins with "How... ", "How... ", "What...", then the approach and method are likely to be qualitative, because the underlying objective of this type of question is an understanding objective where one seeks to relate a set of elements in such a way as to offer a meaningful interpretation of a problematic situation (Quivy & Campenhoudt, 2006).

The general research question is in practice much more important than the space it will occupy in the text. The few lines of the question guide the choice of authors and studies. It allows us to eliminate many texts that are interesting, but not relevant to the question we are asking ourselves. In the same way, it guides our methodological choices (Voss, 1999).

LITERATURE REVIEW

Developing the Theoretical Framework

The aim of the theoretical framework is to clearly present and define the set of terms that will be used to deal with the problem and formulate the specific questions and hypotheses.

Inventory the Concepts and Models

Make an Inventory of the Writings Related to the Explanations

In this part, the researcher presents the studies and authors that have contributed to the understanding of the research problem. He shows that he is familiar with the authors and works that have, before him, in one way or another, tackled the research field and subject that are his own. The aim is to review all the writings (literature review) or other relevant works, i.e. those that correspond to the major concerns of this research, and to select and then organise them intelligently (Quivy & Campenhoudt, 1988).

Present the Factors, Concepts and Approaches
That May Affect the Problem

In this part, the researcher focuses on age, time, duration, language levels, social positioning, attitudes, network structure, etc.; the relationships between the factors and their links with the problem (Germain, 1993).

Basis and Formulation of Research Hypotheses

The research problem explained by precise questions leads to suppositions, proposals and anticipated answer to the questions. This is the meaning of hypotheses.

The hypothesis is an affirmative statement written in the present tense of the indicative, formally declaring the expected relationships between two or more variables. It is a supposition or a prediction, based on the logic of the problem and the defined research objectives. It is the anticipated answer to the research question posed. The formulation of a hypothesis implies the verification of a theory or precisely of its propositions. The hypothesis needs to be confirmed, refuted or qualified by the confrontation of facts.

There are several factors to be taken into account when formulating hypotheses:

- The statement of relationships: relationship between two variables, two phenomena, two or more concepts. This relationship can be causal (cause and effect; for example: "this causes this", "this explains that", "this affects that") or associative (for example: "this has a connection with that", "this is related to that"). In most hypotheses, two main types of concepts are considered: causes (or factors) that have effects (or consequences). Causes are also referred to as independent variables, while effects are referred to as dependent variables. In a relationship between two variables in a hypothesis, the variable to be explained is the dependent variable, and the explanatory factor is the independent variable.

- The meaning of the relationship is indicated by terms such as: "less than", "greater than", "different from", "positive", "negative", etc. The relationship between the two variables is indicated by terms such as: "less than", "greater than", "different from", "positive", "negative", etc.
- Verifiability: the essence of a hypothesis is that it can be verified. It contains variables that are observable, measurable in reality and analysable.
- Plausibility: the hypothesis must be plausible, i.e. it must be relevant to the phenomenon under study.

However, it should not be forgotten:

- There can be a main hypothesis and secondary or operational hypotheses. These must be articulated around the main one and must be called each other in a logic imposed by the research problem.
- In order to verify a hypothesis, the starting attitude must be that of invalidating it. This reinforces doubt and creates the conditions for scientific objectivity by reducing the risks of subjective interpretations and orientations. The hypothesis is confirmed only insofar as none of the data collected invalidates it.
- Validating a hypothesis does not consist in asking the subjects surveyed whether they agree with the idea put forward.

RESEARCH METHODOLOGY

A research methodology starts with a problem to be solved or from a myth of understanding and action. Methods cannot be isolated from the paths opened up by the researcher's interests (the questions, values, ideologies or theories guiding his or her objectives) nor from the characteristics of the information accessible. A method is relevant when it fits the questions asked and the information sought (Heritage, 1987; Feuls, 2022).

During this phase, the researcher explains and justifies the methods and instruments he or she will use to apprehend and collect data, in response to the questions asked and the hypotheses formulated. The researcher also specifies the characteristics of the population (human group or not) on which he will work and from which he will extract the information. Finally, he or she describes the data collection process and indicates the data analysis plan (Ben Aissa, 2001).

Choice of Data Collection Methods and Instruments

At this stage, the researcher presents or explains the methods or paradigms to be used, then describes the instruments or techniques that will be used. Various instruments are used to measure the study variables. These instruments may provide qualitative information (interviews, observation, etc.) or quantitative information (questionnaire, measurement scales, etc.), (Yin, 2002).

Definition of the Population and the Study Sample

The researcher characterises the population by establishing the selection criteria for the study, specifying the sample and determining the size. The target population refers to the population that the researcher wishes to study and from which he will want to make generalisations. The accessible population is the portion of the target population that is within the researcher's reach. It can be limited to a region, a city, a company, an agency, a department, etc. It can also be limited to a particular region, city, company, agency, department, etc. A sample is a subset of items or subjects drawn from the population that are selected to participate in the study (Marie-Laure et al., 2012).

Describe the Process of Data Collection

The researcher anticipates and describes, as far as possible any problems that might arise in the data collection process. In all cases, a research plan must include a description of how the process will be organised: what the population will be surveyed, who exactly will be surveyed, the size of the sample, how the data will be collected, the administrative arrangements, how many interviewers will be available, what logistics will be available, what obstacles are likely to be encountered, etc. The researcher must also describe the data collection process, the methodology to be used, the methodology to be used, the time frame, the time frame, the time frame and the duration of the survey (Schoonenboom, 2016).

Presentation of the Plan for Analysing the Data Collected

The researcher specifies the types of analysis he plans to carry out. For numerical, quantitative data, he will explain how he will establish rankings and statistical links between two variables (distributions, contingency tables, linkage by chance, X2, etc.). He will also explain how he will handle qualitative data (thematic analysis, content analysis of textual data taken from various documents, interviews, reports, press articles, strategic or operational documents, etc.), (Dawnie & Health, 1974; Schoonenboom et al., 2017).

Data Collection

This work is carried out according to an established plan. This systematic collection of information is carried out using the instruments chosen (Beaud & Weber 1997).

Justification of Reliability

The question of the reliability of a research project concerns a priori all phases of the research process. In particular, it concerns the measurement of phenomena, which must be carried out using instruments (measurement scales, questionnaires, etc.) that are reliable in the following sense: if the same phenomenon is measured several times with the same instrument, the same results must be obtained (De Lagarde, 1983).

Justification of the Internal Validity of a Research

The internal validity of a research is based on the internal coherence of the research process, the validity of the construct and the rigour of the research process.

Justification of the External Validity of a Research

External validity refers to the validity of knowledge beyond the empirical basis on which it was developed (i.e., in quantitative research, beyond the sample considered, and, in qualitative research, beyond the cases considered). Regardless of the epistemological framework of the research, the justification of the external validity of knowledge is based on the testing of that knowledge. For generalisation, the researcher's interest is not in knowing what is happening here and now, but in knowing what might happen to other individuals, under other conditions and at other times (Johnson & Larry, 2017; Martinet, 1990).

Analysis of the Results

Analysing means breaking down a phenomenon so as to distinguish its constituent elements. This division of a global phenomenon into smaller elements is carried out with the aim of recognising or explaining the relationships that link these elements together in order to better understand the phenomenon as a whole. The analysis prepares the synthesis, which is the operation of linking the identified elements to form a new coherent whole (Le Moigne, 1990).

Data analysis depends on the type of study and its purpose, depending on whether the aim is to explore or describe phenomena and to understand or verify relationships between variables. Statistics allow for quantitative analysis. Qualitative analysis gathers and summarizes, in narrative form, non-numerical data. It can, for example, make categorizations. Data analysis produces results that are interpreted and discussed by the researcher (Agresti & Barbara, 2008; Aron, Elliot & Elaine, 2010; Tesch, 1990).

Discussions and Interpretations of the Results

As the data is analysed and presented using narrative texts, tables, graphs, figures and others, the researcher explain them in the context of the study and in the light of previous work. On the basis of the results he discusses, checking their authenticity, going back over the hypotheses, calling precisely the theories and authors who have addressed the issue studied, he can make inferences, draw conclusions or develop a theory and make recommendations (Whitley, 1984).

Discussing the results means relating them to each other and to what was already known. Interpreting means trying to make sense. It does not matter whether this effort is applied to a set of numerical observations or to a set of text or image segments. Thus, we interpret the results by organising and linking them together in such a way as to be able to offer an explanation for the phenomena observed. In the same way, discussing the results means relating them to the elements of the initial problem and to what was already known in the scientific literature. Whether the research approach is qualitative or quantitative, the process of interpreting and discussing the results remains in itself a qualitative process of linking various elements in order to give them meaning (Bachelard, 1965).

CONCLUSION

By way of conclusion, published in a high-impact journal requires the writing of an excellent manuscript. Conclusion is an important part of scientific research. The structure of a research conclusion is fairly standardised. Its content is marked out in such a way that a well-written conclusion usually gives the reader a very good idea of the work done. In fact, the conclusion is a detailed summary from which the actual summary can easily be written and placed at the beginning of the research (Kuhn, 1963).

The conclusion usually begins with a brief reminder of the issue being addressed and the general research question. The theoretical or practical relevance of this question and the research work that has been done to answer it is then highlighted.

Then the main elements of the research approach are recalled and the limits of the research are specified (see section Limits and future paths of research). Next, the most crucial or significant results are summarised and their contributions to the understanding of the issue are highlighted. In particular, their scientific and practical implications are highlighted (see research contributions section). Finally, new avenues of research and intervention are indicated (see section limitations and future avenues of research), (Tremblay, 1994).

Research Contributions

Research contributions are generally of three types:

- Theoretical contribution: through the construction and/or testing by past research of a developed theory,
- Methodological contribution: by contributing to the development of new methods,
- Practical contribution: probably leading to the solution of some practical problems.

LIMITATIONS AND FUTURE PATHS OF RESEARCH

Really present the limits of your research. This prepares you to consider the future of your research work. It allows you to better target the avenues of research that seem promising. Tracks that could be taken up in future studies. Broaden the subject dealt with by proposing new avenues of research or reflection in the future. You can formulate new questions. Often you will be quoted because you have put your finger on interesting things that have not yet been studied.

REFERENCES

Reviewing the list of references cited in the research and its formatting is a tedious step. This task can be greatly facilitated by the use of bibliographic management software or by a constant concern to take careful note of each reference throughout the writing process. Unfortunately, this is not always the case. Indeed, wasting time searching for the publisher or the issue of the journal or page, etc., is a frequent occurrence. There is no magic recipe, other than consistency in note-taking. Generally, there are several thousand citation standards that govern the formatting of references. As far as the bibliography is concerned, the researcher remains the authority who gives the standard to be followed. The MLA, APA, Chicago Manual of Style standards are the most widely used. However, in the absence of instructions, it is possible to use the French adaptation of the international standard ISO 690. Respecting a bibliographical standard requires rigour and punctuation rules (Deboin et al., 2012). Usually, the references of research documents must be classified in alphabetical order as follows: - Book: Author, First name (date). *Title of the book*. Place of publication: Publisher, Number of pages. - Book chapter: Author, First name (date). "*Chapter title*" (chap. 0), in Book title. Place of publication: Publisher, Pages. - Section of a Website: Author, First name (date of publication of the section). *Title of the section, in Site Name*. Consulted on (date). Address on the Web.

- Journal article: Author, First name (date). Title of the article. *Place of publication*. Volume. Number. Pages.

ACKNOWLEDGMENTS

Acknowledgements are not obligatory, but it is always nice for those who have given us their support during the research to have their support publicly acknowledged. In addition, if financial or logistical support, public or private, was provided, it is customary to acknowledge the contribution of these organisations to your work.

Stylistically, acknowledgements need not stretch or be poignant. Their mere presence is usually enough to reach the intended audience. They can be brief. It should include the names of the people, their functions, their institutional affiliation and the nature of their contribution. This last part is the one that lends itself best to some personalization.

APPENDICES

At the end, the appendix pages are listed. These pages consist mainly of the list of appendices, the glossary or lexicon (if applicable). An appendix contains information which helps to understand the research: sketches, lists of figures, lists of tables, abbreviations, diagrams, statistics, questionnaires and symbols used. The Annexes are placed in order of mention in the text.

PRACTICAL ADVICE

- The researcher must enter his or her work himself or herself.

- He must manage his time efficiently.
- He must establish a real retroplanning of the research process.
- He must be courageous and hard-working.
- He must read sufficiently.
- He must have his work read for corrections of form.
- Do not hesitate to call on other skills for parts of the work that challenge his knowledge.

BEFORE SUBMISSION OF THE MANUSCRIPT

Before submitting your manuscript, it is essential to check it thoroughly. You have to be satisfied with your work to satisfy the publisher if not, your chance is lost. It is always very useful to have your manuscript evaluated by a competent researcher in your specialty. It is also advisable to check your work with anti-plagiarism software to guarantee its originality. Don't forget to establish the order of authors, to write up their affiliations, to select the author of correspondence. Special attention should be given to the cover letter to the publisher and to conflicts of interest, as explained in the following paragraphs.

MOTIVATION LETTER

In order to prepare a good covering letter and to attract the attention of the publisher, the following points should be taken into account:

- The length of a cover letter should never exceed one page: the editor will only devote a minimum amount of time to your letter. Make sure that it is clear and quick to read.
- Special care should also be taken in writing and presentation: a pleasant read will motivate the editor, or at least not discourage him/her.
- A summary, 15 to 20 lines are sufficient.
- Limit your paragraphs to a maximum of 5 lines, ideally with 12 to 15 words per line, and avoid sentences that are too long.
- A letter occupying three-quarters of a page seems to be a good middle ground. It should be short enough to make the editor want to read it and long enough to present you convincingly.
- Avoid writing the name of the publisher or newspaper in the wrong way.
- Emphasise the added value of your research.
- Explain how your search fits the mission and scope of the newspaper.

- Confirm that your search has not been published elsewhere and is not currently being evaluated by another journal.

CONFLICTS OF INTEREST

During the course of the publication project, the most frequent disagreements between co-authors concern the contribution of each or the way in which the scientific content is presented or interpreted. The best way to avoid conflicts is to establish from the outset of the publication project clear principles and transparent exchanges between all those involved. I recommend that no conflicts of interest be declared (Callon & Latour, 1991).

CHOICE OF JOURNAL

The choice of the journal is a difficult matter. In order to make a successful choice, the following points should be taken into account:

- The quality of the targeted newspaper (impacted newspaper).
- The compatibility of the journal with the subject matter (journal in the field or speciality or research area).
- The target readership is the same as the newspaper's readership.
- The type of article is the responsibility of the journal.
- The language of publication of the journal.
- The notoriety of the journal.
- The publication deadlines and editorial constraints of the journal.
- Knowledge of the financial conditions for free access to the newspaper.
- Use of an electronic solution for the choice of the newspaper.

COMPLIANCE WITH THE NEWSPAPER'S EDITORIAL POLICY

Publishers require authors to follow instructions (Author Guidelines, Instructions for Authors). These instructions include certain rules for being an author or contributor (Authorship, Changes to authorship, Contributors, Ethics in publishing, Conflict of interest, Submission declaration), (Wood, 2006; Karim & Hue, 2022).

The submission instructions of the journal in question must be followed. It is essential to respect the number of words in the manuscript, the formatting, the tables and figures and their locations. After the manuscript is received through the electronic submission system of the journal, compliance with the editorial policy will be assessed and judged by the editorial assistant. An Associate Editor will be assigned to evaluate the manuscript and make the decision to send it for external peer review or to reject it without such a review. The main reasons for instant rejection or external peer review will be explained in the following sections (Ansell & Samuels, 2021).

INSTANT REJECTION

The main reasons for instant rejection of manuscripts submitted to journals are:

- Inappropriate manuscript to the journal.
- Manuscript too basic.
- Manuscript outside the journal's jurisdiction.
- Manuscript lacking novelty.
- Manuscript with a poor study plan.
- Manuscript with no added value....(Fischer et al, 2017).

EXTERNAL PEER REVIEW

The first step in the right direction if the publishers decide that your manuscript has a chance of publication. This chance translates into an external peer review. Getting to this stage is not easy because the percentage of manuscripts selected for peer review varies from one journal to another. The journal with the strongest impact factor is more severe than the others and selects only the best manuscripts (Yin, 1989).

After the return of the reviewers' responses, there are usually three decisions: rejection, major or minor revision and acceptance. Direct acceptance of the manuscript is very rare. A fairly good manuscript requires major revision. A better manuscript still requires minor revision. The main reasons for rejection of a manuscript after peer review are the following:

- The adoption of the wrong methods.
- Design flaws
- Lack of added value and novelty.
- Poor explanations.
- Weak justifications.
- Presence of confusing graphics.
- Insufficient figures or tables.

REQUEST FOR A MAJOR REVISION

Remember that the reviewers are external to the journal and are not paid. They provide a service to the journal and to science. If they request a major revision, the manuscript has a chance of publication. In order to be accepted for publication, their comments must be taken into consideration because they are often fair and designed to improve the quality and structure of your research. In short, it is essential that the reviewers' requests and questions are answered correctly. Answers must be point by point without forgetting any points, even if they are small. If you disagree with their point of view, try to state your opinion clearly and politely. Finally, to respond well to a Request for Review, try to prepare two documents. The first is the manuscript revised with the precision of the corrections made by other colours for example. The second contains the assessors' comments and the answers made, which must be clear. These two documents must be well organised with titles and numbered pages, all to make it easier for the examiners (Kotsis & Chung, 2014).

AFTER THE REJECTION OF THE MANUSCRIPT

The rejection of a manuscript is undoubtedly bad news for the authors. In this situation, the majority of authors feel demotivated and become desperate. This is a natural reaction, but try not to let these horrible emotions disrupt your concentration. Above all, try to rest and take a period of reflection and wisdom. The logic of things says that there is no such thing as a perfect manuscript.

For this, you must not get out of the competition. In my opinion, there are two solutions. The first is to see and read the comments you have received carefully and fairly. Write to the publisher and say that you understand his decision to reject it and the reviewers' comments. Inform him or her that you have rectified the weaknesses in your manuscript. Try to convince the publisher to reverse the rejection decision and give you another chance. If the first solution does not produce a positive result, you should go on to the second. The second solution is to revise and improve your manuscript and propose a new version, overcoming the weaknesses of the first one in a new journal. The chances of publication in this case are higher than the first.

AFTER ACCEPTANCE OF THE MANUSCRIPT

After acceptance of your manuscript and before sharing your successes, it is necessary to complete the copyright assignment and conflict of interest disclosure forms. The department in charge of publication in the journal is working on your manuscript. You are obliged to respond to their requests within a limited time frame. Small corrections may be requested. These rectifications concern the layout of the manuscript, the correction of errors such as incorrect order of figures and tables, mislabelled captions, inaccurate language, updating of all bibliographical references, etc. The next step is the publication of the manuscript online. Then a digital object identification (DOI) number is assigned to the publication.

The DOI (Digital Object Identifier) is an unambiguous and perennial character string designed for the internet. The DOI makes it possible to identify reference, cite and provide a lasting link to resources of all types: publications, research data (tables or databases). The DOI facilitates the identification of a resource by associating metadata with it, i.e. information describing it: author or creator, title, keywords, abstract, publisher, language, date of publication, source, property rights of the resource, location, access conditions, etc. (Ronald et Hites, 2021).

THINKING: H-INDEX AND IMPACTS OF YOUR PUBLICATIONS

First of all, the h-index (or h-factor), is an indicator of the impact of a researcher's publications. It takes into account the number of a researcher's publications and the number of their citations. An author's h-index is equal to the highest number "h" of his publications that received at least "h" citations each. Example: an h-index of 6 means that 6 publications by the author were each cited at least 6 times. The h-index is calculated by ranking and numbering the author's publications from the most cited (n°1) to the least cited. The h-index corresponds to the last issue of the publication which checks: number of citations [3] number of the publication. The h-index of a researcher is increasingly requested in submission files for calls for proposals or in the framework of research evaluations.

Secondly, measuring the impact of a scientific author's publication aims to assess his scientific reputation. The scientific reputation of an author is measured by the number of citations received by all the publications to which he or she is a signatory, whether as sole or co-author.

The number of citations received by a publication is the number of publications that cite the publication in their bibliography. Some impact measures and indicators may exclude citations issued by one of the authors of the publication (self-citation, self-citation).

However, this impact measure depends on the tool and database used: it is limited to the corpus of publications allowed by the database according to its indexing strategy, i.e. the choice of information sources that it analyses and indexes (journals, book publishers, conferences, etc.). When analysing a corpus, it can be interesting to measure the impact of a particular publication.

Finally, an impact measurement can go beyond a given publication or author. By studying all the publications of authors affiliated with an institution, it is possible to measure the impact of this institution as a collective or scientific knowledge-producing entity.

CONCLUSION

By way of conclusion, we have presented some knowledge in the field of scientific research. From this work we discussed how, how to structure and how to prepare a good manuscript for publication in a high impact journal. We detailed several elements in this regard. On the empirical level, we have provided researchers with several scientific implications. We hope to see further work that adds value to this topic.

REFERENCES

Agresti. A / Barbara Finlay (2008): Statistical Methods for the Social Sciences. 4th Edition. Prentice Hall.

Ansell, B. W., & Samuels, D. J. (2021). Desk rejecting: A better use of your time. *PS, Political Science & Politics.*

Aron, A. / Elliot Coups / Elaine N. Aron (2010): Statistics for the Behavioral and Social Sciences: A Brief Course. 5th Edition, Pearson.

Bachelard, G. (1965), La formation de l'esprit scientifique, librairie scientifique Jean Vrin, Paris, 1965.

Balibar, S. (2014). *Chercheur au quotidien.* Seuil.

Callon, M. & Latour, B. (1991). *La science telle qu'elle se fait.* Paris: La découverte.

Dawnie, N.M. / R.W.Health (1974): Basic Statistical Methods. New York: Harper and Row.

De Lagarde, J. (1983). *Initiation à l'analyse des données.* Dunod.

Deboin, M. C., Dedieu, L., Fovet-Rabot, C., & Boussou, C. (2012). *Publier dans une revue en libre accès (ou open access), en 9 points.* CIRAD.

Eileen, F. A. G. D. S. (2017). Why papers are rejected and how to get yours accepted Advice on the construction of interpretive consumer research articles. *Qualitative Market Research, 20*(1), 60–67.

El-Omar, E. M. (2014). How to publish a scientific manuscript in a high-impact journal. *Advances in Digestive Medicine*, *2014*(1), 105–109.

Feuls, M., Plotnikof, M., & Stjerne, I. S. (2022), "Timely methods: a methodological agenda for researching the temporal in organizing", Qualitative Research in Organizations and Management, Vol. ahead-of-print No. ahead-of-print

Fortin, M.-F. (2006). *Fondements et étapes du processus de recherche*. Chenelière Éducation.

Fovet-Rabot, C. (2018), Écrire en style scientifique et technique en 5 points. Montpellier (FRA): CIRAD, 5 p.

Fovet-Rabot, C., & Deboin, M. C. (2019), Définir les auteurs d'une publication, en 8 points. Montpellier (FRA): CIRAD, 6 p.

Gauthier, B. (1992). *Recherche sociale. De la problématique à la collecte des données*. Presses de l'Université du Québec.

Germain, C. (1993). *Évolution de l'enseignement des langues - 5000 ans d'histoire*. CLÉ International.

Hazem Ben Aissa. (2001), quelle méthodologie de recherche appropriée pour une construction de la recherche en gestion? xième conférence de l'association internationale de management stratégique, 13-14-15 juin 2001, 27 P.

Heritage, J. C. (1987). Ethnomethodology. In A. Giddens & J. H. Turner (Eds.), *Social Theory Today*. Stanford University Press.

Hites, R. A. (2021). How to convince an editor to accept your paper quickly. *The Science of the Total Environment*, *798*, 149–243.

Johnson, R. B., & Christensen, L. B. (2017). Educational research: Quantitative, qualitative, and mixed approaches. 6th Los Angeles. *Sage (Atlanta, Ga.)*.

Karim, S., & Hue, M. T. (2022). Researching ethnic minority lives in multicultural contexts: A methodological inquiry in acculturation. *International Journal of Comparative Education and Development*, *24*(3/4), 177–192.

Kotsis, S. V., & Chung, K. C. (2014). Manuscript rejection: How to submit a revision and tips on being a good peer reviewer. *Plastic and Reconstructive Surgery*, *133*, 958–964.

Kuhn, T. S. (1963). *The structure of scientific revolutions*. The University of Chicago Press.

Le Moigne, J. L. (1990). *La modélisation des systèmes complexes*. Dunod.

Marie-Laure, G.-P., Gotteland, D., Haon, C., & Jolibert, A. (2012). *Méthodologie de la recherche en sciences de gestion*. Pearson France.

Martinet, A. C. (1990). (coord.), (1990), Epistemologie et Sciences de gestion, Paris. *Economica*.

Martinsuo, M. & Huemann, M. (2021), The basics of writing a paper for the International Journal of Project Management, *International Journal of Project Management* 38 (2020) pp. 340–342.

NEET, Hanna E. (1989) *À la recherche du mot clé. Analyse documentaire et indexation alphabétique*. Genève, les éditions 1ERS, coll. « Les cours de le 1ER », n° 2.

Patriotta, G. (2017). Crafting papers for publication: Novelty and convention in academic writing. *Journal of Management Studies*, 54(5), 747–759.

Quivy, R., & Van Campenhoudt, L. (2006), *Manuel de recherche en Sciences Sociales*, Paris, Dunod, 3e éd.

Quivy Raymond Et Van Campenhoudt Luc. (1988). *Manuel de recherche en sciences sociales*. Dunod.

Schoonenboom, J. (2016). The multilevel mixed intact group analysis: A mixed method to seek, detect, describe and explain differences between intact groups. *Journal of Mixed Methods Research*, *10*, 129–146.

(2017). (in press). Schoonenboom, Judith, R. Burke Johnson, and Dominik E. [Combining multiple purposes of mixing within a mixed methods research design. *International Journal of Multiple Research Approaches*.]. *Froehlich*.

Beaud Stéphane, Weber Florence (1997), *Guide de l'enquête de terrain. Produire et analyser des données ethnographiques*, Paris, la découverte (Repères)

Tesch, R. (1990). *Qualitative Research, Analysis Types & Software Tools*. Falmer Press.

Tinker, T., & Lowe, T. (1982). The Management Science of Management Sciences. *Human Relations*, *35*(4), 331–347.

Tremblay, R. (1994). *Savoir faire – Précis de méthodologie pratique*. McGraw Hill.

Voss V. (1999), Research Methodology in operation management, *Eden seminar*, Brussels, February.

Whitley, R. (1984). The Fragmented State of Management Studies: Reasons and Consequences. *Journal of Management Studies*, *21*(4), 369–390.

Wood, E. J. (2006). The Ethical Challenges of Field Research in Conflict Zones. *Qualitative Sociology*, *29*(3), 373–386.

Yin, R. K. (1989). Applied Social Research Methods Series: Vol. 5. *Case Study Research, Design and Methods*. Sage Publications.

Yin, R. K. (2002). *Case Study Research Design and Methods*. Sage Pub.

Chapter 18
Publishing:
Selecting Journals, Writing Abstracts, and Addressing Issues Raised by Reviewers

Michael J. Merten
University of Nebraska, Lincoln, USA

Amanda Terrell
University of Arkansas, Fayetteville, USA

ABSTRACT

This chapter will provide valuable information to readers about several important issues in the publishing process. This chapter will concentrate on issues specific to: (1) selecting the appropriate journal for a manuscript; (2) writing effective abstracts that convey the main points of a manuscript; and (3) effectively addressing issues and comments raised during the peer review process. This chapter will discuss the importance of identifying a potential journal early in the writing process and reassessing goodness of fit once the manuscript is complete. Additionally, this chapter suggests ways to construct effective abstracts that provide an accurate picture of what the paper is about, which allows readers to determine whether or not they are interested in reading the article further. Lastly, this chapter will provide step-by-step instruction for researchers to effectively address comments that journal reviewers have provided, including the importance of addressing all comments thoroughly and the organization and presentation of the authors' comments in response to the reviewers.

DOI: 10.4018/978-1-6684-6859-3.ch018

SELECTING JOURNALS

The process of selecting a journal to review and publish your manuscript involves a series of considerations and decisions. The primary concern is whether a journal's subject area encompasses a potential publication's topic and scientific approach. This is not always readily apparent and may require a decision-making process. An example decision tree is provided in Figure 1, with steps outlined in greater detail below:

Does This Journal Publish the Topic or Method of Research You Aim to Publish?

One approach to finding a potential publication outlet for your manuscript is an in-depth examination of specific journals that appear to publish on your topic. Although the title of a journal may indicate that it is in your field, that does not necessarily mean that they regularly (or ever) publish research on specific topics. Even if the topic of your manuscript aligns with previous topics published in the journal, it might not be a good methodological fit. For example, some journals might prioritize longitudinal research and rarely or never publish cross-sectional studies. Similarly, some journals might solely publish qualitative research, so that would not be an appropriate place to submit a quantitative study. Authors can get direction on the type of publications and topics journals prioritize by reading the description and aims and scope on the journal's website. In addition, it is recommended for authors to review the most recent editions of the journal and see what topics and methods have been published lately. If the journal has not published on a topic in many years, authors need to review more recent publications to determine of the topic is no longer of interest to the journal or if it is an opportunity to publish an update on the subject. The journal's publication history can give authors a sense of whether their manuscript would be of interest and a priority to the journal.

If you are not readily familiar with specific journals on a topic, another approach is searching for articles focused on a similar topic (and using a similar methodology) as your paper. Some journals routinely publish studies on topics that might not have an obvious link to the journal title. For example, the *American Journal of Orthopsychiatry* (*AJO*) "articles that clarify, challenge, or reshape the prevailing understanding of factors in the prevention and correction of injustice and in the sustainable development of a humane and just society" (AJO Journal Scope Statement, 2022, para. 1). AJO's scope statement specifically states they publish:

Contemporary topics in AJO's topical scope include, but are not limited to, public behavioral health and prevention; institutional reform; causes and solutions to behavioral healthcare disparities; adaption of behavioral health methods to the needs of racial, ethnic, cultural and other minority groups; responses to natural and human-made disasters; immigrants and refugees; underserved behavioral health populations; protection of vulnerable people; and sociocultural dimensions of behavioral health problems.

What might not be readily apparent from this journal's title and scope description is that they regularly publish research on homelessness. When writing up a study on homelessness, authors may find that they are repeatedly citing research from the same journal – that should be a clear sign that the journal could be an ideal place to submit the manuscript for publication. Similarly, journals with a more medical orientation (such as publications focused on nursing) can and often do publish research on specific topics that might not be readily apparent by the journal title or scope description. So, whether authors are starting with a specific journal in mind or reviewing the literature to find appropriate journals, becoming highly familiar with published research on the topic is imperative for publication success. If authors are struggling to determine whether a journal they aim to publish in is a good fit, they can always consult with colleagues or email the editor or an associate editor and ask if their topic and methodological approach would be of interest.

Reputation of the Journal in Your Field of Study

So, you have identified a potential journal for your work. What is the reputation of the journal in your specific field? Is it considered a top-level publication with a high level of readership? Indicators of how prestigious a journal is can be found in a couple different metrics:

- *Impact factor:* This number indicates how "important" the journal is in the field as it is calculated based on the number of times it has been read and cited (Sharma, Sarin, Gupta, Schdeva, & Desai, 2014). A journal with a high readership and citation history is typically considered important and top tier.
- *Acceptance rate:* A journal's acceptance rate is simply a calculation based on how many manuscripts are submitted and accepted vs. rejected. A journal who rejects many more manuscripts than accepts is considered selective, rigorous, and a desirable target for publication.
- *Rankings and other metrics:* Different professional and analytics organizations offer rankings and readership/citations metrics for journals. This can help authors contextualize how a certain journal compares to other, similar publications. Google Scholar offers rankings, by category, that are based on how often publications from the journal are read and cited (Google Scholar,

n.d.). Other sources of journal metrics include Web of Science, Scopus, Elsevier, Springer, and the directory of open access journals (Droog, 2020.

If authors are aiming to publish in a top-tier journal, they should seriously and realistically consider whether their study findings are "good enough" for a highly selective journal. While "good enough" is subjective, if findings are limited in significance or impact, or based on simple cross-sectional data with limited generalizability, a journal with a low acceptance rate might not be the best first attempt at publication. Reading previous publications in the journal under consideration is the best way to determine how a potential submission compares in terms of topic importance, research methodology, and robustness of findings.

Is It Peer-Reviewed?

In order for a journal to be considered "peer reviewed," it must have a rigorous review process where experts in the field and on the topic of paper submissions weigh in on the scientific merit and writing style of submitted manuscripts. More and more, "open source" journals are popping up and many of these do not have a scholarly peer review process. While it might seem desirable to have any easy route to publication – or even a pay-to-publish route – the peer review process is critical to ensuring that only high quality and credible research is published.

Does your article/paper fit the mission/scope of the journal. Generally, all/most journals have an explicit mission/scope. (lots of examples here: (1) cope talks a lot about international samples/focus, but your work is not that; (2) scope specifically says it only focuses on longitudinal studies, but your study is cross-sectional).

What Are the Guidelines?

Make sure that your paper adheres to the journal's submission guidelines. For example, authors should not submit a 6,000-word paper to a journal that has a word limit of 3,500 words. Also pay close attention to how many tables, figures, and references are allowed and whether or not they are counted in the journal's page limit. Journal's use different publication styles, so it is important to follow the appropriate style guidelines. There is also variation in how manuscripts should be structured – from the abstract to the headings to the references – so pay close attention to the instructions for authors provided by the journal.

Timeline

What is the typical amount of time it takes to get reviews back? Many journals provide this information on their website. Authors may need to get their papers published in a timely manner (for example, before going on the job market, for annual review or tenure purposes, or because the topic addresses a time-sensitive current event). Thus, examining the timeline helps authors avoid submitting to journals that have historically taken a much longer time to receive reviews and publish the article.

WRITING ABSTRACTS

In the English language, the word "abstract" has several different meanings ranging from a vague type of art, an immaterial thought or idea, to a summary of a longer document or speech (Oxford University Press, 2022). In some instances, the word abstract refers to a brief summary of a conference presentation that is published with a compilation of other abstracts from the same conference. In social research, an abstract is most commonly a brief written summary that is provided at the beginning of an article. This is the use of abstracts that is described in detail here.

The purpose of an abstract in a published article is to provide a very brief overview of the entire project. The abstract should make complete sense on its own, separate from the full article. Readers of the article (typically other researchers, practitioners, students, and journalists) usually read the abstract first before even downloading or printing the article. This quick summary of the overall project tells them if it is on the topic they are interested in, studied a population that is relevant to their work, used a methodology that is appropriate or useful for their purposes, and had results that can inform their own work. After reviewing the abstract, the reader decides whether they want to read the article or discard it and search for other articles. This makes the abstract one of, if not *the* most important part of a publication. The abstract often determines whether the full article is ever read!

An important skill in social research is to write an abstract that leads people to read the entire article (in other words, a high impact abstract). Abstracts are almost never more than 250 words (and often limited by journals to 150 words; APA, 2020). This limitation means that authors must convey a lot of compelling information in a small amount of text. Below, the key elements of high impact abstracts are reviewed. Keep in mind that different journals will have different specifications for the structure and content of an abstract. Some journals will simply ask authors to provide an abstract within a specific word limit, while other journals specify a certain format and content for structured sections of the abstract. Thus, it is important to pay close attention to journal and style guidelines.

For a general, unstructured abstract, the recommended format starts by explaining the topic area, the purpose of the current study, the sample and methodology used, brief statement about type of analysis conducted, major findings, and a final concluding statement. The first sentence of the abstract should be attention-grabbing and communicate the importance of the research. This can be a generalized summary statement or "take away message" based on the entire literature review in the article. It is a high-level summary of the substantive points and, as such, does not need citation in the abstract. Following this first sentence (or couple of sentences), should be a purpose statement that identifies the scope of the present study. Then, the sample studied (including basic descriptors and sample size) and general methodological approach should be stated. When stating the major results of the study, authors should indicate what analytic approach was used and any other key information that should be provided in a brief summary of that approach. The results provided in the abstract should be in plain language, avoid overly technical language (often called jargon), and clearly address the purpose stated at the beginning of the abstract. The final sentence or two should restate the importance and significance of the study and indicate practical, research, or policy applications of the work. The ideal format of an abstract can be thought of as a circle that begins with an idea, flows through the method and results, and closes the circle by showing how the study filled the research gaps indicated at the beginning of the abstract (see Figure 2).

Some journals require a specific type of structure abstract. In those instances, the most common format requires structured headings within the abstract. Though the headings required will vary by journal, the format often looks similar to this:

- **Study Aims:** This should include several sentences specifying the scope of the study, why it is important, and why it should be considered novel or innovative. The aims should also briefly summarize the research questions and hypotheses.
- **Method:** The methodology used in the study (sampling, measures, procedure, and analytic approach) should be briefly stated. Potential readers will scan this information to see if it is focused on their population of interest and make a quick judgement of whether the study approach was appropriate and rigorous.
- **Results:** In this section, authors should summarize the most important and meaningful findings from the study. If the reader is intrigued by these results, they will read the entire paper to learn more about the findings in detail, including more nuanced results, such as mediation and moderation. The abstract summary of results should present the most compelling results in brief.

- **Conclusion:** The conclusion to the abstract should, in a sentence or two, reiterate why the study was needed/important and should link the results to the broader field in terms of future research needed, practical implications, or policy work that is needed – all based on present study results.

Occasionally, certain journals will also require additional information, such as how the study is novel or new and how it addresses a significant current issue. APA provides a very thorough guide to developing an abstract, available at https://apastyle.apa.org/instructional-aids/abstract-keyword s-guide.pdf. There is also a brief but useful video tutorial from Scribbr: https://youtu.be/lbCh94nJqIo.

All abstracts should be followed by a series of three to five keywords that indicate the major themes of the research found in the article. These keywords are critical for the article to be found when scholars are searching topics in databases and when they are scanning the abstract to see if it is a good fit for what they are studying and deciding if they should even read it. A successful, well-written abstract will 1) increase the chances an article is found in a search and 2) enhance the likelihood that the full article will get read and cited in other scholars' work.

ADDRESSING REVIEWER COMMENTS

The initial step in the peer-review process is the submission of the manuscript to a journal. Not every article that is submitted to a journal will be sent out for peer review. Generally, the editor will assess the submission and determine whether the manuscript will be sent out to be reviewed by reviewers. Editors evaluate whether submitted manuscripts fit the scope of the journal, possess scientific rigor, and contribute new knowledge to field. These are some of the main characteristics that will determine whether the paper gets reviewed. It can take a bit of time for reviewers to be invited and to accept to review a manuscript. Thus, recruiting and assigning reviewers to submitted manuscripts can delay the overall timeline of the publication process.

For papers that are sent out for review, reviewers provide written comments that are then compiled by the journal editor. Along with written comments, the reviewer is asked to provide a recommendation for the manuscript. In general, those recommendations are as follows: (1) accept manuscript as is; (2) accept with minor revisions; (3) not accept, but grant opportunity to revise and resubmit; (4) reject with no opportunity for revisions. Two of the possible recommendations provides the author(s) an opportunity to revise their manuscript and ultimately resubmit their revised paper for consideration. Of course, an author may choose not to revise their manuscript and, instead, decide to submit it to a different journal. Regarding recommendation (3) mentioned above (revise and resubmit – often referred to as an R&R), the editor will generally specify in their feedback whether your revision is a "minor" or "major" revision. This is often determined by the number of comments as well as the scope and depth of the recommended edits. *As an example:* An author may receive feedback from reviewers that instructs them to re-organize their literature review as well as re-run some analyses after including a new variable into the model. These kinds of revisions generally require substantial time and effort, thus would be considered a "major" revision. Alternatively, a journal editor may render a "minor revisions" decision, based on a number of issues the editor believes can be easily addressed. An example of a minor revision may include the correction of grammar/ punctuation in a few places in the manuscript and or adding clarity and/or small pieces of information in the manuscript. Due note that "minor revisions" are things that should not take significant time and effort to address, because the quantity of those revisions are generally low. However, grammar/punction and clarity issues can be considered "major revisions" if those issues are numerous throughout the manuscript.

The important thing to remember is that the purpose of the feedback provided by reviewers is to strengthen an existing paper or manuscript. The following suggestions andguidelines are provided relative to things to consider when addressing issues raised by reviewers.

1. Be prompt in submitting your revisions to the journal. Many journals will provide you anywhere from 1 to 3 months to address your revisions. If you need more time, please let the journal editor know and provide a justification. *Example:* You may not have had the opportunity to meet with your research team, thus you are requesting an extension. Also, we suggest that you provide an alternative date when to expect your submission, preferably, no more than one week past the original due date.

2. Be polite and appreciative. The cover letter in response to the comments should thank the reviewers and editor for providing helpful feedback and the opportunity to revise and resubmit the manuscript. As a result of the feedback, authors have been able to strengthen the original manuscript submission. Acknowledge the reviewer(s) for making a helpful suggestion and show appreciation for the opportunity to revise your paper.

3. Make sure you understand reviewers' comments. If a revision comment from a reviewer is unclear or authors do not understand what they are asking for, they should contact the editor to seek clarification. It is never advisable to simply ignore a reviewer's comment because authors did not understand it.

4. Be responsive to every comment. Authors do not have to agree with every comment made by a reviewer and authors are not required to make the suggested edit. However, authors disagree with the revision recommendation, be clear and specific as to why the suggested change is not being made. *In this instance, a response to the reviewer could look like this:* "We appreciate the reviewer's suggestion about adding an additional variable in our analyses. Because our data set does not contain this variable, we are not able to include it in our analyses. We have addressed this in our limitations section of our revised paper (see lines 18-22 on page 17)." There are also instances where authors *could* make the suggested revision, but do not feel it is appropriate for legitimate scientific reasons. In these instances, authors should explain their rationale for not making the revision and support their reasoning with previous research and/or theory. In all instances, authors should use professional and friendly language when responding to reviewers. Remember – reviewers are authors' peers who have donated their time and energy to the journal in an effort to support the scholarly development of other researchers and the field.

5. Be thorough in addressing reviewer comments. In your responses to the editor, authors should restate each reviewers' comments word-for-word. Authors should be clear in addressing each comment, what changes were made in the paper, and where (specifically) in the paper reviewers will find the changes. For example, authors might write that, "We added a paragraph in the introduction (second paragraph on page 3) that provides additional justification for our study." Authors should create a document that includes all reviewer comment listed out one-by-one. For example:

Reviewer Comment #1: *The literature review in your paper needs to be updated to include more recent studies published in the last 5 years. The current version does not cite recent studies in this area that have been published in the last several years.*

Authors' response: *Thank you for this helpful feedback. We have updated our literature review section of the paper to include several studies that have been published in the last several years. Specifically, we have added the following references and discussion of them:*

Anderson, 2022 (page 4)
Bosick (2021) (page 6)
Braun (2019) (page 7)
Gentry (2020) (page 8)

6. There are no guarantees. Addressing reviewer comments does not guarantee the paper will ultimately be accepted for publication, but it will certainly go a long way in increasing the chances that your paper will be published.

REFERENCES

American Journal of Orthopsychiatry (AJO). (2022). *Journal scope statement.* AJO. https://www.apa.org/pubs/journals/ort

American Psychological Association (APA). (2020). *APA Style.* APA. https://apastyle.apa.org/instructional-aids/abstract-keywords-guide.pdf

Droog, A. (2020). Choosing a journal to publish in: A Toolkit. *Huskie Commons: Northern Illinois University.* https://huskiecommons.lib.niu.edu/cgi/viewcontent.cgi?article=1509&context=allfaculty-peerpub

Google Scholar. (n.d.). *Google Scholar metrics.* Google. https://scholar.google.com/intl/en/scholar/metrics.html#overview

Oxford University Press. (2022). *Abstract and Keyword Guide,* (7th ed.). OED. https://www.oed.com

Sharma, M., Sarin, A., Gupta, P., Sachdeva, S., & Desai, A. V. (2014). Journal impact factor: Its use, significance and limitations. *World Journal of Nuclear Medicine, 13*(2), 146. doi:10.4103/1450-1147.139151 PMID:25191134

Compilation of References

Abrahim, S., Mir, B. A., Suhara, H., Mohamed, F. A., & Sato, M. (2019). Structural equation modeling and confirmatory factor analysis of social media use and education. *International Journal of Education Technology and Higher Education.*, *16*(1), 32. doi:10.118641239-019-0157-y

Agresti. A / Barbara Finlay (2008): Statistical Methods for the Social Sciences. 4th Edition. Prentice Hall.

Ali, S. I., Yusoff, Z. M., & Ayub, Z. A. (2017). Legal Research of Doctrinal and Non-Doctrinal. *International Journal of Trend in Research and Development*, *4*(1), 493–495. http://www.ijtrd.com/papers/IJTRD6653.pdf

Alvesson, M. & Sköldberg, K. (2009). Reflexive Methodology: New Vistas for Qualitative Research. London. Sage

American Journal of Orthopsychiatry (AJO). (2022). *Journal scope statement.* AJO. https://www.apa.org/pubs/journals/ort

American Psychological Association (APA). (2020). *APA Style.* APA. https://apastyle.apa.org/instructional-aids/abstract-keywords-guide.pdf

Anderson, J. C., & Gerbing, D. C. (1988). Structural equation modeling in practice: A review and recommended two-step approach. *Psychological Bulletin*, *103*(3), 411–423. doi:10.1037/0033-2909.103.3.411

Ansell, B. W., & Samuels, D. J. (2021). Desk rejecting: A better use of your time. *PS, Political Science & Politics.*

Aron, A. / Elliot Coups / Elaine N. Aron (2010): Statistics for the Behavioral and Social Sciences: A Brief Course. 5th Edition, Pearson.

Ary, D., Jacobs, L., & Sorenson, C. Asghar. (2006). Introduction to Research in Education. (8th edition). Wadsworth Cengage Learning .

Asim, A. E., Idaka, I. E., & Eni, E. I. (2017). *Research in education: Concepts and techniques.* University of Calabar Press.

Bachelard, G. (1965), La formation de l'esprit scientifique, librairie scientifique Jean Vrin, Paris, 1965.

Bailey, C. A. (2007). *A Guide to qualitative field research*. Sage. doi:10.4135/9781412983204

Bailey, J. (2008, April). First steps in qualitative data analysis: Transcribing. *Family Practice*, *25*(2), 127–131. doi:10.1093/fampra/cmn003 PMID:18304975

Balibar, S. (2014). *Chercheur au quotidien*. Seuil.

Baron, R. M., & Kenny, D. A. (1986). The moderator-mediator variable distinction in social psychological research: Conceptual, strategic, and statistical considerations. *Journal of Personality and Social Psychology*, *51*(6), 1173–1182. doi:10.1037/0022-3514.51.6.1173 PMID:3806354

Baxi, U. (1975). Socio-legal Research in India-A Programschrift, 416-449. Indian Council of Social Science Research (ICSSR).

Beaud Stéphane, Weber Florence (1997), *Guide de l'enquête de terrain. Produire et analyser des données ethnographiques*, Paris, la découverte (Repères)

Bentler, P. M. (1995). *EQS structural equations program manual*. Multivariate Software.

Bhat, I. P. (2019). *Idea and Methods of Legal Research*. Oxford University Press.

Blumer, H. (1969). *Symbolic interactionism: Perspective and method*. Prentice-Hall.

Boral, K., Burman, J., & Sembiah, S. M. (2020). A cross-sectional study on menstrual hygiene among rural adolescent girls of West Bengal. *International Journal of Contemporary Medical Research*, *7*(10), J10–J14.

Branson, R. D. (2004). Anatomy of a Research Paper. *Respiratory Care*, *49*, 10. PMID:15447807

Brough, P. (2019). *Advanced Research Methods for Applied Psychology (Design, Analysis and Reporting)* (1st ed.). Routledge, Taylor & Francis.

Browne, M. W., & Cudek, R. (1993). Alternative ways of assessing model fit. In K. A. Bollen & J. S. Long (Eds.), *Testing structural equation models* (pp. 136–162). Sage.

Bryman, A., & Bell, E. (2011) Business Research Methods. Oxford University Press.

Bude, H. (2004). The art of interpretation. In U. Flick, E. von Kardorff, & I. Steinke (Eds.), *A companion to qualitative research*. Sage.

Bude, H. (2004). The art of Interpretation. In U. Flick, E. von Kardorff, & I. Steinke (Eds.), *A companion to qualitative research*. SAGE.

Callon, M. & Latour, B. (1991). *La science telle qu'elle se fait*. Paris: La découverte.

Cameron, A. C., & Windmeijer, F. A. (1997). An R-squared measure of goodness of fit for some common nonlinear regression models. *Journal of Econometrics*, *77*(2), 329–342. doi:10.1016/S0304-4076(96)01818-0

Carlsen, A., & Mantere, S. (2007). Pragmatism. In *International Encyclopedia of Organization Studies*. Sage publications.

Chenail, R. J., Duffy, M., St. George, S., & Wulff, D. (2011). Facilitating coherence across qualitative research papers. *Qualitative Report*, *16*(1), 263–275. http://www.nova.edu/ssss/QR/QR16-1/coherence.pdf

Cheng, E. W. L., & Li, H. (2004). Contractor selection using the analytic network process. *Construction Management and Economics*, *22*(10), 1021–1032. doi:10.1080/0144619042000202852

Chicco, D., Warrens, M. J., & Jurman, G. (2021). The coefficient of determination R-squared is more informative than SMAPE, MAE, MAPE, MSE and RMSE in regression analysis evaluation. *PeerJ. Computer Science*, *7*, e623. doi:10.7717/peerj-cs.623 PMID:34307865

Christensen, L. B., Johnson, R. B., & Turner, L. A. (2014). *Research Methods, Design, and Analysis* (12th ed.). Pearson.

Cohen, L., Manion, L., & Morission, K. (2018). *Research methods in education* (8th ed.). Routledge., doi:10.4324/9781315456539

Cornell Law School. Legal Information Institute, Stare decisis. Retrieved from https://www.law.cornell.edu/wex/stare_decisis

Cornell, J. A., & Berger, R. D. (1987). Factors that influence the value of the coefficient of determination in simple linear and nonlinear regression models. *Phytopathology*, *77*(1), 63–70. doi:10.1094/Phyto-77-63

Coulter, K., & Sarkis, J. (2005). Development of a media selection model using the analytic network process. *International Journal of Advertising*, *24*(2), 193–215. doi:10.1080/02650487.2005.11072914

Council of Australian Law Deans. (2005) Statement on the Nature of Legal Research. CALD. https://cald.asn.au/wp-content/uploads/2017/11/cald-statement-on-the-nature-of-legal-research-20051.pdf

Creswell, J. W. (2007). *Qualitative Inquiry and Research Design; Choosing among five traditions*. Sage.

Creswell, J. W. (2014). *Research Design: Qualitative, Quantitative and Mixed Method Approaches* (4th ed.). Sage.

CSCU. (2005). *Assessing the Fit of Regression Models*. The Cornell Statistical Consulting Unit.

Dalal, M., & Saini, P. (2015). An Exploratory Survey to Assess the Menstrual Characteristics and Prevalence of Dysmenorrhea in College Going Girls. *International Journal of Scientific Research*, *6*(4), 754–757.

Davis, K. C. (1964-65). Behavioural Science and Administrative Law, 17. *Journal of Legal Education*, 137–148.

Dawnie, N.M. / R.W.Health (1974): Basic Statistical Methods. New York: Harper and Row.

De Lagarde, J. (1983). *Initiation à l'analyse des données*. Dunod.

Deboin, M. C., Dedieu, L., Fovet-Rabot, C., & Boussou, C. (2012). *Publier dans une revue en libre accès (ou open access), en 9 points*. CIRAD.

Demetri, L. M. (2015). Criticality in Qualitative Research. *Qualitative research: Bridging the conceptual, theoretical, and methodological*. Thousand Oaks. https://works.bepress.com/demetrilmorgan/11/

Denzin, N. K., & Lincoln, Y. S. (2005). *The landscape of qualitative Research: theories and issues*. Sage.

Dewey, J. (1938). *Logic: The Theory of Inquiry*. Henry Holt.

Dewey, J. (1986). How we think: A restatement of the relation of reflective thinking to the educative process. In *John Dewey: The Later Works, 1925–1953* (Rev. ed., Vol. 8). Southern Illinois University Press.

Dillon, D. R., O'Brien, D. G., & Heilman, E. E. (2000). Literacy research in the next millennium: From paradigms to pragmatism and practicality. *Reading Research Quarterly*, *35*(1), 10–26. doi:10.1598/RRQ.35.1.2

Dobinson, I., & Johns, F. (2007). Legal Research as Qualitative Research. In M. McConville & W. H. Chui (Eds.), *Research Methods For Law* (pp. 18–47). Edinburgh University Press.

Droog, A. (2020). Choosing a journal to publish in: A Toolkit. *Huskie Commons: Northern Illinois University*. https://huskiecommons.lib.niu.edu/cgi/viewcontent.cgi?article=1509&context=allfaculty-peerpub

Dummett, M. (1978). *Truth and Other Enigmas*. Harvard University Press.

Eaton, W. W., Badawa, M., & Melton, B. (1995). Prodromes and precursors: Epidemiological data for primary prevention of disorders with slow onset. *The American Journal of Psychiatry*, *152*(7), 967–972. doi:10.1176/ajp.152.7.967 PMID:7793466

Edmonds, W. A., & Kennedy, T. D. (2017). *An Applied Guide to Research Designs Quantitative, Qualitative, and Mixed Methods* (2nd ed.). Sage. doi:10.4135/9781071802779

Eileen, F. A. G. D. S. (2017). Why papers are rejected and how to get yours accepted Advice on the construction of interpretive consumer research articles. *Qualitative Market Research*, *20*(1), 60–67.

El-Omar, E. M. (2014). How to publish a scientific manuscript in a high-impact journal. *Advances in Digestive Medicine*, *2014*(1), 105–109.

Fan, Y., Chen, J., Shirkey, G., John, R., Wu, S. R., Park, H., & Shao, C. (2016). Applications of structural equation modeling (SEM) in ecological studies: An updated review. *Ecological Processes*, *5*(1), 19. doi:10.118613717-016-0063-3

Ferligoj, A., & Kramberger, A. (1995). Some Properties of R 2 in Ordinary Least Squares Regression.

Feuls, M., Plotnikof, M., & Stjerne, I. S. (2022), "Timely methods: a methodological agenda for researching the temporal in organizing", Qualitative Research in Organizations and Management, Vol. ahead-of-print No. ahead-of-print

Figueiredo Filho, D. B., Júnior, J. A. S., & Rocha, E. C. (2011). What is R2 all about? *Leviathan (São Paulo)*, (3), 60–68. doi:10.11606/issn.2237-4485.lev.2011.132282

Fortin, M.-F. (2006). *Fondements et étapes du processus de recherche*. Chenelière Éducation.

Fovet-Rabot, C. (2018), Écrire en style scientifique et technique en 5 points. Montpellier (FRA): CIRAD, 5 p.

Fovet-Rabot, C., & Deboin, M. C. (2019), Définir les auteurs d'une publication, en 8 points. Montpellier (FRA): CIRAD, 6 p.

Gauthier, B. (1992). *Recherche sociale. De la problématique à la collecte des données*. Presses de l'Université du Québec.

Gelman, A., Goodrich, B., Gabry, J., & Vehtari, A. (2019). R-squared for Bayesian regression models. *The American Statistician*, *73*(3), 307–309. doi:10.1080/00031305.2018.1549100

Germain, C. (1993). *Évolution de l'enseignement des langues - 5000 ans d'histoire*. CLÉ International.

Gestel, R. V., & Micklitz, H. W. (2011). Revitalizing Doctrinal Legal Research in Europe: What About Methodology? *European University Institute Working Papers Law*.

Goldkuhl, G. (2012). Pragmatism vs interpretivism in qualitative information systems research. *European Journal of Information Systems*, *21*(2), 135–146. doi:10.1057/ejis.2011.54

Google Scholar. (n.d.). *Google Scholar metrics*. Google. https://scholar.google.com/intl/en/scholar/metrics.html#over view

Gournelos, T., Hammonds, J.R., & Wilson, M.A. (2019). Doing Academic Research: Perlego.

Gournelos, T., Hammonds, J. R., & Wilson, M. A. (2019). *Doing Academic Research: A Practical Guide to Research Methods and Analysis*. Sage.

Gournelos, T., Hammonds, J. R., & Wilson, M. A. (2019). *Doing Academic Research: A Practical Guide to Research Methods and Analysis., Taylor & Francis Group*. Routledge.

Government of India. (n.d.). An MHRD Project under its National Mission on Education through ICT (NME-ICT) Pathshala. Government of India. http://epgp.inflibnet.ac.in/epgpdata/uploads/epgp_content/law/09._research_methodology/08.qualitativeanddoctrinalmethodsinresearch/et/8155etet.pd

Gray, E. D. (2018). Doing Research in the Real World (4t ed.). London, Sage.

Gray, R., Owen, D., & Adams, C. (Eds.). (1996). Accounting and Accountability Changes and Challenges in Corporate Social and Environmental Reporting. Prentice Hall. ISBN 9780131758605

Grbich, C. (2013). *Qualitative Data Analysis- An Introduction* (2nd ed.). Sage. doi:10.4135/9781529799606

Green, S. B., Thompson, M. S., & Babyak, M. A. (1998). A Monte Carlo investigation of methods for controlling Type I errors with specification searches in structural equation modeling. *Multivariate Behavioral Research*, *33*(3), 365–383. doi:10.120715327906mbr3303_3 PMID:26782719

Guba, E. (1990). *The Paradigm Dialog*. Sage.

Guba, E. G., & Lincoln, Y. S. (1988). Do inquiry paradigms imply inquiry methodologies? In D. M. Fetterman (Ed.), *Qualitative approaches to evaluation in education: Thesilent scientific revolution* (pp. 89–115). Praeger.

Guba, E. G., & Lincoln, Y. S. (1989). What is This Constructivist Paradigm Anyway? In *Fourth Generation Evaluation*. Sage.

Guba, E. G., & Lincoln, Y. S. (1994). Competing paradigms in qualitative research. In N. K. Denzin & Y. S. Lincoln (Eds.), *The Handbook of Qualitative Research* (3rd ed., pp. 105–117). Sage.

Guba, E. G., & Lincoln, Y. S. (2005). Paradigmatic controversies, contradictions, and emerging confluences. In N. K. Denzin & Y. S. Lincoln (Eds.), *The SAGE handbook of qualitative research* (3rd ed., pp. 191–215). Sage.

Guba, E. G., & Lincoln, Y. S. (2005). *Paradigmatic controversies, contradictions, and emerging confluences. The SAGE handbook of qualitative research. N. K. Denzin and Y. S. Lincoln*. Sage.

Gujarati, D. N., Porter, D. C., & Gunasekar, S. (2012). *Basic econometrics*. Tata Mcgraw-Hill Education.

Gummesson, E. (2003). All research is interpretive! *Journal of Business and Industrial Marketing*, *18*(6/7), 482–492. https://doi.org/10.1108/08858620310492365

Hagle, T. M., & Mitchell, G. E. (1992). Goodness-of-fit measures for probit and logit. *American Journal of Political Science*, *36*(3), 762–784. doi:10.2307/2111590

Hagquist, C., & Stenbeck, M. (1998). Goodness of fit in regression analysis–R 2 and G 2 reconsidered. *Quality & Quantity*, *32*(3), 229–245. doi:10.1023/A:1004328601205

Halil, Y., & Petek, A. (2013). Learning programming, problem solving and gender: A longitudinal study. *Procedia: Social and Behavioral Sciences*, *83*, 605–610. doi:10.1016/j.sbspro.2013.06.115

Hart, H. L. A. (1961). The Concept Of Law. Clarendon Press, Oxford. Cited in Chynoweth Paul, (2008) Legal Research in the Built Environment: A Methodological Framework. In Andrew Knight & Les Ruddock (Eds.), Advanced Research Methods in the Built EnvironmentWiley-Blackwell.

Hazem Ben Aissa. (2001), quelle méthodologie de recherche appropriée pour une construction de la recherche en gestion? xième conférence de l'association internationale de management stratégique, 13-14-15 juin 2001, 27 P.

Helen, E. L. (1990). *Science as Social Knowledge: Values and Objectivity in Scientific Inquiry.* Princeton University Press.

Heritage, J. C. (1987). Ethnomethodology. In A. Giddens & J. H. Turner (Eds.), *Social Theory Today.* Stanford University Press.

Hesse-Biber., S. (2011). *The practice of Qualitative Research.* Sage.

Hill, R. C., Griffiths, W. E., & Lim, G. C. (2018). *Principles of econometrics.* John Wiley & Sons.

Hites, R. A. (2021). How to convince an editor to accept your paper quickly. *The Science of the Total Environment, 798,* 149–243.

Hoyle, RH. (1995). *Structural equation modeling: concepts, issues, and applications.* Sage, Thousand Oak.

Hsu, P.F. (2010). Selection model based on ANP and GRA for independent media agencies. Quality & Quantity). doi:10.1007/s11135-010-9323-y

Hsu, P. F. (2009). Evaluating advertising spokespersons via the ANP-GRA selection model. *Journal of Grey System, 21*(1), 35–48.

Hsu, P.-F., & Kuo, M.-H. (2011). Applying the ANP model for selecting the optimal full-service advertising agency. *International Journal of Operations Research, 8*(4), 48–58.

Hsu, P.-F., & Kuo, M.-H. (2011). Applying the ANP Model for Selecting the Optimal Full-service Advertising Agency. *International Journal of Operations Research, 8*(4), 48–58.

Hu, L. T., & Bentler, P. M. (1995). Evaluating model fit. In R. H. Hoyle (Ed.), *Structural equation modeling: Concepts, issues and applications* (pp. 76–99). Sage.

Hutchinson, T. (2015). The Doctrinal Method: Incorporating Interdisciplinary Methods in Reforming the Law, *Erasmus. Law Review, 3,* 130–138.

Hutchinson, T., & Duncan, N. (2012). Defining and Describing What We Do: Doctrinal Legal Research, *Deakin. Law Review, 17*(1), 83–119. https://ojs.deakin.edu.au/index.php/dlr/article/view/70/75

Ijomah, M. A. (2019). On the Misconception of R-square for R-square in a Regression Model. [IJRSI]. *International Journal of Research and Scientific Innovation, 6*(12), 71–76.

Isangedighi, A. J., & Bassey, B. A. (2012). Research report writing. In A. J. Isangedighi (Ed.), *Essentials of research and statistics in education and social sciences* (pp. 287–292). Eti-Nwa Associates.

Jain, S. N. (1982). Doctrinal and Non-Doctrinal Legal Research. *Journal of the Indian Law Institute, 24*(2/3), 341–361.

James, W. (2000). What pragmatism means. In J. J. Stuhr (Ed.), *Pragmatism and the Classical American Philosophy: Essential Readings and Interpretive Essay* (2nd ed., pp. 193–202). Oxford University Press.

Jerome Hall Law Library. (2019) *Legal Dissertation: Research and Writing Guide.* Maurer School of Law. https://law.indiana.libguides.com/dissertationguide#:~:text= Doctrinal,%2C%20statutes%2C%20or%20regulations)

Jharkharia, S., & Shankar, R. (2007). Selection of logistics service provider: An analytic network process (ANP) approach. *Omega, 35*(3), 274–289. doi:10.1016/j.omega.2005.06.005

Johnson, R. B., & Christensen, L. B. (2017). Educational research: Quantitative, qualitative, and mixed approaches. 6th Los Angeles. *Sage (Atlanta, Ga.).*

Johnson, R. B., & Onwuegbuzie, A. J. (2004). Mixed Methods Research A Research Paradigm Whose Time Has Come. *Educational Researcher, 33*(7), 14–26. doi:10.3102/0013189X033007014

Jöreskog, K. G., & Sörbom, D. (1981). *Analysis of linear structural relationships by maximum likelihood and least squares methods* (Research Report No. 81-8). Uppsala, Sweden: University of Sweden.

Kahn, J. H. (2006). Factor analysis in counseling psychology research, training, and practice: Principles, advances, and applications. *The Counseling Psychologist, 34*(5), 684–718. doi:10.1177/0011000006286347

Karim, S., & Hue, M. T. (2022). Researching ethnic minority lives in multicultural contexts: A methodological inquiry in acculturation. *International Journal of Comparative Education and Development, 24*(3/4), 177–192.

Kemigisha, E., Rai, M., Mlahagwa, W., Nyakato, V. N., & Ivanova, O. (2020). A Qualitative Study Exploring Menstruation Experiences and Practices among Adolescent Girls Living in the Nakivale Refugee Settlement, Uganda. *International Journal of Environmental Research and Public Health, 17*(18), 6613. doi:10.3390/ijerph17186613 PMID:32932817

Kerlinger, F. N. (2000). *Foundations of behavioural research.* Holt, Rinehart and Wilson.

Kerlinger, P., & Lein, M. R. (1986). Differences in winter range among age-sex classes of Snowy Owls Nyctea scandiaca in North America. *Ornis Scandinavica*, •••, 1–7.

Kinash, S. (n.d.). Fatal mistakes in academic writing. [Internet source]. http:// www.bong.edu.gu/prod_ext/groups/public@pub-tis-gen/do cuments/genericwedocument/bd3_12330pdf

King, G. (1986). How not to lie with statistics: Avoiding common mistakes in quantitative political science. *American Journal of Political Science, 30*(3), 666–687. doi:10.2307/2111095

King, G. (1990). Stochastic Variation: A Comment on Lewis-Beck and Skalaban's "The R-Squared". *Political Analysis*, *2*, 185–200. doi:10.1093/pan/2.1.185

Kothari, C. R. (2008). *Research Methodology, Methods and Techniques* (2nd ed.). New Age International Publication.

Kotsis, S. V., & Chung, K. C. (2014). Manuscript rejection: How to submit a revision and tips on being a good peer reviewer. *Plastic and Reconstructive Surgery*, *133*, 958–964.

Krathwohl, D. R. (2009). Methods of Education and Social Science Research: An Integrated Approach (2nd ed). Waveland Press, Inc. Long Grove, Il.

Kuhn, T. S. (1963). *The structure of scientific revolutions*. The University of Chicago Press.

Kuhn, T. S. (1977). The essential tension: Tradition and innovation in scientific research. In *The essential tension: Selected studies in scientific tradition and change* (pp. 225–239). University of Chicago Press. doi:10.7208/chicago/9780226217239.001.0001

Kuhn, T. S. (2012). *The Structure of Scientific Revolutions*. University of Chicago Press. doi:10.7208/chicago/9780226458144.001.0001

Laughlin, R. C. (1995). *Middle Range Thinking*. Accounting, Auditing and Accountability.

Le Moigne, J. L. (1990). *La modélisation des systèmes complexes*. Dunod.

Leavy, P. (2017). *Research Design- Quantitative, Qualitative, Mixed Methods, Arts based, and Community based Participatory research approaches* (1st ed.). The Guilford Press.

Leedy, P. D., & Ormrod, J. E. (2010). *Practical research: Planning and design* (9th ed.). Merril.

Lee, J. W., & Kim, S. H. (2000). Using analytic network process and goal programming for interdependent information system project selection. *Computers & Operations Research*, *27*(4), 367–382. doi:10.1016/S0305-0548(99)00057-X

Lewis-Beck, C., & Lewis-Beck, M. (2015). *Applied regression: An introduction* (Vol. 22). Sage publications.

Lewis-Beck, M. S., & Skalaban, A. (1990). The R-squared: Some straight talk. *Political Analysis*, *2*, 153–171. doi:10.1093/pan/2.1.153

Libguides. (2022). Research Guides, Literature Review - Finding the Resources: Evaluating Sources. (2022). *Libguides*. https://libguides.library.cityu.edu.hk/litreview/evaluating-sources/

Library Highline College. (2022) *Primary and Secondary Legal Sources*. Highline College. https://library.highline.edu/c.php?g=344547&p=2320319

Lincoln, Y. S., & Guba, E. G. (1985). *Naturalistic inquiry*. Sage. doi:10.1016/0147-1767(85)90062-8

Little, T. D. (2013). *Longitudinal structural equation modeling*. Guilford Press.

Macdonald, S., & Birdi, B. (2019). The concept of neutrality: A new approach. *The Journal of Documentation, 76*(1), 333–353. doi:10.1108/JD-05-2019-0102

Madhavika, W.D.N., Nagendrakumar, N., Colombathanthri, P.S.H., Rathnayake, R.M.T., Jayaweera, J.H.M.P.S.B., & Buddhika M.S. (2021). " Resource Optimization in Paddy Cultivation, for Developing Countries; A Sector Synergetic Approach *" Alinteri Journal of Agricultural Science,* vol.36, Issue 2, 2021, pp.122 131, EBSCO, 22/09/2021, doi:10.47059/alinteri/V36I2/AJAS21124

Madhavika, N., Jayasinghe, N., Ehalapitiya, S., Wickramage, T., Fernando, D., & Jayasinghe, V. (2022). Operationalizing resilience through collaboration: The case of Sri Lankan tea supply chain during Covid-19. *Quality & Quantity.* doi:10.100711135-022-01493-8 PMID:35971419

Marczyk, G., DeMatteo, D., & Festinger, D. (2005). *Essentials of Research Design and Methodology* (1st ed.). John Wiley & Sons, Inc.

Marie-Laure, G.-P., Gotteland, D., Haon, C., & Jolibert, A. (2012). *Méthodologie de la recherche en sciences de gestion.* Pearson France.

Mario, L. (2013). *Brilliant Blunders: From Darwin to Einstein - Colossal Mistakes by Great Scientists That Changed Our Understanding of Life and the Universe.* Simon & Schuster.

Martinet, A. C. (1990). (coord.), (1990), Epistemologie et Sciences de gestion, Paris. *Economica.*

Martinsuo, M. & Huemann, M. (2021), The basics of writing a paper for the International Journal of Project Management, *International Journal of Project Management* 38 (2020) pp. 340–342.

Maulingin-Gumbaketi, E., Larkins, S., Gunnarsson, R., Rembeck, G., Whittaker, M., & Redman-MacLaren, M. (2021). 'Making of a Strong Woman': A constructivist grounded theory of the experiences of young women around menarche in Papua New Guinea. *BMC Women's Health, 21*(1), 144. doi:10.118612905-021-01229-0 PMID:33832465

Maxcy, S. J. (2003). Pragmatic threads in mixed methods research in the social sciences: The search for multiple modes of inquiry and the end of the philosophy of formalism. In A. Tashakkori & C. Teddlie (Eds.), *Handbook of Mixed Methods in Social and Behavioral Research* (pp. 51–89). Sage.

Maxwell, J. A. (2013). *Qualitative research design: An interactive approach.* SAGE.

Maydeu-Olivares, A., & Garcia-Forero, C. (2010). Goodness-of-fit testing. *International encyclopedia of education, 7*(1), 190-196.

Maykut, P. S. (1994). *Beginning Qualitative Research: A Philosophic and Practical Guide.* Falmer Press.

McLeod, S. A. (2020), May 01). Karl popper - theory of falsification. *Simply Psychology.* https://www.simplypsychology.org/Karl-Popper.html

McNally, K. (2022). Library Guides: Literature Review: Types of literature reviews. *Libguides.* csu.edu.au. https://libguides.csu.edu.au/review/Types

Meade, L. M., & Sarkis, J. (1998). Strategic analysis of logistics and supply chain management systems using the analytic network process. *Transportation Research Part E, Logistics and Transportation Review, 34*(3), 201–215. doi:10.1016/S1366-5545(98)00012-X

Melnikovas, A. (2018). Towards an Explicit Research Methodology: Adapting Research Onion Model for *Futures Studies. Journal of Futures Studies, 23*(2), 29–44. doi:10.6531/JFS.201812_23(2).0003

Mertler, C. A., & Charles, C. M. (2008). *Introduction to educational research*. Allyn and Bacon.

Miles, J. (2005). *R-squared, adjusted R-squared*. Encyclopedia of statistics in behavioral science.

Minow, M., M. (2013). Archetypal Legal Scholarship – A Field Guide. *Journal of Legal Education, 63*(1), 65–73.

Mittra, A. (2021) Analytical School of Jurisprudence, *Lawcorner.in.* https://lawcorner.in/analytical-school-of-jurisprudence/

Montgomery, P., Hennegan, J., Dolan, C., Wu, M., Steinfield, L., & Scott, L. (2016). Menstruation and the Cycle of Poverty: A Cluster Quasi-Randomised Control Trial of Sanitary Pad and Puberty Education Provision in Uganda. *PLoS One, 11*(12), e0166122. doi:10.1371/journal.pone.0166122 PMID:28002415

Morgan, D. L. (2007). Paradigms lost and pragmatism regained: Methodological implications of combining qualitative and quantitative methods. *Journal of Mixed Methods Research, 1*(1), 48–76. doi:10.1177/2345678906292462

Morgan, D. L. (2014). *Integrating Qualitative and Quantitative Methods: A Pragmatic Approach*. Sage. doi:10.4135/9781544304533

Mukherjee, S. P. (2020). *A Guide to Research Methodology: An Overview of Research Problems, Tasks and Methods* (1st ed.). Taylor & Francis.

Mulaik, S. A., & Millsap, R. E. (2000). Doing the four-step right. *Structural Equation Modeling, 7*(1), 36–73. doi:10.1207/S15328007SEM0701_02

Mushtaq, B., & Mir, J.A. (2019). A Pre Experimental Study To Assess The Effectiveness Of Structured Teaching Programme On Knowledge Regarding Menstrual Hygiene Among Fmphw Ist Year Students At Ramzaan Institute Of Paramedical Sciences Nowgam Srinagar. *Indian Journal of Applied Research, 9* (7).

Muthén, L. K., & Muthén, B. O. (2012). *Mplus user's guide* (7th ed.). Authors.

myneni. S.R. (Ed.). (2006) Legal Research Methodology, (1st ed.). Allahabad Law Agency.

Nagendrakumar, N., De Silva, L. M. H., Weerasinghe, R. M., Pathirana, T. D., Rajapaksha, C. M., Perera, K. R., & Kaneshwaren, S. (2022). Corporate social responsibility and financial performance: A study of the tourism industry in Sri Lanka. *Corporate Ownership & Control, 19*(4), 103–110 (B rank). doi:10.22495/cocv19i4art9

Nagendrakumar, N. (2017). Public Sector Accounting and Financial Reporting Reforms: Public Entities Perspectives, Sri Lanka. *International Journal on Governmental Financial Management*, *17*(1), 17–34.

Nakhmanson, R. (2003). Quantum mechanics as a sociology of matter *Quantum Physics*. https://doi.org/ doi:10.48550/arXiv.quant-ph/0303162

Nakhmanson, R. (2003). Quantum mechanics as a sociology of matter. eprint arXiv:quant-ph/0303162. https://ui.adsabs.harvard.edu/abs/2003quant.ph.3162N/abstract

National Law University. (n.d.). *Delhi, Handbook for Research Project Writing*. National Law University. https://nludelhi.ac.in/download/publication/2015/NLU%20old.pdf

Ndiyo, N. A. (2005). *Fundamentals of research in behavioural sciences and humanities*. Wusen Publishers.

NEET, Hanna E. (1989) *À la recherche du mot clé. Analyse documentaire et indexation alphabétique*. Genève, les éditions 1ERS, coll. « Les cours de le 1ER », n° 2.

Nworgu, B. G. (2005). *Educational research: Basic issues and methodology*. Wisdom Publishers Limited.

O'Leary, Z. (2004). *The essential guide to doing research*. Sage.

O'Leary, Z. (2005). *Researching real-world problems*. Sage.

O'Leary, Z. (20014). *The essential guide to doing research*. London: Sage.

Onyutha, C. (2020). From R-squared to coefficient of model accuracy for assessing" goodness-of-fits." *Geoscientific Model Development Discussions*, 1-25.

Ormerod, R. J. (2006). The history and ideas of pragmatism. *The Journal of the Operational Research Society*, *57*(8), 892–909. doi:10.1057/palgrave.jors.2602065

Owan, V. J., & Bassey, B. A. (2018). Comparative study of manual and computerised software techniques of data management and analysis in educational research. [IJIEM]. *International Journal of Innovation in Educational Management*, *2*(1), 35–46.

Oxford University Press. (2022). *Abstract and Keyword Guide*, (7th ed.). OED. https://www.oed.com

Pansiri, J. (2005). Pragmatism: A methodological approach to researching strategic alliances in tourism. *Tourism and Hospitality Planning and Development*, *2*(3), 191–206. doi:10.1080/14790530500399333

Patriotta, G. (2017). Crafting papers for publication: Novelty and convention in academic writing. *Journal of Management Studies*, *54*(5), 747–759.

Patten, M. L., & Newhart, M. (2018). Understanding Research Methods; An Overview of the Essentials (10th ed.). Routledge, Taylor & Francis Group. New York and London.

Pearce, D., Campbell, E., & Harding, D. (1987). *Australian Law Schools: A Discipline Assessment for the Commonwealth Tertiary Education Commission*. Australian Government Publishing Service.

Peirce, C. S. (1934). Pragmatism and Abduction. In C. Hartshorne & P. Weiss. Cambridge, (eds). The Collected Papers of Charles Sanders Peirce, Vol. 5, Pragmatism and Pragmaticism [sic],180-212. Harvard University Press.

Peirce, C.S. (1878). How to Make Our Ideas Clear. *Popular Science Monthly, 12*, 286–302.

Peirce, C. S. (1878). Illustrations of the Logic of Science. *Popular Science Monthly, 13*, 470–482.

Poonikom, K., O' Brien, C., & Chansangavej, C. (2004). An application of the analytic network process (ANP) for university selection decisions. *Science Asia, 30*(4), 317–326. doi:10.2306cie nceasia1513-1874.2004.30.317

Popper, K. (1959). The Logic of Scientific Discovery (2002 pbk; 2005 ebook ed.). Routledge.

Quivy Raymond Et Van Campenhoudt Luc. (1988). *Manuel de recherche en sciences sociales*. Dunod.

Quivy, R., & Van Campenhoudt, L. (2006), *Manuel de recherche en Sciences Sociales*, Paris, Dunod, 3e éd.

Rebecca, W., & Paul, A. G. (2006). A Brief Guide to Structural Equation Modeling. *The Counseling Psychologist, 34*(5), 719–751. doi:10.1177/0011000006286345

Reisinger, H. (1997). The impact of research designs on R2 in linear regression models: An exploratory meta-analysis. *Journal of Empirical Generalisations in Marketing Science, 2*(1).

Rubin, D. B. (1976). Inference and missing data. *Biometrika, 61*(3), 581–592. doi:10.1093/biomet/63.3.581

Rückert, J. (2006) Friedrich Carl von Savigny, the Legal Method, and the Modernity of Law, *Juridica International XI*. https://www.juridicainternational.eu/public/pdf/ji_2006_1_55.pdf

Saaty, R. W. (1987). The analytic hierarchy process—what it is and how it is used. *Mathematical Modelling, 9*(3–5), 161-176.

Saaty, T. L. (1977). A scaling method for priorities in hierarchical structures. *Journal of Mathematical Psychology, 15*(3), 234–281. doi:10.1016/0022-2496(77)90033-5

Saaty, T. L. (1980). *The Analytic Hierarchy Process*. McGraw-Hill.

Saaty, T. L. (1987). Rank generation, preservation, and reversal in the analytic hierarchy decision process. *Decision Sciences, 18*(2), 157–177. doi:10.1111/j.1540-5915.1987.tb01514.x

Saaty, T. L. (1988). What is the analytic hierarchy process? In *Mathematical models for decision support* (pp. 109–121). Springer. doi:10.1007/978-3-642-83555-1_5

Saaty, T. L. (1996). *Decision Making with Dependence and Feedback: The Analytic Network Process*. RWS Publications.

Saaty, T. L. (2001). *Decision making for leaders: the analytic hierarchy process for decisions in a complex world*. RWS publications.

Saaty, T. L. (2001). *Decision Making with Dependence and Feedback: the Analytic Network Process* (2nd ed.). RWS Publications.

Saaty, T. L. (2008). Decision making with the analytic hierarchy process. *International Journal of Services Sciences*, *1*(1), 83–98. doi:10.1504/IJSSCI.2008.017590

Saliya, C. A. (2010). *The Role of bank lending in sustaining income/wealth inequality in Sri Lanka*. [PhD Thesis, Auckland University of Technology, New Zealand.] https://openrepository.aut.ac.nz/handle/10292/824

Saliya, C. A. (2017), Doing Qualitative Case Study Research in Business Management, International Journal of Case Studies Journal ISSN (2305-509X), 6 (12), pp. 96 – 111.

Saliya, C. A. (2017). Doing Qualitative Case Study Research in Business Management. *International Journal of Case studies, 6* (12), pp. 96 – 111. http://www.casestudiesjournal.com/Volume%206%20Issue%2012%20Paper%2010.pdf

Saliya, C. A. (2022). Doing social research and publishing results. Springer. https://link.springer.com/book/10.1007/978-981-19-3780-4

Saliya, C. A. (2022). Doing Social Research and Publishing Results. Springer. https://link.springer.com/book/10.1007/978-981-19-3780-4

Saliya, C. A. (2012). The oldest profession. *Accounting, Auditing & Accountability Journal*, *25*(6), 1072–1072. doi:10.1108/09513571211250279

Saliya, C. A. (2021). Conducting Case Study Research: A Concise Practical Guidance for Management Students. *International Journal of KIU*, *2*(1), 1–13. https://doi.org/10.37966/ijkiu20210127

Saliya, C. A. (2022). *Doing Social Research: A Guide to Non-native English Speakers*. Springer., https://link.springer.com/book/10.1007/978-981-19-3780-4

Saliya, C. A. (2023). *Doing social research and publishing results*. Springer.

Saliya, C. A., & Wickrama, K. A. S. (2021). Determinants of Financial Risk Preparedness. *Advances in Climate Change Research*. Advance online publication. doi:10.1016/j.accre.2021.03.012

Salmerona, J. L., & Smarandacheb, F. (2010). Redesigning Decision Matrix Method with an indeterminacy-based inference process. Multispace and Multistructure. Neutrosophic Transdisciplinarity. *100 Collected Papers of Sciences, 4*, 151.

Samaddar, R. (2015). The Red Closet: Narrative Concept of Menstruation in Indian Advertisement. Thesis for: Masters in Mass Communication Journalism.

Satorra, A., & Bentler, P. (1994). Corrections to test statistics and standard errors on covariance structure analysis. In A. Von Eye & C. C. Clogg (Eds.), *Latent variables analysis* (pp. 399–419). Sage.

Satyajit, & Kaur, I. (2017). A Quasi Experimental Study to Assess the Effectiveness of Ginger Powder on Dysmenorrhea among Nursing Students in Selected Nursing Colleges, Hoshiarpur, Punjab. *International Journal of Innovative Research in Medical Science, 2* (8), 1204-1210.

Saunders, M., Lewis, P., & Thornhill, A. (2012) *Research methods for business students, International Journal of the History of Sport*. Pearson Education Limited.

Saunders, M., Lewis, P., Thornhill, A., & Bristow, A. (2019). Research Methods for Business Students Chapter 4: Understanding research philosophy and approaches to theory development. Harlow, United Kingdom. Pearson.

Saunders, M., Lewis, P., & Thornhill, A. (2019). *Research methods for business students* (8th ed.). Pearson Education Limited.

Schoonenboom, J. (2016). The multilevel mixed intact group analysis: A mixed method to seek, detect, describe and explain differences between intact groups. *Journal of Mixed Methods Research, 10*, 129–146.

Schurz, G. (2008). Patterns of abduction. *Synthese, 164*(2), 201–234. doi:10.100711229-007-9223-4

Sekaran, U., & Bougie, R. (2016). *Research Methods for Business*. Wiley & Sons Ltd., doi:10.1007/978-94-007-0753-5_102084

Shah, J. N. (2015). How to write "introduction" in scientific journal article. *Journal of Patan Academy of Health Sciences, 2*(1), 1–2. doi:10.3126/jpahs.v2i1.20331

Sharma, M., Sarin, A., Gupta, P., Sachdeva, S., & Desai, A. V. (2014). Journal impact factor: Its use, significance and limitations. *World Journal of Nuclear Medicine, 13*(2), 146. doi:10.4103/1450-1147.139151 PMID:25191134

Sheoran, P., Kaur, S., Sadhanu, H., & Sarin, J. (2020). A descriptive study of menstrual hygiene practices among women at the rural area of Haryana. *Journal of Nursing and Midwifery Sciences, 7*(4), 269. doi:10.4103/JNMS.JNMS_18_20

Simon, H. A. (1977). *The New Science of Management Decision*. Prentice-Hall.

Simon, M. K. (2011). *Assumptions, limitations and delimitation*. [Excerpt from dissertation and scholarly research: Recipe for success. Seatle, W. A.] Dissertation Success, LLC.

Singh, A. K. (2006). *Tests, Measurements and Research Methods in Behavioral Sciences* (5th ed.). Bharati Bhawan.

Singh, G., Bartaula, S., Dhakal, N., Gurung, Y., Shrestha, S. K., Basnet, M., Poudel, M., & Sherpa, L. Y. (2017, December 15)... . *BMC Women's Health*, *21*, 410. doi:10.118612905-021-01544-6

Sivakumar, P. S., Bibudha, P., Raghu, N. D., & Anantharaman, M. (2014). Determinants of computer utilization by extension personnel: A structural equations approach. *Journal of Agricultural Education and Extension*, *20*(2), 191–212. doi:10.1080/1389224X.2013.803986

Smith, J. K., & Heshusius, L. (1986). Closing down the conversation: The end of the quantitativequalitative debate among educational inquirers. *Educational Leadership*, *15*(1), 4–12. doi:10.3102/0013189X015001004

Snyder, J. (2015). Exploitation and Sweatshop Labour: Perspectives and Issues. *Society for Business Ethics*. 20(2), 187–213. . doi:10.5840/beq201020215

Spearman, C. (1904). General Intelligence: Objectively determined and measured. *The American Journal of Psychology*, *5*(2), 201–293. doi:10.2307/1412107

Spiess, A. N., & Neumeyer, N. (2010). An evaluation of R2 as an inadequate measure for nonlinear models in pharmacological and biochemical research: A Monte Carlo approach. *BMC Pharmacology*, *10*(1), 1–11. doi:10.1186/1471-2210-10-6 PMID:20529254

Steiger, J. H., & Lind, J. C. (1980). *Statistically based tests for the number of common factors*. Paper presented at the annual meeting of the Psychometric Society, Iowa City, IA.

Steiger, J. H. (1990). Structural model evaluation and modification: An internal estimation approach. *Multivariate Behavioral Research*, *25*(2), 173–180. doi:10.120715327906mbr2502_4 PMID:26794479

Strauss, A. L., & Corbin, J. (1996). *Basics of Qualitative Research: Techniques and Procedures for Developing Grounded Theory*. Sage.

Swales, J. M., & Feak, C. B. (2014). Commentary for academic writing for graduate students: Essential tasks and skills (5th ed.). University of Michigan Press/ESL.

Tanya, N. B., & Claudio, V. (2010). Structural equation modeling in medical research: A primer. *BMC Research Notes*, *3*, 26. PMID:20969789

Tarka, P. (2018). An overview of structural equation modeling: Its beginnings, historical development, usefulness and controversies in the social sciences. *Quality & Quantity*, *52*(1), 313–354. doi:10.100711135-017-0469-8 PMID:29416184

Tesch, R. (1990). *Qualitative Research, Analysis Types & Software Tools*. Falmer Press.

Thompson, A. (1997). Political pragmatism and educational inquiry. In F. Margonis (ed.) Philosophy of Education, pp. 425–34. Urbana: Philosophy of Education Society.

Tinker, T., & Lowe, T. (1982). The Management Science of Management Sciences. *Human Relations, 35*(4), 331–347.

Tiwary, S. (2020) Doctrinal and Non-Doctrinal. *Academia.* https://www.academia.edu/40656281/Doctrinal_and_Non_Doctrinal_Methods_of_Legal_Research

Tremblay, R. (1994). *Savoir faire – Précis de méthodologie pratique.* McGraw Hill.

Ugodulunwa, C. A. (2016). *Basics of academic writing: A guide for students.* Fab Anieh Nigeria Ltd.

Varga, L. (2018). Mixed methods research: A method for complex systems. In E. Mitleton-Kelly, A. Paraskevas, & C. Day (Eds.), *Edward Elgar handbook of research methods in complexity science* (pp. 34–39). Edward Elgar Publishing.

Vibute, K. I. & Filipos, A. (2009) *Legal Research Methods: Teaching Material, Justice and Legal System Research Institute.* Wordpress. chilot.wordpress.com

Voss V. (1999), Research Methodology in operation management, *Eden seminar*, Brussels, February.

Whitley, R. (1984). The Fragmented State of Management Studies: Reasons and Consequences. *Journal of Management Studies, 21*(4), 369–390.

Wickrama, K. A. S., Lee, T. K., O'Neal, C. W., & Lorenz, F. O. (2016). *Higher-order growth curves and mixture modeling with Mplus: A practical guide.* Routledge/Taylor & Francis Group.

Wickrama, K. A. S., Conger, R. D., & Abraham, W. T. (2008). Early family adversity, youth depressive symptoms trajectories, and young adult socioeconomic attainment: A latent trajectory class analysis. *Advances in Life Course Research, 13*, 161–192. doi:10.1016/S1040-2608(08)00007-5

Wickrama, K. A. S., & Wickrama, T. (2011). Perceived community participation in tsunami recovery efforts and the mental health of tsunami affected mothers: Findings from a study in rural Sri Lanka. *The International Journal of Social Psychiatry, 57*(5), 518–527. doi:10.1177/0020764010374426 PMID:20603268

Wickrama, K. A. T., Wickrama, K. A. S., & Bryant, C. M. (2016). Community Influence on Adolescent Obesity: Race/Ethnic Differences. *Journal of Youth and Adolescence, 35*(4), 647–657.

Wickrama, T., Wickrama, K. A. S., Banford, A., & Lambert, J. (2017). PTSD symptoms among tsunami exposed mothers in Sri Lanka: The role of disaster exposure, culturally specific coping strategies, and recovery efforts. *Anxiety, Stress, and Coping, 30*(4), 415–427. doi:10.1080/10615806.2016.1271121 PMID:27960534

Willet, J. B. (1988). Questions and answers in the measurement of change. In E. Z. Rothkpf (Ed.), *Review of Research in Education* (Vol. 15, pp. 345–422). American Educational Research Association. doi:10.2307/1167368

Willet, J. B., & Sayer, A. G. (1994). Using covariance structure analysis to detect correlates and predictors of individual change over time. *Psychological Bulletin, 116*(2), 363–381. doi:10.1037/0033-2909.116.2.363

Wood, E. J. (2006). The Ethical Challenges of Field Research in Conflict Zones. *Qualitative Sociology, 29*(3), 373–386.

Wright, S. (1918). On the nature of size factors. *Genetics, 3*(4), 367–374. doi:10.1093/genetics/3.4.367 PMID:17245910

Yin, R. K. (1989). Applied Social Research Methods Series: Vol. 5. *Case Study Research, Design and Methods*. Sage Publications.

Yin, R. K. (2002). *Case Study Research Design and Methods*. Sage Pub.

About the Contributors

Candauda Arachchige Saliya holds a PhD in Finance/Banking from the Auckland University of Technology (AUT), New Zealand. He is a Fellow Chartered Accountant and a member of the Association of Professional Bankers (Sri Lanka), CPA (Australia), MICM (UK) and a founder member of the Society of Certified Management Accountants of Sri Lanka. He also holds a Diploma of Central Banking from the Central Bank of Sri Lanka and is a TESOL qualified teacher.

* * *

Ranasinghe Amaradasa is the Dean of the School of Business & Economics of the University of Fiji. Dr. Ranasinghe has been engaged in teaching Management & Business Administration subjects since July 2009. Dr. Amaradasa holds a BSc Degree in Physics & Master of Science Degree in Physics from University of Peradeniya, Sri Lanka (1982 & 1985 respectively) and PhD Degree in Management from University of Wollongong, Australia (2004). He gained a considerable insight of Research & Technology Management and Science Policy Analysis while he was working at National Science Foundation in Sri Lanka during 1985 to 2008. Dr Amaradasa has received extensive training in these areas from University of Sussex in U.K. and University of Wollongong, Australia. He worked as Director (Planning & Monitoring) at National Enterprise Development Authority of Sri Lanka for one year before joining University of Fiji in Fiji Islands in 2009. He has contributed to the World Science Report 2010, 2015 & 2020 of UNESCO, covering status of Science & Technology in Pacific Islands.

Bassey Bassey is a Faculty member (Lecturer) in the Department of Educational Foundations, University of Calabar. He rose to the rank of a full Professor in 2022, all to the glory of Almighty God. Prof. Bassey has some relevant and cognate experiences over the years, typical of which are: - Academic Librarian in UNICAL Library (1999 to 2007) - Academic Adviser to Diploma and Undergraduate students in Library & Information Science, UNICAL (1999 to 2007). He has served as the deputy Dean, Faculty of Education, University of Calabar (2018 till 2020) and Senate Member (Faculty Representative), University of Calabar. He has published many peer-reviewed articles in international journals that are indexed in both Scopus and Web of Science.

Ruwan Gopura received the B.Sc. Eng. Degree (Hons.) in Mechanical Engineering in 2004 and the M.Eng. degree in Manufacturing Systems Engineering from the University of Moratuwa, Sri Lanka. He received his PhD degree in robotics and intelligent systems from Saga University, Japan, in 2009 and subsequently carried out postdoctoral research on bio-robotics at Saga University, Japan. He is a professor in the Department of Mechanical Engineering, University of Moratuwa, and head, Medical Technology, Faculty of Medicine in the same university.

Kavita Gupta is an Assistant Professor in the Department of Psychology, Faculty of Education and Psychology at The Maharaja Sayajirao University of Baroda, Vadodara (Gujarat). She is Pursuing her Ph.D. in Psychology from Sardar Patel University, Vallabh Vidyanagar, Anand (Gujarat). Besides, she has her Doctoral thesis on 'Quality of Life in Cancer Patients undergoing Chemotherapy and Radiotherapy'. She is working with the university students targeting their Personal, Emotional, Psychological problems and enhancement of their mental health and well-being. Her area of interest includes Positive Psychology, Clinical Psychology, Social Psychology, Research Methodology, Educational Psychology. Her research findings have been published as 20+ research papers and 10+ chapters in edited book in national and international referred/indexed journals and presented 10 research papers at National and International conferences.

Nisha Jayasuriya is an Assistant Professor and head of the department, of business management at the Sri Lanka Institute of Information Technology. Her main fields of research are education, social marketing, advertising, consumer behaviour and brand management.

Chandimal Jayawardena received his B.Sc.Eng.(Hons) and M.Eng. in Electronic and Telecommunication Engineering from the University of Moratuwa, Sri Lanka, and his Ph.D. in Robotics and Intelligent Systems from Saga University, Japan. From 1999 to 2001, he was with Sri Lankan Airlines and from 2001 to 2003 he was with Sri Lanka Telecom as an Engineer. From 2003 to 2006 he was a doctoral research student in Saga University, Japan. In 2006 he joined the Sri Lanka Institute of Information Technology (SLIIT) as a Senior Lecturer and in 2009 joined the University of Auckland as a Research Fellow. From 2011 to 2016 he was with the Department of Computer Science, Unitec Institute of Technology, New Zealand as a Senior Lecturer. Currently, he is a professor of the Faculty of Computing, SLIIT. His research interests include service robotics, human–robot interaction, software engineering for robotics, and machine intelligence.

Thantirige Sanath Siroshana Jayawardena, PhD, received a B.Sc. (Eng.) degree in Electronics and Telecommunications from the University of Moratuwa, an M.Sc. in Operations Research from the same university and Ph.D. in Robotics and Systems Control from the Saga University Japan in 1996, 2003, and 2005 respectively. Currently, he is serving as a Professor attached to the Department of Textile and Clothing Technology, Faculty of Engineering, University of Moratuwa, Sri Lanka. Dr. Jayawardana became a Senior Member (SM) of IEEE and a Fellow of Textile Institute (UK) in 2017. He is also a charted Engineer, a founding member of the Applied Statistics Association, Sri Lanka, and a member of the Institute of Engineers Sri Lanka. Dr. Jayawardena served as the Chair of the IEEE Sri Lanka Section in 2017 and he also served as the editor of the Sri Lanka Section for two years. He authored more than 20 journal papers and more than 30 conference papers. He renders his service as a reviewer to many internationally reputed journals including IEEE journals and SCI-indexed journals.

Wadanambilage Dona Madhavika is a Senior Lecturer attached to Department of Information Management at SLIIT Business School. Her research interest is in Sustainable Supply Chain Management, Resilience Management and Gender studies. She has over ten journal articles published in peer-reviewed journals including Quality and Quantity Journal, Empirical Economic Letters, Operations and Supply Chain Management: An International Journal, Design Engineering (Toronto), Test Engineering & Management and etc within the academic career of 5 years. She has also presented in more than 10 international and national conferences held in Sri Lanka, India and Singapore.

Michael Merten is a Professor in the Department of Child, Youth and Family Studies at the University of Nebraska-Lincoln. In his studies of adolescents and young adults, he focuses on the determinants of physical and mental health considering both family and community contexts, specifically in both rural and urban populations.

Moez Ltifi is a Ph.D in Business Administration. He is currently associate professor (HDR) in marketing at the University of Shaqra in Saudi Arabia and at the University of Sfax in Tunisia. Dr Ltifi is a reviewer in various international academic journals. His research work focuses on consumer attitudes, online shopping, customer satisfaction, customer trust, acceptance of new technologies, electronic loyalty, retailing, bank marketing, m.mobile, consumer behaviour, corporate governance, performance, branding. His most recent articles are published in refereed international ranked and impacted journals such as International Journal of Bank Marketing, Management and Organization Review, Management Decision, Journal of Management Science, Management 2000, Journal of Global Marketing, International Journal of Law and Management, Corporate Governance: The International Journal of Business in Society, Journal of Knowledge Management, Journal of Air Transport Management.

Nagendrakumar Nagalingam is the current Associate Dean at SLIIT Business School. He is also a University Professor specializing in Accounting and Finance at Global Humanistic University, Curacao. He is the formers Head- of Department of Information Management and the former Coordinator for MBA, Faculty of Graduate Studies, SLIIT, Sri Lanka. He is the current Adviser, Academic Affairs-Institute of Chartered Accountants of Sri Lanka. Further he is the Former Head of Education and Training, Institute of Chartered Accountants of Sri Lanka, Former Rector, Trincomalee Campus of Eastern University, Sri Lanka (TCEUSL), Former Dean, Faculty of Communication and Business Studies (FCBS), TCEUSL. And the Former Head, Department of Business & Management Studies, TCEUSL. He has published more than 50 articles in refereed journals.

Valentine Owan is a postgraduate student of Research, Measurement and Evaluation in the Department of Educational Foundations at the University of Calabar, Nigeria. He is the founder of the Ultimate Research Network (URN), a multidisciplinary research initiative aimed at raising the next generation of scholars for knowledge creation and problem-solving through self-development. His research interests include item-response theory, research and statistics, structural equation modelling, program evaluation, quantitative research methodology, Rasch measurement theory, and higher education. Due to his early interest in research, Owan has published internationally and domestically in many journals. He is an established reviewer for several WoS- and Scopus-indexed academic journals.

Peterson Ozili is an economist at the Central Bank. He is a leading scholar in development and financial sector economics. He works extensively in economic policymaking and is actively involved in rigorous academic research. He has experience in economic policy, financial inclusion, financial stability, financial innovation, banking regulation and supervision. His research areas of specialisation are in financial economics, international development, accounting, development finance, the economics of financial markets and bank financial reporting. He has published extensively in many accounting, finance and economics journals.

Kenneth Peprah is a Professor of Agricultural Geography and Environmental Studies. He a product of the University of Ghana, Legon, a Commonwealth Scholar and an alumnus of the University of East Anglia, Norwich, UK. He convenes Philosophy of the Social Sciences for graduate students of the Simon Diedong Dombo University of Business and Integrated Development Studies in Ghana.

W.A. Perera is a graduate of University of Kelaniya-Sri Lanka. Currently, Perera is in the final semester of M.Sc. in Psychological Counselling.

Gaurav Shukla has a Ph.D., LL.M, and B.A.LL.B. At present working as a Lecturer at the University of South Pacific, with over 16 years of experience teaching public laws at different tertiary educational institutions in various jurisdictions. I am a Max Planck scholar. I have obtained B.A.LL.B (Hons), LL.M, and Ph.D. in legal studies. Utilizing my expertise in teaching and research, I have been pivotal in ensuring the overall development of the students at the UG and PG levels. I have several publications mostly on the contemporary issues of Public Law, like Constitutional Law, Tax Laws, Criminal Law, etc..

Amanda Terrell is an Associate Professor of Human Development and Family Sciences in the School of Human Environmental Sciences at the University of Arkansas. In her studies of adolescence and emerging adults, she focuses on psychosocial and physical health, cumulative risks and life course resilience, social media technology, and program evaluation.

Kandauda Wickrama PhD is an Emeritus Professor, Human Development and Family Science The University of Georgia, USA. He has more than 200 publications in indexed journals, and the main author of the book *Higher Order Growth Curves and Mixure Modeling with Mplus: A Practical Guide.*

Thulitha Wickrama is a Senior Research Associate University of Nebraska. Lincoln. My academic and research training and subsequent work have been in the area of research methods, and individual, family, and community relations and health. My education has been in human development and family studies (PhD from Pennsylvania State University) with concentrations in research methods and family relations. I have also studied community health (MS from Minnesota State University) and statistics (BS in Statistics, from Iowa State University). For over two decades, I have engaged in health research, program formulation, funding, implementation, and monitoring in these areas. I have worked as a researcher and lecturer at Iowa State University, Minnesota State University, and Pennsylvania State University, while I worked as a professor and faculty member at Auburn University and the University of Nebraska-Lincoln, USA.

Krishantha Wisenthige is a Senior Lecturer (Higher Grade) attached to Department of Business Management, School of Business, Sri Lanka Institute of Information Technology (SLIIT), Sri Lanka. Krishantha Received his B.Sc. (Hons) and MBA from University of Peradeniya and his Ph.D in Management Science and Engineering from School of Management, Wuhan University of Technology, China. He process more than 15 years of experiences in industry in various capacities including his services as consultant / expert to number of projects in multilateral agencies. He is currently holing the responsibility as research coordinator of the faculty and published number of journal and conference papers.

Index

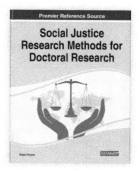

Ensure Quality Research is Introduced to the Academic Community

Become an Evaluator for IGI Global Authored Book Projects

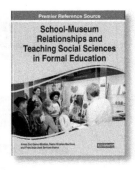
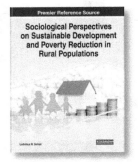

The overall success of an authored book project is dependent on quality and timely manuscript evaluations.

Applications and Inquiries may be sent to:
development@igi-global.com

Applicants must have a doctorate (or equivalent degree) as well as publishing, research, and reviewing experience. Authored Book Evaluators are appointed for one-year terms and are expected to complete at least three evaluations per term. Upon successful completion of this term, evaluators can be considered for an additional term.

If you have a colleague that may be interested in this opportunity, we encourage you to share this information with them.

CPSIA information can be obtained
at www.ICGtesting.com
Printed in the USA
LVHW021316260723
753438LV00007B/527

9 781668 468630